VIOLENCE
IN DATING
RELATIONSHIPS

VIOLENCE IN DATING RELATIONSHIPS

EMERGING SOCIAL ISSUES

Edited by
Maureen A. Pirog-Good and Jan E. Stets

New York
Westport, Connecticut
London

Library of Congress Cataloging-in-Publicaton Data

Violence in dating relationships : emerging social issues / edited by
    Maureen A. Pirog-Good and Jan E. Stets.
        p.   cm.
    Bibliography: p.
    Includes index.
    ISBN 0-275-93004-1 (alk. paper)
    ISBN 0-275-93353-9 (pbk. : alk. paper)
    1. Dating violence—United States. 2. Acquaintance rape—
United States. 3. Aggressiveness (Psychology)—United States.
4. Family violence—United States.   I. Pirog-Good, Maureen A. II. Stets, Jan E.
HQ801.83.V56   1989
362.1'532—dc19   88-31894

Library of Congress Catalog Card Number: 88-31894
ISBN: 0-275-93004-1
ISBN: 0-275-93353-9 (pbk.)

First published in 1989

Praeger Publishers, One Madison Avenue, New York, NY 10010
An imprint of Greenwood Publishing Group, Inc.

Printed in the United States of America

The paper used in this book complies with the
Permanent Paper Standard issued by the National
Information Standards Organization (Z39.48-1984).

10 9 8 7 6 5 4 3 2

Contents

Preface

Included in this volume are 14 pioneering chapters on physical and sexual abuse in dating relationships. With contributors from a wide variety of disciplines, including sociology, criminology, psychology, psychiatry, women's studies, and policy analysis, this book provides an interdisciplinary and comprehensive review of the fields of physical and sexual abuse in dating relationships. Additionally, new and provocative empirical work on dating abuse is presented.

The first section, "Physical Abuse in Dating Relationships," provides estimates of the prevalence of physical abuse in dating relationships and compares dating violence with cohabiting and marital violence. It also provides the reader with new theoretical and empirical research on the *antecedents* and *consequences* of physical abuse while dating. First, Sugarman and Hotaling review the literature on physical abuse while dating and provide estimates of the incidence of dating violence. They highlight the risk factors associated with dating violence, and discuss how dating violence compares with marital violence.

In the chapter that follows, Stets and Straus compare physical abuse among those who date, cohabit, or are married. Using the same measure of physical abuse across these different marital status groups, they find that abuse is more common and severe in cohabiting relationships than in the other groups. They posit that the high rate of assault among cohabiting couples may be due to social isolation, issues of autonomy and control, and lack of investment in the relationship. The first two chapters provide the reader with a general understanding against which the remaining chapters in this section of the book can be read.

Riggs and O'Leary present a theoretical model of courtship aggression. Their model contains two general categories of variables: contextual (such as individual characteristics) and situational (such as precipitating events). The former variables predict *which* people will behave aggressively and the latter variables predict *when* individuals will behave aggressively. The chapter is designed to provide the reader with a framework with which to approach the subject of dating violence.

In the chapter that follows, Burke, Stets, and Pirog-Good build a model of physical and sexual abuse while dating in order to test the direct and indirect effects of gender identity and self-esteem on dating violence. They find that while self-esteem is not directly related to either physical or sexual abuse, men and women with a more feminine gender identity are more likely to inflict and sustain both physical and sexual abuse. Because the effect of gender identity is the same for both genders, the authors suggest that we reconsider the male-oriented theories of the past when trying to understand physical and sexual abuse.

Makepeace examines physical abuse for five stages of courtship: first date, casual dating, steady dating, engagement, and living together. He indicates that there are two types of courtship violence: predatory violence, which is more characteristic of early-stage relationships, especially first dates, and relational violence, which is more characteristic of later-stage relationships, including those couples who are engaged and live together. Makepeace discusses the consequences of the violence in terms of whether or not a relationship remains intact, pointing out that whether it remains intact depends upon the partners' investment in the relationship.

Pirog-Good and Stets address one consequence of dating abuse by examining the help-seeking behavior of men and women who are physically and sexually abused. Several patterns are revealed. Women are more likely to report abuse than men, and both men and women are more likely to report physical abuse than sexual abuse. Individuals are most likely to tell friends about the abuse, followed by parents. Very few people seek help from counselors, physicians, or criminal justice authorities. Whether or not abused individuals seek help is largely determined by whether or not they *perceive* that they have been abused.

Conceptualizing dating violence within a conflict perspective, Lloyd, Koval, and Cate compare conflictual-violent relationships with conflictual-non-violent relationships. They find that individuals in conflictual-violent relationships characteristically use persistence in conflict negotiation. Additionally, individuals in conflictual-violent relationships have been in their relationships longer, have a greater investment in the relationship, and have greater belief that change within the relationship is possible.

The second section of the book, "Sexual Abuse in Dating Relationships," is devoted to sexual aggression in dating relationships. The section begins with Koss's work on sexual aggression and victimization. Koss reveals that women's experience of sexual aggression is pervasive. For example, she finds that about 54 percent of women respondents report some form of sexual victimization. Comparing this figure with the 25 percent of men admitting to sexually aggressive behavior, Koss concludes that men are underreporting their sexual aggression. Many women experience rape. About 15 percent of her sample of women reported experiencing rape. Most incidents of rape involved close acquaintances or dates. Koss's research presents a comprehensive profile not only of the prevalence and incidence of sexual aggression, but also the most serious victimization and sexually aggressive act as seen from the women's and men's point of view, respectively.

There are three objectives to Lundberg-Love and Geffner's chapter. First, they identify the prevalence, risk factors, and potential long-term consequences of date rape. Second, they propose an additional risk factor for date rape: childhood or adolescent sexual abuse, particularly incest. Finally, they offer a theoretical model that explains why date rape occurs. This model integrates the risk-factor data in both the date rape and child sexual abuse literature. Lundberg-Love and Geffner view date rape as one step in a possible lifespan cycle of sexual victimization of women that often begins in childhood.

Gwartney-Gibbs and Stockard investigate the effect of friendship networks on inflicting and sustaining sexual aggression while dating. They find that for both males and females, having sexually aggressive male friends is sufficient to guarantee having sexually victimized female friends. They also find that males who have no friends who inflict sexual aggression are less likely to inflict sexual aggression themselves, and females who have no friends who sustain sexual aggression are also less likely to sustain aggression. Thus, peer groups appear to play an important role in sexual relations.

Belknap examines unmarried women who experienced attempted rape or rape by a nonrelative acquaintance or person well-known to them. Her work goes beyond the usual focus on a college population. Among several important results, Belknap finds that young women (ages 12–15) are more likely to experience rape by an acquaintance than by a well-known person, and that attempts of rape by a well-known person are more likely to result in completed rapes than attempts by an acquaintance. Further, victims of rape by a well-known person are more likely to be injured than victims of acquaintance rape.

Malamuth's examines predictors of sexual aggression by men against women. He finds that the following factors are related to men's sexual aggression: sexual arousal in response to aggression, dominance as a motive for sexual acts, hostility toward women, attitudes accepting of violence against women, psychoticism, and sexual experience. He also finds that the combined predictors work better in explaining sexual aggression than any single predictor by itself.

Muehlenhard examines various dating behaviors and their relationship to the risk of date rape. Respondents were given a series of scenarios and were asked to respond in terms of the degree to which they thought that the woman wanted sex (sex-willingness ratings) and how justified the man would be in having sex with her against her wishes (rape-justifiability ratings). Her results reveal that sex-willingness and rape-justifiability ratings are highest when the woman initiates the date, when they go to the man's apartment, and when the man pays the dating expenses. No matter who initiates the date, who pays, or where the couple goes, men are always more likely than women to interpret the dating behavior as a sign that the woman wants sex. Muehlenhard suggests that men may overestimate their date's interest in sex, and could lead men later to feel "led on." This, in turn, may lead some males to regard rape as justifiable. Finally, she finds that rape-justifiability ratings are higher for men than for women and higher for traditional individuals, especially traditional men, then for nontraditional individuals.

In the final article, Fenstermaker addresses the issue of acquaintance rape. She investigates this problem in the same way as Muehlenhard in that she provides respondents with a series of vignettes about sexual coercion. Respondents indicate the degree to which the man and woman in each of the scenarios is responsible for the sexually coercive act and decide whether a crime has been committed. Fenstermaker finds that female respondents progressively assign more and more responsibility to the female as the vignettes depict greater implied female complicity or greater ambiguity concerning the situation. Additionally, the percentage of respondents who think a crime has been committed drops when they confront vignettes that imply at least initial consent by the female. Finally, prior experience with sexual coercion influences attributions of responsibility. For example, in situations in which there is implied female complicity, those who have actually experienced sexual coercion are less likely to attribute responsibility to the female.

Many people have made this book possible. We want to especially thank the book's contributors. These leading scholars gave up their valuable time to make an important contribution to this volume. Without their hard work, we would not have been able to accomplish our task. We would also like to thank Sue Fiscus, who spent many hours preparing the manuscripts and tables for this volume.

I Physical Abuse in Dating Relationships

1 Dating Violence: Prevalence, Context, and Risk Markers

David B. Sugarman and
Gerald T. Hotaling

Less than a decade ago, Makepeace (1981) reported that a substantial proportion of college students engaged in violence in their dating relationships. This seemed to contradict the contentions of some who believed that dating was a time of innocent exploration and that intimate violence was more a feature among conflict-ridden married couples (Gelles, 1972). However, it confirmed the expectations of others. In a historical analysis of marital violence, May (1978) cited Mayhew's (1861) observations of London street life, which depicted severe beating as being accepted by women as consonant with their role not only in marital relationships but during courtship as well. More recently, Dobash and Dobash's (1979) analysis of the relationship between battered women and patriarchy offered cursory evidence that violence was also present in dating relationships. After witnessing the revelations of high rates of child and wife battering (Straus, Gelles & Steinmetz, 1980) and after beginning to understand the prevalence of sexual child abuse (Finkelhor, 1979), sibling violence (Straus, Gelles & Steinmetz, 1980), and elder abuse (Block & Sinnott, 1979), the high reported rates of dating violence did not evoke a great deal of surprise in the research community.

Within this context, it was also easy for researchers to directly link dating violence to family violence. Dating violence was discovered and seen as one more example of how violence can permeate intimate and close relationships. This perception of dating violence as closely aligned, if not identical, to violence in the family takes many forms and has largely structured what we currently know about violence between dating partners. For example, Makepeace (1981) saw dating violence as a mediating stage between the experiencing of violence in one's family of origin and in one's family of procreation, a training ground hypothesis. Others have employed the marital violence literature as a framework for investigating dating violence. DeMaris (1987) and Thompson (1986) conceptualized dating violence theoretically in terms of the factors associated with marital violence. With regard to method, the vast majority of the researchers have employed some form or modification of the Conflict Tactics Scale (CTS: Straus, 1979), a widely used assessment tool for domestic violence. With regard to therapy, Flynn (1987) argues that marital violence counselors should expand their clientele to include violent dating partners and conclude that dating violence and marital violence are "forms of the same phenomenon" (p. 295). Essentially, violence is violence regardless of who is doing it to whom.

If one accepts the argument of dating–marital violence equivalence, does this imply that dating is like marriage? Laner and Thompson (1982) offer a number of common characteristics of both marital and serious dating relationships in contrast to other dyads: (1) a greater degree of mutual interaction in terms of time spent together, range of activities in which they are engaged, and higher levels of involvement; (2) a greater exchange of personal information; (3) a greater presumed right to influence the partner; and (4) a greater likelihood of conflict due to the need to negotiate roles and responsibilities and to cope with environmental stressors. However, Carlson (1987) correctly points out that certain differences emerge as well. Married couples often have children, whereas dating couples typically do not. In marriage in contrast to dating, the couple are economically bound to each other, usually with the woman dependent on her spouse.

While these arguments are intriguing, empirical evidence is rarely used to support the notion of equivalence in dating and marital violence. In order to more clearly understand the relationship between dating and marital violence, we review empirical work on dating violence, and then compare these findings with what we know about marital violence. This chapter, which reviews over 40 published and unpublished studies of dating violence, addresses three major issues: prevalence, contextual factors, and risk markers. The first issue focuses on the amount of dating violence that research has uncovered and the second examines the meanings people attach to violence in dating. The third issue concentrates on the factors that place an individual at risk of sustaining or inflicting violence in a dating relationship. In summary, this chapter reviews what we currently know about the amount and correlates of dating violence and compares these conclusions with those of a similar analysis of marital violence (Hotaling & Sugarman, 1986).

THE DEFINITION OF DATING VIOLENCE

One problem that plagues the study of interpersonal violence is how to define it. For the present purposes, violence is defined as the use or threat of physical force or restraint carried out with the intent of causing pain or injury to another. Three points should be raised about this definition. First, psychological abuse is excluded. Although psychological strategies are the primary means of controlling another person, little work has focused on operationalizing this construct within the dating context. Second, while sexual aggression is a form of physical violence and has an extensive research literature, it is reviewed by Lundberg-Love and Geffner (this volume, Chapter 9). Consequently, sexual aggression is not included in this chapter. Third, our definition emphasizes acts of physical aggression in contrast to the injuries that may result from these acts. Interestingly, only Makepeace (1984) focused on injuries sustained during acts of dating violence.

Researchers of dating violence have utilized a number of definitions. Puig (1984), for example, considered courtship partner abuse to be "acts of physical aggression directed at one dating partner by another dating partner" (p. 268). Carlson (1987) defined dating violence as "violence in unmarried couples who are romantically involved" (p. 17), while Thompson (1986) conceived of courtship violence as "any acts and/or threat of acts that physically and/or verbally abuse another person" (p. 166) and that occur during "any social interaction related to the dating and/or mate selection process" (p. 165).

One of the difficulties with these definitions is that the terms "dating" and "courtship" are not adequately defined and seem to apply to a broad range of persons and social activities. For our purposes, the process of dating is seen as a dyadic interaction that focuses on participation in mutually rewarding activities that may increase the likelihood of future interaction, emotional commitment, and/or sexual intimacy. Consequently, dating violence involves the perpetration or threat of an act of physical violence by at least one member of an unmarried dyad on the other within the context of the dating process. Our definition of dating violence (1) excludes married individuals and divorced couples who are not attempting to reconcile their relationships; (2) incorporates a range of relationships from the first dates to cohabitation and engagement; and (3) can apply to homosexual as well as to heterosexual relationships.

THE PREVALENCE OF DATING VIOLENCE

Even though research in this area is relatively new, there are over 20 data sets that have resulted from attempts to estimate the prevalence of dating violence. A majority of these studies have counted cases in terms of lifetime prevalence, allowing for an estimation of the proportion of respondents who had ever inflicted or sustained physical violence in a dating relationship.

Meaningful comparisons across data sets, however, are not always easy to make because of variations in sampling, research design, and analysis decisions. These problems are complicated further by the various operationalizations of dating violence. For example, some authors include in their counts only acts of physical force as measures of violent behavior, some include threats of violence, and some include other forms of verbal aggression as well. All in all, the comparison of prevalence estimates across studies must proceed with caution in order to avoid a series of misleading comparisons. Tables 1.1 and 1.2 summarize several of the methodological features of these studies as well as the overall prevalence rates and rates broken down by the gender and role of the respondent (victim or offender) in the violent interaction.

Lifetime Prevalence Rates

Prevalence studies are based on the assumption that since dating violence is rarely officially reported, the most accurate estimate of the size of the problem will have to come directly from the self-reports of victims and offenders. This strategy has produced a broad array of estimates. In Table 1.1, levels of involvement in dating violence range from 9 percent to 65 percent. It should be kept in mind that "involvement" here concerns either expressing or sustaining violence. Even so, these findings have a frightening tone. The low estimates point to a problem that is sizable, while the high estimates indicate a problem of epidemic proportions. Several possible factors could account for the broad range of estimates found in these studies, and they are discussed below.

Characteristics of the Measure of Violence. Almost all studies reviewed here have used the Conflict Tactics Scale (CTS) (Straus, 1987), a shorter version of these scales, or single items about the level of dating violence involvement. No major differences in prevalence rates are produced by this methodological decision. As would be expected, rates are higher in studies that include threats as well as actual violence (O'Keefe, Brockopp & Chew, 1986) and in studies that include verbal aggression as well as acts of physical violence (Laner, 1983; Laner & Thompson, 1982). Also, as is true in the spousal-abuse literature, the more severe the violence being measured, the lower the prevalence rate (Gelles & Straus, 1988; Straus, Gelles & Steinmetz, 1980).

Sample Characteristics. Two characteristics of the samples used in these studies might account for the variation in the reported rates: age (high school versus college samples) and the proportion of females in the sample. Rates of involvement in interpersonal violence have been found to be higher for the young and for females in spousal-abuse research (Straus et al., 1980) and could also be true of dating violence. Since all these studies surveyed college and/or high school students, the age range is rather constricted. Nevertheless, college samples produce higher average (*M*) prevalence rates (*M* = 31.9%) than samples of high school students (*M* = 22.3%). Also, mean prevalence rates are higher for samples in which at least 65 percent of respondents are women (*M* = 34.6%) than for those samples with a lower proportion of women (*M* = 27.7%).

Year of Publication. More recent studies report slightly higher overall prevalence rates than older studies. The mean prevalence rate in studies published between 1985 and 1987 is 31.2 percent compared to a mean prevalence rate of 29.2 percent in studies published before 1985. The reason for this is unclear. It could be that dating violence has actually increased in the past few years, but it is more likely due to improvements in methodological technique.

Table 1.1
Overall Life Time Dating Violence Prevalence Rates and Survey Characteristics

Study	Rate	Sample Size	Female Percentage of Sample	Region[1]	Sample Type[2]
Bernard & Bernard, 1983	30.0%	461	63.6	S	C
Billingham & Sack, 1987	32.1%	526	68.2	MW	C
Bogal-Allbritten & Allbritten, 1985	19.0%	510	80.0	*	C
Cate et al., 1982	22.3%	355	57.0	W	C
Comins, 1984	52.0%	354	100.0	S	C
Deal & Wampler, 1986	47.0%	410	72.0	S	C
Ferraro & Johnson, (a)	24.8%	418	NR	W	C
1984[3] (b)	22.2%	502	NR	W	C
(c)	37.0%	521	NR	W	C
(d)	41.3%	367	NR	W	H
Henton et al., 1983	12.1%	644	45.1	W	H
Lane & Gwartney-Gibbs, 1985	33.0%	325	49.1	W	C
Laner, 1983	64.9%[4]	371	65.2	MW	C
Makepeace, 1981	21.2%	202	51.0	MW	C
Makepeace, 1986	16.7%	NR	54.7	*	C
Matthews, 1984	22.8%	351	65.0	E	C
McKinney, 1986a	66.2%	163	52.1	S	C
Murphy, 1984	40.4%	485	52.5	MW	C
O'Keefe, Brockopp & Chew, 1986	26.9%	256	52.7	W	H
Roscoe & Callahan, 1985	9.0%	212	53.0	MW	H
Sack, Keller & Howard 1984	24.0%	211	56.4	S	C

[1]Abbreviations for the regions are: E, Eastern States; S, Southern states; MW, Midwestern states; W, Western states; *; Institutions in more than one region were surveyed.
[2]Sample type abbreviations are: C, college sample; H, High school sample.
[3]This study involves four separate surveys.
[4]Includes verbal abuse.

Region. One intriguing pattern is the substantial difference in prevalence rates by geographical region. Grouping studies by region of data collection yields a mean prevalence rate for the eastern United States of 22.8 percent; for the Midwest, 25.7 percent; for the western states, 27.5 percent; and for the South, 43.8 percent. This regional pattern is similar in rank and magnitude to murder and aggravated assault rates presented yearly by the Federal Bureau of Investigation (1985). Southern states consistently report the highest rates of criminal violence followed by the western states, with the East and Midwest reporting the lowest.

It is difficult to know how much confidence to place in this finding, given the small number of available studies and the fact that college and university populations contain people from more than one region. To examine the combined effects of the variables listed in Table 1.1 on prevalence rates, we performed a backward elimination regression analysis using year of publication, college versus high school sample, size of sample, and region (two dummy-coded variables) as predictors of prevalence rates. Several studies had to be excluded from this analysis. Bogal-Allbritten and Allbritten (1985) and Makepeace (1986) were omitted because the students they surveyed came from institutions located in more than one region. Matthews (1984) was eliminated since it was the only survey in the eastern region. Finally, Laner's (1983) data were excluded from this analysis because the reported overall prevalence rate included verbal aggression. Seventeen samples remained in the analysis.

The analysis revealed that the model including region and publication year significantly predicted prevalence rates [$F(3, 13) = 3.56$, $p = .044$, $R^2 = .45$]. Both dummy-coded regional variables significantly contributed to this effect. The southern studies exhibited a significantly higher prevalence rate than either the midwestern studies [$t(1, 13) = -2.275$, $p = .040$] or western studies [$t(1,13) = -2.416$, $p = .031$]. Furthermore, there was a strong but nonsignificant positive relationship between prevalence rate and year of publication [$t(1, 13) = 1.855$, $p = .086$]. The persistence of regional differences suggests support for a culture-of-violence effect (Wolfgang & Ferracuti, 1967) in the context of secondary and postsecondary educational environments. Future research may want to more directly examine whether the culture-of-violence theory of violent behavior can fruitfully be applied to dating violence by specifying the respondent's place of origin.

Prevalence Rates by Gender and Victim-Offender Relationship

The prevalence rates in Table 1.2 are from studies in which the results were categorized by gender and role in violence. Overall, there is little sex difference in self-reported victimization in dating. Females are somewhat more likely than males to report ever having been victimized by an act of violence in the context of dating (male: $M = 33.3\%$; female: $M = 36.2\%$), based on studies reporting victimization rates for *both* males and females. On average, over one-third of those surveyed report an experience of violence victimization at some point in their dating history. This proportion is high but similar to the lifetime prevalence rate that has been reported in studies of spousal violence. For example, Straus, Gelles, and Steinmetz (1980) found that over the entire length of a marriage 28 percent of respondents report at least one violent incident.

A more surprising finding contained in Table 1.2 is the higher proportion of females than males who self-report having expressed violence in a dating relationship (male: $M = 32.9\%$; female: $M = 39.3\%$). Almost four out of every ten women and almost one-third of the males are reported to have been violent at some point in their dating careers. It is difficult to fully understand this pattern of findings because of the manner in which much data on dating violence are analyzed and presented. For example, the vast majority of studies in dating

Table 1.2
Prevalence Rates of Expressed and Sustained Dating Violence for Men and Women

Measure	Study	Expressed Violence Men	Women	Sustained Violence Men	Women
Overall violence including verbal abuse	Lane & Gwartney-Gibbs, 1985	63.9	61.7	68.7	65.7
Overall violence including threats	Billingham & Sack, 1987	21.6	28.4	24.6	25.1
	Marshall, 1987[1]	63.0	66.0	33.0	48.0
	Marshall, 1987[2]	57.0	61.0	46.0	49.6
	O'Keefe, Brockopp & Chew, 1986	19.0	22.0	22.0	28.9
Overall violence excluding threats	Arias, Samios & O'Leary, 1987[3]	30.0	32.0	49.0	26.0
	Arias, Samios & O'Leary, 1987[4]	30.0	49.0	50.0	38.0
	Bernard & Bernard, 1983	15.0	21.0	19.0	38.0
	DeMaris, 1987	23.5	31.1	28.6	22.5
	Lane & Gwartney-Gibbs, 1985	20.0	40.5	34.2	42.2
	Makepeace, 1983	13.7	9.7	9.8	10.6
	Marshall & Rose, 1987[5]	45.0	59.0	52.0	57.0
	Marshall & Rose, 1987[6]	39.0	46.0	46.0	49.0
	McKinney, 1986b[7]	22.0	17.0	28.0	31.0
	McKinney, 1986b[8]	21.0	26.0	47.0	38.0
	Roscoe & Benaske, 1985	----	23.2	----	51.0
	Sigelman, Berry & Wiles, 1984	53.6	52.1	58.9	47.8
Severe violence	Arias, Samios & O'Leary 1987[3]	10.0	10.0	23.0	3.0
	Arias, Samios & O'Leary 1987[4]	10.0	19.0	27.0	8.0
	Lane & Gwartney-Gibbs, 1985	5.4	1.0	9.7	7.0
	Makepeace, 1983	6.9	2.6	5.9	9.3

[1]Rate of violence in relationships over the current 2 years.
[2]Rate of violence in relationships prior to the current 2 years.
[3]Rate of violence in current relationship.
[4]Rate of violence in past relationships.
[5]Respondents were currently in a dating relationship.
[6]Respondents were not currently in a dating relationship.
[7]Respondent's self-defined rate of dating violence.
[8]Rate at which the respondent reported expressing or sustaining violent dating behaviors.

violence have used the CTS (Straus, 1979). These scales ask about the occurrence of a number of acts of physical violence ranging from pushing and shoving to beating up someone to the use of a weapon by one partner against the other. Unfortunately, these various acts are often not broken down in data analysis into subtypes of violent behavior.

Some studies do allow for an examination of rates of serious violence by gender. Both Makepeace (1983) and Lane and Gwartney-Gibbs (1985) found that males were from two to four times more likely than females to have used severe violence against dating partners. However, Arias, Samios, and O'Leary (1987) found no gender difference in the use of severe violence when respondents were asked about current relationships but found females twice as likely as males to have used violence in past relationships.

Focusing on injuries rather than acts of violence, the evidence on gender differences in injuries is meager but less equivocal than that on serious violent acts. Makepeace (1984) found that 53 percent of the females and 18 percent of the males reported sustaining an injury inflicted by their partner in the dating context. While males and females seem to be equally likely in the context of dating to use physical violence, women are significantly more likely to experience injury due to this violence. A similar pattern of results has been found in the spousal-abuse literature (see Berk et al., 1983). The risk of female injury is still larger if only severe forms of injury are considered. Four times as many females as males report a "moderate" or "severe" injury resulting from violent episodes while dating (Makepeace, 1986).

Another issue on which information is needed to help interpret gender differences in prevalence is the set of motives people disclose for engaging in violent behavior. Of particular importance are the data presented by Makepeace (1984) and Olday and Wesley (1983). Women were over twice as likely as men to have interpreted their own violent behavior as being the result of self-defense and/or retaliation. Men, on the other hand, were over three times more likely than women to cite intimidation, intention of striking fear into the other, or intention of forcing the other person to do something as their major motive for using violence.

One consistent finding in this literature is that violence is largely mutual. The correlation between expressing and sustaining violence is large and significant (Billingham & Sack, 1987; Marshall, 1987; Marshall & Rose, 1987). The available evidence indicates that males initiate severe violence more often than females and females are victimized more severely by males' severe violence.

There may be many reasons for gender differences in prevalence rates of dating violence, and several authors have offered their interpretations. One interpretation holds that males are more reluctant to admit expressing violence against dating partners because of its stigmatizing nature (Arias & Johnson, 1986). But if this interpretation is correct, it also would have to account for the high proportion of males claiming dating violence victimization; another stigmatizing admission. A second explanation may be that through the dating process, males learn the cultural norms concerning the use of violence against females. Realizing that their violence has the potential for causing severe physical harm, they may be socialized to practice restraint and concentrate on minor acts of violence (Arias, Samios & O'Leary, 1987). Third, females may have greater power in dating than they do in other relationships with males. They may be more successful in communicating that they will not stand for violence on the part of dating partners. Also, they can more easily end dating relationships and may be less reluctant to report violence directed against them than married women (Plass & Gessner, 1983).

DATING VIOLENCE CONTEXT

A large amount of dating violence research is descriptive. In most studies, there is no comparison between violent and nonviolent dating couples to allow for the identification of risk markers that differentiate the two groups. Instead, a profile of the violent person or couple is constructed. This literature provides a fuller picture of the context of dating violence by focusing on the meanings that participants attach to their involvement in violent episodes. This phenomenological approach highlights the interpretations people construct about what caused the violence, what effects the violence had on their relationship, their perceived role in the violence, and what they did in response to the violence.

Perhaps the greatest value of this research is what it tells us about the cultural norms that surround violence in dating. Is violence stigmatized or is it seen as an acceptable part of dating? It has often been argued that there are a number of cultural norms that support and encourage the use of violence in marital and other close adult relationships (Greenblat, 1983; Straus, 1980a), but this issue has not been extensively discussed in the literature on dating. In the following section, descriptive studies will be reviewed with a special emphasis on the meanings that participants hold about their involvement in dating violence.

Descriptions of Dating Violence

Dating violence occurs primarily on weekends (Olday & Wesley, 1983) and in private settings. It takes place most often in the residence of one of the partners or the parents of the partners, followed in frequency by vehicles and, lastly, out of doors (Makepeace, 1981; Olday & Wesley, 1983; Roscoe & Benaske, 1985; Roscoe & Kelsey, 1986). Anywhere from 70 to 93 percent of violent incidents take place in private settings, outside of the view of third parties (Laner, 1983; Roscoe & Kelsey, 1986). When the violence takes place in public, attempts by others to intervene occur less than half the time (Laner, 1983).

The available evidence indicates that if violence occurs once in a dating relationship, it is likely to occur again. Among those who experienced violence in a relationship, the mean number of such incidents was 9.6 (Roscoe & Benaske, 1985) which is similar to the mean frequency of violent episodes (8.8) based on a national sample of married persons (Straus, 1980b). Given this frequency, it is not surprising that physical injury is a common outcome of dating violence (see Makepeace, 1986).

Perceptions of Why Dating Violence Occurred

Victim-Offender Roles. Studies that have asked about the initiation of violence in dating relationships rarely find that people indict themselves. Across studies, the majority of respondents (ranging from 75 to 100 percent) do *not* label themselves as initiators of the violence. This is consistent with findings from attribution theory that people tend to label themselves as victims rather than as initiators of aggression (Tedeschi, Smith & Brown, 1974). Males and females seem equally likely to label the other partner as the initiator or to attribute blame to both partners equally. There does not seem to be a clear pattern to the assignment of blame across these studies. Approximately equal proportions of people blame both themselves and their partners as blame the other partner exclusively (Henton, et al., 1983; Makepeace, 1986; Matthews, 1984; Roscoe & Callahan, 1985; Roscoe & Kelsey, 1986). When respondents are asked whether they see themselves as victims or as aggressors in the violent episodes rather than being asked who initiated the violence, a sex difference emerges. Females are two to three times more likely than males to perceive themselves as victims in the violent episodes. Males are also significantly more likely to label themselves as offenders.

Perceived Causes of Violent Behavior. Studies have asked a variety of questions about perceived causes of the occurrence of dating violence; many of the studies involve either open-ended questions or fixed choice lists. Unfortunately, many studies do not specify whether respondents are interpreting their own or their partner's behavior, making analysis difficult. Regardless of these methodological shortcomings, it is clear that jealousy is perceived to be the most pressing cause of dating violence. In every study in which a respondent has had a chance to check or list jealousy as a cause, it is the most frequently mentioned reason (Makepeace, 1981; Matthews, 1984; Roscoe & Benaske, 1985; Roscoe & Callahan, 1985; Roscoe & Kelsey, 1986). The actual role of jealousy in violence may be understated in these studies. For example, some studies that do not include jealousy in the choices presented to the respondents typically find that "uncontrollable anger" is the most frequently cited cause. It is likely that much of this "uncontrollable anger" results from issues surrounding sexual jealousy. Jealousy and uncontrollable anger are listed as primary causes of dating violence equally by males and females (Makepeace, 1986).

Drinking behavior or disagreements about drinking are typically the next most frequently cited cause of violence, but far less often than jealousy. Certainly, the mention of alcohol and, for that matter, other drugs, occurs less often among violent daters than among violent spouses (Kantor & Straus, 1987).

Females most frequently mention uncontrollable anger, self-defense, jealousy, and retaliation as causes of their own violent behavior. Females who are victimized see the violence of their male partner as largely due to sexual denial. This is consistent with the perceptions of a significant number of males who use violence in a dating context. While frequently citing uncontrollable anger and jealousy, between a quarter to over a third of males report that the primary cause of their violence was to "intimidate," "frighten," or "force the other person to give me something." The boldness of these claims separates violent married males from their dating counterparts. Violent husbands typically do not readily volunteer the instrumentality of their aggression but rather rely heavily upon a set of "loss of control" reasons, such as anger, alcohol, or drugs (Adams, 1986; Sonkin, Martin & Walker, 1985).

Related to the investigation of causal attribution is a group of studies that seek to understand emotional attributions. In other words, what emotion or set of emotions motivated the violence. This research clearly indicates that violence is seen as springing from anger and confusion (Cate, et al., 1982; Henton et al., 1983; Matthews, 1984; Roscoe & Benaske, 1985; Roscoe & Kelsey, 1986). This is consistent with the perceived role of sexual jealousy as a cause of dating violence. Between a quarter to over a third of respondents interpreted the violence of their partner as signifying love. The belief that violence is a sign of love points to the normative confusion that surrounds dating violence. Whether these findings are due to the youthfulness of the research subjects or to the nature of dating in the U.S., the merging of love with violence occurs among a sizable number of people.

Responses to Dating Violence

People involved in dating violence respond in predictable ways to violent episodes. Among victims, the most common response is anger, followed closely by fear and surprise (Henton et al., 1983; Matthews, 1984). Among offenders, the most common response is sorrow. A majority of both victims and offenders, whether male or female, report some degree of emotional trauma because of the violence. While the trauma is considered mild in the majority of cases, almost three times as many women ($M = 31.2$) than men ($M = 12.0$) reported major emotional trauma as an outcome of the violent episodes (Makepeace, 1986).

While a good deal of dating violence involves severe force, dating partners rarely seek professional help. On average, about 1 in 25 victims seeks out the assistance of either a teacher, counselor, member of the clergy, or law officer (Henton et al., 1983; Makepeace, 1981; Olday & Wesley, 1983). Studies do show, however, that a very high proportion of people talk to someone about violent episodes. A majority talk to friends, while between 20 and 40 percent talk to family members (Henton et al., 1983; Roscoe & Benaske, 1985; Stets & Pirog-Good, 1987b). In one study of gender differences in help seeking, it was found that more females than males talk to someone about dating violence experiences (Stets & Pirog-Good, 1987b).

Does the experience of dating violence ultimately lead to the termination of the relationship? The available research reports a wide range across studies in the proportion of relationships that end because of the violent behavior (from

12 to 70 percent). Multivariate analyses are not currently available to allow us to know what factors lead to termination or what types of persons are more or less likely to end the violent relationship.

Among those who are still dating following the onset of violence, responses are quite mixed. On average, the relationship has worsened because of the violence in about 40 percent of the cases, but in roughly six of every ten relationships that did not terminate, the violence is reported to have had no effect on, or to have actually improved, the relationship (Cate et al., 1982; Henton et al., 1983; Makepeace, 1981; Marshall, 1987; Matthews, 1984; Murphy, 1984; O'Keefe, Brockopp & Chew, 1986; Roscoe & Benaske, 1985; Roscoe & Callahan, 1985; Roscoe & Kelsey, 1986).

RISK MARKERS OF DATING VIOLENCE

A risk marker (Last, 1983) refers to an attribute or exposure that is associated with an increased probability of the reception and/or expression of dating violence but that is not an outcome (or suspected outcome) of the violence. The term risk marker simply indicates association, not causation. For example, lowered self-esteem may be correlated with higher rates of dating violence victimization as a cause, an effect, or as the result of a third variable. A risk marker alerts us to factors that may be responsible for the existence of the phenomena under study.

Several studies have examined the issue of risk. They are classified according to their focus into one of six categories: intrapsychic, personality, family history, interpersonal, stress, and sociodemographic.

Intrapsychic Factors

Attitudes toward Premarital and Marital Violence. Six studies evaluated the relationship between attitudes on violence and violent dating behavior. Across these studies, there is considerable consistency. Cate et al. (1982) and Henton et al. (1983) reported that respondents who were more accepting of premarital and marital violence exhibited a greater likelihood of dating violence involvement. Deal and Wampler (1986) noted that a more accepting attitude was associated with violence involvement in both past and current relationships.

Stets and associates (Burke, Stets & Pirog-Good (this volume, Chapter 4) Stets & Pirog-Good, 1987a; Stets & Pirog-Good, 1987c) and McKinney (1986b) examined the relationship between violence attitudes and violence involvement separately for male and female offenders and victims. Each study revealed that there was no relationship between female respondents' violence attitudes and whether they had either inflicted or sustained dating violence, but male victims and offenders exhibited greater acceptance of violence than their nonviolent counterparts. Consequently, the male's attitude regarding violence is more predictive of dating violence involvement than the female's attitude.

Overall, these findings indicate that men have more accepting views of violence. There is a problem, however, with assuming a causal relationship between attitudes and behavior (Ajzen & Fishbein, 1980). Currently, the research seems to assume that these attitudes are a function of socialization processes that teach men that it is permissible to control women through the use of violence. Alternatively, Bem (1967) has argued that one's attitudes are formed on the basis of observation of one's own behavior. Hence, someone who uses violence in an intimate situation begins to perceive this behavior as acceptable.

Sex-Role Attitudes. Eight studies examined the relationship between sex-role attitudes and participation in violent dating relationship, employing a range of sex-role measures: Bem sex-role inventory (BSRI: Bernard, Bernard & Bernard, 1985; Comins, 1984), attitude-toward-women scale (AWS: Bernard & Bernard, 1983; McKinney, 1986b; Sigelman, Berry & Wiles, 1984), personality attribute questionnaire (PAQ: Stets & Pirog-Good, 1987c); Osmond-Martin sex-role attitude scale (OMSRAS: Deal & Wampler, 1986); and semantic differential scales (Burke et al., (this volume, Chapter 4)).

Among studies employing the AWS scale, Bernard and Bernard (1983) reported no differences between abusive and nonabusive men or between abused and nonabused women. McKinney (1986b) noted that women who hold more liberal sex-role attitudes were more likely to define themselves as being victims or offenders in a violent relationship. However, Sigelman, Berry, and Wiles (1984) indicated that violent men showed less liberal attitudes than nonviolent men; yet no significant differences were revealed for women. Using the BSRI, Comins (1984) could not discriminate between violent and nonviolent respondents, but Bernard et al. (1985) reported that abusive men exhibited a more masculine sex typing than their nonviolent counterparts and that abused women exhibited less feminine sex typing than nonabused women.

Stets and Pirog-Good (1987c) examined the relationship between dating violence and scores on the instrumentality and expressiveness scales of the PAQ. Both men and women who scored low on the instrumentality scale were more likely to have sustained dating violence. This scale did not predict the use of violence for either gender. In contrast, low scores on the expressiveness scale were correlated only with male's inflicting and sustaining violence. Using semantic differential scales, Burke, Stets, and Pirog-Good (this volume, Chapter 4) reported that men and women who perceived themselves as more feminine were more likely to inflict violence on their partner. Finally, Deal and Wampler (1986) noted that the OMSRAS, which assesses "traditional" versus "modern" attitudes, did not significantly correlate with the frequency of violent acts.

This lack of research consensus on the relationship between sex-role attitudes and dating violence may indicate that it is not the individual's specific sex-role attitude that predicts dating violence involvement; rather, it is the sex-role attitudinal difference between the dyadic members that is associated with violence. Sigelman, Berry, and Wiles (1984) had respondents assess their own and their partners sex-role traditionalism. The researchers found that victimized women were more likely to be five or more points higher or lower than their partners, in contrast to nonvictimized women, who held attitudes more in agreement with those of their partners. A nonsignificant tendency for violent men to hold more traditional attitudes than their partners, in contrast to nonviolent men, was revealed. Possibly, the sex-role attitudinal conflict that exists between partners may predispose the relationship toward violence.

Personality. Six studies investigated the relationship between measures of personality and psychopathology and involvement in dating violence. The majority of these studies focused on self-esteem; each of them employed the Rosenberg self-esteem scale (Burke et al., this volume, Chapter 4; Comins, 1984; Deal & Wampler, 1986; Stets & Pirog-Good, 1987a). Comins (1984) noted that those individuals who had experienced dating violence had poorer self-esteem scores than those who did not. Deal and Wampler (1986) indicated that the frequency of abuse in both past and current relationships negatively correlated with self-esteem. Both Burke, Stets, and Pirog-Good (this volume, Chapter 4) and Stets and Pirog-Good (1987a) reported that men and women who had sustained physical abuse also had lower self-esteem scores. Burke, Stets, and Pirog-Good (this volume, Chapter 4) reported that self-esteem was unrelated to the infliction of physical abuse for either gender. However, Stets and Pirog-Good (1987a) uncovered a negative association between the likelihood that men would inflict violence on their partner and male self-esteem.

Using the Symptom Check List-90, SCL-90 (Derogatis, 1977), a measure of psychiatric symptomatology, Comins (1984) noted that victims of dating violence reported higher levels of emotional distress. Deal and Wampler (1986) found that lower levels of self-confidence and greater overdependence were associated with the higher amounts of violence. Yet Arias, Samios, and O'Leary (1987) reported that respondents' feelings of inferiority were not related to the degree of violence in a current dating situation. Finally, lower scores on the Crowne-Marlowe social desirability scale predicted a greater likelihood that a women will report either having been the recipient or inflictor of violence; however, no relationship seems to be present for men (Sigelman, Berry & Wiles, 1984).

Familial Factors

Family History. Do persons who are involved in dating violence have particular family histories that set them apart from the nonviolent? The available evidence is meager and based almost entirely on victim effects. Those who experienced dating violence are more likely to have grown up in homes marked by divorce or separation and periods of parental absence of either the father or mother (Makepeace, 1987; O'Keefe, Brockopp & Chew, 1986). Victims of dating violence are also more likely than nonvictims to describe their relationship to their mother and father as distant (Makepeace, 1987), to have spent less time with their mothers (Murphy, 1984), and to characterize the discipline used by their parents as more harsh (Makepeace, 1987). Growing up in a large family ·has also been indicated as a risk marker, at least for males (Murphy, 1984). While the evidence is tentative, it appears that victims of dating violence grew up in unhappy families and are clearly dissatisfied with their family experience as children. Whether this is also true of offenders is, unfortunately, not known but should be a priority on any dating violence research agenda.

Experiencing and Witnessing Family-of-Origin Violence. One aspect of family history extensively studied in the spousal and child abuse literatures is the experience of violence and abuse while growing up (see Hotaling & Sugarman, 1986; Kaufman & Zigler, 1987). Dating violence surveys have typically asked about these childhood events; so an abundance of data exists concerning the association of those events with violence during dating.

The relationship between *experiencing* violence as a child and using violence while dating is inconsistent. Seven studies find a positive relationship between childhood maltreatment and the later use of dating violence (Bernard & Bernard, 1983; Comins, 1984; DeMaris, 1987; Laner & Thompson, 1982; Marshall, 1987; Marshall & Rose, 1988; Sigelman, Berry & Wiles, 1984), but five do not (McKinney, 1986a; Murphy, 1984; O'Keefe, Brockopp & Chew, 1986; Stets & Pirog-Good, 1987a, 1987b). The same murky picture appears when examining the effects of experiencing violence as a child on later victimization in the context of dating. There is a fairly even split between studies finding evidence of a link between both forms of victimization (DeMaris, 1987; Laner & Thompson, 1982; Marshall, 1987; Marshall & Rose, 1988; Sigelman, Berry & Wiles, 1984) and studies finding no relationship at all (Comins, 1984; Murphy, 1984; O'Keefe, Brockopp & Chew, 1986; Stets & Pirog-Good, 1987a, 1987b). It should be mentioned that, unlike those studies finding a link, most of the studies that found *no* link between experiencing violence as a child and dating violence performed multivariate analyses on their data.

There is also little evidence of a relationship between *witnessing* violence as a child and involvement in dating violence. For example, Gwartney-Gibbs, Stockard, and Brohmer (1987) found that witnessing violence had significant univariate effects for males who sustained or inflicted violence; however, these effects disappeared when certain other factors were controlled. For the women's data, no univariate effect was even found. Seven other studies that have examined this variable found no support for a modeling interpretation of dating violence (DeMaris, 1987; Marshall & Rose, 1988; Murphy, 1984; O'Keefe, Brockopp & Chew, 1986; Sigelman, Berry & Wiles, 1984; Stets & Pirog-Good, 1987a, 1987c). Four studies do support this contention (Bernard & Bernard, 1983; Gwartney-Gibbs, Stockard & Brohmer, 1987; Marshall, 1987; Sack, Keller & Howard, 1982). Neither offenders nor victims of dating violence are any more likely to have been exposed to violence between parents during childhood than their nonviolent counterparts.

The lack of uniformity across studies is noteworthy, given the central role accorded the hypothesis of the ''intergenerational transmission of violence'' in the dating violence literature. Dating is often viewed as a training ground for violence in marriage or other more lasting relationships (Makepeace, 1981).

Interpersonal Factors

Past Dating Experiences. These risk markers can be divided into three categories: (1) dating history, (2) history of dating violence, and (3) sexual experiences. Focusing first on dating history, Makepeace (1987) and Murphy (1984) indicated that the younger the age at which individuals started dating, the more likely they were to be involved in dating violence. Murphy (1984) also reports a positive relationship between the number of times respondents have gone steady and the probability of violence involvement. However, Stets and Pirog-Good (1987b, 1987c) found that for both men and women, the number of dating partners was unrelated to the likelihood of the respondents' inflicting violence on their partners. But with the use of violence, higher probabilities were associated with a *lower* number of dating partners (Stets & Pirog-Good, 1987c). Their other study (1987b) revealed that this effect was present only among female respondents. Examining the impact of dating frequency, Stets and Pirog-Good (1987c) reported that for women, higher dating frequencies were related to greater frequencies of sustaining violence, but they could not replicate this effect (Stets & Pirog-Good, 1987b). Finally, Makepeace (1987) revealed no relationship between involvement in dating violence and respondents' evaluation of their dating success.

One potential hypothesis is that individuals who are currently in a violent relationship are simply replaying the type of interactions in which they have engaged in previous relationships. While Stets and Pirog-Good (1987b) indicated that very few of their respondents had been involved in more than one violent dating relationship, Roscoe and Benaske (1985) reported that their sample of battered women reported being participants in an average of 2.45 violent dating relationships. Further, a sizable minority of individuals who were members of a violent relationship indicated that this violence was present in other dating relationships as well (34 percent: Matthews, 1984; 29 percent: Roscoe & Callahan, 1985; 20 percent: Roscoe & Kelsey, 1986). Finally, Deal and Wampler (1986) correlated respondents' total violence CTS scores for past relationships and current relationships and uncovered a moderately high association ($r = .41$).

A single study examined the effect of sexual experience on dating violence (Murphy, 1984). Men and women involved in violent dating relationships were more likely to have engaged in sexual intercourse, were younger when they had their first coital experience, and had a higher number of coital partners than individuals who were not involved in dating violence.

Level of Interpersonal Commitment. A number of potential risk markers can be grouped in this category, and they are discussed below. Descriptive statistics (Cate et al., 1982; Henton et al., 1983, Olday & Wesley, 1983; Plass & Gessner, 1983; Roscoe & Benaske, 1985; Roscoe & Kelsey, 1986; Sigelman, Berry & Wiles, 1984) would lead us to believe that the majority of dating violence incidents occur during the steady or serious dating phase of the relationship (range of reported proportions: 47 to 86 percent).

However, researchers who attempted to more clearly assess commitment found no relationship between respondents' status level and experiencing or inflicting dating violence (Arias, Samios & O'Leary, 1987; Billingham, 1987; Billingham & Sack, 1987; Deal & Wampler, 1986). Two factors may account for this apparent contradiction. First, the above noted descriptive statistics may just represent the distribution of dating relationships types in the populations from which the samples were drawn, that is, more serious dating is representative of college samples while casual dating is more characteristic of high school samples. Some support for this contention is given by survey reports that higher levels of violence are found to occur during casual dating in high school samples than in college samples. A second account is offered by Comins (1984), who found that violent relationships tended to be rated as more intimate than nonviolent relationships. Consequently, when participants are requested to simply indicate the relationship stage at which the violence occurred, they may perceive the relationship as more serious than it was.

Arias, Samios, and O'Leary (1987) indicated that the length of time that an individual dated a partner was positively associated with male and female perpetration and female victimization in a current dating situation. In addition, the longer that a female had *known* her partner the greater was the likelihood that she would both inflict and sustain violence. Marshall and Rose (1987) reported a similar finding for males who used violence but not for female users or victims. Stets and Pirog-Good's (1987b) report, however, that the number of months a partner dated was no different for people who had sustained violence than those who had not. However, men's use of violence was more likely the longer the length of time they had been dating their partners (Stets & Pirog-Good, 1987c).

Stets and her associates (Burke, Stets & Pirog-Good, 1987; Stets & Pirog-Good, 1987a) created an "involvement" scale by combining data on the length of time a respondent dated the same person and the number of dates with that person. For both men and women, greater involvement, as measured here, was associated positively with inflicting and sustaining abuse. Commitment can also be measured by examining living arrangements. Stets and Straus (1988) report a higher rate of assault and more severe violence in cohabiting relationships than in either dating or marital relationships. Lane and Gwartney-Gibbs (1985) noted that the likelihood of experiencing and expressing violence was higher in the cohabiting situation than if the respondent was single or married. This result was replicated by Sigelman, Berry, and Wiles (1984). However, Billingham and Sack (1987) reported no significant differences between cohabiting and noncohabiting respondents.

Love as a motive for violence has been looked at by Arias, Samios, and

O'Leary (1987). They noted that loving a partner was uncorrelated with the extent to which an individual sustained or used violence. However, lower levels of liking and less positive feelings for one's partner were associated with a higher frequency of female, but not male, involvement with dating violence.

Finally, Stets and Pirog-Good (1987c) looked at jealousy. They measured this by coding individuals as jealous if they reported being in a serious relationship but their partner still dated other individuals. Being coded as jealous was predictive of whether females (but not males) employed or experienced violence.

Interpersonal Communication. One intriguing study (Vivian & O'Leary, 1987) audiotaped couples while they discussed a relationship problem for ten minutes. The content and affect of the couples' speech were coded into positive, negative, and neutral categories. Aggressive couples did not differ from nonaggressive couples with respect to the frequency of positive and neutral content and affect; however, they did exhibit more negative content and affect. While this finding has limited generalizability, since the couples were engaged, it does suggest that patterns of behaviors found in distressed married couples (Billings, 1979) may have roots in the premarital relationship

Power and Resource Availability. Sigelman, Berry, and Wiles (1984) examined the role of dominance in dating violence. No significant findings were revealed for the males; but female respondents who indicated that there was equal splitting of power within the relationship reported significantly lower levels of inflicting or sustaining violence. DeMaris (1987) noted that males were more likely to have inflicted or sustained violence if they believed that males should control the relationship and if their partners had greater resources than they did. For the female respondents, belief in female control of the relationship, regardless of resource distribution, predicted a greater likelihood that they would inflict violence on their partners.

Sexual Aggression. Makepeace (1986) noted that 24 percent of the female dating violence victims reported that they were also forced to have sex. This descriptive information suggests that sexual aggression may be a correlate of physical aggression; however, other research findings only tentatively support this view (Stets & Pirog-Good, 1987b).

Stress Factors

The research on the relationship between stress and dating violence reveals few consistent facts. It suggests a relationship between undesirable non-health-related life events and dating violence, at least among males. Makepeace (1983) finds that males who have experienced recent undesirable nonhealth life events (such as academic problems, job loss, role loss, or financial problems) are significantly more likely than males who have not experienced these events to become both users and victims of dating violence. No relationship was found between undesirable health life events and dating violence. Among males but not females, the absence of desirable life events predisposed them to dating abuse and victimization. Some of these findings were replicated by Marshall and Rose (1987) who found a relationship between undesirable non-health-related life change events and being a male victim of dating violence. In a later study, Marshall (1987) found no relationship between stress and violence for women, but found a link for males between the experience of positive stress and the use of violence on dating partners. This contradicts the finding by Makepeace (1983) of a negative relationship between desirable life events and dating violence.

Negative sources of stress may not be limited to recent events. Makepeace (1987) reports that among both male and female college students, those who received D's as a frequent high school grade were more than twice as likely as students who mostly received A's and B's in high school to report involvement in dating violence. Higher rates were also found among those who had been fired from a job. Furthermore, people who have been fired from more than one job were four times more likely to report a dating violence experience than someone who was never fired.

Sociodemographic Factors

Race. Five studies examined racial differences in the occurrence of dating violence. Once again, the results are mixed. In terms of white-black differences, three studies find higher rates of dating violence among blacks (Makepeace, 1987; O'Keefe, Brockopp & Chew, 1986; Plass & Gessner, 1983). One finds no white-black differences (Matthews, 1984), and a fifth study finds a higher rate of dating assault among whites (Lane & Gwartney-Gibbs, 1985). Asians report lower levels of involvement in dating violence, and reported Hispanic rates are generally slightly higher than white rates across these samples. The bulk of dating violence studies exclude nonwhites from their analyses because of small sample sizes, thus limiting the available information on racial differences.

Family Income. Seven studies have examined family income as a risk marker of dating violence. Even with the constricted range in family income levels in college samples, there does appear to be a relationship between income level and involvement in dating violence. Three studies find significantly higher rates of dating violence experience among those with lower family incomes, while two studies report nonsignificant findings but a definite overrepresentation of individuals from lower economic strata among the ranks of the violent. Matthews (1984) finds no relationship between dating violence and family income, but his sample is largely middle class, and Makepeace (1987) found higher rates of involvement in dating violence among the lowest and highest family income groupings. In studies that controlled for gender, this finding holds for males but not for females (Sigelman, Berry & Wiles, 1984).

There is also some evidence of a "status-incongruence" effect (Lane & Gwartney-Gibbs, 1985; Makepeace, 1987; Plass & Gessner, 1983) with victims of dating abuse being overrepresented in higher family income groups and offenders more likely to come from poorer backgrounds.

Religion. While no religious affiliation differences have been found (Matthews, 1984), there is evidence of effects due to religious participation. Makepeace (1987) has reported that persons who rarely or never attend religious services are twice as likely as frequent attenders to report involvement in dating violence. Stets and Pirog-Good (1987c) focused on whether religious incompatibility (that is, differences in religious affiliation) prompted higher rates of dating violence and reported little effect.

Age. Dating violence has been studied almost exclusively as an issue of adolescence. Not only are noncollege young people usually excluded from the conceptual domain of dating violence, but so are large numbers of people over college age. Four studies find no relationship between age and dating violence. In these studies, neither victims nor offenders were significantly younger or older than their nonviolent counterparts (Arias, Samios & O'Leary, 1987; Marshall & Rose, 1987; Matthews, 1984; Sigelman, Berry & Wiles, 1984). One study finds a relationship between age and the use of violence in dating situations, but only for males (Stets & Pirog-Good, 1987c). Plass & Gessner (1983) in a sample of both high school *and* college students find generally higher rates of dating violence for the high schoolers, but this result could be due to myriad factors rather than solely to the effects of age. Even so, this study does suggest that even higher rates of dating violence may exist among younger populations.

Another avenue that has been pursued regarding age is the issue of age discrepancy. Perhaps couples with significant age differences are more likely to engage in violence? Stets & Pirog-Good (1987c) could find no evidence for this hypothesis. Separately examining the role of age differences among both males and females and among victims and offenders of dating violence, they reported no significant findings.

Place of Origin. Two studies examined the relationship between the size of the community in which respondents were reared and current dating violence. Both studies find that persons involved in dating violence are more likely than nonviolent daters to have been raised in urban environments. Makepeace (1987) reported a positive relationship between size of place of upbringing and involvement in dating violence. This pattern is most exaggerated in the comparison between those growing up in rural areas and those growing up in cities of over 100,000 population. Those reared in large urban areas are over 50 percent more likely to report involvement in dating violence compared to those from small rural areas. Lane and Gwartney-Gibbs (1985) found that the use of violence against dating partners as well as being victimized by dating violence is also more common among those from urban compared to rural backgrounds. One study has also assessed the relationship between dating violence and current residence and has found that males who use violence are more likely to currently reside in rural areas but females who use violence in dating are less likely to be rural residents (Sigelman, Berry & Wiles, 1984).

COMPARISON OF DATING AND MARITAL VIOLENCE

Dating violence has been seen as closely linked with other forms of family violence, particularly marital violence (cf. Carlson, 1987), but three questions must be addressed about this claim. First, are the prevalence rates reported for dating violence of similar magnitudes to marital violence rates? Second, are there substantial differences between the contextual factors associated with dating violence and the factors associated with marital violence? Finally, do similar risk markers tend to be associated with these two types of interpersonal violence?

Prevalence Comparisons

The first major issue is whether marital and dating violence have similar or dissimilar prevalence rates. Using the 1975 National Family Violence Survey (NFVS) data, Straus, Gelles, and Steinmetz (1980) reported a 28.0 percent lifetime prevalence rate, that is, over one-fourth of their married respondents indicated that they had either sustained or expressed marital violence over the lifetime of their relationships. Across the 20 studies in Table 1.1 (excluding Laner, 1983) that reported overall lifetime prevalence rates of dating violence, a 30.0 percent average rate is revealed. While these rates are strikingly similar, they are very crude estimates that may hide important distinctions. Using the NFVS data, Yllo and Straus (1981) divided the sample into cohabitants and married respondents and reported that the former exhibited a higher rate of violence than the latter. However, a number of confounding variables could account for these findings, particularly respondent's age and socioeconomic status. Furthermore, cohabiting couples represent only a minority of possible dating relationships.

Stets and Straus (this volume, Chapter 2) compared the rates of dating, cohabiting, and marital violence. Using data from the 1986 National Family Violence Resurvey (NFVR) and from a survey of dating couples at a midwestern university, Stets and Straus reported that cohabitants exhibited more overall violence and a greater amount of severe violence during a time frame of a year than either married or dating couples, after controlling for age and socioeconomic status. Furthermore, dating violence was only slightly more frequent than marital violence. This corroborates the above reported similarities between lifetime involvement rates for marital and dating violence. Still, the Stets and Straus results indicate that not all forms of dating violence have equivalent rates. Consequently, studies that have higher proportions of cohabiting respondents may report higher rates of dating violence. Unfortunately, few studies offer a breakdown of the violence rates based on the relationship level.

While these surveys suggest similar rates between marital and dating violence (excluding cohabitation), Erez's (1986) research offers a different picture. She examined all domestic violence incident reports filed in 1978 by 28 police departments of a midwestern county. Of the 1,764 incidents involving adult intimate relationships, 56.5 percent involved married couples; 22.7 percent involved boyfriends or girlfriends; and 20.8 percent involved ex-spouses. It is questionable whether these data accurately reflect the frequencies of dating and marital violence. First, Erez is unclear as to whether the boyfriend/girlfriend reports involve cohabitation or not. Second, it is difficult to compare these percentages because figures on the number of dating individuals or divorced individuals in the general population are unavailable to permit the computation of comparative rates. Third, these data represent the frequencies of intimate violence that becomes known to legal authorities and thus may underestimate the actual prevalence rate.

Context Comparison

Some aspects of the context in which marital violence takes place are similar to earlier mentioned findings from the dating violence literature. For example, Coleman (1980), Giles-Sims (1983), and Roy (1982) reported that individuals involved in marital violence cited jealousy and disagreements over alcohol and drug usage as explanations for the violence. However, they also mentioned a number of other reasons for the violence that do not emerge in the dating violence research, such as disputes over money, children, the woman's working outside the home. Still, the thematic similarities are striking. These similarities are confirmed by Roscoe and Benaske (1985), who requested battered wives to report about their violent experiences with their husbands and the men they dated prior to marriage. Similarities were reported in the type of violent acts received and inflicted and the perceived causes of the violence.

Still, these two types of violent experiences may not be contextually equivalent. In the police report study, Erez (1986) noted that among the three types of violent incidents (boyfriend/girlfriend, spousal, and ex-spousal) a number of contextual differences were revealed. Dating violence participants were more likely to be younger and black, while marital violence participants were more likely to be older and white. Furthermore, compared with marital violence, dating violence was more likely to involve the use of objects or criminal weapons, to be related to drug use, and to occur during the fall. The racial difference is particularly important, given the low number of minority respondents in the dating violence survey research.

Risk Marker Comparison

If one were to assume that dating and marital violence are representations of the same phenomenon, one would be led to predict that similar markers will be associated with these two forms of intimate violence. Four problems arise with this type of comparison. First, the primary concentration of marital violence research has been on husband-to-wife violence, unlike the dating violence literature that has examined both male-to-female and female-to-male violence. Second, since some markers were evaluated in only one or two studies, it is hard to be certain of the effect's stability and generalizability. This is particularly true with the dating violence findings. The third problem involves differences in the operationalization of these markers. For example, in the marital violence research, family income may refer to the monies available to the family of procreation while dating respondents would report the income of their family of origin. Although both literatures may report a negative association between family income and intimate violence, one must be cautious not to overstate the similarity of these findings. The fourth obstacle is that many of the risk markers that have been evaluated in the marital violence literature have not been assessed in regard to dating violence. One notable example is alcohol usage. Hotaling and Sugarman (1986) noted that alcohol consumption by men was a consistent risk marker for marital violence; however, the presently reviewed research offers no data on this marker's relationship to dating violence. Unfortunately, a number of risk markers that were associated with marital violence were not investigated in dating violence research, including frequency of verbal arguments, relationship satisfaction or adjustment, age, and assertiveness.

Even given these comparison problems, agreements and disagreements between these two literatures can be cited. Using Hotaling and Sugarman's (1986) review as the marital violence literature comparison, three risk markers appear to exhibit similar statistical associations with violence in these two contexts. Higher levels of male sexual aggression, higher stress levels, and lower income levels are related to higher levels of both forms of intimate violence. In addition, the research in these two areas suggests that four other markers are either unrelated to intimate violence or offer mixed or inconsistent findings: experiencing violence as a child, race, sex-role attitudes, and psychiatric symptomology.

More intriguing are the differences in these two literatures. According to Hotaling and Sugarman (1986), lower educational attainment, greater religious incompatibility, and the witnessing of marital violence as a child were associated with a greater likelihood of being involved in marital violence. These effects were not consistently found in the dating violence research. Part of these differences can be accounted for by methodological issues. For example, the education effect may have been concealed in the dating studies, given that the respondents were mostly college students. However, the lack of a witnessing effect in the dating violence studies is more problematic. This strikes at the heart of the assumption that dating violence serves as an intermediate stage between violence in the family-of-origin and in the family-of-procreation. In addition, two effects emerged in the dating violence research that did not appear in the marital violence literature. Low self-esteem and more positive attitudes toward the use of violence in intimate situations were predictive of dating violence involvement but inconsistently related to marital violence involvement. Based on this type of analysis, it is premature to conclude that dating and marital violence represent the same phenomenon.

Does Dating Violence Lead to Marital Violence?

Research on this important point is lacking. Roscoe and Benaske (1985), who surveyed 82 battered women seeking help at a women's shelter, found that 51 percent of these women reported that they were physically abused in a dating relationship. While this percentage is high, it is difficult to argue that this is firm evidence for the relationship between dating and marital violence. First, the researchers did not survey a nonvictimized comparison group. Second, compared to other prevalence rates noted in the dating violence research, this rate is high but not totally out of line with the observed rate distribution. Third, their assessment of dating violence involved the women's reporting of the type of violent acts inflicted or sustained in the four most recent dating relationships prior to marriage. It is unclear whether the researchers excluded the dating relationships with the men the battered women eventually married. This is important, given that Gayford (1975) reported that in 25 percent of the violent relationships that he studied, the violence began before marriage. Based upon the lack of research focused on this question, it is impossible to ascertain whether one of the major dating violence hypotheses has been supported or not.

CONCLUSION

Although dating violence research has had a relatively short history, a review of this knowledge base does permit some conclusions and suggests a number of implications. They can be organized under three headings: methodology, theory, and policy.

Methodology

A number of criticisms can be leveled at this research, including sample selection, violence measurement, and results reporting. First, researchers have primarily surveyed college or high school student samples; little is known about dating violence among older couples or nonstudent populations. Most of these samples have been convenience samples and thus potentially nonrepresentative of even the subpopulations surveyed. Furthermore, few researchers (for example, Olday & Wesley, 1983) have attempted to examine whether their sample characteristics matched the characteristics of the population from which the sample was drawn, such as racial, grade level, and age distribution characteristics. Also, the inclusion of married participants in dating samples raises questions about what is being studied. If we are assessing violence in existing relationships then we may be including marital violence, which may be totally different from dating violence. Finally, research has depended on a single respondent's responses instead of obtaining data from dating couples (cf. Szinovacz, 1983).

A second problem involves the operationalization of dating violence. Almost all of the studies employed some variation of the CTS; however, the measures that were derived from this scale often changed with these variations. Some measures include only acts of violence, others counted both acts and threats of violence, and some expanded the measure to contain acts of verbal abuse. Another problem is time frame: Some surveys employ a lifetime time frame, some use a period of a year, and still others use a period of two years. Obviously, the number of types of behaviors to be included and the length of the time frame will have a direct effect on the rates reported and make it difficult to do a comparative analysis across studies. By implication, this suggests a need to study multiple indicators of dating violence, preferably both acts and injuries. Simple reliance on the CTS may allow comparison of study results (which is questionable, given the variation in CTS usage); however, it opens the entire literature to the criticisms that have been leveled at the CTS (Straus, 1987). Clearly, further instrument development is needed.

A third issue surrounds the reporting of data analysis and findings. Researchers can derive a variety of measures from the CTS, using the same information. They may simply dichotomize their sample into violent or nonviolent groups or they can compute a continuous violence index using a weighting procedure and sometimes excluding nonviolent respondents. Findings can be dramatically affected by the scale of measurement used, and interpretation is difficult if the measure that was used is not clearly specified. A related problem is that many studies do not disaggregate their data into victim/offender-male/female categories.

Overall, there is a methodological parochialness in this literature. The survey is king. Alternative strategies have to be employed to examine factors that may be associated with dating violence, such as behavioral observation of violent and nonviolent dating relationships within laboratory settings. Part of this parochialness is in the continued emphasis on prevalence rates. While monitoring trends is important, it should not be the only focus of future research. A shift in attention to examining the factors that support or inhibit violent behavior should begin. Prevalence indicates that there is a need to intervene, but not how to intervene.

Theory

The major theoretical assumptions within this field have not gained sufficient empirical support. Dating violence appears to be inconsistently related to witnessing and experiencing violence in the family of origin and the data regarding its relationship to marital violence are missing. These findings would appear to undercut any social learning theory or "training ground" interpretation of dating violence.

Certain findings, however, may offer important keys to a better theoretical understanding of dating violence. Since lower family income, poorer academic performance, and greater levels of stress are related to higher levels of dating violence involvement, an emphasis on the application of conflict theory to dating should be explored. Also, several pieces of evidence suggest that the support of patriarchal norms is not uncommon among those involved in dating violence. First, a sizable proportion of abusive men readily admitted that the purpose of their violent behavior was to control the woman's behavior. Second, a vast majority of the individuals who were involved in violence reported having told others about the incident(s) regardless of their role in the violent act. This suggests that little social stigma is attached to dating violence involvement and that it may be viewed as normative behavior. Third, the high rate of violence would suggest that it is more the rule than the exception for both men and women. Finally, the regional differences in prevalence rates may represent subcultural variations in the acceptance of patriachical norms. These norms may have a greater impact in dating relationships than in marital relationships due to the greater ambiguity that characterizes interactional roles in dating.

Other perspectives also may be fertile sources of theoretical direction. Perhaps dating violence research should be integrated with the more general courtship research (cf. Murstein, 1980). For example, the impact of physical attractiveness and sexual jealousy within this context has gone unexamined. Similarly, the attributional literature may offer some intriguing leads (Fletcher et al., 1987; Sugarman & Hotaling, in press). In some ways, dating violence research examines a phenomenon that is searching for a theory.

Policy

Even given our limited knowledge of dating violence, certain policy implications deserve to be mentioned. The high prevalence rate of such behavior in our secondary and postsecondary educational institutions mandates that those facilities confront this issue directly. Student services personnel should be educated in identifying individuals who may be at risk of being involved in dating violence. Human relations workshops should be offered to educate students in nonviolent means of resolving interpersonal conflict and coping with jealousy. These efforts should be dovetailed with attempts to prevent the rising rates of sexual aggression on campus. Shelters or dating violence hotlines should be created on campus. Dating violence is likely a large problem off campus as well. Companies that offer computer dating services also have a responsibility to screen candidates for a history of dating violence as part of their routine data collection efforts.

REFERENCES

Adams, D. C. (1986, August). Counseling men who batter: A profeminist analysis of clinical models. Paper presented at the annual meeting of the American Psychological Association, Washington, DC.

Ajzen, I., & Fishbein, M. (1980). *Understanding attitudes and predicting social behavior.* Englewood Cliffs, NJ: Prentice-Hall.

Arias, I., & Johnson, P. (1986, November). Evaluations of physical aggression in marriage. Paper presented at the meeting of the Association for Advancement of Behavior Therapy, Chicago.

Arias, I., Samios, M., & O'Leary, K. D. (1987). Prevalence and correlates of physical aggression during courtship. *Journal of Interpersonal Violence,* 2(1), 82–90.

Bedford, A., & Foulds, G. (1978). *Manual of the Personality Deviance Scales (PDS).* Windsor: National Foundation for Educational Research in England and Wales.

Bem, D. (1967). Self-perception: An alternative interpretation of cognitive dissonance phenomena. *Psychological Review,* 74, 188–200.

Berk, R. A., Berk, S. F., Loseke, D. B., & Rauma, D. (1983). "Mutual Combat and Other Family Violence Myths." In D. Finkelhor, R. J. Gelles, G. T. Hotaling, & M. A. Straus (eds.), *The dark side of families: Current family violence research,* 197–212. Beverly Hills, CA: Sage.

Bernard, M. L., & Bernard, J. L. (1983). Violent intimacy: The family as a model for love relationships. *Family Relations,* 32, 283–86.

Bernard, J. L., Bernard, S. L., & Bernard, M. L. (1985). Courtship violence and sextyping. *Family Relations,* 34, 573–76.

Billingham, R. E. (1987). Courtship violence: The patterns of conflict resolution strategies across seven levels of emotional commitment. *Family Relations,* 36, 283–89.

Billingham, R. E., & Sack, A. R. (1987). Conflict resolution tactics and the level of emotional commitment among unmarrieds. *Human Relations,* 40, 59–74.

Billings, A. (1979). Conflict resolution in distressed and nondistressed married couples. *Journal of Counseling and Clinical Psychology,* 47(2), 368–76.

Block, M. R., & Sinnott, J. D. (1979). *The battered elder syndrome: An exploratory study.* College Park, MD: Center on Aging.

Bogal-Allbritten, R., & Allbritten, W. L. (1985). The hidden victims: Courtship violence among college students. *Journal of College Student Personnel,* 19, 201–4.

Carlson, B. (1987). Dating violence: A research review and comparison with spouse abuse. *Social Casework,* 68(1), 16–23.

Cate, R. M., Henton, J. M., Koval, J., Christopher, F. S., & Lloyd, S. (1982). Premarital abuse: A social psychological perspective. *Journal of Family Issues,* 3, 79–90.

Coleman, K. H. (1980). Conjugal violence: What 33 men report. *Journal of Marriage and the Family,* 6, 207–13.

Comins, C. A. (1984). Courtship violence: A recent study and its implications for future research. Paper presented at the Second National Family Violence Research, Conference, University of New Hampshire, Durham, NH.

Deal, J. E., & Wampler, K. S. (1986). Dating violence: The primacy of previous experiences. *Journal of Social and Personal Relationships,* 3(4), 457–71.

30   Sugarman & Hotaling

DeMaris, A. (1987). The efficacy of a spouse abuse model in accounting for courtship violence. *Journal of Family Issues,* 8(3), 291–305.

Derogatis, L. R. (1977). *SCL-90 administration, scoring and procedures manual-I for the R(evised) version.* Baltimore, MD: Johns Hopkins University School of Medicine.

Dobash, R. E., & Dobash, R. (1979). *Violence against wives: A case against the patriarchy.* New York: Free Press.

Erez, E. (1986). Intimacy, violence and the police. *Human Relations,* 39(3), 265–81.

Federal Bureau of Investigation (1985). *Uniform crime reports for the United States.* Washington, DC: U.S Department of Justice.

Ferraro, K. J., & Johnson, J. M. (1984, August). The meanings of courtship violence. Paper presented at the Second National Family Violence Research Conference, University of New Hampshire, Durham, NH.

Finkelhor, D. (1979). *Sexually victimized children.* New York: Free Press.

Fletcher, G., Fincham, F., Cramer, V., & Heron, N. (1987). The role of attributions in the development of dating relationships. *Journal of Personality and Social Psychology,* 53, 481–89.

Flynn, C. P. (1987). Relationship violence: A model for family professional. *Family Relations,* 36, 295–99.

Gayford, J. J. (1975). Wife battering: A preliminary survey of 100 cases. *British Medical Journal,* 1, 194–97.

Gelles, R. J. (1972). *The violent home.* Beverly Hills, CA: Sage.

Gelles, R. J., & Straus, M. A. (1988). *Intimate violence.* New York: Simon & Schuster.

Giles-Sims, J. (1983). *Wife-battering: A systems theory approach.* New York: Guilford.

Greenblat, C. S. (1983). A hit is a hit is a hit . . . Or is it? Approval and tolerance of the use of physical force by spouses. In D. Finkelhor, R. J. Gelles, G. T. Hotaling, & M. A. Straus (eds.), *The dark side of families: Current family violence research,* 235–60. Beverly Hills, CA: Sage.

Gwartney-Gibbs, P. A., Stockard, J., & Brohmer, S. (1987). Learning courtship violence: The influence of parents, peers, and personal experiences. *Family Relations,* 36, 276–82.

Henton, J., Cate, R., Koval, J., Lloyd, S., & Christopher, S. (1983). Romance and violence in dating relationships. *Journal of Family Issues,* 4, 467–82.

Hotaling, G. T., & Sugarman, D. B. (1986). An analysis of risk markers in husband to wife violence: The current state of knowledge. *Violence and Victims,* 1(2), 101–24.

Kantor, G. K., & Straus, M. A. (1987). The drunken bum theory of wife abuse. *Social Problems,* 34, 213–30.

Kaufman, J., & Zigler, E. (1987). *Do abused children become abusive parents?* Yale University, New Haven, CT. Unpublished.

Lane, K. E., & Gwartney-Gibbs, P. A. (1985). Violence in the context of dating and sex. *Journal of Family Issues,* 6(1), 45–59.

Laner, M. R. (1983). Courtship abuse and aggression: Contextual aspects. *Sociological Spectrum,* 3, 69–83.

Laner, M. R., & Thompson, J. (1982), Abuse and aggression in courting couples. *Deviant Behavior,* 3, 229–44.

Last, J. M. (1983). *A dictionary of epidemiology.* New York: Oxford University Press.

Makepeace, J. M. (1981). Courtship violence among college students. *Family Relations, 30*, 97–102.

———. (1983). Life events, stress and courtship violence. *Family Relations, 32*, 101–109.

———. (1984, August). The severity of courtship violence injuries and individual precautionary measures. Paper presented at the Second National Family Violence Research Conference, University of New Hampshire, Durham, NH.

———. (1986). Gender differences in courtship violence victimization. *Family Relations, 35*, 383–88.

———. (1987). Social factors and victim offender differences in courtship violence. *Family Relations, 36*(1), 87–91.

Marshall, L. L. (1987, July). Gender differences in the prediction of courtship abuse from family of origin violence, anxiety proneness and recent positive and negative stress. Paper presented at the Third National Family Violence Research Conference, University of New Hampshire, Durham, NH.

Marshall, L. L., & Rose, P. (1987). Gender, stress and violence in adult relationships of a sample of college students. *Journal of Social and Personal Relationship, 4*, 299–316.

———. (1988). Family of origin and courtship violence. *Journal of Counseling and Development, 66*(9), 414–18.

Matthews, W. J. (1984). Violence in college couples. *College Student Journal, 18*, 150–58.

May, M. (1978). Violence in the family: An historical perspective. In J. P. Martin (ed.), *Violence and the family*, 135–68. New York: Wiley.

Mayhew, H. (1861). *London labour and the London poor*. 4 vols. London: Griffen, Bohn.

McKinney, K. (1986a). Measures of verbal, physical, and sexual dating violence by gender. *Free Inquiry into Creative Sociology, 14*(1), 55–60.

———. (1986b). Perceptions of courtship violence: Gender difference and involvement. *Free Inquiry into Creative Sociology, 14*(1), 61–66.

Murphy, J. E. (1984, August). Date abuse and forced intercourse among college students. Paper presented at the Second National Family Violence Research Conference, University of New Hampshire, Durham, NH.

Murstein, B. I. (1980). Mate selection in the 1970s. *Journal of Marriage and the Family, 42*, 51–66.

O'Keefe, N., Brockopp, K., & Chew, E. (1986). Teen dating violence. *Social Work, 31*, 465–68.

Olday, D., & Wesley, B. (1983). *Premarital courtship violence: A summary report*. Moorhead State University, Moorhead, KY. Unpublished.

Plass, M. S., & Gessner, J. C. (1983). Violence in courtship relations: A Southern example. *Free Inquiry into Creative Sociology, 11*, 198–202.

Puig, A. (1984). Predomestic strife: A growing college counseling concern. *Journal of College Student Personnel, 25*, 268–69.

Roscoe, B., & Benaske, N. (1985). Courtship violence experienced by abused wives: Similarities in patterns of abuse. *Family Relations, 34*, 419–24.

Roscoe, B., & Callahan, J. E. (1985). Adolescents' self-report of violence in families and dating relations. *Adolescence, 20*, 545–53.

Roscoe, B., & Kelsey, T. (1986). Dating violence among high school students. *Psychology*, 23(1), 53–59.

Roy, M. (1982). Four thousand partners in violence: A trend analysis. In M. Roy (ed.), *The abusive partner*, 17–38. New York: Van Nostrand Reinhold.

Rubin, Z. (1970). Measurement of romantic love. *Journal of Personality and Social Psychology*, 16, 265–73.

Sack, A. R., Keller, J. F., & Howard, R. D. (1982). Conflict tactics and violence in dating situations. *International Journal of the Sociology of the Family*, 12, 89–100.

Sigelman, C. K., Berry, C. J., & Wiles, K. A. (1984). Violence in college students' dating relationships. *Journal of Applied Social Psychology*, 5, 6, 530–48.

Sonkin, D. J., Martin, D., & Walker, L. E. A. (1985). *The male batterer: A treatment approach*. New York: Springer.

Stets, J. E., & Pirog-Good, M. A. (1987a). Control and dating violence. Family Research Laboratory, University of New Hampshire, Durham, NH. Unpublished.

————. (1987b). Patterns of physical and sexual abuse for men and women in dating relationships: A descriptive analysis. Paper presented at the American Society of Criminology Meetings, Montreal, August.

————. (1987c). Violence in dating relationships. *Social Psychology Quarterly*, 50(3), 237–46.

Straus, M. A. (1979). Measuring intrafamily conflict and violence: The conflict tactics (CT) scales. *Journal of Marriage and the Family*, 41, 75–86.

————. (1980a). The marriage license as a hitting license: Evidence from popular culture, law, and social science. In M. A. Straus & G. T. Hotaling (eds.), *The social causes of husband-wife violence*, 39–50. Minneapolis, MN: University of Minnesota Press.

————. (1980b). Social stress and marital violence in a national sample of American families. *Annals of the New York Academy of Science*, 347, 229–50.

————. (1987, November). The conflict tactics scales and its critics: An evaluation and new data on validity and reliability. Paper presented at the annual meeting of the National Council on Family Relations, Atlanta, GA.

Straus, M. A., Gelles, R. J., & Steinmetz, S. K. (1980). *Behind closed doors: Violence in the American family*. Garden City, NY: Anchor.

Sugarman, D. B., & Hotaling, G. T. (in press). Violent men in intimate relationships: An analysis of risk markers. *Journal of Applied Social Psychology*.

Szinovacz, M. E. (1983). Using couple data as a methodological tool: The case of marital violence. *Journal of Marriage and the Family*, 45, 633–44.

Tedeschi, J. T., Smith, R., & Brown, R. (1974). A reinterpretation of research on aggression. *Psychological Bulletin*, 81, 540–62.

Thompson, W. E. (1986). Courtship violence: Toward a conceptual understanding. *Youth and Society*, 18(2), 162–76.

Vivian, D., & O'Leary, K. D. (1987, July). *Communication patterns in physically aggressive engaged couples*. Paper presented at the Third National Family Violence Research Conference, University of New Hampshire, Durham, NH.

Wolfgang, M. E., & Ferracuti, F. (1967). *The subculture of violence*. New York: Tavistock.

Yllo, K., & Straus, M. A. (1981). Interpersonal violence among married and cohabiting couples. *Family Relations*, 30, 339–47.

2   The Marriage License as a Hitting License: A Comparison of Assaults in Dating, Cohabiting, and Married Couples

Jan E. Stets and Murray A. Straus

Gelles and Straus coined the term "the marriage license as a hitting license" in the early 1970s in response to the discovery that the assault rate among married couples was many times greater than the assault rate between strangers. They argued that the common law rule which gave husbands the right to "physically chastise an errant wife," although not formally recognized by the courts since the mid 1800s, lived on in popular culture and in the way the criminal justice system actually operated (Straus, 1975; 1976). Since then, the pervasiveness of violence in intimate relationships has been well documented by the two National Family Violence Surveys and by other investigations. Each year, more than 3 million married couples experience one or more severe assaults (Straus & Gelles, 1988).[1]

Subsequent investigations revealed that violence in cohabiting relationships is also quite common. In fact, physical assaults may be more common and more severe among cohabiting couples than married couples (Yllo & Straus, 1981; Lane & Gwartney-Gibbs, 1985). Given that cohabitation as an alternative living arrangement has steadily increased since 1970 (Glick & Spanier, 1980; Spanier, 1983), more individuals may be at risk not only of minor violence, but severe violence.[2]

The most recent research shows that dating violence is also pervasive and is a hidden serious social problem (Bogal-Allbritten & Allbritten, 1985). About 20 percent of college students have been physically assaulted by a dating partner (Makepeace, 1981; Cate et al., 1982; Stets & Pirog-Good, 1987).

The findings on violence between cohabiting couples and between dating couples raise questions about the implication that the status of being married is

This chapter is reprinted with permission from *Journal of Family Violence*, 41(2), 1989.

one of the factors accounting for the high rate of violence among married couples. While some research suggests that the overall assault rate in dating may be comparable to or higher than that found in marriage (Bernard et al., 1985; Makepeace, 1986), the comparisons are questionable because the rates are not based on the same measure (for example, Makepeace, 1981). Even when the same measure is used, researchers do not usually identify which partner is violent, the severity of the assault, or whether the behavior is different from that found in marriage or cohabiting relationships (for example, Cate et al., 1982). A similar problem occurs when cohabiting and marital violence are compared because of the failure to identify which partner is violent and the severity of the assault. In response to these problems, the present research compares physical assaults across dating, cohabiting, and marital relationships using the same measure. Additionally, we examine which partner is violent and the form of abuse used across marital status groups.

It should be pointed out that there has been a long tradition in sociology of studying group differences in terms of rates in order to better understand the phenomenon under study. For example, Durkeim (1951) found that suicide was related to social integration only after comparing suicide rates of Catholics versus Protestants, married versus single people, men versus women, and young versus old people. A comparison of group rates is also used in epidemiology studies. However, in order to study group differences, accurate comparative rates are needed. Consequently, in this study, the rate of physical assault not only has to be measured in the same way across the different groups, but also other factors that may influence the group rates must be controlled. We do this in the present study by controlling on key demographic variables, including age, education, and occupation.

RESEARCH QUESTIONS

The primary objective of this research is to compare the frequency and form of violence among those who date, cohabit, or are married. The following questions will be addressed.

1. *Are there differences in the frequency of assault across marital status groups?* Given prior research, we anticipate that violence will be more common in cohabiting than marital relationships (Yllo & Straus, 1981; Lane & Gwartney-Gibbs, 1985). Researchers have not adequately explained why cohabitors are more violent than married individuals. Later, we discuss why this pattern might arise. We do not know how those who date will compare with the other marital status groups.

2. *Does the severity of the assault vary by marital status?* Based on prior research (Yllo & Straus, 1981), we expect that violence will be more severe in cohabiting than in dating or marital relationships. Later, we discuss why this might occur.

3. *Does the partner who is violent vary by marital status?* Prior research has

not directly examined whether the use of violence by men and women varies across different marital status groups. There is evidence that husbands are victims of marital violence as often as wives [Steinmetz, 1978; Nisonoff and Bitman, 1979; Straus, Gelles & Steinmetz, 1980; Straus & Gelles, 1986 (see also the summary in Straus and Gelles, 1988; Stets & Straus, 1989)]. However, other studies reveal that most offenders are men (Dobash & Dobash, 1979) and that if women hit, it is usually for self-defense (Saunders, 1986). The finding that women are more likely to hit for retaliation or self-defense (Straus, 1980) has not been supported by the most recent studies on this issue, which show that women *initiate* violence as often as men (Straus & Gelles, 1988; Stets & Straus, 1989).

The mixed results may be due to the use of different samples. On the one hand, studies based on clinical populations find that men are more violent than women and that when women hit, it is for self-defense. On the other hand, community surveys find that women are as violent as men and that women initiate violence as often as men (see Stets & Straus, 1989).

Evidence on the frequency with which men and women use violence while dating is also mixed (see the summary in Straus & Gelles, 1988). For example, some researchers have found no difference in the assault rate by sex (Deal & Wampler, 1986; Arias, Samios & O'Leary, 1987; Stets & Pirog-Good, 1987). Others reveal that men are more likely than women to be the aggressors (Makepeace, 1983), and that if women hit, it is usually for self-defense (Makepeace, 1986). Still others find that women are more likely than men to be the aggressors (Plass & Gessner, 1983). More research is needed to resolve these contradictory findings.

This chapter examines violence by both men and women in dating, cohabiting, and marital relationships. We view violence as a mutual problem of both sexes (Breines & Gordon, 1983), even though, when injury occurs, it is probably not as grave for men as for women because men, on average, are physically stronger (Straus, Gelles & Steinmetz, 1980; Greenblat, 1983). Indeed, recent research reveals that female victims of violence are more likely than male victims to experience physical and psychological injury (Stets & Straus, 1989).

This research attempts to answer the above questions and controls for age, education, occupational status, and gender of the respondent. These controls are introduced to help rule out spurious relationships. Because many other controls could be introduced, our results are suggestive and not definitive of physical assaults across marital status groups.

METHOD

Samples

For the dating couples, a survey was administered to a probability sample of students at a large midwestern university during the spring of 1987. The response rate was 83 percent. A total of 526 individuals had complete information on physical violence and were included in our analysis.

The data on married and cohabiting couples is from the National Family Violence Resurvey conducted in the summer of 1985 (Straus & Gelles, 1986). The interviews were conducted by telephone, using random digit dialing to select a nationally representative sample. The respondent was the husband (or male partner) for a random half of the cases, and the wife (or female partner) for the other half. A total of 6,002 people were interviewed. However, the number used in this chapter is lower because single parent families are excluded, and because data on certain questions are missing. The response rate, calculated as completed interviews as a portion of eligible interviews was 84 percent. The sample is described in more detail in Straus and Gelles (1986, 1988). In this study, we analyze 5,005 married and 237 cohabiting couples.

Violence Measures

Conflict Tactics Scale (CTS). The CTS (Straus, 1979, 1987b) was used to measure the incidence of violence in dating, cohabiting and marital relationships. Respondents were asked how often, within the past year, they engaged in each of the following acts of physical violence against their partner: (1) threw an object; (2) pushed, grabbed or shoved; (3) slapped; (4) kicked, bit, or punched; (5) hit or tried to hit with an object; (6) beat up; (7) threatened with a knife or gun; or (8) used a knife or gun. If any violent acts occurred, then violence was coded one; otherwise, it was coded zero. Following this, respondents again filled out the CTS, but in reference to how often, within the past year, their partner used violence against them. Again, if violence occurred, a score of one was given; otherwise, violence was scored zero.

Minor and severe categories of violence were also calculated. If acts 1–3 above occurred, a score of one was given for minor violence; otherwise, this category was zero. If acts 4–8 occurred, a score of one was given for severe violence; otherwise, this category was zero. When severe violence occurred, there was almost always minor violence. Consequently, the "severe violence" measure does not exclude minor assaults. In other words, one who used any of acts 4–8 also could have used any of acts 1–3.

Assault Rate and Violence Type Percentages. Three different but overlapping measures of violence are used in this chapter because each serves to illuminate a different facet of interpersonal violence. The first measure is the *assault rate* per 100 couples. This provides information on the incidence of physical violence among married, cohabiting, and dating couples. These data will be shown in the form of figures.

The second and third measures are typologies. These violence types are used for a more detailed analysis of the subset of respondents who experienced one or more violent acts during the year of the survey. These data will be given in tables.

Two violence types are identified: *Physical Violence I* and *Physical Violence II*. Physical Violence I identifies the violent partner: male only, female only, or both. Physical Violence II uses the same categories of violent actors, but also accounts for the severity and mutuality of assaults. There are eight categories:

1. Male used minor violence, and female did not use violence.
2. Male did not use violence, and female used minor violence.
3. Both used minor violence.
4. Male used severe violence, and female did not use violence.
5. Male did not use violence, and female used severe violence.
6. Male used severe violence, and female used minor violence.
7. Male used minor violence, and female used severe violence.
8. Both used severe violence.

Demographic Measures

The married and cohabiting respondents were individuals who resided in households containing a currently married or cohabiting heterosexual couple. Households with a single parent or recently terminated marriage were excluded. The dating respondents were individuals who had dated during 1986. Married individuals were excluded.

For married and cohabiting respondents, the respondents were grouped into four age categories: 18–24, 25–34, 35–44, and 45 and over. The dating respondents included only those ages 18–24.

Married and cohabiting respondents were grouped into five education categories: no education through eighth grade, some high school education, high school graduate, some college, and college graduate and postgraduate work.

The occupational status of those who date was not collected because all respondents were attending school full-time. Married and cohabiting respondents were classified as "blue collar" and "white collar" (which are somewhat parallel to "working class" and "middle class"), using the Bureau of Labor Statistics revised Occupational Classification system. Each Bureau of Labor Statistics occupation code was classified as either blue collar or white collar using Rice's list of occupations classified by these categories (see Robinson et al., 1969).

If respondents were currently unemployed or were housewives, their occupational code was based on their most recent paid job. If they never held a job for pay, they were coded as missing. To establish the occupational status of the relationship, the respondent's occupational status was used. When we examined the relationship between husbands' and wives' occupations, we found that two-thirds of the cases were concordant. Therefore, respondent's occupational status approximates the occupational status of the relationship.

RESULTS

Figure 2.1 shows that cohabiting couples are more likely to have experienced violence than those in dating or marital relationships ($\chi^2 = 84.4$, $p < .01$, df $= 6$).[3] The line for "either" shows that almost 35 out of every 100 cohabiting couples experienced a physical assault during the previous year compared to 20 per 100 dating couples and 15 per 100 married couples. Moreover, cohabiting couples have the highest rates for each of the three specific types of violence. For example, in 18 out of every 100 cohabiting couples, both were violent, which is about double the rates for dating and married couples.

Two other points worth noting about the rates in Figure 2.1 are that female only violence is less common among the married than the other marital status groups, and the lowest rate for male only violence is among dating couples.

Table 2.1 focuses on the subsample who reported one or more assaults. It shows the distribution of types of violence among those couples who experienced violence. Comparison of the percentages in the first column shows that female only violence type is a larger proportion of the violence among dating couples (39.4 percent) than other marital status groups (28.6 percent and 26.9 percent for those who are married and cohabit, respectively). Male only vio-

Figure 2.1
Assault Rates by Marital Status
("either" category is sum of the other three)

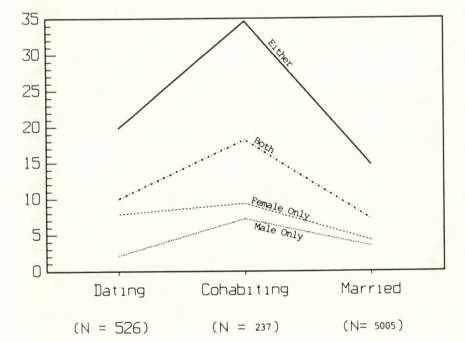

Table 2.1
Violent Couples: Percent In Physical Violence Type I by Marital Status

Marital Status	Physical Violence Type I			
	Female Only	Male Only	Both	N
Dating	39.4%	10.5%	50.0%	104
Cohabit	26.9%	20.7%	52.4%	82
Married	28.6%	23.2%	48.2%	736

$X^2 = 10.4$, p <.05, df=4

lence is a larger proportion of the violence in cohabiting (20.7 percent) and marital (23.2 percent) than dating (10.5 percent) relationships. There is little difference among marital status groups with respect to the both violent category.

In general, these results answer research questions 1 and 3. Figure 2.1 indicates that among all couples, there is a tendency for assaults to be most common in cohabiting relationships and slightly more common in dating than marital relationships. In couples among whom there is an assault, female only violence most often occurs in dating relationships and male only violence mostly occurs in marital and cohabiting relationships, as shown in Table 2.1. Situations in which both partners are violent occur about equally often in all marital status groups.

Figure 2.2 and Table 2.2 extend the analysis by taking into account the *severity* of assault by men and women in marital, cohabiting, and dating relationships. With two exceptions, the plot lines in Figure 2.2 show that cohabiting couples have the highest assault rate ($\chi^2 = 135.4$, $p < .01$, df = 16). For minor violence committed by both partners, cohabiting couples have roughly double the rate of the other two groups (8.0 versus 4.2 and 4.2; sixth category in Figure 2.2). For severe violence committed by both partners, cohabiting couples have more than six times the rate of the dating and married couples (first category in Figure 2.2). Exceptions to the tendency for assault to be greatest among cohabiting couples involve a more severe level of violence by the female partner than the male partner (second and seventh categories in Figure 2.2).

Turning to the subsample of violent couples, Table 2.2 indicates some types of violence in which there is little difference among dating, married, and cohabiting couples, and other types in which the difference is large. There is little difference in the percentage of violent couples who are in the both minor category (both partners engaged in minor assaults). However, there is a large difference in the both severe category (both severely violent). For 22 percent of violent cohabiting couples, both partners used severe violence compared to less than 11 percent for violent dating or married couples. Furthermore, the

Figure 2.2
Assault Rates (II) by Marital Status

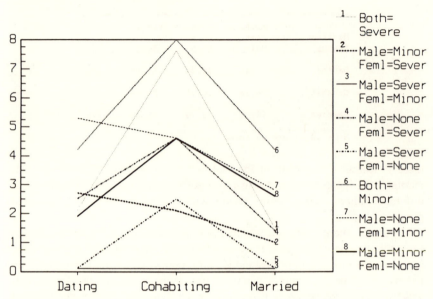

high percentage of female only violence while dating and male only violence while cohabiting and married typically manifests itself in minor violence.

In sum, the results in Figure 2.2 and Table 2.2 answer research question 2. They suggest that not only are cohabiting couples at greatest risk for violence, but, in addition, the most dangerous forms of violence occur when individuals cohabit. This is because severe violence that is carried out by both partners is most common in cohabiting relationships.

These conclusions are the type that might be made across different studies, if the dependent variable (physical assault) is measured in the same way in each case. However, these comparisons do not take into account the fact that

Table 2.2
Violent Couples: Percent in Physical Violence Type II by Marital Status

	Physical Violence Type II								
	M-Minor F-None	M-None F-Minor	Both Minor	M-Sev F-None	M-None F-Sev	M-Sev F-Minor	M-Minor F-Sev	Both Sev	N
Dating	9.6%	26.9%	21.2%	.1%	12.5%	4.8%	13.5%	10.6%	104
Cohabit	3.5%	13.4%	23.2%	7.3%	13.4%	1.2%	6.1%	22.0%	82
Married	7.5%	18.9%	28.3%	5.7%	9.6%	2.4%	7.1%	10.5%	736

$X^2 = 33.9$, p <.01, df=14

married, cohabiting, and dating couples vary in other characteristics that might affect their overall violence rates. Unless those other factors are controlled, or otherwise standardized, incorrect conclusions may be drawn. To see this, we turn first to age-controlled results.

Age

It is possible that the relationship between marital status and physical assault is spurious because age exerts an influence on both marital status and violence. Dating and cohabiting couples are likely to be younger than married couples. Additionally, studies have found that marital violence and cohabiting violence declines with age (Straus, Gelles & Steinmetz, 1980; Yllo & Straus, 1981). Therefore, the relationship between marital status and violence may change or disappear when age is controlled.

To investigate this possibility, we analyzed the relationship between (1) age and marital status; (2) age and assault, and (3) marital status and assault with age controlled. With respect to age and marital status, younger couples are more likely to cohabit, and older couples are more likely to be married ($\chi^2 = 298.0$; $p < .01$, df = 3). With respect to age and violence, age negatively influences the assault rate ($\chi^2 = 357.3$; $p < .01$, df = 6). This is not surprising given that criminal violence is most common among the young (Uniform Crime Reports, 1984). These findings indicate the importance of controlling for age in reducing a spurious relationship between marital status and assault.

We then examined the effects of age and marital status on violence, using log-linear analysis (Knoke & Burke, 1980). This provides a test of the effect of age (net of marital status), marital status (net of age), and the interaction of age and marital status on violence. The dating category is omitted from the log-linear analysis because individuals are between ages 18 and 24. However, the descriptive statistics for the dating group are shown in Figure 2.3 discussed below.

The results indicate that, while age and marital status exert their own influence on violence, the interaction between age and marital status is nonsignificant (n.s.): (χ^2 for age = 30.6, $p < .01$, df = 9; marital status = 10.5, $p < .05$, df = 3; age $\times$ marital status = 11.0, n.s., df = 9). Thus, age and marital status each have its own independent effects on violence. The age effects are not contingent on marital status, and the marital status effects are the same for all age groups.

The rates for each of the cells in the log-linear analysis are displayed in Figure 2.3. All but 3 of the 16 marital status comparisons in Figure 2.3 show a higher rate for cohabiting than married couples, and most of the differences are large.

Table 2.3, like the other tables, is focused on the subsample of respondents who reported one or more assaults. The data for age-controlled respondents show that there is no strong tendency for age to be related to Physical Violence I or marital status.

Figure 2.3
Assault Rates by Marital Status and Age

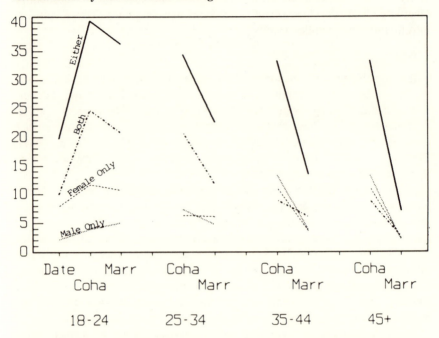

The importance of controlling for age is brought out by comparing the assault rate for those of ages 18–24 who are married, cohabiting, and dating. Without the age control, it seems as though dating couples are more violent than married couples (for example, see the line entitled "Either" in Figure 2.1). However, comparison of the violence rate for dating couples with the rates for married and cohabiting couples of the same ages (18–24) in the left panel of Figure 2.3 shows that violence is most common in cohabiting relationships and more common in marital than in dating relationships.

Education

The low rate of violence among dating couples after controlling for age may be due to the fact that they have a higher education than the other marital status groups. Since education negatively influences husband-to-wife violence (Hotaling & Sugarman, 1986), the violence rate in the dating sample may be depressed. We tested this by controlling for education in the age group 18–24 for married and cohabiting couples. We found that education did not significantly influence the rate of violence (χ^2 for marital status = 0.9, n.s., df = 3; for education = 0.7, n.s., df = 3; for marital status * education = 3.4, n.s., df = 3). Consequently, education does not explain the lower rate of violence among dating couples as compared to married and cohabiting couples.

Table 2.3
Violent Couples: Percent Physical Violence Type I by Age and
Occupational Status

Control	Marital Status	Physical Violence Type I			
		Female Only	Male Only	Both	N
Age					
18-24	Cohabiting	29.0%	9.7%	61.3%	31
	Married	29.1%	13.6%	56.4%	110
25-34	Cohabiting	18.2%	21.2%	60.6%	33
	Married	26.9%	20.7%	52.4%	309
35-44	Cohabiting	33.3%	40.0%	26.7%	15
	Married	26.9%	28.0%	45.1%	175
45+	Cohabiting	66.7%	33.3%	0%	3
	Married	34.2%	29.4%	36.4%	142

X^2 for Age - 12.3, p <.10, df-6; Marital Status - 0.1, n.s., df-2;
Age*Marital Status - 3.6, n.s., df-6

Occupational Status					
Blue C.	Cohabiting	19.0%	31.0%	50.0%	42
	Married	30.8%	24.5%	44.7%	302
White C.	Cohabiting	38.2%	11.8%	50.0%	34
	Married	27.1%	23.5%	49.4%	399

X^2 for Occ. Status - 4.8, p <.10, df-2; Marital Status - 1.0, n.s., df-2;
Occ. Status*Marital Status - 6.0, p <.05, df-2

Occupation

The relationship between marital status and assault may also be influenced by occupational status. For example, Straus, Gelles & Steinmetz (1980) found a lower rate of marital violence among white collar than blue collar workers. Similar results are found in this survey; that is, violence is more common in blue collar than white collar relationships ($\chi^2 = 10.2$, $p < .05$, df = 4).

A log-linear analysis of violence by occupational status and marital status reveals significant main effects for marital status, occupational status, and a significant marital status by occupation status interaction (χ^2 for Occupational Status = 10.2, $p < .05$, df = 3; for marital status = 47.3, $p < .001$, df = 3; for occupational status $\times$ marital status = 7.9, $p < .05$ df = 3). Figure 2.4 displays the rates.

Figure 2.4 shows an overall tendency for the assault rate to be lower among marital couples compared to cohabiting couples, and for white collar rates to be lower than blue collar rates, but the difference between married and cohab-

Figure 2.4
Assault Rates by Marital Status and Occupational Class

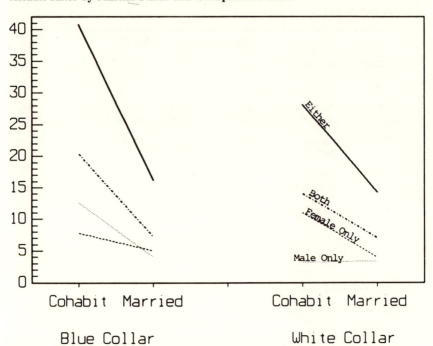

iting couples is somewhat less pronounced among white collar couples than blue collar couples.

The Occupational Status-controlled data in Table 2.3 show that among violent couples, there is no significant main effect for either marital status or occupational status. However, there is a significant interaction effect between these variables: The proportion of female only and male only changes from blue collar to white collar, but only for those who cohabit.

In summary, our results reveal that after controlling for age, education, and occupation, the marital status difference in assault rates remain; that is, cohabiting couples have the highest assault rate, followed by dating and married couples. However, it should be pointed out that after controlling for age, dating couples have a lower rate of assault than married couples.

Gender of Respondent

Returning to Figure 2.1, we find that female only violence is more common than male only violence in every marital status group. These differences may be due to gender differences in *reporting* assaults. In other words, the percentage of female only violence may be higher than the percent of male only violence, not because the former actually occurs with greater frequency, but because men are less likely than women to report their violence, as previous research revealed (Szinovacz, 1983; Jouriles & O'Leary, 1985; Edleson & Brygger, 1986). It has been suggested that men who batter may deny their use of violence (Coleman, 1980; Pagelow, 1981; Walker, 1979) more than women. The gender difference in reporting violence may be another example of the "his/her marriage" (Bernard, 1982) or Rashomon effect (Condran and Bode, 1982) where wives have different perceptions of their marriage than the husbands.

The analysis to investigate whether violence by gender is due to differences in reporting violence was conducted for respondents aged 18–24 (the only age group for which we have data on all three marital status groups). The results are presented in Figure 2.5.

The left side of Figure 2.5, which displays the violence rates as described by male respondents, is clearly different from the right side, which is based on information provided by female respondents. However, in every marital status category, the female only assault rate is greater than the male only assault rate (χ^2 for sex = 10.0, $p < .05$, df = 3; for marital status = 27.5, $p < .01$, df = 6; for sex × marital status = 6.6, n.s., df = 6).

Figure 2.5
Assault Rates by Marital Status and Gender of Respondent

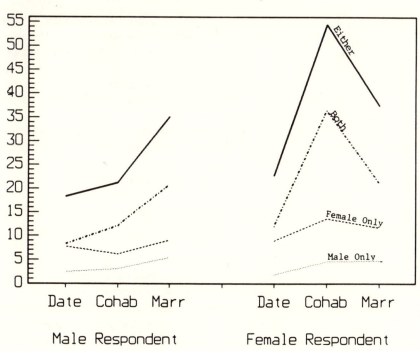

We investigated two factors that might explain the high rate of female violence in this study. First, we examined minor and severe violence separately to see if the higher rate of female only violence was mainly due to more minor violence by women, but we found no support for this (χ^2 for sex = 3.7, n.s., df = 7; for marital status = 7.9, n.s., df = 14; for sex × marital status = 9.6, n.s., df = 14).

Another possibility is that the high rate of female only assaults in Figure 2.5 occurs because those data refer to young couples (ages 18–24). We therefore replicated the analysis for men and women of ages 25 and older who were married or cohabiting. The results showed that, consistent with other research, the female only assault rate is similar to the rate of male only assaults (χ^2 for sex = 2.6, n.s., df = 3; for marital status = 2.5, n.s., df = 3; for age = 8.3, n.s., df = 6; for sex × marital status = 1.3, n.s., df = 3; for sex × age = 2.4, n.s., df = 6; for marital status × age = 6.2, n.s., df = 6; for sex × marital status × age = 6.4, n.s., df = 6).

These analyses rule out the possibility that the results are due to confounding with age and gender. However, they leave unresolved the reasons for the high rate of female only violence among young couples and indeed the even more fundamental question of why violence by females primarily occurs within the family (see Straus, 1980 and Straus & Gelles, 1988 for some suggestions).

DISCUSSION

This study compared the rate of physical assault between partners in 526 dating couples, 237 cohabiting couples, and 5,005 married couples. Three research questions were investigated. The findings indicate that (1) the highest *rate* of assault is among the cohabiting couples; (2) violence is most *severe* in cohabiting couples; and (3) for all three marital status groups, the most frequent pattern is for both partners to be violent, followed by female only, and the least frequent pattern is male only violence.

We examined whether the high rate of female only violence is due to gender differences in reporting violence. After controlling for gender of respondent, female only violence is still more common than male only violence in all three marital status groups. After controlling for age, female only violence is similar to male only violence.

This may seem like a surprising finding, but similar results have been reported in a number of previous studies (summarized in Straus & Gelles, 1988). The high rate of assaults by women in this study is also consistent with the data on homicidal assaults. The rate of homicides committed by women overall is one-fifth the rate of homicides by men, but within the family, women commit nearly half (48 percent) of all homicides (Plass & Straus, 1987).

Without controlling for age, dating couples have a higher rate of assault than married couples. When age is controlled, dating couples have the lowest assault rate of the three marital status groups. However, controls for age, education, and occupational status do not alter the finding that there is much more violence, and more severe violence, among cohabiting than married or dating couples. These findings are consistent with an earlier study (Yllo & Straus, 1981). Thus, the greater risk of assault typically occurs when individuals live together but are not married.

If age, education, and occupation do not explain the differences in assault rates by marital status, then what does? What is unique about cohabiting couples when compared to dating and married couples that might explain the higher assault rate? We offer some suggestions.

Cohabiting couples may be more likely to be isolated from their network of kin than dating or married couples. For those who are dating or are married, being tied to one's kin may have the unintended consequence of helping to monitor violent behavior. Whether cohabiting couples are isolated by choice or because of a lingering stigma attached to this type of relationship, physical violence may be less likely to be recognized or challenged (Cazenave & Straus, 1979).

Issues of autonomy and control also may be relevant in explaining why assaults are more common in cohabiting than dating or married relationships. It is possible that some enter cohabitation rather than marriage in order to keep more of their own independence, only to find that there are frequent arguments over rights, duties, and obligations that may lead to violence. This suggests that successfully controlling another, or being controlled by another, may be more problematic in cohabiting than in married relationships and thus may lead to more incidents of violence. Indeed, research indicates that where the issue of control frequently arises, violence often occurs (Burke, Stets, & Pirog-Good, this volume, Chapter 4; Stets & Pirog-Good, 1987; Stets & Pirog-Good, 1988; Stets, 1988).

The issue of control may not be as problematic among dating and married couples as it is among cohabiting couples. On the one hand, those who date but are not serious about their partner may feel that they do not have the right to control the other. Consequently, conflict over control may be less likely to arise and hence explain the lower rate of dating assault. On the other hand, those who are married and are more committed to one another may not only feel that they have the right to control the other but also may agree to be controlled. Married individuals may "give in" to their partner's wishes, believing that they need to make sacrifices or compromises for the sake of keeping the relationship intact. In this sense, the marriage license may also be a control license.

It should be pointed out that as dating relationships become more serious, control may take precedence and violence may become more frequent. Therefore, research that has shown that the more serious and involved the partners, the more likely that violence will occur (Hotaling & Straus, 1980; Cate et al., 1982; Laner & Thompson, 1982; Laner, 1983; Henton et al., 1983; Sigelman, Berry & Wiles, 1984; Roscoe & Benaske, 1985; Arias, Samios & O'Leary,

1987) may, in part, be explained by conflict arising over control (Stets & Pirog-Good, 1987).

Finally, the investment in the relationship may help explain the high rate of assaults while cohabiting. Cohabiting couples may be more violent than married couples because although both relationships tend to share certain features that give rise to conflict, the former may lack some features of marriage that serve to constrain the conflict from escalating into physical assaults. The feature that cohabiting couples share with married couples is the conflict inherent in a primary group relationship (Straus & Hotaling, 1980; Straus, 1987a). To take one example, in a marital or cohabiting relationship, everything about the partner is of concern to the other and hence little or nothing is off-limits for discussion and conflict. Consequently, there is an inherently high level of conflict in marriage and cohabiting.

Nevertheless, conflict does not necessarily lead to violence. There are other modes of resolving conflicts, or one party may implicitly decide that the potential costs of violence cannot be risked. These costs may be greater for married, than for cohabiting couples to the extent that married couples have a greater material, social, and psychological investment as well as a greater long-term interest in the relationship. Consequently, married couples may be more constrained to control assault in order to avoid the risk of such acts terminating the marriage and to lessen the risk of the partners' being injured or even killed, resulting in a greater loss (Straus, 1987a). Thus, although the marriage license may be an implicit hitting license in a normative sense (Straus, 1976), the structural realities of marriage also tend to impose a ceiling on the frequency and severity of violence, whereas the similar normative tolerance of violence in cohabiting couples is not subject to the same structural constraints.

Dating couples may be less violent because they are less involved in a relationship, and thus the conflict-generating characteristics do not apply as strongly in their case as they do among cohabiting and married couples. In this respect, they are different from cohabiting couples. However, they share with cohabiting couples the low investment in the relationship as compared to married couples. It is possible that as a dating relationship becomes more serious, the rate of assault may approximate that found in cohabiting relationships, given not only their increased level of conflict and low investment in the relationship, but also, as discussed above, the more frequent issue of control.

Our suggestions on the cause for the high rate of assault among cohabiting as compared to dating and married couples is speculative and not definitive. Future research needs to directly examine these factors. Identifying what might explain cohabiting violence may help us obtain a better understanding of why violence occurs at all.

ACKNOWLEDGMENTS

This chapter was presented at the 1988 meeting of the American Sociological Association. This research was part of the Family Violence Research Program of the Family Research Laboratory, University of New Hampshire, Durham, NH, 03824. A program description and publications list will be sent on request.

The work of the first author was supported by a post doctoral research fellowship program funded by the National Institute of Mental Health (grant T32 MH15161.) The data on married and cohabiting couples are from the National Family Violence Resurvey, funded by the National Institute of Mental Health grant R01MH40027 (Richard J. Gelles and Murray A. Straus, co-investigators). It is a pleasure to acknowledge the support of these organizations and to express appreciation to the members of the 1987–88 Family Violence Research Program Seminar for valuable comments and suggestions.

NOTES

1. For purposes of this chapter, the term "violence" refers to *physical* violence. Violence is defined as an act carried out with the intention or perceived intention of causing physical pain or injury. This definition is synonymous with the legal concept of "assault" and the concept of "physical aggression" used in social psychology. Consistent with the legal concept of assault, physical injury is *not* a criterion. As Marcus (1983:89) puts it, "Physical contact is not an element of the crime" or as the *Uniform Crime Reports* of the FBI (1984:21) puts it, "Attempts are included [in the tabulation of aggravated assault] because it is not necessary that an injury result."

The theoretical ambiguity of the terms "abuse" and "violence" and a conceptual analysis of these and other related terms is given in Gelles (1985) and Gelles and Straus (1979). See also Straus and Lincoln (1985) for a theoretical analysis of the "criminalization" of family violence.

2. However, it is projected that by 1990 only about 3 percent of all households and 5 percent of all couple households will comprise cohabitors (Glick, 1984).

3. Since the X-axis variable is not continuous, readers familiar with graphing conventions will wonder why line graphs were used rather than bar charts. Graphs were explored because the tables were difficult to comprehend. However, the bar chart versions were equally or more difficult to comprehend, especially Figures 2.2, 2.3, and 2.5. The line graphs, in our opinion, bring out the main points more clearly than any other mode of presentation.

REFERENCES

Arias, I., Samios, M., & O'Leary, K. D. (1987). "Prevalence and Correlates of Physical Aggression During Courtship." *Journal of Interpersonal Violence* 2: 82–90.

Bernard, J. (1982). *The Future of Marriage*. New Haven, CT: Yale University Press.

Bernard, J. L., Bernard, S. L., & Bernard, M. L. (1985). "Courtship Violence and Sex Typing." *Family Relations* 34:573–76.

Bogal-Allbritten, R. B., & Allbritten, W. (1985). "The Hidden Victims: Courtship Violence Among College Students." *Journal of Student Personnel* 19:201–4.

Breines, W., & Gordon, L. (1983). "The New Scholarship on Family Violence." *Signs: Journal of Women in Culture and Society* 8:490–531.

Cate, R., Henton, J., Koval, J., Christopher, F. S., & Lloyd, S. (1982). "Premarital Abuse: A Social Psychological Perspective." *Journal of Family Issues* 3:79–80.

Cazenave, N. A., & Straus, M. A. (1979). "Race, Class, Network Embeddedness and Family Violence: A Search for Potent Support Systems." *Journal of Comparative Family Studies* 10:280–99.

Coleman, K. Howes. (1980). "Conjugal Violence: What 33 Men Report." *Journal of Marital and Family Therapy* 6:207–13.

Condran, J. G., & J. G. Bode. (1982). "Rashomon, Working Wives, and Family Division of Labor: Middletown, 1980." *Journal of Marriage and the Family* 44:421–26.

Deal, J. E., & Wampler, K. S. (1986). "Dating Violence: The Primacy of Previous Experience." *Journal of Social and Personal Relationships* 3:457–71.

Dobash, R. E., & R. P. Dobash. (1979). *Violence Against Wives: A Case Against the Patriarchy.* New York: Free Press.

Durkeim, E. (1951). *Suicide.* New York: Free Press.

Edleson, J. L., & M. P. Brygger. (1986). "Gender Differences in Reporting of Battering Incidences." *Family Relations* 35:377–82.

Gelles, R. J. & M. A. Straus. (1979). "Determinants of Violence in the Family: Toward a Theoretical Integration." In W. R. Burr et al. (eds.) *Contemporary Theories About the Family,* 549–81. New York: Free Press.

Glick, P. C. (1984). "Marriage, Divorce and Living Arrangements: Prospective Changes." *Journal of Family Issues* 5:7–26.

Glick, P. C. & Spanier, G. B. (1980). "Married and Unmarried Cohabitation in the United States." *Journal of Marriage and the Family* 42:19–30.

Greenblat, C. (1983). "Physical Force by Any Other Name . . . : Quantitative Data, Qualitative Data, and the Politics of Family Violence Research." In D. Finkelhor, R. Gelles, G. Hotaling, & M. Straus (eds.) *The Dark Side of Families: Current Family Violence Research,* 235–60. Beverly Hills, CA: Sage.

Henton, J., Cate, R., Koval, J., Lloyd, S., & Christopher, S. (1983). "Romance and Violence in Dating Relationships." *Journal of Family Issues* 4:467–82.

Hotaling, G. T., & Sugarman, D. B. (1986). "An Analysis of Risk Markers in Husband to Wife Violence: The Current State of Knowledge." *Violence and Victims* 1:101–24.

Jouriles, E. N., & O'Leary, K. D. (1985). "Interspousal Reliability of Reports of Marital Violence." *Journal of Consulting and Clinical Psychology* 53:419–21.

Knoke, D., & Burke, P. J. (1980). *Log-Linear Models.* Beverly Hills, CA: Sage.

Lane, K. E., & Gwartney-Gibbs, P. (1985) "Violence in the Context of Dating and Sex." *Journal of Family Issues* 6:45–59.

Laner, M. R. (1983). "Courtship Abuse and Aggression: Contextual Aspects." *Sociological Spectrum* 3:69–83.

Laner, M. R., & Thompson, J. (1982). "Abuse and Aggression in Courting Couples." *Deviant Behavior: An Interdisciplinary Journal* 3:229–44.

Makepeace, J. M. (1981). "Courtship Violence Among College Students." *Family Relations* 30:97–102.

———. (1983). "Life Events Stress and Courtship Violence." *Family Relations* 32:101–09.

———. (1986). "Gender Differences in Courtship Violence Victimization." *Family Relations* 35:383–88.

Marcus, P. (1983). "Assault and Battery." In Sanford H. Kadish (ed.), *Encyclopedia of Crime and Justice,* 88–90. New York: Free Press.

Nisonoff L., & I. Bitman. (1979). "Spouse Abuse: Incidence and Relationship to Se-
lected Demographic Variables." *Victimology* 4:131–40.
Pagelow, M. Daley. (1981). *Woman-Battering: Victims and Their Experiences.* Beverly
Hills, CA: Sage.
Plass, M. S., & Gessner, J. C. (1983). "Violence in Courtship Relations: A Southern
Example." *Free Inquiry in Creative Sociology* 11:198–202.
Plass, P. S., & Straus, M. A. (1987). "Intra-Family Homicide in the United States:
Incidence, Trends, and Differences by Region, Race, and Gender." Paper pre-
sented at the Third National Family Violence Research Conference, University
of New Hampshire, Durham, NH.
Robinson, J. P., Athanasiou, R., & Head, K. B. (1969). *Measures of Occupational
Attitudes and Occupational Characteristics.* Ann Arbor, MI: Survey Research
Center of the Institute for Social Research, University of Michigan.
Roscoe, B., & Benaske, N. (1985). "Courtship Violence Experienced by Abused Wives:
Similarities in Patterns of Abuse." *Family Relations* 34:419–24.
Saunders, D. G. (1986). "When Battered Women Use Violence: Husband-Abuse or
Self-Defense?" *Violence and Victims* 1:47–60.
Sigelman, C. K., Berry, C. J., & Wiles, K. A. (1984). "Violence in College Students'
Dating Relationships." *Journal of Applied Social Psychology* 5,6:530–48.
Spanier, G. B. (1983). "Married and Unmarried Cohabitation in the United States:
1980." *Journal of Marriage and the Family* 45:277–88.
Steinmetz, S. K. (1978). "The Battered Husband Syndrome." *Victimology: An Inter-
national Journal* 2:499–509.
Stets, J. E. (1988). *Domestic Violence and Control.* New York: Springer-Verlag.
Stets, J. E., & Pirog-Good, M. A. (1987). "Violence in Dating Relationships." *Social
Psychology Quarterly* 50:237–46.
———. (1988). "Violence and Control in Dating Relationships." Unpublished.
Stets, J. E., & Straus, M. A. (1989). "Gender Differences in Reporting Marital Vio-
lence and Its Medical and Psychological Consequences." In M. A. Straus and
R. J. Gelles (eds.), *Physical Violence in American Families: Risk Factors and
Adaptations to Violence in 8,145 Families,* Chapter 9. New Brunswick, NJ:
Transaction Press.
Straus, M. A. (1976). "Sexual Inequality, Cultural Norms, and Wife Beating." *Victimology: An International Journal* 1:54–76.
———. (1979). "Measuring Intrafamily Conflict and Violence: The Conflict Tactics
(CT) Scales." *Journal of Marriage and the Family* 41:75–88.
———. (1980). "Victims and Aggressors in Marital Violence." *American Behavioral
Scientist* 23:681–704.
———. (1987a). "Primary Group Characteristics and Intra-family Homicide." Paper
presented at the 3rd National Family Violence Research Conference, University
of New Hampshire, Durham NH.
———. (1987b). "The Conflict Tactics Scales: An Evaluation and New Data on Validity, Reliability, Norms, and Scoring Methods." Paper presented at the National
Council on Family Relations Meetings.
Straus, M. A., & Gelles, R. J. (1986). "Societal Changes and Change in Family Violence from 1975 to 1985 as Revealed by Two National Surveys." *Journal of
Marriage and the Family* 48:465–79.
———. (1988). "How Violent are American Families? Estimates from the National

Family Violence Resurvey and Other Studies.'' In G. T. Hotaling et al. (eds.), *New Directions in Family Violence Research*. Beverly Hills, CA: Sage.

Straus, M. A., Gelles, R. J., & Steinmetz, S. (1980). *Behind Closed Doors: Violence in the American Family*. Garden City, New York: Anchor.

Straus, M. A., & Hotaling, G. T. (1980). ''Culture, Social Organization, and Irony in the Study of Family Violence.'' In M. A. Straus & G. T. Hotaling (eds.), *The Social Causes of Husband-Wife Violence*, 3–22. Minneapolis: University of Minnesota Press.

Straus, M. A., & Lincoln, A. J., (1985). ''A Conceptual Framework for Understanding Crime and the Family.'' In A. J. Lincoln & M. A. Straus (eds.), *Crime and the Family*. New York: C. C. Thomas.

Szinovacz, M. E. (1983). ''Using Couple Data as a Methodological Tool: The Case of Marital Violence.'' *Journal of Marriage and the Family* 45:633–44.

Uniform Crime Reports (1984). U.S. Department of Justice. Washington, D.C.: U.S. Government Printing Office.

Walker, L. E. (1979). *The Battered Woman*. New York: Harper & Row.

Yllo, K., & Straus, M. A. (1981). ''Interpersonal Violence Among Married and Cohabiting Couples.'' *Family Relations* 30:339–47.

3 A Theoretical Model of Courtship Aggression
David S. Riggs and K. Daniel O'Leary

Adolescence has been identified as a potentially important period of development (Feinstein & Ardon, 1973; Feinstein, Giovacchini & Miller, 1971). Within this stage, the formation of intimate dating relationships is important to the continued healthy development of the individual (Feinstein & Ardon, 1973; McCabe, 1984). Recently, however, it has become apparent that physical aggression between partners occurs in a significant percentage of dating relationships (Makepeace, 1981; Sigelman, Berry & Wiles, 1984). As research on the phenomenon of courtship aggression has grown, little or no attempt has been made to develop a theory of such aggression. In this chapter, we will review the available empirical literature and theories of aggression and present a theoretical model of dating aggression.

ADOLESCENT DATING

Social dating as practiced by adolescents in the United States is a relatively new phenomenon. Dating has been established as an acceptable practice and has been developing into its present forms since the end of World War I (Ehrmann, 1959). Prior to that time, interactions between unmarried men and women were chaperoned by family and community or were nonexistent, as in the case of arranged marriages (Mead, 1959). Dating relationships may take a variety of forms, and often an individual will encounter several of these forms in his or her own dating history. The most common pattern of premarital relationship is serial monogamy (Sorensen, 1973). Such relationships are often termed "going steady." These "steady" relationships are intense and monogamous, but they are of uncertain length.

As the practice of social dating has evolved, one change in the pattern appears consistent: People are beginning to ''go steady'' at younger and younger ages (Ehrmann, 1959; Ellis, 1962). Additionally, the age at which people marry is slowly increasing (McCabe, 1984). The lengthening of the period of dating has resulted in the dating relationship becoming an end in itself rather than just a part of the courtship process (Smith, 1962).

The development of steady relationships leads to behavioral changes that indicate an increased level of intimacy between the partners during courtship. Ehrmann (1959) reported that people involved in steady relationships were more likely to experience sexual activity in their current relationships. Bell (1969) found that going steady makes sexual intimacy more legitimate. Similar findings regarding appropriate and actual sexual behavior were reported by Roche (1986). Increased levels of intimacy also increase the levels of conflict between partners (Cate et al., 1982; Laner & Thompson, 1982) and contribute to the problem of aggression in dating relationships.

THE PREVALENCE AND CORRELATES OF COURTSHIP AGGRESSION

The systematic study of aggression between people who are dating has a short history. There are a few early reports of sexual aggression within dating relationships. Ehrmann (1959) reported that 26 percent of the female subjects in his study had been forced into unwanted sexual activity by acquaintances, 18 percent by friends, and 8 percent by lovers. Kanin (1969) reported that 25 percent of a sample of unmarried college students admitted performing an act of sexual aggression. Other early indications that there was a problem of courtship aggression came from retrospective reports of the victims of spousal abuse. Starr et al. (1979), for example, reported that 49 percent of their sample of battered women had witnessed or been the victims of their husbands' violence prior to marriage.

Makepeace (1981) published the first study on physical aggression in courtship. He reported that 21 percent of the college students in his sample had experienced some form of aggression in a dating relationship at some point in their lives. A year later, Cate et al. (1982) reported a similar prevalence rate, 22 percent in their sample of college students. Bernard and Bernard (1983) found that 38 percent of the women in the sample had been victimized by a partner while 21 percent of the women had engaged in aggression against a date. Of the men surveyed, 15 percent had behaved aggressively toward a partner, while 19 percent had been victims of such aggression. Sigelman, Berry & Wiles, (1984) reported higher rates of aggression among college students. In their sample, 48 percent of the women had been victims of aggression by a boyfriend, and 52 percent of the women had engaged in aggression against a date. Of the men, 59 percent had been victimized, while 54 percent had been aggressive.

Some researchers assessed the rates of aggression in specific dating relationships, that is, in a current or the most recent relationship rather than throughout the individual's dating history. The rates of dating aggression in specific relationships are also quite high. Arias, Samios, and O'Leary (1987) found that 30 percent of the men in their college student sample and 32 percent of the women had engaged in aggression against their current partners. Additonally, 49 percent of the men and 26 percent of the women had been the victims of aggression in a current relationship. Riggs (1986) reported that 23 percent of the men and 39 percent of the women in a sample of college students had engaged in aggression against their current or most recent partner. The wide discrepancies found in prevalence estimates of courtship aggression indicate that it is difficult to draw clear conclusions about the extent of the problem. However, it appears that as many as 50 percent of college students experience instances of courtship aggression at some point in their lives, and 30 percent of these students may currently be involved in aggressive relationships.

In order to predict, treat, and prevent courtship aggression, it is necessary to understand the factors related to it. To this end, researchers have searched for causes and correlates of dating aggression. A detailed summary of the factors previously found to relate to courtship aggression is included below in the description of a proposed model of aggression in dating relationships. To date, none of the studies has attempted to use correlates to predict the future occurrence of courtship aggression.

THEORETICAL MODELS OF RELATIONSHIP AGGRESSION

Little of the research examining the correlates of dating aggression has been guided by an underlying theoretical framework that would facilitate the prediction of aggression. The result of the search for factors associated with dating aggression is simply a list of variables, each found to relate to aggression in at least one study, with little attempt to examine the relationship between variables. Alternatively, previous models were either too complex to use (for example, Gelles & Straus, 1979) or constructs were included that were too broad to be testable, such as couple characteristics or societal characteristics (O'Leary & Arias, 1987). Because of these difficulties, O'Leary (1988) suggested that theoretical models be limited to empirically verifiable variables that are thought to be most relevant to interpartner aggression.

The current literature on courtship aggression provides an ample supply of variables that have been empirically related to such aggression. In the following pages, we will outline a model of courtship aggression based on the social learning model presented by O'Leary and Arias (1987). Data from studies of courtship aggression will be emphasized, but because such studies are limited in number, data related to interspousal aggression and aggression in general will also be used.

WHY HAVE A MODEL SPECIFIC TO COURTSHIP
AGGRESSION?

Most theories developed specifically to explain spousal abuse are based on studies of severely battered women. These theories tend to focus on social and cultural factors, such as sexism, power differentials, and societal acceptance of aggression, that have an impact on spousal aggression and the continuation of aggressive relationships (for example, Dobash & Dobash, 1978; Pleck et al., 1978; Rounsaville, 1978; Straus, 1976; Walker, 1981). When attempting to apply these theories to courtship aggression, one is faced with the problem of explaining the large number of women who report aggressive behavior against their dating partners (cf. Laner & Thompson, 1982; Sigelman, Berry & Wiles, 1984). Clearly, if aggression perpetrated by husbands against their wives is the result of the greater power that men possess, then women's aggression would likely be a result of some factor other than greater power. Similarly, the connections among sexism, sex-role–specific behavior, and aggression must be different for men and women.

Additionally, the application of marital aggression theories to the problem of courtship aggression is problematic because of the differences between dating relationships and marriages. The clearest difference between dating and marital relationships is the nature of the relationship. While dating relationships often include strong emotional commitment, the legal, financial, and moral constraints of marriage do not exist. Thus, it is much less difficult to end a dating relationship than to dissolve a marriage. In addition, dating relationships are frequently limited in duration. The individuals involved often do not intend for the relationship to last forever or to lead directly to marriage.

A second important difference between aggression in dating and in marriage is the perceived approval of such aggression. While it has been argued that there is an implied right to use physical force among family members (Straus, 1976), there appears to be no such implicit approval for courtship aggression.

Dating relationships are similar to marriages in terms of privacy, intensity of emotional involvement, and the perceived right of the partners to exert influence on each other. These similarities, though, are greatly influenced by the level of intimacy shared by the specific dating couple. More intimate dating relationships (that is, steady, serious, monogamous relationships) tend to be more private and to have more emotional involvement, and the individuals will perceive a greater right to influence their partners' behavior. These characteristics may contribute to the finding that physical aggression is more likely in more serious dating relationships than in those that are less serious (Comins, 1984; Lane & Gwartney-Gibbs, 1985). This finding suggests that a model that treats characteristics such as level of emotional involvement and amount of privacy as variables to be assessed would be appropriate for describing courtship aggression.

In sum, dating relatinships share some characteristics with marriages. Specifically, more serious dating relationships will be more similar to married relationships in terms of privacy and emotional involvement. There are, however, several differences that exist. These differences suggest that a theoretical model specific to courtship aggression would be beneficial to those attempting to better understand relationship aggression. Because of the similarities between dating and marital relationships, a model of dating aggression will share some elements with models of spousal aggression. For example, both married and dating couples will likely vary in stress, time, amount of activities, commitment, and expectations, and these factors need to be considered in modeling both courtship and spousal aggression.

A CAUSAL MODEL OF COURTSHIP AGGRESSION

The prediction of interpartner aggression requires an understanding of two related but separate elements. First, it is necessary to understand what factors will cause a person to behave aggressively toward any dating partner in any situation. Second, it is necessary to know what factors contribute to a person's becoming aggressive toward a partner in a specific situation. In other words, one must know which people will behave aggressively and when they will become aggressive. Previous models of interpartner aggression have attempted to address both of these factors with a single set of predictors and, as a result, have become overly complex. The model proposed in the current paper separates the two factors necessary for the prediction of aggression and provides distinct sets of predictors for each.

The model of interpartner aggression proposed by O'Leary and Arias (1987) provides a good illustration of the two factors involved in the prediction of interpartner aggression. The model includes two general categories of variables: contextual and situational. The contextual variables (such as societal characteristics, individual characteristics) are primarily related to predicting who will behave aggressively toward a partner. The situational variables (such as specific precipitating events) are involved in predicting when or in what situations the aggression will occur. In addition, the model describes a potential feedback mechanism through the consequences of the aggressive behavior. Because of its lack of specificity, the O'Leary and Arias model offers few concrete measures to assess in order to predict the occurrence of interpartner aggression. In other words, while the impact of individual, couple, and societal characteristics may provide a complete set of predictors of spousal aggression, each characteristic is itself a category of numerous more specific variables.

The model developed in the present chapter is composed of two interrelated components that are extensions of the contextual and situational variables in the O'Leary and Arias model. The first component (Figure 3.1) is analogous to the contextual variables and includes constructs selected to predict *who* will become aggressive. The second component (Figure 3.2) represents situational variables and predicts *when* or in what situation a person will become aggressive toward a dating partner. The two components are separated in the present model to simplify the description of the model. Each component includes a number of constructs. While these constructs are more specific than those found in the O'Leary and Arias model, there are still finer distinctions and additional paths that could be added to the model.

Component One: Contextual Variables

The first component of Figure 3.1 contains seven constructs that have been empirically or theoretically related to courtship aggression or to other forms of aggression: (1) models of aggression in intimate relationships; (2) parental aggression toward the child; (3) acceptance of aggression as an appropriate response to conflict, frustration, or threat; (4) psychopathology and neuropathology; (5) arousability and emotionality; (6) personality; and (7) prior use of aggression. In the current model, all the constructs, with the exception of neuropathology and psychopathology, relate directly to courtship aggression. Neuropathology and psychopathology are related to courtship aggression only through their impact on more general levels of aggression.

Models of Aggression in Intimate Relationships. In the current model of courtship aggression, exposure to models of aggression in intimate relationships (construct 1) is predicted to increase the likelihood that a person will behave aggressively toward a partner. Models of aggression in intimate relationships are important theoretically because they provide the primary source of early modeling of aggression. Models of aggression in intimate relationships are thought to influence the likelihood of courtship aggression both directly and through several indirect paths. Witnessing aggression between one's parents may increase aggressive tendencies, both behaviorally (that is, increasing the use of aggression in general) and in terms of incorporating aggressiveness into their personality style. Also, witnessing aggression within intimate relationships should increase the acceptance of aggression as a response to problems. Spousal aggression also is related to parental aggression toward children (Jouriles, Barling & O'Leary, 1987; Straus, Gelles & Steinmetz, 1980), which is predicted to relate to courtship aggression.

Some studies have found a positive relationship between reports of courtship aggression and witnessing aggression between one's parents. Bernard and Bernard (1983) reported that 73 percent of the aggressive males and 50 percent of the aggressive females in their sample had experienced or observed abuse in their families of origin. Only 32 percent of the nonaggressive males and 23 percent of the nonaggressive females had experienced or observed aggression in their families of origin. These results are difficult to interpret because no distinction was made between witnessing interparental aggression and being the victim of a parent's aggression. Sigelman, Berry & Wiles (1984) reported a significant correlation between interparental aggression and courtship aggression reported by women. Riggs (1986) found a significant correlation between maternal aggression toward the father and men's courtship aggression.

Figure 3.1
Contextual Variables Associated with Courtship Aggression

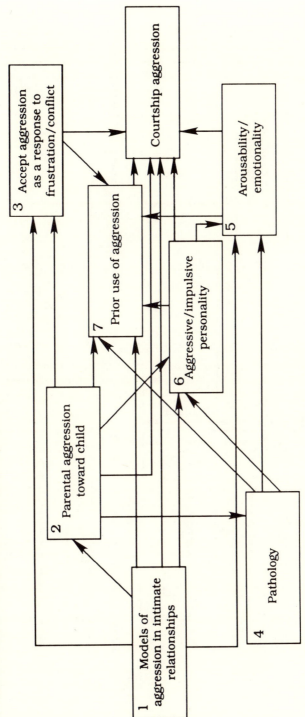

Figure 3.2
Situational Variables Associated with Courtship Aggression

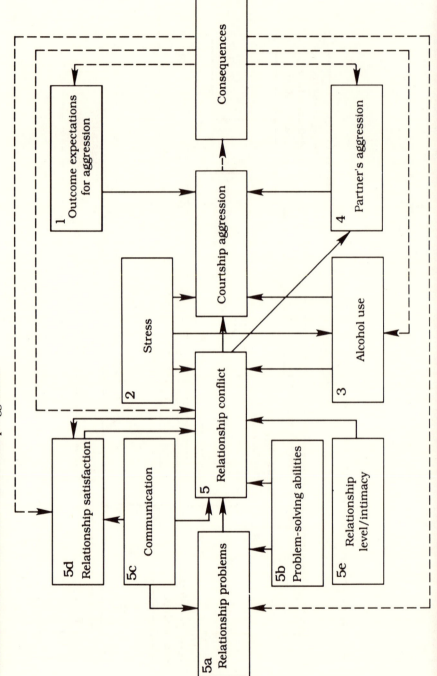

Arias (1984) found that the relationship between interparental aggression and courtship aggression was mediated by personality variables. For the men in her sample, interparental aggression was related to courtship aggression both directly and through its impact on personality variables. Interparental aggression was related to women's courtship aggression only through the personality variables.

The construct of witnessed aggression also includes the perceived consequences of that aggression. According to social learning theory, the perceived consequences of a witnessed behavior are important in predicting whether the behavior will be initiated by the witness. For example, to accurately predict the occurrence of interpartner aggression based on previously witnessed aggression it is necessary to know whether the witness perceived positive or negative consequences of the aggression. The consequences of witnessed aggression have not been examined empirically. However, negative memories of interparental aggression may inhibit some people from using aggression against their partners. Differences in perceived consequences of aggression may explain the inconsistent relation between witnessed aggression and the use of aggression against a dating partner.

Parental Aggression toward the Subject. The relationship between parental aggression toward the subject (construct 2) and dating aggression by the subject has also been examined by a number of researchers. In the proposed model, parental aggression is thought to directly increase the likelihood of aggression in dating relationships. In addition, parental aggression toward the subject is predicted to increase the use of aggression during courtship indirectly through the constructs of personality, acceptance of aggression, and the general use of aggression.

Researchers have found that college students who had experienced parental aggression were more likely to have behaved aggressively in a dating relationship than were subjects who had not experienced parental aggression. In general, the data indicate that being the victim of parental aggression increases the likelihood that a person will behave aggressively in a dating relationship. Like the effects of interparental aggression, the effects of child victimization appear different for men and women and are probably mediated by other factors.

Acceptance of Aggression as a Response to Conflict. The third construct related to courtship aggression is the acceptance of aggression as a response to conflict, stress, or threat. According to the proposed model, the acceptance of aggression is related to courtship aggression both directly and through the general use of aggression. In other words, if one accepts the use of aggression as a response to conflict, then one is more likely to behave aggressively both in general and in dating relationships. The acceptance of interpartner aggression is likely to be influenced by the observation of interpartner aggression (between parents or within other partnerships) and the parents' use of aggression toward the child.

Cate et al. (1982) found that the subjects who had experienced aggression in a dating relationship had less negative attitudes toward both courtship and marital aggression. Stets & Pirog-Good (1987) found that acceptance of aggression toward women was associated with an increased likelihood that men would act aggressively against dating partners. Clearly, not all persons who act aggressively against a dating partner feel that such aggression is good, nor do all those who feel that interpartner aggression is appropriate actually act aggressively. Less negative attitudes toward aggression between partners, however, appear to be an important determinant of the likelihood that such aggression will take place.

Psychopathology and Neuropathology. The role of psychopathology and neuropathology (construct 4) in dating aggression has been largely neglected. Comins (1984) associated women's courtship aggression with their scores on the Symptom Check List–90 (SCL-90: Derogatis, Rickels & Rock, 1976). Unfortunately, it was not possible to determine if the psychological problems existed prior to the experience of aggression. However, aggressive behavior is recognized as a symptom of a number of psychological disorders (American Psychiatric Association, 1987).

There is evidence that neurological (Detre, Kupfer & Taub, 1975; Reis, 1975) and hormonal (Lloyd & Weisz, 1975) factors may influence human aggressive behavior. There are also data linking lesions and seizures of the limbic system, head trauma, and viral encephalomyelitis to violent behavior (Detre, Kupfer & Taub, 1975).

Arousability and Emotionality. Arousability and emotionality (construct 5) are seen as important predictors of aggressive behavior. A number of theorists (Bandura, 1973; Berkowitz, 1965; Feshbach, 1970) have used the construct of arousal or emotional responsivity as a link to actual aggressive behavior. According to Zillmann (1979), the relationship between arousal and aggression is quite complex. For arousal to lead to aggression, it must be accompanied by provocation and the arousal must be attributed to the source of the provocation. With regard to courtship aggression, it is therefore important that the emotional arousal be attributed to provocation by the partner. In the proposed model, arousability contributes to the occurrence of courtship aggression directly and by increasing the likelihood that aggression will be used more generally.

Studies have linked courtship aggression and various measures of emotionality and arousal. Cate et al. (1982) reported that the courtship aggression experienced by their sample was most often a reflection of anger or confusion on the part of the aggressor. Makepeace (1981) found that the emotional reaction of jealousy was often the source of the disagreement that led to the aggressive incident. Both Riggs (1986) and Stets and Pirog-Good (1987) reported a relationship between jealousy and courtship aggression for women. Additionally, Stets and Pirog-Good (1987) reported that the men in their sample who had acted aggressively against a partner showed higher levels of emotionality. According to the present model of courtship aggression, higher levels of emotionality and arousability should be associated with increased use of aggression between dating partners.

Personality. Though personality variables (construct 6) have received little attention from behavioral theorists in recent years, they are important in understanding courtship aggression. In the proposed model, personality variables serve as a mediating variable between the historical constructs (that is, interparental aggression and parent-child aggression) and the current use of aggression in dating relationships.

The role and importance of personality variables is demonstrated by the work of Arias (1984). Her results indicated that certain aggressive personality characteristics, mediated the relationship between witnessing interparental aggression, and courtship aggression. Riggs (1986) found similar results. According to the present model, high ratings of certain personality characteristics, such as aggressiveness and impulsiveness, should increase the likelihood that dating aggression will occur.

Prior Use of Aggression and Coercion. The use of earlier aggression against others is a particularly important factor for courtship aggression. Comins (1984) found that the women in her sample who had acted aggressively against a dating partner were more likely to report a history of fighting with their siblings than were the women who had not acted aggressively against a dating partner. Similarly, Riggs (1986) found that a history of fighting with other people (siblings, friends, classmates) was significantly related to men's and women's use of aggression against a dating partner.

According to social learning theory, the consequences of a behavior are important for predicting the future occurrence of that behavior. To date, no research has examined the relation between the consequences of earlier aggression and the use of aggression against a dating partner. However, consequences of the aggression should influence the frequency with which an individual acts aggressively against another. Thus, individuals who have frequently behaved aggressively in the past and thus are more likely to behave aggressively against a dating partner (Riggs, 1986) should also have experienced more positive outcomes of their aggressive behavior. In the current model, frequent use of aggression in the past and the positive consequences resulting from that behavior will function to increase the probability that a person will behave aggressively against a dating partner.

Component Two: Situational Variables

The second component of the model (Figure 3.2) is conceptualized as predicting *when* a person will behave aggressively. There are five major predictors of courtship aggression in the second component of the model: (1) the expectation of a positive outcome to the aggression, (2) stress, (3) the use of alcohol, (4) the partner's use of aggression, and (5) relationship conflict. Five constructs are related to relationship conflict (relationship problems, problem-solving ability, couple communication, relationship satisfaction, relationship level/intensity) rather than to the aggression itself. In general, the constructs in the second (situational) component of the model have received less attention in the literature involving courtship aggression than have the constructs in the first component.

Expectations of Outcome Aggression. The expectations associated with the use of aggression (construct 1) are central to the social learning model of aggression as described by Bandura (1973). Despite their important role in social learning theory, almost no empirical studies of the role of expectations in either dating aggression or spousal aggression exist. Breslin et al. (1988) compared the expected consequences of aggression of college students who report aggressive behavior toward their dating partners and those who do not report aggression. The aggressive subjects anticipated negative consequences less frequently than did the nonaggressive subjects. In accordance with social learning theory, if individuals anticipate positive outcomes of their use of aggression toward others, then they will be more likely to actually behave aggressively toward others.

Stress. The role of stress (construct 2) in the initiation of courtship and marital aggression has been the subject of much empirical study. While there is evidence that stress is an important factor underlying spouse abuse (see Straus, Gelles & Steinmetz, 1980), the literature linking stress and courtship aggression is not as substantial nor as clearly interpretable.

Makepeace (1983) reported that both desirable and undesirable stress were related to courtship aggression experienced (both as aggressors and as victims) by the men in his sample, but no relation existed between stress and courtship aggression experienced by the women. In another study (Rose and Marshall, 1985), courtship aggression experienced by both men and women was associated with undesirable stressful events. In a third study (Riggs, 1986), undesirable stress was related to men's dating aggression, and women's courtship aggression was negatively correlated to desirable stress. In conclusion, stress levels, particularly levels of undesirable stress, seem important in the prediction of men's courtship aggression. For women, however, the relation between stress and dating aggression is unclear.

Alcohol Use. Several studies have examined the role of alcohol use in courtship aggression. Makepeace (1981) reported that aggression often occurred during disagreements about drinking. Cate et al. (1982) revealed that both the aggressors and the victims attributed their aggression to alcohol consumption. In a more direct test, Comins (1984) found that consumption of alcohol by both the respondents and their partners led to aggressive as opposed to nonaggressive conflicts. In the current model, alcohol use is thought to be a situational predictor of courtship aggression. Increased alcohol consumption prior to or during an argument should increase the likelihood that aggression will occur.

Partner's Aggression. The use of aggressive or coercive behavior by the subject's dating partner (construct 4) is closely related to the subject's own use of aggression. Many studies of courtship aggression have revealed it to be a phenomenon that is reciprocal in nature (Bernard & Bernard, 1983; Cate et al., 1982). Courtship aggression is not reciprocal in all relationships. In at least one study (Comins, 1984) it was not even the most frequently reported pattern. Aggression by one's partner, however, appears to increase the likelihood that the other partner will also behave aggressively in a dating relationship.

Relationship Conflict. Researchers have often assumed that some form of relationship conflict (construct 5) must exist for interpartner aggression to occur. Despite this, little research has examined the role of conflict in the development of aggressive interactions. In the current model, relationship conflict is conceptualized as the frequency and severity of disagreements that a couple experiences. Disagreements and conflict are experienced by a large majority of people in dating relationships. Lane and Gwartney-Gibbs (1985) found that over 95 percent of the college students they sampled had experienced some form of conflict in a dating relationship. Approximately one-third of these subjects also reported the use of aggression. Clearly, not all disagreements result in physical aggression, but more frequent and severe conflicts make aggression more probable.

Five constructs in the current model (relationship problems, problem-solving ability, communication ability, relationship satisfaction, and relationship level) are thought to be causally related to relationship conflict. Each of the five constructs has been directly or indirectly associated with interpartner aggression. It is proposed here that these constructs increase the likelihood of aggression by increasing the frequency and severity of relationship conflict.

Relationship problems (construct 5a) including the number of problems (Riggs, 1986) and topics of disagreement (Riggs, O'Leary & Weiss, 1988) influence conflict in relationships and, in turn, courtship aggression. Several specific problems, including jealousy (Makepeace, 1981), drinking (Comins, 1984; Makepeace, 1981) and sexual conflict (Comins, 1984; Makepeace, 1981), have been associated with dating aggression.

There is some evidence that individuals with better problem-solving abilities (construct 5b) report less dating aggression (Riggs, 1986). Couples with good problem-solving skills should face fewer conflict situations and, therefore, be less likely to engage in courtship aggression. Additionally, conflicts that do arise are likely to be solved in more appropriate ways than by the use of physical aggression.

Good communication skills (construct 5c) should also reduce the amount and severity of conflict within a couple. As with problem-solving skills and the number of relationship problems, communication patterns have been associated with relationship aggression. Vivian & O'Leary (1987) reported that aggressive married couples (who had been assessed during their engagement period) were more negative in their communication than nonaggressive couples. Smith and O'Leary (1987) found that aggressive couples expressed more negative emotion than did the nonaggressive couples. There are no data relating communication to aggression in dating couples, but the relation is expected to be similar to that found in married couples.

Relationship dissatisfaction (construct 5d) has been strongly correlated to spousal aggression (Rosenbaum & O'Leary, 1981). In at least one proposed model of spousal aggression (Rosenbaum, 1980) marital discord was the most important causal factor in the development of physical aggression between spouses.

Recent data from individuals in dating relationships (Arias, Samios & O'Leary, 1987) and early marriages (Murphy & O'Leary, 1987; O'Leary et al., 1988) question the direct causal link of relationship discord to interpartner aggression. Arias, Samios, and O'Leary (1987) found that for men in dating relationships, aggression against one's partner was not related to liking the partner, loving the partner, having positive feelings toward the partner, or feeling commitment to the partner. For women in dating relationships, aggression was negatively related to liking the partner and to having positive feelings toward the partner, but was not significantly related to love for the partner or commitment to the partner. Data from a longitudinal study of early marriages (Murphy & O'Leary, 1987; O'Leary et al., 1988) indicate that relationship discord does not precede the occurrence of interpartner aggression, but repeated aggressive incidents result in or are associated with dissatisfaction with the relationship. In the current model, there is no direct causal link between relationship discord and physical aggression. However, discord is still thought to influence the likelihood of interpartner aggression by increasing the severity and frequency of conflict situations.

As noted earlier, dating relationships vary greatly in the level of intensity or seriousness of involvement (construct 5e). Empirically, researchers have found that aggression is more likely to occur in more serious and intense relationships (Comins, 1984; Lane & Gwartney-Gibbs, 1985). The current model proposes that this relation is the result of increased sources of conflict apparent in more serious relationships. The intensity with which partners are involved with one another also contributes to the intensity of their disagreements and the importance placed on reaching a settlement (Gelles & Straus, 1979). The extent to which a couple is unable to solve the problems arising from their deeper involvement will increase the conflict within the relationship and thus contribute to the level of aggression.

THE ROLE OF CONSEQUENCES IN THE MODEL OF DATING AGGRESSION

In the current model of courtship aggression, the consequences of aggression provide the feedback mechanism in the system. According to the social learning theory of aggression (Bandura, 1973), consequences act to change the likelihood of aggression primarily by altering the expected outcome of such aggression. If the consequences of an aggressive interaction are perceived as positive (for example, winning the argument, regaining lost control, ending a negative interaction) then the expectation of similar positive outcomes from future aggression is increased and aggression becomes more likely. Alternatively, if the consequences of an aggressive incident are negative (for example, refusal of one's partner to talk, social disapproval, arrest) then the expectations for future consequences will be more negative, and it will become less likely that aggression will occur.

In addition to changing the outcome expectations related to the use of aggression, the consequences of dating aggression have an impact in other ways on the future use of aggression. For example, the use of aggression may result in increased consumption of alcohol. In turn, the use and abuse of alcohol may increase the level of aggression. As another example, aggression may increase the amount of conflict experienced by the couple. In turn, increased conflict may lead to increased levels of aggression.

It is clear that the consequences that follow an aggressive interaction between dating partners may affect the future use of such aggression. However, understanding the relation between the consequences of aggression and the future use of aggression is complicated. The positive or negative value of a particular consequence is specific to the individuals involved and to the situation. For example, social disapproval may greatly trouble one person while it has little or no impact on another. Even for the same individual, the social repercussions may be important at one time but not at another.

A second difficulty involved in the study of consequences is that a particular act of aggression will result in numerous consequences. For example, the use of aggression may win an argument (usually perceived as a positive outcome) and also result in the partner's threatening to end the relationship (usually perceived as a negative outcome). Consequences of an aggressive act may also differ over time. The use of aggression may decrease the immediate level of conflict (by ending the argument), but result in an increased level of future conflict (by decreasing satisfaction and increasing problems). In the study of courtship aggression, the role of consequences is further complicated by the differential impact of the aggression on each partner. The consequences related to the use of aggression by one partner may decrease the probability that that person will use aggression and simultaneously increase the probability that the other partner will use aggression.

THE INTERACTION OF THE TWO COMPONENTS

In the description of the current model the two components (Figures 3.1 and 3.2) were separated for ease of description. The contextual and situational characteristics that lead to the use of aggression, though, are closely related. The most apparent point of interaction of the two components is the construct of outcome expectations (Figure 3.2, Construct 1). Many of the contextual constructs in Figure 3.1 (such as prior use of aggression, models of aggression) directly affect the expected consequences of aggression. These and other contextual constructs (such as parental aggression toward the subject, personality) probably affect the level of conflict experienced by the couple. Certain contextual variables, particularly those involving the family-of-origin and personality variables, are also likely to relate to alcohol use. The relation of the contextual constructs to the stress experienced by a person is less clear, but the subjective evaluation of stressful events is probably affected by family-of-origin variables. The contextual variables may serve to increase the chances that a conflict situation becomes aggressive. For example, the acceptance of aggression as justified may not increase the conflict experienced by a couple, but will increase the likelihood that a conflict will become aggressive.

RECOMMENDATIONS FOR FURTHER RESEARCH

The proposed model holds a number of advantages for future researchers in the area of courtship aggression. The model includes constructs that are both specific enough to allow measurement and broad enough to make the overall model useful. As such, the model serves both as an empirically testable model appropriate for use with time series data and as a general framework for planning studies regarding specific variables and for understanding the results of such studies.

The proposed model includes a manageable number of measurable constructs and specifies the relationships among the constructs. The hypothesized relationships among the constructs, the overall power of the model to predict the occurrence and severity of courtship aggression, and the contribution of the individual constructs to such prediction may all be evaluated empirically. In addition, although the model as presented here does not propose any specific sex differences, the potential for understanding the differential impact of variables on men and women is testable within the framework of the model. Finally, the model specifies a set of constructs that potentially change over time (situational variables) and thus change the likelihood that aggression will occur. Specific predictions regarding these changes may be made and tested.

This model serves as a theoretical framework for designing and interpreting studies. The theoretical distinction between background and situational variables that is emphasized in the current model provides a source of many new research questions and a means of interpreting results. The background variables provide a means for predicting which individuals are likely to be aggressive against a partner. As the model is developed and tested, the set of background variables may provide a means of identifying individuals at high risk for future relationship aggression and allow preventative measures to be taken. This will be particularly important if it becomes possible to identify specific patterns among the background variables that predict severe forms of aggression.

The set of situational variables is important because it includes variables that should predict future changes in the aggressive pattern. Specifically, changes in the situational variables should precede the future occurrence of aggression and any change in the severity or frequency of the aggression. Thus the model will allow researchers to begin to predict future aggression and its potential escalation.

More importantly, the situational variables serve as potential points of intervention. Both the variables predicted to relate directly to dating aggression and those thought to increase relationship conflict might be targeted. Treatment programs might attempt to help aggressive couples cope with stress, improve communication and problem-solving skills, deal with specific problem areas, or alter outcome expectations related to aggression.

Much work is necessary before the model developed here can be termed complete. Variables and paths may be added or deleted. In the future, the role of the consequences of the aggression should be better specified. Finally, the possible interaction of characteristics of the two dating partners should be examined.

ACKNOWLEDGMENTS

The authors especially thank Marie Caulfield for her help in the preparation of this chapter.

REFERENCES

American Psychiatric Association. (1987). *Diagnostic and Statistical Manual of Mental Disorders*. 3rd ed. rev. Washington, DC: American Psychiatric Association.

Arias, I. (1984). "A Social Learning Theory Explication of the Intergenerational Transmission of Physical Aggression in Intimate Heterosexual Relationships." Ph.D. diss., State University of New York at Stony Brook.

Arias, I., Samios, M., & O'Leary, K. D. (1987). "Prevalence and Correlates of Physical Aggression During Courtship. *Journal of Interpersonal Violence*, 2:82–90.

Bandura, A. (1973). *Aggression: A Social Learning Analysis*. Engelwood Cliffs, NJ: Prentice-Hall.

Bell, R. R. (1966). *Premarital Sex in a Changing Society*. Engelwood Cliffs, NJ: Prentice-Hall.

Berkowitz, L. (1965). "The Concept of Aggressive Drive: Some Additional Considerations." Pp. 301–29. In L. Berkowitz (ed.), *Advances in Experimental Social Psychology*, Vol. 2. New York: Academic.

Bernard, M. L. & Bernard, J. L. (1983). "Violent Intimacy: The Family as a Model for Love Relationships." *Family Relations*, 32:283–86.

Breslin, F. C., Riggs, D. S., O'Leary, K. D., & Arias, I (1988). "The Impact of Interparental Violence on Dating Violence: A Social Learning Analysis." Unpublished.

Cate, C. A., Henton, J. M., Koval J., Christopher, F. S., & Lloyd, S. (1982). "Premarital Abuse: A Social Psychological Perspective." *Journal of Family Issues*, 3:79–90.

Comins, C. A. (1984). "Violence Between College Dating Partners: Incidence and Contributing Factors." Doctoral diss., Auburn University.

Derogatis, L. R., Rickels, K., & Rock, A. F. (1976). "The SCL-90 and the MMPI: A

Step in the Validation of a New Self-Report Scale." *British Journal of Psychiatry,* 128:280–89.

Detre, T., Kupfer, D. J., & Taub, S. (1975). "The Nosology of Violence." In W. S. Fields & W. H Sweet (eds.), *Neural Bases of Violence and Aggression,* 294–316. St. Louis, MO: Green.

Dobash, R. E., & Dobash, R. P. (1978). "Wives: The 'Appropriate' Victims of Marital Violence." *Victimology,* 2:426–42.

Ehrmann, W. (1959). *Premarital Dating Behavior.* New York: Holt.

Ellis, A. (1962). *The American Sexual Tragedy.* New York: Grove.

Feinstein, S. C., & Ardon, M. S. (1973). "Trends in Dating Patterns and Adolescent Development." *Journal of Youth and Adolescence,* 2:157–66.

Feinstein, S. C., Giovacchini, P., & Miller, A. (1971). Introduction, *Adolescent Psychiatry.* Vol. 1. New York: Basic Books.

Feshbach, S. (1970). "Aggression." In P. H. Mussen (ed.), *Carmichael's Manual of Child Psychology,* Vol. 2, 159–260. New York: Wiley.

Gelles, R. J., & Straus, M. A. (1979). "Determinants of Violence in the Family: Toward a Theoretical Integration." In R. B. Wesley, R. Hill, F. I. Nye, & I. L. Reiss (eds.), *Contemporary Theories About the Family,* 549–81. New York: Free Press.

Jouriles, E., Barling, J., & O'Leary, K. D. (1987). "Predicting Child Behavior Problems in Maritally Violent Families." *Journal of Abnormal Child Psychology,* 15:165–73.

Kanin, E. J. (1969). "Selected Dyadic Aspects of Male Sexual Aggression." *Journal of Sex Research,* 5.

Lane, K. E., & Gwartney-Gibbs, P. A. (1985). "Violence in the Context of Dating and Sex." *Journal of Family Issues,* 6:45–59.

Laner, M. R., & Thompson, J. (1982). "Abuse and Aggression in Courting Couples." *Deviant Behavior,* 3:229–44.

Lloyd, C. W., & Weisz, J. (1975). "Hormones and Aggression." In W. S. Fields & W. H Sweet (eds.), *Neural Bases of Violence and Aggression,* 92–127. St. Louis, MO: Green.

Makepeace, J. (1981). "Courtship Violence Among College Students." *Family Relations,* 30:97–102.

———. (1983). "Life Events, Stress and Courtship Violence." *Family Relations,* 32:101–9.

McCabe, M. P. (1984). "Toward a Theory of Adolescent Dating." *Adolescence,* 19, 159–70.

Mead, M. (1959). Introduction to Ehrmann (1959).

Murphy, C. M., & O'Leary, K. D. (1987, July). "Verbal Aggression as a Predictor of Physical Aggression in Early Marriage." Paper presented at the Third National Family Violence Research Conference, University of New Hampshire, Durham, NH.

Murphy, J. E. (1984). "Date Abuse and Forced Intercourse Among College Students." Paper presented at the Second Annual Family Violence Research Conference, University of New Hampshire, Durham, NH.

O'Leary, K. D. (1988). "Physical Aggression Between Spouses: A Social Learning Theory Perspective." In V. B. Van Hasselt, R. L. Morrison, A. S. Bellack, & M. Hersen (eds.), *Handbook of Family Violence,* 31–55. New York: Plenum.

O'Leary, K. D., & Arias, I. (1987). "Prevalence, Correlates and Development of Spouse

Abuse." In R. deV. Peters & R. J. McMahon eds.), *Marriage and Family: Behavioral Treatments and Processes*. New York: Brunner/Mazel.

O'Leary, K. D., Barling, J., Arias, I., Rosenbaum, A., Malone, J., & Tyree, A. (1988). "Prevalence and Stability of Spousal Aggression." Unpublished.

Pleck, E., Pleck, J., Grossman, M., & Bart, P. (1978). "The Battered Data Syndrome: A Comment on Steinmetz' Article." *Victimology*, 2:680–83.

Reis, D. J. (1975). "Central Neurotransmitters in Aggressive Behavior." In W. S. Fields & W. H. Sweet (eds.), *Neural Bases of Violence and Aggression*, 57–89. St. Louis, MO: Green.

Riggs, D. S. (1986). "Conflict in Dating Couples: A Multiple Predictor Approach." Master's thesis, State University of New York at Stony Brook.

Riggs, D. S., O'Leary, K. D., & Weiss, I. (1988). "Problems in Dating Relationships and Their Relation to Interpartner Aggression." In preparation.

Roche, J. P. (1986). "Premarital Sex: Attitudes and Behavior by Dating Stage." *Adolescence*, 21:107–21.

Rose, P., & Marshall, L. L. (1985). "Gender Differences: Effects of Stress on Expressed or Received Abuse." Paper presented at the American Psychological Association Meetings.

Rosenbaum, A. (1980). *Wife Abuse: Characteristics of the Participants and Etiological Considerations*. Ph.D. diss., State University of New York at Stony Brook.

Rosenbaum, A., & O'Leary, K. D. (1981). "Marital Violence: Characteristics of Abusive Couples." *Journal of Consulting and Clinical Psychology*, 49:63–71.

Rounsaville, B. J. (1978). "Theories in Marital Violence: Evidence From a Study of Battered Women." *Victimology*, 3:11–31.

Sigelman, C. K., Berry, C. J., & Wiles, K. A. (1984). "Violence in College Students' Dating Relationships." *Journal of Applied Social Psychology*, 5,6:530–48.

Smith, D. A., & O'Leary, K. D. (1987). "Affective Components of Problem-Solving Communication and Their Relationships With Interspousal Aggression." Paper presented at the Third National Family Violence Research Conference, University of New Hampshire, Durham, NH.

Smith, E. A. (1962). *American Youth Culture: Group Life in Teen-Age Society*. New York: Free Press.

Sorensen, R. C. (1973). *Adolescent Sexuality in Contemporary America*. New York: World.

Starr, B., Clarke, C. B., Goetz, K. M., & O'Malia, Li. (1979). "Psychosocial Aspects of Wife-Battering." *Social Casework*, 60:479–87.

Stets, J. E., & Pirog-Good, M. A. (1987). "Violence in Dating Relationships." *Social Psychology Quarterly*, 50(3):237–46.

Straus, M. A. (1976). "Sexual Inequality, Cultural Norms and Wife-Beating." *Victimology*, 1:54–76.

Straus, M. A., Gelles, R. J., & Steinmetz, S. (1980). *Behind Closed Doors: Violence in the American Family*. New York: Anchor.

Vivian, D., & O'Leary, K. D. (1987). "Communication Patterns in Physically Aggressive Engaged Couples." Paper presented at the Third National Family Violence Research Conference, University of New Hampshire, Durham, NH.

Walker, L. E. (1981). "A Feminist Perspective on Domestic Violence." In R. B. Stuart (ed.), *Violent Behavior: Social Learning Approaches to Prediction, Management and Treatment*. New York: Brunner/Mazel.

Zillmann, D. (1979). *Aggression and Hostility*. Hillsdale, NJ: Erlbaum.

4   Gender Identity, Self-Esteem, and Physical and Sexual Abuse in Dating Relationships

Peter J. Burke, Jan E. Stets, and Maureen A. Pirog-Good

Physical and sexual abuse while dating is pervasive. Roughly 20 to 50 percent of men and women who date have sustained physical abuse at some point during courtship (Arias, Samios & O'Leary, 1987; Cate et al., 1982; Deal & Wampler, 1986; Lane & Gwartney-Gibbs, 1985; Makepeace, 1981; Sigelman, Berry & Wiles, 1984; Stets & Pirog-Good, 1987). Moreover, 20 to 50 percent of women have sustained sexual coercion at least once while dating (Kanin & Parcell, 1977; Korman & Leslie, 1982; Koss, Gidycz & Wisniewski, 1987; Koss & Oros, 1982), and 15 to 25 percent of men have reported inflicting forceful attempts at intercourse (Kanin, 1967; Rapaport & Burkhart, 1984; Wilson, Faison & Britton, 1983).

Because individuals are dating longer before marriage, an increasing number of individuals may be at risk for physical and sexual abuse while dating. In addition, in view of the high incidence of physical abuse in marriage (Straus & Gelles, 1986; Straus, Gelles & Steinmetz, 1980) and marital rape (Finkelhor & Yllo, 1985; Russell, 1982), physical and sexual abuse while dating may be precursors to abuse in marriage (Roscoe & Benaske, 1985). For these reasons, this chapter examines abuse during courtship.

For purposes of this chapter, the term "physical abuse" refers to an act carried out with the intention or perceived intention of causing physical pain or injury. This definition is synonymous with the concept of "physical aggression" used in social psychology (Bandura, 1973; Berkowitz, 1983), and the term "violence" used in family violence research (Gelles & Straus, 1979; Stets & Straus, this volume, Chapter 2; Straus & Gelles, 1986). "Sexual abuse" refers to any unwanted or coercive erotic or sexual behavior; this definition is

This chapter is reprinted with permission from *Social Psychology Quarterly*, 51(3):272–85, 1988.

synonymous with the term "sexual aggression" (Garrett-Gooding & Senter, 1987; Korman and Leslie, 1982; Koss et al., 1985; Stets & Pirog-Good, 1988b; Wilson, Faison & Britton, 1983).[1] Throughout this chapter, the terms "inflicting" and "sustaining" abuse are used to refer to abuse that one person imposes on another and receives from another, respectively.

To understand physical abuse, many researchers have focused on identifying the traits of the male aggressor (for example, Goldstein & Rosenbaum, 1985; Walker, 1979). One important theme in this work deals with the abuser's gender identity (Toby, 1966). Essentially, it has been held that abusive men have an extreme and compulsive masculine identification and inflict abuse to display their masculinity.

Our research examines whether this idea explains physical *and* sexual abuse for males and females in dating relationships. A measure of gender identity based upon identity theory (Burke & Tully, 1977; Stryker, 1980) is developed and incorporated into models of physical and sexual abuse. The models are tested on a large sample of males and females involved in dating relationships.

BACKGROUND

Parsons (1947:305ff) argued that as industrialization moved men out of the home, a problem of gender identification emerged for males. Without the father in the home, boys identified initially with the mother. As they grew older, however, they realized that they must learn to behave as adult males rather than females. To renounce their initial feminine identification and establish their own masculine gender identity, boys engaged in "compulsive masculinity" to prove they were "men."

Toby (1966) drew upon Parsons' theme by noting that one response to concern about one's masculinity was to be *compulsively masculine;* to exaggerate the characteristics that differentiate males from females. Toby argued that violence was one of the masculine ideals: therefore, men inflicted violence to demonstrate their masculinity. Straus (1976) also used this point to explain why men inflict physical abuse.

A major problem with this argument is that it has been made in the absence of any real data (Rosenbaum, 1986). Only recently has research examined how gender identity affects abuse. To date, however, this research has examined these effects only as they relate to inflicting (and not sustaining) physical abuse, and little has been published. In general, studies find weak or nonexistent effects for gender identity and very little support for the compulsive-masculinity idea (Barnett & Ryska, 1986; Barnett & Sweet, 1986; Bernard & Bernard, 1984; Bernard, Bernard, & Bernard, 1985; Caesar, 1985; Rosenbaum, 1986; Rosenbaum & Barling, 1984).

Barnett and Ryska (1986) concluded from their review of prior work on gender identity and physical abuse that maritally violent men do differ from other comparison groups in terms of masculinity and/or femininity, but because the results are mixed and depend upon the type of measure used, no firm conclusions can be reached. We argue that the results of previous studies are not only mixed, but also are flawed in one way or another: (1) The samples tend to be very small; (2) the samples are drawn from clinical as opposed to general populations; (3) the samples consist of men only; (4) the measures of gender identity are confounded with potential uncontrolled self-esteem effects; (5) these studies lack control or other appropriate comparison groups; and (6) subjects have been dropped inappropriately from analyses. We need more theoretically grounded measures of masculine/feminine identity; a clear model of relationships among the variables with controls for self-esteem and other confounding variables; and a large, nonclinical sample.

Regarding gender identity and sexual abuse, the issue of masculinity/femininity is not discussed in the sexual-abuse literature. We know, however, that adherence to traditional sex-role attitudes is related directly and indirectly (through acceptance and sexual coercion and rape myths) to sexual abuse by men (Burt, 1980; Garrett-Gooding & Senter, 1987; Koss et al., 1985; Muehlenhard & Linton, 1987; Wilson, Faison & Britton, 1983), although some research questions this relationship (Rapaport & Burkhart, 1984). Adherence to traditional sex roles may also influence sexual victimization (Russell, 1984), although Korman and Leslie (1982) suggest this relationship is open to some question.

Our study addresses the relationship between gender identity and both physical and sexual abuse in dating relationships. We examine physical and sexual abuse for men and women separately because we view abuse as a mutual problem of both sexes (Breines & Gordon, 1983). This observation is especially true for physical abuse in dating because research finds no difference in the physical abuse rate by sex (Arias, Samios & O'Leary, 1987; Deal & Wampler, 1986; Laner & Thompson, 1982). In addition, although women sustain sexual abuse more often than men, anywhere from 10 percent to 20 percent of men have reported sustaining sexual abuse from women (Sigelman, Berry & Wiles, 1984; Stets & Pirog-Good, 1988b).

We begin by discussing the background for the improved measure of gender identity we will use. Based on identity theory, our measure of gender identity is consistent with the views of Parsons and Toby, who imply that gender identity is bipolar, with masculinity at one end and femininity at the other.

GENDER IDENTITY: AN INTERACTIONIST APPROACH

The interactionist view of gender identity was first presented by Burke and Tully (1977) as part of an ongoing program of research on identities and their impact on behavior (see below). This view grows out of a body of work and ideas known as identity theory (Stryker, 1980). According to this theory the self is an organized collection of *identities,* which directly shape our behavior in interactive situations.[2]

Identities are the internal reactions to oneself as an object; these reactions are self-meanings (Osgood, Suci & Tannenbaum, 1957). For example, a ''masculine'' identity is based on the meanings we have internalized from our association with the role of a male. Roles provide the shared meanings through which an individual and others are able to establish an identity. The work of Burke and others (Burke & Franzoi, 1988; Burke & Hoelter, 1988; Burke & Reitzes, 1981; Burke & Tully, 1977; Mutran & Burke, 1979) suggests that identities are relatively stable and are a source of motivation, leading people to behave in ways that are ''consistent with'' their identities.

It is axiomatic in sociology that roles do not stand in isolation, but presuppose and are related to counterroles (Lindesmith & Strauss, 1956). This is true of identities; the meaning of ''student'' as an identity is understood in relation to that of ''teacher,'' the meaning of ''male'' is relative to that of ''female,'' and so on.

When these ideas are applied to gender identity, we can say that people know what it means to be a male and what it means to be a female on the basis of roles in their own culture. These meanings relate to one another as opposite ends on a single continuum. People also respond to themselves as objects (self-meaning) along the male-female dimension of meaning.[3] In identity theory, gender identity consists of self-meaning on this gender dimension. Because it is embedded in the societal roles of male and female in society, gender identity is bipolar. In this respect, our measure is similar to the bipolar MF scale of the personality attribute questionnaire (PAQ).

THE MODEL

We include a number of variables in our model of abuse (see Figure 4.1) in order to test more accurately the potential direct and indirect effects of gender identity, with proper controls for other variables. In each case, the variables we include were shown in prior research to be important determinants of abuse. We view our model as a tentative and exploratory first attempt at modeling abuse explicitly.

In the model, both physical and sexual abuse are influenced by the exogenous variables observing (parental) and sustaining (child) physical abuse in childhood. Examining these background factors enables us to determine whether physical abuse is transmitted from childhood experiences to dating experiences. Research on physical abuse in marriage shows that *witnessing* physical abuse in childhood influences involvement in physical abuse, but *experiencing* physical abuse in childhood is not related consistently to physical abuse in marriage (Hotaling & Sugarman, 1986). In the dating literature, some researchers have found that witnessing and experiencing physical abuse as a child influences physical abuse (Bernard & Bernard, 1983; Laner & Thompson, 1982; Roscoe & Benaske, 1985), but others have found that it is relevant only in explaining men's involvement in abusive dating relationships (Gwartney-Gibbs, Stockard & Bohmer, 1987; Stets & Pirog-Good, 1987). Although the results have been

Figure 4.1
Inflicting and Sustaining Abuse

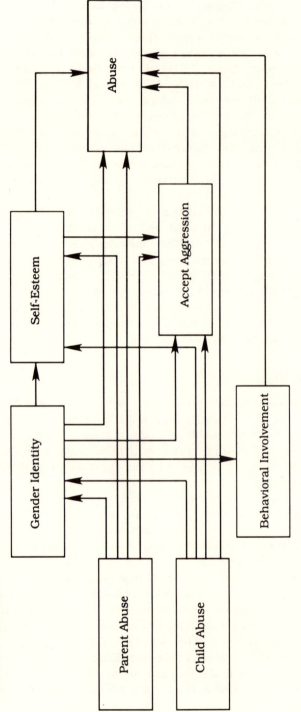

somewhat inconsistent regarding the transmission of physical abuse from childhood to dating to marriage, these characteristics continue to be important predictors of abuse (Hotaling & Sugarman, 1986) and thus are included in our analysis.

Growing up in a violent home may influence sexual abuse as well. Wilson, Faison & Britton (1983) suggest that this influence is due to learning that aggressive behavior is appropriate. Therefore we examine the effect of observing and experiencing physical abuse on sexual abuse.

Other variables that we expect to influence abuse in dating include gender identity, behavioral involvement, self-esteem, and acceptance of aggression. As mentioned above, we will test the compulsive masculinity theory.

Research shows that physical abuse among dating couples is more likely to occur in more serious dating relationships (Arias, Samios & O'Leary, 1987; Cate et al., 1982; Henton et al., 1983; Laner & Thompson, 1982; Sigelman, Berry & Wiles, 1984; Stets & Pirog-Good, 1987). In addition, Garrett-Gooding and Senter (1987) found that sexual coercion is more likely to be viewed as acceptable by both men and women in more serious relationships. Serious relationships are characterized by the men and women knowing each other for a longer time, seeing each other more frequently, experiencing a deeper level of commitment, each knowing what is expected of himself and of the other, and possessing information about the other's insecurities and weaknesses. If any of these are threatened (for example, if commitment to the relationship is breached by dating another), that threat may be the basis for inflicting or sustaining abuse. We anticipate that behavioral involvement (a characteristic of serious relationships) will influence physical and sexual abuse positively.

Among interactionists, self-esteem is an important aspect of the self that influences behavior (Kaplan, 1982a; Rosenberg, 1979). The marital and dating literature shows that low self-esteem influences physical abuse (Deal & Wampler, 1986; Goldstein & Rosenbaum, 1985; Hotaling & Sugarman, 1986; Walker, 1979). This finding is consistent with Kaplan's (1982b) proposition that low self-esteem influences deviant behavior. We anticipate that sexual abuse while dating, like physical abuse, will be shown to be characteristic of individuals with low self-esteem.[4]

Finally we examine the relationship between acceptance of aggression and physical and sexual abuse. Acceptance of aggression has been shown to be a component of physical abuse (Cate et al., 1982; Henton et al., 1983; Stets & Pirog-Good, 1988a; Ulbrich & Huber, 1981). In addition, sexually coercive men are more likely to view aggression against women as legitimate (Burt, 1980; Rapaport & Burkhart, 1984). Thus, we expect that acceptance of aggression will have a positive influence on inflicting and sustaining physical and sexual abuse.

When we note the relationships among the other variables in the model (see Figure 4.1), we view potential determinants of acceptance of aggression to be self-esteem (those with lower self-esteem may be more likely to accept aggression), gender identity (acceptance of aggression being a masculine trait), and witnessing and experiencing physical abuse as a child (these experiences lead to the acceptance of aggression). We view self-esteem as an outcome of gender identity[5] (low self-esteem is more characteristic of a feminine gender identity), and of witnessing and experiencing physical abuse in childhood (these experiences lead to low self-esteem). Finally, behavioral involvement is seen as an outcome of gender identity; persons with a feminine identity seeking more involvement (DeLamater, 1987; Rubin, 1986).

METHODS

Sample

During the spring of 1986, we obtained a random sample of 56 upper-level classes at a large midwestern university.[6] We sent letters to the professor of each sampled class, explaining the research and asking if they would agree to have their students participate in a survey. Thirty-one professors agreed to participate. The refusals were distributed evenly across disciplines and class size. The reasons for refusing to participate included "class was cancelled," "insufficient class time," and "student and professor met on a one-on-one basis, and confidentiality of the questionnaire could not be insured." Thus, the nonsystematic self-selection of professors from the study is not likely to compromise the representativeness of the responses obtained. The low frequency of nonwhites in the sample (2 males and 11 females) prompted us to exclude them from our analysis. The final sample included 505 (298F, 207M) respondents. A comparison of our sample to the general distribution of upperclass students showed no significant departures for age, sex, and area of study.

Measures

Physical Abuse. We use the Conflict Tactics Scale (CTS) to measure physical abuse (Straus, 1979). Although this scale does not incorporate the context in which violent behavior arises, the injury that results (Breines & Gordon, 1983; Ferraro & Johnson, 1983), or whether the abuse is "offensive" or "defensive" (Stets & Straus, 1989), it is the most comprehensive index of the frequency and form of tactics used to resolve conflict.[7] It has relatively high reliability (0.83 for male-to-female violence and 0.82 for female-to-male violence; Straus, Gelles & Steinmetz, 1980) and has been used in numerous studies on dating abuse (Arias, Samios & O'Leary, 1987; Cate et al., 1982; Deal & Wampler, 1986; Henton et al., 1983; Lane & Gwartney-Gibbs, 1985; Laner & Thompson, 1982; Sigelman, Berry & Wiles, 1984; Stets & Pirog-Good, 1987, 1988a).

The scale is divided into three major types of conflict resolution tactics: reasoning, verbal, and violent. We asked respondents how often in the past year they had inflicted each of these forms of abuse on each of up to four people they had dated. The *total* physical abuse measure was the sum of the frequencies of the following types of physical abuse that respondents stated they had inflicted during the past year:

1. Threw something at the partner.
2. Pushed, grabbed, or shoved the partner.
3. Slapped or spanked the partner.
4. Kicked, bit or hit the partner with fist.
5. Hit or tried to hit the partner with something.
6. Beat up the partner.
7. Threatened the partner with a knife or gun.
8. Used a knife or gun.

The frequency for each item could range from 0 (never) to 104 ("more than once a week," coded as twice a week for 52 weeks). In addition to the *total* measure, we divided the items into two severity groups: *minor* physical abuse (items 1–3) and *severe* physical abuse (items 4–8) (Straus & Gelles, 1986). The correlation between inflicting minor and severe forms of physical abuse is 0.90.

The CTS also was used to measure sustaining physical abuse. We asked respondents how often their partner(s) had inflicted each of the violent tactics on them within the past year. Using the above procedures, scales measuring sustaining, *minor, severe,* and *total* abuse were obtained. The correlation between sustaining minor and severe physical abuse is 0.53.

Sexual Abuse. To measure sexual abuse, we asked respondents to indicate the frequency with which they inflicted (or sustained) each of the following sexual activities *against their partner's (or own) will* in the past year: (1) breast fondling, (2) genital fondling, (3) attempted intercourse that was not successful, and (4) intercourse. As above, each item had a potential range of 0 (none) to 104 ("more than once a week," coded as twice a week for 52 weeks). Following the procedures used to measure physical abuse, *minor* (items 1 and 2), *severe* (items 3 and 4), and *total* sexual abuse scales were constructed for both inflicting and sustaining sexual abuse. The omega reliabilities (Heise & Bohrnstedt, 1970) on the *total* scales for inflicting and sustaining sexual abuse are 0.78 and 0.80, respectively. The correlation between inflicting minor and severe sexual abuse in the sample is 0.67. The correlation between sustaining minor and severe sexual abuse is 0.41.

Parental Abuse and Child Abuse. The violent items of the CTS also were administered to measure the degree to which respondents witnessed and/or sustained physical abuse in childhood. We asked respondents to think about the worst year of their childhood when disputes between their parents occurred most frequently and to state how often their parents inflicted the violent tactics on one another (parental) and toward the respondent (child).

Gender Identity. On the basis of the conceptualization of gender identity discussed earlier, Burke and Tully (1977) have developed a highly reliable and valid method of measuring gender identity[8] (as well as identities in general). This two-step method assesses the meanings that people attribute to themselves and others on the basis of gender. The first step is the selection of items to measure gender meanings.[9] Following the symbolic interactionist precept that the meanings of the people under study must be used (as opposed to those assumed by the researchers or those derived from some other population), Burke and Tully suggest how to find items relevant to being male or female in a particular population, using the semantic differential (Osgood, Suci & Tannenbaum, 1957). Using discriminant function analysis, researchers select items that discriminate best between the meanings of male selves and female selves. In the second step the self-ratings on the most discriminating items are summed to form a scale of gender identity.

Note that a scale constructed along these lines has certain properties. First, as interactionist theory dictates, it is based on the meanings (as measured with the semantic differential) of maleness in relation to femaleness that *actually are held in the population from which the sample is drawn.* Second, on the basis of the theory of the semantic differential (Osgood, Suci & Tannenbaum, 1957), the measure incorporates the symbolic interactionist view that meaning is contrastive. In this sense it captures the essential bipolar social nature of gender identity (cf. Storms, 1979).

For the study, initial items to capture the self-meaning of male and female were drawn from the M, (Masculinity) F, (Femininity) and MF scales of the PAQ (Spence & Helmreich, 1978). Results of the discriminant function analysis showed that nine of these items were particularly discriminating:

1. Not at all emotional . . . Very emotional.

2. Very active . . . Very passive.

3. Very competitive . . . Not at all competitive.

4. Feels very superior . . . Feels very inferior.

5. Not at all excitable in a major crisis . . . Very excitable in a major crisis.

6. Indifferent to others' approval . . . Highly needful of others' approval.

7. Feelings not easily hurt . . . Feelings easily hurt.

8. Never cries . . . Cries very easily.

9. Very little need for security . . . Very strong need for security.

These items were summed to form the gender identity scale.

Five of the nine items that were meaningful to the population under study were from the PAQ MF scale, showing the relative importance of the MF. In view of this outcome, one might want to adopt the MF scale in its entirety as a measure of gender identity, but not all items of the MF scale are meaningful. Further, three items from the M scale and one item from the F scale did contribute to the overall meaningfulness of the gender identity scale for this population. This finding illustrates the importance of making the measure meaningful to the population under study, as suggested by identity theory. The resulting scale had an omega reliability of 0.81 (Heise & Bohrnstedt, 1970). High scores indicate a more masculine identity; low scores indicate a more feminine identity. The correlation between gender identity as measured here and the M, F, and MF scales of the PAQ are 0.396, −0.402 and 0.817, respectively. Clearly, gender identity as measured here is different from the instrumentality and expressiveness measures of the PAQ, though they overlap somewhat in regard to items. Our scale is most similar to the bipolar MF scale of the PAQ, though the latter was not designed specifically for the population considered here and did not use interactionist principles.

Self-Esteem. Self-esteem was measured using the ten-item Rosenberg self-esteem scale; the reliability of this scale is 0.85 (Rosenberg, 1979). It has been used in other studies on physical and sexual abuse in dating relationships (Deal & Wampler, 1986; Stets & Pirog-Good, 1988a; 1988b).

Acceptance of Aggression. Verbal aggression items and violent items from the CTS were used to measure the degree to which respondents felt that each of the various tactics was an act of violence against a woman: "always," "depends," or "never" was scored 1; otherwise the item was scored zero. Scores were summed across items. Higher scores reflect greater acceptance of aggression.

Behavioral Involvement in the Relationship. Two items were designed as indicators of behavioral involvement: the number of months that the respondent had been dating a partner, and the number of dates per year with the dating partner (we asked how often they dated, from once every six months to more than once a week, but translated this frequency to a standardized rate of dates per year). Each of these variables was standardized (to zero mean and unit variance), and they were summed to form the scale. The correlation between these two indicators was 0.71.

Analysis

Several components of our analysis require comment. First, the outcome variables of sexual and physical abuse (like the variables of parent abuse and child abuse) are censored variables with a lower limit of zero. They are skewed highly, with a large preponderance of zeros. Such variables should not be analyzed with ordinary least squares (OLS) procedures (Muthén, 1984, 1988). For this reason we analyzed the model by means of the program LISCOMP (Muthén, 1988). This program does not assume normally distributed variables, but allows for the specification of variables as censored in the way as the single-equation Tobit approach.

A second feature of the data is that each person was asked to describe his or her relationship with up to four other partners. Dating relationships are unique in that people are often involved with more than one partner; neglecting to include multiple partners results in a failure to represent the population of dating relationships. Including these data, however, may result in correlated errors. Although the presence of correlated errors would not bias the parameter estimates, it would inflate the tests of significance somewhat. To check this possibility we used Durbin-Watson statistics (Hanushek & Jackson, 1977), following the procedure of Good, Pirog-Good, and Sickles (1986). Although the results were too numerous to report in detail, we found no significant correlation among the errors for the variables that changed across partners (physical and sexual abuse, and behavioral involvement), but we noted significant correlation for those variables which did not change across partners (gender identity, self-esteem, and acceptance of violence). To correct the tests of significance in the equations where there were correlated errors, we used the number of independent observations (not counting multiple partners) to calculate the t-ratios. This procedure provides somewhat conservative tests of significance which are based only on the number of independent observations.

The number of cases for each analysis varied because of missing data. The total number of cases for each equation (along with the number of independent observations, after multiple partners were excluded) are as follows: males (in the equation for inflicting physical abuse), 151 (68); males (sustaining physical abuse), 256 (122); females (inflicting physical abuse), 236 (125); females (sustaining physical abuse), 345 (169); males (inflicting sexual abuse), 243 (117); males (sustaining sexual abuse), 251 (132); females (inflicting sexual abuse), 345 (167); females (sustaining sexual abuse), 339 (163).

RESULTS

Table 4.1 presents the range, mean, and standard deviations for each of the variables used in our model. Seven of the 18 variables have significantly different means for men and for women. Table 4.1 reveals that women have a more feminine gender identity than men, and that men are more likely than women to accept aggression.

We find no significant difference between men and women in reporting inflicting or sustaining physical abuse.[10] This finding supports past research, which showed that men and women inflict physical abuse at about the same rate (Arias, Samios & O'Leary, 1987; Deal & Wampler, 1986; Laner & Thompson, 1982, Sigelman, Berry & Wiles, 1984) and that they have similar rates of sustaining physical abuse (Laner & Thompson, 1982). Although the frequencies of physical abuse inflicted and sustained by men and women are similar, we must recognize that the consequences of such abuse may be more severe for women than men because of men's greater average strength (Stets & Straus, 1989). With respect to sexual abuse, we find that men report inflicting it much

Table 4.1
Means and Standard Deviation of All Variables

Variable	Males Range		Mean	SD	Females Range		Mean	SD
Parent Abuse	0	- 155	4.1	14.2	0.	- 447	·7.2	36.6
Child Abuse	0	- 214	13.8	23.0	0.	- 377	11.3	28.2
Gender Identity	4.	- 26	15.3**	4.2	1.	- 20	11.6**	4.0
Behavioral Involve.	-2.1-	5.4	-0.2	1.7	-2.2-	5.4	0.0	1.7
Self-Esteem	22.	- 40	32.4	4.0	17.	- 40	32.1	4.3
Accept Aggression	0	- 9	0.7**	1.5	0	- 5	0.4**	0.9
Inflict Sexual Abuse								
Mild	0	- 104	5.1**	19.5	0	- 120	1.7**	12.1
Severe	0	- 64	2.5*	10.2	0	- 60	1.2*	7.7
Total	0	- 168	7.0*	27.4	0	- 180	2.6*	17.3
Inflict Physical Abuse								
Mild	0	- 23	0.4	2.0	0	- 47	1.0	4.9
Severe	0	- 38	0.3	3.2	0	- 65	0.6	4.8
Total	0	- 60	0.7	5.1	0	- 112	1.5	9.3
Sustain Sexual Abuse								
Mild	0	- 67	0.8	5.2	0	- 120	1.8	11.2
Severe	0	- 64	0.9*	6.0	0	- 63	2.1*	9.8
Total	0	- 131	1.5*	10.3	0	- 183	4.0*	17.2
Sustain Physical Abuse								
Mild	0	- 61	0.8	4.8	0	- 84	1.1	7.1
Severe	0	- 74	0.4	4.8	0	- 25	0.2	1.6
Total	0	- 77	1.1	6.9	0	- 102	1.2	8.4

*   Difference between males and females significant at .05 level.
** Difference between males and females significant at .01 level.
SD: standard deviation.

more than women; women report sustaining such abuse more than men.[11] These findings are similar to results of other research on sexual abuse in dating (Sigelman, Berry & Wiles, 1984; Lane & Gwartney-Gibbs, 1985; Stets & Pirog-Good, 1988a).

When we attempt to match inflicting and sustaining abuse, some interesting anomalies appear. Women tend to report sustaining sexual abuse significantly less than men report inflicting it. We find also that men tend to report sustaining physical abuse significantly less than women report inflicting it. It would appear that men either are more likely to take some physical abuse for granted or do not recognize it fully as such (in the sense that it is a "normal crime"; cf. Sudnow, 1965). In either case they tend to underreport sustaining such physical abuse. Women, underreport sustaining sexual abuse, perhaps for the same reasons.

Inflicting Abuse

Gender Identity. The effects of gender identity on inflicting abuse are presented in Table 4.2. For males, gender identity directly affects inflicting total

Table 4.2
Standardized Betas for the Model of Inflicting Abuse

MALES: Independent Variables

Dep. Vars.	Parent Abuse (1)	Child Abuse (2)	Gender Identity (3)	Behav Involvement (4)	Self-Esteem (5)	Accept Aggression (6)	Total Sexual Abuse (7)	Total Physical Abuse (8)
(3)			0	0	0	0	0	0
(4)	0	0		0	0	0	0	0
(5)			.22***	0	0	0	0	0
(6)				0	-.16***	0	0	0
(7)			-.14**	.21***			0	0
(8)		.17***		.31***		.33***	0	0

N (physical abuse) = 151; N (sexual abuse) = 243.

FEMALES: Independent Variables

Dep. Vars.	Parent Abuse (1)	Child Abuse (2)	Gender Identity (3)	Behav Involvement (4)	Self-Esteem (5)	Accept Aggression (6)	Total Sexual Abuse (7)	Total Physical Abuse (8)
(3)	-.16**	-.11**	0	0	0	0	0	0
(4)	0	0	-.13***	0	0	0	0	0
(5)	-.28***		.34***	0	0	0	0	0
(6)			.25***	0	-.20***	0	0	0
(7)				.29***		.14**	0	0
(8)			-.29**	.24***			0	0

N (physical abuse) = 236; N (sexual abuse) = 345.

**	p < .05
***	p < .01
Blank	Estimated effect not significant.
0	Estimated effect constrained to be zero.

sexual abuse independently of self-esteem and the other variables in the model. In separate analyses not reported in Table 4.2, this effect holds for severe sexual abuse; for minor sexual abuse it is in the same direction, though not quite significant. With respect to the direction of effect, the *less masculine* (more feminine) these males are, the more likely they are to be sexually abusive to their dating partner(s). Gender identity also affects inflicting physical abuse for males; this effect operates indirectly through self-esteem and acceptance of aggression. Again, the *less* masculine (more feminine) the males are, the more likely they are to be physically aggressive. This pattern also holds for mild and severe levels of physical abuse as well as for total physical abuse.

For females, gender identity directly affects inflicting physical abuse (total, minor, and severe). The *less* masculine the gender identity, the more likely the individual will inflict physical abuse. Gender identity also has indirect effects on inflicting physical abuse (minor, severe, and total) through behavioral involvement in the relationship. In addition, gender identity has indirect effects on inflicting sexual abuse (minor, severe, and total) through behavioral involvement in the relationship and acceptance of aggression.

Self-Esteem. For both males and females, self-esteem has no direct effects on inflicting sexual or physical abuse in dating relationships. Indirect effects of self-esteem occur through acceptance of aggression, which influences inflicting sexual abuse for women and inflicting physical abuse for men.

Other Variables. In addition to the above findings, behavioral involvement has strong effects on inflicting both sexual and physical abuse for both males and females, and does so for minor, severe, and total levels of abuse. Inflicting physical abuse, for males, is influenced additionally by experiencing abuse in childhood. For males, acceptance of aggression influences inflicting physical abuse (at all levels of severity), but not sexual abuse. For females, acceptance of aggression influences total sexual abuse (though it does not show up as significant in separate analyses of either severe or minor sexual abuse), but has no effect on inflicting physical abuse.

Sustaining Abuse

Gender Identity. The effects of gender identity on sustaining abuse are shown in Table 4.3. For males, gender identity has direct and indirect effects on sustaining sexual abuse. The *less* masculine (more feminine) the gender identity, the more likely men will sustain sexual abuse. In separate analyses not reported in Table 4.3, this effect holds for severe sexual abuse; and it is in the same direction, though not quite significant, for minor sexual abuse. For total and minor physical abuse, gender identity has indirect effects through self-esteem and acceptance of aggression. For severe levels of physical abuse, gender identity also has direct effects. All of these effects show *fewer* masculine respondents sustaining more abuse.

For females, gender identity has direct and indirect effects on sustaining physical abuse (minor, severe, and total). Indirectly, gender identity influences sustaining sexual abuse (at all levels) through its effect on behavioral involvement and self-esteem. Again, in both cases, the *less* masculine (more feminine) females are likely to sustain this abuse.

Self-Esteem. For females, self-esteem has direct effects on sustaining sexual abuse (minor, severe, and total), but no direct effects on sustaining physical abuse. For males, self-esteem has no direct effects on sustaining either sexual or physical abuse (at any level of severity), though it has indirect effects on both outcomes through acceptance of aggression.

Table 4.3
Standardized Betas for the Model of Sustaining Abuse

MALES: Independent Variables

Dep. Vars.	Parent Abuse (1)	Child Abuse (2)	Gender Identity (3)	Behav Invol-vement (4)	Self-Esteem (5)	Accept Aggres-sion (6)	Total Sexual Abuse (7)	Total Physical Abuse (8)
(3)			0	0	0	0	0	0
(4)	0	0		0	0	0	0	0
(5)			.22***	0	0	0	0	0
(6)				0	-.16***	0	0	0
(7)	.32***	.12**	-.18**	.21***		.20***	0	0
(8)	.20***	.20***		.22***		.19**	0	0

N (physical abuse) = 256; N (sexual abuse) = 251.

FEMALES: Independent Variables

Dep. Vars.	Parent Abuse (1)	Child Abuse (2)	Gender Identity (3)	Behav Invol-vement (4)	Self-Esteem (5)	Accept Aggres-sion (6)	Total Sexual Abuse (7)	Total Physical Abuse (8)
(3)	-.16**	-.11**	0	0	0	0	0	0
(4)	0	0	-.13***	0	0	0	0	0
(5)	-.28***		.34***	0	0	0	0	0
(6)			.25***	0	-.20***	0	0	0
(7)		.11***		.14**	-.18***		0	0
(8)			-.20**	.26***			0	0

N (physical abuse) = 345; N (sexual abuse) = 339.

**	p < .05
***	p < .01
Blank	Estimated effect not significant.
0	Estimated effect constrained to be zero.

Other Variables. In addition to the effects discussed above, sustaining sexual abuse, for men, is influenced by witnessing and experiencing abuse as a child, by being more involved with dating partners, and by acceptance of aggression. These same factors also influence the likelihood that they will sustain physical abuse.

For women, the pattern is somewhat different. Increased involvement with dating partners directly influences sustaining both sexual and physical abuse. Experiencing abuse in childhood also increases the likelihood of sustaining sexual abuse.

DISCUSSION

Gender Identity and Abuse

We find that males and females with more feminine gender identities are likely to inflict and sustain both sexual and physical abuse. The argument that physical abuse results from the adoption of extreme masculine identities and behaviors (Parsons, 1947; Toby, 1966), was the result of a male-oriented theory that was developed in part by examining only males as abusers. Direct research has failed to provide support for this argument.

First, while Bernard and Bernard (1984) imply the truth of this argument, they have no data to indicate it directly; the only hard data they have on the abusive males' gender identity (the MMPI MF scale) suggest that such identities are in the normal range. Second, Barnett and Sweet (1986) failed to find support for this hypothesis in a direct test. Finally, in examining both male and female abuse, we find that the effects of gender identity on abuse are generally the same for men and women: A more feminine identity increases abuse directly or indirectly. The "compulsive masculinity" argument fails to acknowledge that women who have more feminine gender identities act in the same abusive ways as men. Therefore, an understanding of the dynamics of abuse must involve an understanding of gender identity mechanisms that work for both males and females.

We can only speculate about this result. In doing so, we also attempt to stay within the interactionist framework of identity theory. The first dictate of identity theory, which research has supported (for example, Burke & Franzoi, 1988; Burke & Hoelter, 1988; Burke & Reitzes, 1981; Chassin et al., 1981; Mutran & Burke, 1979), is that *people behave in ways that are consistent with their identities*. In the absence of similar results for males and for females, it would be tempting to say (for example) that males who have more feminine gender identities are inflicting abuse to "compensate" for their more feminine identity. This statement, however, would be inconsistent with identity theory and would not make sense for females. Instead we must try to see the abusive behaviors as consistent with the acting out of a feminine gender identity, whether the identity is held by a male or by a female.

With respect to inflicting sexual abuse, it is possible that people with more feminine gender identities are more emotionally expressive and more oriented toward their dating relationship (DeLamater, 1987; Rubin, 1986). Being relationship-oriented, and perhaps wanting heightened involvement, men and women with more feminine gender identities may initiate sexual activity in an attempt to demonstrate or attain that higher involvement (DeLamater, 1987). If their partner does not agree to such activity or resists it, then it becomes sexual abuse.

With respect to inflicting physical abuse, it is possible that the emotional expressiveness of the feminine gender identity plays an important role. It is easy to see emotional expressiveness in outbursts that might be characterized as "losing control of oneself" and leading to physical abuse (Stets, 1988).

Finally, with respect to sustaining abuse, the results show again that individuals with more feminine gender identities are more likely to sustain physical and sexual abuse. Although it is possible that persons with more feminine gender identities are more vulnerable to abuse, there is no evidence to substantiate this "blaming the victim" explanation. Our tentative interpretation of this result draws upon the findings of Cate et al. (1982), Henton et al. (1983) and Sigelman, Berry & Wiles, (1984) that violence tends to be reciprocal; sustaining physical abuse is related to inflicting physical abuse. Indeed, our research revealed that inflicting and sustaining abuse are positively correlated. People who inflict abuse are likely also to be the people who sustain abuse.[12]

Self-Esteem and Abuse

We found in general that self-esteem was not related directly to either physical or sexual abuse for men or for women. We know that a moderate relationship exists between gender identity and self-esteem such that people with a more feminine identity have low self-esteem (females: $r = -.33$, $p \le .01$; males: $r = -.21$, $p \le .01$). As a result, the independent effects of self-esteem on inflicting abuse generally are not strong enough to achieve statistical significance. This is important; although direct research on this issue is lacking severely, the literature on physical abuse assumes that self-esteem is included in the causal equation (Deal & Wampler, 1986; Hotaling & Sugarman, 1986; Walker, 1979). Our work shows that the way in which self-esteem is related to inflicting physical abuse for women and sexual abuse for men is spurious in part because of the common cause of a more feminine gender identity.

CONCLUSION

In trying to understand physical and sexual abuse, researchers have suggested that abuse is influenced by gender identity in the form of compulsive masculinity for men. To test this idea we used a large sample of both males and females from a general population, a reliable and theoretically based measure of gender identity, and a model with proper controls for self-esteem and other variables known to influence abuse.

Our results suggest that a more feminine identity is associated with both inflicting and sustaining abuse for both males and females. We speculate that this relationship may be the result of two components of a more feminine gender identity: an emotional excitability, which may result in physical outbursts, and an orientation to the dating relationship, which may lead the respondent to seek greater sexual involvement than desired by the dating partner. Because these results hold for both males and females, they should cause us to reconsider the male-oriented theories of the past in trying to understand physical and sexual abuse.

ACKNOWLEDGMENTS

An earlier version of this chapter was presented at the 1987 meeting of the North Central Sociological Association. The work of the second author was supported in part by a grant from the National Institute of Justice (86-IJ-CX-67) and a postdoctoral research fellowship from the National Institute of Mental Health (T34 MH15161).

NOTES

1. When the term "abuse" is used without modification, it refers to *both* physical and sexual abuse.

2. See Markus and Wurf (1988) for a review of an independent but related tradition of research on the self-concept in psychology.

3. Storms (1979) found this idea to be empirically true in his study of sex-role identities, attributes, and stereotypes. He states that "although the instrument contained separate masculine and feminine identity items, thus allowing for multidimensional responses, subjects conceptualized their sex role identity along a single, bipolar dimension. This is not surprising, given that until very recently everyone, including psychologists, viewed masculinity and femininity as diametric" (1979:1786).

4. While self-esteem ultimately may be both a cause and an outcome of abuse, such a model cannot be estimated without longitudinal data. Because low self-esteem has been implicated in the literature as a cause of abuse, we modeled it in this fashion.

5. We distinguish between *gender identity* scales, such as the Bem sex-role inventory (BSRI), which consistently show nonmasculine gender identity to be associated with low self-esteem (Spence & Helmreich, 1978), and *gender,* which shows little relationship with self-esteem (Maccoby & Jacklin 1974).

6. We wanted to study only college students' dating experiences. We selected upper-level classes to avoid freshmen, whose dating experiences over the past year may go back to high school.

7. Although our data do not distinguish between offensive and defensive physical abuse, Stets and Straus (1989) found that men and women do not differ in their relative amounts of offensive and defensive physical abuse.

8. The omega reliability (Heise & Bohrnstedt, 1970) of their measure of gender identity was 0.82. Construct validity was assessed and was shown to be acceptable by relating the measure of gender identity to several behavioral outcomes.

9. Although identities are tied to roles, they are self-meanings and must be measured as such. For this purpose, as in the Burke-Tully procedure, bipolar traits (adjective pairs) are presented in a semantic differential format to measure the *direction* and *intensity* of the internal response (Osgood, Suci & Tannenbaum, 1957).

10. Treating physical abuse as dichotomous (present vs. absent), we find that 14 percent of the men and 18 percent of the women inflict physical abuse, while 10 percent of the men and 14 percent of the women sustain physical abuse.

11. Treating sexual abuse as dichotomous, we find that 27 percent of the men and 7 percent of the women inflict sexual abuse, while 9 percent of the men and 18 percent of the women sustain sexual abuse.

12. Treating abuse as dichotomous, we correlate inflicting and sustaining physical abuse and find that phi is 0.55 ($X^2 = 40.85$, df $= 1$, p $< .01$) for men, and 0.52 ($X^2 = 56.68$,

df $= 1$, p $< .01$) for women. With respect to inflicting and sustaining sexual abuse, the phi for men is 0.42 ($X^2 = 45.08$, df $= 1$, p $< .01$); for women is .24 ($X^2 = 18.99$, df $= 1$, p $< .01$).

REFERENCES

Arias, Ileana, Mary Samios & K. Daniel O'Leary. (1987). "Prevalence and Correlates of Physical Aggression During Courtship." *Journal of Interpersonal Violence* 2:82–90.

Bandura, Albert. (1973). *Aggression: A Social Learning Analysis.* Englewood Cliffs, NJ: Prentice-Hall.

Barnett, Ola W., & Todd A. Ryska. (1986). "Masculinity and Femininity in Maritally Violent Males." Paper presented at the American Society of Criminology meetings.

Barnett, Ola W., & J. Steven Sweet. (1986). "Sex-Role Perceptions and Masculinity of Male Spouse Abusers." Paper presented at the American Psychological Association meetings.

Berkowitz, Leonard. (1983). "The Goals of Aggression." In *The Dark Side of Families: Current Family Violence Research,* ed. D. Finkelhor, R. Gelles, G. Hotaling, and M. Straus, pp. 166–81. Beverly Hills, CA: Sage.

Bernard, J. L., & M. L. Bernard. (1984). "The Abusive Male Seeking Treatment: Jekyll and Hyde." *Family Relations* 33:543–47.

Bernard, J. L., S. L. Bernard & M. L. Bernard. (1985). "Courtship Violence and Sex-Typing." *Family Relations* 34:573–76.

Bernard, M. L., & J. L. Bernard. (1983). "Violent Intimacy: The Family as a Model for Love Relationships." *Family Relations* 32:283–86.

Breines, Wini, & Linda Gordon. (1983). "The New Scholarship on Family Violence." *Signs: Journal of Women in Culture and Society* 6:490–531.

Burke, Peter J., & Stephen L. Franzoi. (1988). "Situations and Identities: An Experimental Sampling Study." *American Sociological Review* 53:559–68.

Burke, Peter J., & Jon W. Hoelter. (1988). "Identity and Sex-Race Differences in Educational and Occupational Aspirations Formation." *Social Science Research* 17:29–47.

Burke, Peter J., & Donald C. Reitzes. (1981). "The Link Between Identity and Role Performance." *Social Psychology Quarterly* 44:83–92.

Burke, Peter J., & Judy C. Tully. (1977). "The Measurement of Role Identity." *Social Forces* 55:881–97.

Burt, Martha. (1980). "Cultural Myths and Supports for Rape." *Journal of Personality and Social Psychology* 38:217–30.

Caesar, P. L. (1985). "The Wife Beater: Personality and Psychosocial Characteristics." Doctoral diss., California School of Professional Psychology, Berkeley.

Cate, Rodney M., June M. Henton, James Koval, F. Scott Christopher & Sally Lloyd. (1982). "Premarital Abuse." *Journal of Family Issues* 3:79–90.

Chassin, L., C. C. Presson, R. D. Young & R. Light. (1981). "Self-Concepts of Institutionalized Adolescents: A Framework for Conceptualizing Labeling Effect." *Journal of Abnormal Psychology* 20:143–51.

Deal, James E., & Karen Smith Wampler. (1986). "Dating Violence: The Primacy of Previous Experience." *Journal of Social and Personal Relationships* 3:457–71.

DeLamater, John. (1987). "Gender Differences in Sexual Scenarios." In *Females, Males and Sexuality: Theories and Research,* ed. Katheryn Kelley, pp. 127–38. Albany: SUNY.

Ferraro, Kathleen J., & John M. Johnson. (1983). "How Women Experience Battering: The Process of Victimization." *Social Problems* 30:325–38.

Finkelhor, David, & Kersti Yllo. (1985). *License to Rape: Sexual Abuse of Wives.* New York: Holt, Rinehart & Winston.

Garrett-Gooding, Joy, & Richard Senter. (1987). "Attitudes and Acts of Sexual Aggression on a University Campus." *Sociological Inquiry* 57:348–71.

Gelles, Richard J., & Murray A. Straus. (1979). "Determinants of Violence in the Family: Toward a Theoretical Integration. In *Contemporary Theories About the Family,* ed. W. R. Burr, R. Hill, F. I. Nye & I. L. Reiss, pp. 549–81. New York: Free Press.

Goldstein, Diane, & Alan Rosenbaum. (1985). "An Evaluation of the Self-Esteem of Maritally Violent Men." *Family Relations* 34:425–28.

Good, David, Maureen Pirog-Good & Robin C. Sickles. (1986). "An Analysis of Youth Crime and Employment Patterns." *Journal of Quantitative Criminology* 2:219–36.

Gwartney-Gibbs, Patricia A., Jean Stockard & Susanne Bohmer. (1987). "Learning Courtship Aggression: The Influence of Parents, Peers, and Personal Experiences." *Family Relations* 36:276–82.

Hanushek, Eric A., & John E. Jackson. (1977). *Statistical Methods for Social Scientists.* New York: Academic.

Heise, David R., & George W. Bohrnstedt. (1970). "Validity, Invalidity, and Reliability." In *Sociological Methodology,* ed. Edgar F. Borgatta and George W. Bohrnstedt, pp. 104–29. San Francisco: Jossey-Bass.

Henton, June, Rodney Cate, James Koval, Sally Lloyd & Scott Christopher. (1983). "Romance and Violence in Dating Relationships." *Journal of Family Issues* 4:467–82.

Hotaling, Gerald T., & David B. Sugarman. (1986). "An Analysis of Risk Markers in Husband to Wife Violence: The Current State of Knowledge." *Violence and Victims* 1:101–24.

Kanin, Eugene J. (1967). "Reference Groups and Sex Conduct Norms." *Sociological Quarterly* 8:495–504.

Kanin, Eugene J., & Stanley Parcell. (1977). "Sexual Aggression: A Second Look at the Offended Female." *Archives of Sexual Behavior* 6:67–76.

Kaplan, Howard B. (1982a). "Prevalence of the Self-Esteem Motive." In *Social Psychology of the Self-Concept,* ed. Morris Rosenberg and Howard B. Kaplan, pp. 139–51. Arlington Heights, IL: Harlan Davidson.

————. (1982b). "Self-Attitudes and Deviant Response." In *Social Psychology of the Self-Concept,* ed. Morris Rosenberg and Howard B. Kaplan, pp. 452–65. Arlington Heights, IL: Harlan Davidson.

Korman, Sheila A., & Gerald R. Leslie. (1982). "The Relationship of Feminist Ideology and Date Expense Sharing to Perceptions of Sexual Aggression in Dating." *Journal of Sex Research* 18:114–29.

Koss, Mary P., C. A. Gidycz & N. Wisniewski. (1987). "The Scope of Rape: Incidence and Prevalence of Sexual Aggression and Victimization in a National Sample of Higher Education Students." *Journal of Consulting and Clinical Psychology* 55:162–70.

Koss, Mary P., Kenneth E. Leonard, Dana A. Beezley & Cheryl J. Oros. (1985). "Nonstranger Sexual Aggression: A Discriminant Analysis of the Psychological Characteristics of Undetected Offenders." *Sex Roles* 12:981–92.

Koss, Mary P., & Cheryl J. Oros. (1982). "Sexual Experiences Survey: A Research Instrument Investigating Sexual Aggression and Victimization." *Journal of Consulting and Clinical Psychology* 50:455–57.

Lane, Katherine E., & Patricia Gwartney-Gibbs. (1985). "Violence in the Context of Dating and Sex." *Journal of Family Issues* 6:45–59.

Laner, Mary Riege, & Jeanine Thompson. (1982). "Abuse and Aggression in Courting Couples." *Deviant Behavior: An Interdisciplinary Journal* 3:229–44.

LaViolette, A. D., Ola W. Barnett & C. L. Miller. (1984). "A Classification of Wife Abusers on the Bem Sex Role Inventory." Paper presented at the Second Annual Conference of Domestic Violence Researchers.

Lindesmith, A., & A. Strauss. (1956). *Social Psychology.* New York: Holt, Rinehart & Winston.

Maccoby, Eleanor E., & Carol N. Jacklin. (1974). *The Psychology of Sex Differences.* Stanford, CA: Stanford University Press.

Makepeace, James M. (1981). "Courtship Violence Among College Students." *Family Relations* 30:97–102.

Markus, Hazel, & Elissa Wurf. (1987). The Dynamic Self-Concept: A Social Psychological Perspective. *Annual Review of Psychology* 38:299–337.

Muehlenhard, Charlene L., & Melaney A. Linton. (1987). "Date Rape and Sexual Aggression in Dating Situations: Incidence and Risk Factors." *Journal of Counseling Psychology* 34:186–96.

Muthén, Bengt O. (1984). "Modeling with Censored Variables: Estimating Correlations." Paper presented at the Psychometric Society meeting, Santa Barbara, CA.

————. (1988). *LISCOMP: Analysis of Linear Structural Equations with a Comprehensive Measurement Model.* Mooresville, IN: Scientific Software.

Mutran, Elizabeth, & Peter J. Burke. (1979). "Personalism as a Component of Old Age Identity." *Research on Aging* 1:37–63.

Osgood, Charles E., George J. Suci & Percy H. Tannenbaum. (1957). *The Measurement of Meaning.* Urbana, IL: University of Illinois Press.

Parsons, Talcott. (1947). "Certain Primary Sources and Patterns of Aggression in the Social Structure of the Western World." In *Essays in Sociological Theory,* ed. T. Parsons, pp. 298–322. New York: Free Press.

Rapaport, K., & B. R. Burkhart. (1984). "Personality and Attitudinal Characteristics of Sexually Coercive College Males." *Journal of Abnormal Psychology* 93:216–21.

Roscoe, Bruce, & Nancy Benaske. (1985). "Courtship Violence Experienced by Abused Wives: Similarities in Patterns of Abuse." *Family Relations* 34:419–24.

Rosenbaum, Alan. (1986). "Of Men, Macho, and Marital Violence." *Journal of Family Violence* 1:121–29.

Rosenbaum, Alan, & J. Barling. (1984). "Maritally Violent Men." Paper presented at the American Psychological Association meetings.

Rosenberg, Morris. (1979). *Conceiving the Self.* New York: Basic Books.

Rubin, Lillian B. (1986). *Just Friends: The Role of Friendship in Our Lives.* New York: Harper & Row.

Russell, Diana E. (1982). *Rape in Marriage*. New York: Macmillan.

————. (1984). *Sexual Exploitation: Rape, Child Sexual Abuse and Workplace Harassment*. Beverly Hills, CA.: Sage.

Sigelman, Carol K., Carol J. Berry & Katharine A. Wiles. (1984). "Violence in College Students' Dating Relationships." *Journal of Applied Social Psychology* 5,6:530–48.

Spence, Janet T., & Robert L. Helmreich. (1978). *Masculinity and Femininity: Their Psychological Dimensions, Correlates and Antecedents*. Austin, TX: University of Texas Press.

Stets, Jan E. (1988). *Domestic Violence and Control*. New York: Springer-Verlag.

Stets, Jan E., & Maureen A. Pirog-Good. (1987). "Violence in Dating Relationships." *Social Psychology Quarterly* 50:237–46.

————. (1988a). "Control and Dating Violence." Durham, NH: Family Research Laboratory.

————. (1988b). "Sexual Aggression and Control in Dating Relationships." Durham, NH: Family Research Laboratory.

Stets, Jan E., & Murray A. Straus. (1989). "Gender Differences in Reporting Marital Violence and Its Medical and Psychological Consequences." In *Violence in American Families*, ed. M. Straus and R. Gelles, Chapter 9. New York: Transaction.

Storms, Michael D. (1979). "Sex Role Identity and Its Relationship to Sex Role Attributes and Sex Role Stereotypes." *Journal of Personality and Social Psychology* 37:1779–89.

Straus, Murray A. (1976). "Sexual Inequality, Cultural Norms, and Wife-Beating." *Victimology: An International Journal* 1:54–70.

————. (1979). "Measuring Intrafamily Conflict and Violence: The Conflict Tactics (CT) Scales." *Journal of Marriage and the Family* 41:75–88.

Straus, Murray A., & Richard J. Gelles. (1986). "Societal Changes and Change in Family Violence from 1975 to 1985 as Revealed by Two National Surveys." *Journal of Marriage and the Family* 48:465–79.

Straus, Murray A., Richard J. Gelles & Suzanne Steinmetz. (1980). *Behind Closed Doors: Violence in the American Family*. Garden City, NY: Anchor.

Stryker, Sheldon. (1980). *Symbolic Interactionism: A Social Structural Version*. Menlo Park, CA: Cummings.

Sudnow, David. (1965). "Normal Crimes: Sociological Features of the Penal Code in a Public Defender's Office." *Social Problems* 12:250–61.

Toby, Jackson. (1966). "Violence and the Masculine Ideal: Some Qualitative Data." *Annual American Academic Political Social Science* 364:19–28.

Ulbrich, Patricia, & Joan Huber. (1981). "Observing Parental Violence: Distribution and Effects." *Journal of Marriage and the Family* 44:623–31.

Walker, Lenore E. (1979). *The Battered Woman*. New York: Harper & Row.

Weis, D. D. (1983). "Domestic Violence: Personality Characteristics of Men Who Batter." Unpublished master's thesis, California State University, Long Beach.

Wilson, Kenneth, Rebecca Faison & G. M. Britton. (1983). "Cultural Aspects of Male Sex Aggression." *Deviant Behavior: An Interdisciplinary Journal* 4:241–55.

5 Dating, Living Together, and Courtship Violence
James Makepeace

Decades ago, Willard Waller (1937) described the emerging U.S. courtship system as participant run and characterized by conflict and exploitation between the sexes. Before long, however, the new system gained normative acceptance, and subsequent descriptions were functionalist in tone—that is, the system came to be described in professional and popular literature as benign and well-suited to the needs of the family and the larger society. There were a few exceptions to this, such as work following Kanin (1957), but they were the exceptions that proved the rule, as no focused tradition recognizing and analyzing conflict within courtship emerged. Indeed, significant interest in this area re-emerged only after the appearance of an analysis by Makepeace (1981) that identified violence as a significant feature of modern courtship.

A second emphasis that has appeared in the courtship literature in recent years is a focus on heterosexual cohabitation or "living together," as it is more commonly called. This was not, like violence, a previously overlooked aspect of U.S. courtship, but, apparently, a genuinely new custom within the system. Not that living together had never occurred before—it had. But it became, beginning in the early 1970s, a much more widespread and somewhat normatively accepted practice (Glick & Spanier, 1980). The early literature on living together frequently focused on its functionality, especially in its sexual aspect and as an "alternative" to traditional marriage and family. Further, living together was usually viewed as a functional revision to the extent that it permitted mutual exploration of roles and personalities by the couple prior to marriage.

In the 1980s, however, some reconsideration of the functionality of living together took place. Thus, research has found violence to be a significant feature of living together (Yllo & Straus, 1981) and has challenged its functionality as a "testing ground" for marriage, showing that marital maladjustment and divorce are more frequent among those who lived together before marriage (Yllo, 1978).

Pertinent questions stand at the interface of these two interpretations and within the broader area of research on couple violence. How do rates of violence in living together relationships compare with rates in more traditional courtship stages? Is the violence that occurs in the former like the violence in other courtship stages, or more like violence within marriage?

Before proceeding, it will perhaps be helpful to review several interpretations of the relationship between violence in premarital and in marital relationships. A first perspective is that premarital and marital violence are sui generis: one and the same. This perspective is adopted de facto in a large number of studies that treat all cases of couple violence as instances of "spousal abuse" or "wife beating," irrespective of the couple's marital status (see Walker, 1979, and Roscoe & Benaske, 1985, as examples of this perspective). This is, by far, the most widespread perspective in the couple violence literature.

A second perspective is that it is the dynamics of marriage that are the primary source of couple violence and, therefore, couple violence will increase as relationships more closely approximate traditional marriage. According to this view, the marriage license is a cultural "hitting license." Therefore, violence should occur only within marriage, or should increase as relationships more closely approximate marriage. This view differs from the first in that it recognizes that premarital relationships are qualitatively different from marital relationships. Also, it would predict increasing rates of violence as couples proceed along the courtship continuum rather than either no violence before marriage or equivalent amounts of violence in living together and marriage (two contradictory positions that have been held by those maintaining the first perspective). That is, violence would be least common in the "least marriagelike" stages, such as first dates or casual dates, and most common in the "most marriagelike" stages of engagement and living together (as an example, see Straus, Gelles & Steinmetz, 1980).

A third perspective assumes that premarital relationships are particularly nonviolent; that is, that courtship is the female's finest hour, a romantic interlude of distinguished consideration that has the social function of seducing the female into marriage, upon entering which she immediately experiences an abrupt loss of individual rights and power. From this point of view courtship seems to be a sort of last meal before execution (as an example, see Dobash & Dobash, 1979).

To summarize, the first view would imply that the rates and dynamics of courtship and marital violence would be identical. The second would imply increasing couple violence over the courtship continuum. The third would imply, essentially, the nonexistence of couple violence prior to marriage (a position already contradicted by studies of courtship violence).

A final issue that deserves consideration before proceeding is the thesis of entrapment. Many authors have argued that the failure of victims to extricate themselves from abusive relationships is due to psychological and/or physical entrapment. The thesis that many victims of *marital* violence are entrapped has been elaborated upon by many writers. But the possibility of entrapment in violent *courtship* relationships has not been addressed. Certainly, the "legal" bonds of laws of property and chastisement are not pertinent to premarital relationships nor are economic dependence or the difficulty of making an escape with children in tow. Possible entrapping features, however, could include a continued strong emotional bond, a sustained commitment to continuing the relationship through difficult times, fear of retaliation following any attempt to flee, nonavailability of alternative housing options, or actual physical entrapment within a dwelling (the last two considerations would seem most pertinent to living together relationships.)

METHODS

The data for this report are from a nationwide study of courtship violence that was initiated by the author in 1981. The data consist of questionnaire responses of 2,650 students from eight colleges and universities, including institutions from all major regions of the United States except the Northeast. The research procedures were designed to ensure inclusion of a broad range of academic majors and 40–60 percent representation each of male, female, upper-division, and lower-division students.

The procedures used do not ensure that the sample is representative of any known population of college students, but only that it includes a broad range of students who vary on race, sex, class standing, rural-urban, region, and type of institution. Indeed, in designing the study, it was concluded that representative sampling was not feasible since there was no population "list" from which a representative sample could be drawn. Even had this been possible, classroom sampling was judged to be superior to mailing questionnaires or telephone interviewing, because it provided a controlled situation with prima facie evidence of validity that the questionnaires were completed confidentially, in a serious manner, and by the intended respondents.

Of the 2,650 students in the sample, 437 reported experiencing courtship violence. As indicated in a previous report (Makepeace, 1986), there was some attrition in responses due to the length of the questionnaire (15 pages), and some respondents did not complete the "worst incident" section of the questionnaire, thinking it simply repeated the "first incident" section. The results presented in this report are based on information from those respondents who had courtship violence experience; perceived themselves as victims; and provided complete information on the worst incident, including courtship stage and the nature of the physical, emotional, and sexual harm endured. The decision to limit analysis to the reports of "victims" was made because assailants' perceptions of the consequences to the victim were judged to be of questionable validity since (1) the data indicate that they were often intoxicated, (2) their recollections seem highly likely to be subject to selective recall and social desirability bias, and (3) victims frequently hide their injuries.

FINDINGS

In this section, the differences in "worst incident" courtship violence will be compared for traditional first-date, casual dating, steady dating, engagement, living together, and "other" relationships in terms of the following dimensions: rate, direct effects, whether the relationship broke up as a result of the incident, precipitating disagreement, and whether the violence was observed by witnesses.

Rate

In descending order, the worst incidents of courtship violence occurred in steady dating (61.4 percent), casual dating (12.2 percent), living together (11.9 percent), engagement (5.7 percent), "other" (5.2 percent), and first-date (3.5 percent) relationships. This confirms previous studies that have found courtship violence to occur most often among steady daters (Cate et al., 1982; Laner & Thompson, 1982; Henton et al., 1983; Sigelman, Berry and Wiles, 1984). This should not be interpreted as indicating that the danger of violence is greater among "steadies" than among daters in other courtship stages. The much higher percentage of incidents that occurred among steady daters may be due in part to their having had many more dates with one another than had first or casual daters. Similarly, the lower percentages of incidents that occurred among engaged and living together couples may be due not to the lower risk in such relationships, but to the much smaller percentages of students who had ever been engaged or lived together. In effect, the "per date" risk of violence may or may not vary across stages. It is not possible to tell with these data. In addition, as the following results show, violence that occurs in the steady-date stage *is* significantly less dangerous than that which occurs in other stages.

Direct Effects

Respondents were asked the following questions to determine the seriousness of the physical, emotional, and sexual consequences of the incidents of violence:

Physical. Using the four levels described below, how would you assess the extent of the harm or injury you experienced as a result of this incident?
1. No injury or pain resulted.
2. Mild—small cuts, lumps, bruises, minor pain, black eye, swollen lip, or similar injury.
3. Moderate—lacerations requiring 1–4 stitches, extensive bruising and swelling, fractured extremities (nose, finger), outpatient emergency room treatment, or similar injury.

4. Severe—injuries requiring hospitalization, fractured limbs, permanent disability or impairment, loss of consciousness, surgery, termination of a pregnancy, knife or gunshot wounds of any severity, death.

Emotional. Which of the following best describes the effect of this incident on your emotional state?

1. No particular effect; didn't bother me much.
2. Upset, but had no major trauma, and there were no serious long-term effects.
3. Experienced substantial trauma; disturbed about it for a long time afterward.

Sexual. Did a sex act actually occur against the will of the victim?

1. Yes.
2. No.

For the present analysis, incidents were defined as having serious physical effects if they were at level 2, 3, or 4; as emotionally serious if they were at level 3, and as sexually serious if a sex act occurred against the will of the victim. Individuals who experienced serious physical, emotional, and sexual effects are additionally categorized as having experienced compound effects.

In the present study, there were significant differences between stages in resulting effects (see Table 5.1). First, while courtship violence occurred most often in steady-dating relationships, serious effects were far more characteristic of relationships at the "ends" of the dating continuum (80 percent of first-date and 75 percent of living together) than in intermediary stages.

Secondly, there were very significant differences between stages in types of effects. First-date incidents were highly prone to serious effects of all types and were more significantly characterized by compound harm than any other stage. Intermediate stages—casual and steady dating—were characterized by relatively more physical than emotional or sexual harm, but still less physical harm than first-date or living together couples. Advanced relationships—engagement and living together—were characterized more by the combination of physical and emotional harm (and relatively little sexual violence). Physical injury was more characteristic of living together than any other type of relationship: Serious injury resulted in nearly two out of three of the incidents.

Breakup

The rates of "breaking up" as a result of the incidents were as follows: first date, 100.0 percent; casual date, 70.4 percent; living together, 38.2 percent; steady date, 32.9 percent; engagement, 11.1 percent. It is noteworthy that both the rate of breakup and the severity of the violence were greatest in first-date violence, where emotional and physical "entrapment" would presumably be

Table 5.1
Courtship Stage by Effects of Courtship Violence Among College Students[a]

	First Date	Casual Dating	Steady Dating	Eng'd	Living Tog'er	N
			Courtship Stage			
Any Serious Effect	80.0 (8)	42.3 (11)	47.6 (70)	55.6 (10)	75.0 (24)	
Physical Injury	50.0 (5)	34.6 (9)	40.1 (59)	38.9 (7)	65.6 (21)	
Emotional Trauma	50.0 (5)	15.4 (4)	12.9 (19)	38.0 (7)	40.6 (13)	
Forced Sex Act	60.0 (6)	11.5 (3)	9.5 (14)	0.0 (0)	6.3 (2)	
Compound Effects	40.0 (4)	7.7 (2)	3.4 (5)	0.0 (0)	6.3 (2)	
Subgroup n:	10	26	147	18	32	233

a. The numbers in Table 5.1 are the percentages of <u>victims</u> in each courtship stage who experienced the specified outcome of a courtship violence incident. The number of observations corresponding to the percentages is given in parentheses.

lowest. However, the breakup rate was *not* lowest in the living together stage, as the thesis of "physical" entrapment would seem to imply, but among the engaged.

If entrapment consists of an inability of the victim to break up with the partner, these results would seem to suggest that entrapment resides not so much in the physical demands and constraints of household life, which would be relatively more characteristic of living together, but in the emotional attachment and commitment that are, presumably, more characteristic of engagement. Indeed, rather than breaking up, victims in engagement relationships were the most likely of all to have stayed with their partners explicitly *because* of continued emotional attachment and/or because they had found ways to make up (See Table 5.2).

Another important feature of the results (see Table 5.2) is that fear of retaliation, promised reform, and giving in to "pleading" were rarely indicated as reasons for staying. A very influential theme in the marital violence literature has been Walker's (1979) "cycle of violence," which states that victims remain in violent spousal relationships because, following violence, they experi-

Table 5.2

Courtship Stage by Relationship Termination and Reasons for Nontermination among College Students[a]

	Courtship Stage					
	First Date	Casual Dating	Steady Dating	Eng'd	Living Tog'er	N
Terminated	100.0 (9)	70.4 (19)	32.9 (46)	11.1 (2)	38.2 (13)	
Reasons for Nontermination:						
Emotional Attachment	0.0 (0)	3.7 (1)	18.6 (26)	27.8 (5)	11.8 (4)	
Made up	0.0 (0)	11.1 (3)	12.9 (18)	22.2 (4)	11.8 (4)	
Promise of Reform	0.0 (0)	0.0 (0)	1.4 (2)	0.0 (0)	2.9 (1)	
Fear	0.0 (0)	0.0 (0)	0.0 (0)	0.0 (0)	5.9 (2)	
Pleading	0.0 (0)	0.0 (0)	0.0 (0)	5.6 (1)	0.0 (0)	
"No big deal"	0.0 (0)	0.0 (0)	17.9 (25)	16.7 (3)	11.8 (4)	
Other	0.0 (0)	14.8 (4)	16.4 (23)	16.7 (3)	17.6 (6)	
Totals	100.0 (9)	100.0 (27)	100.0 (140)	100.0 (18)	100.0 (34)	228

a.   The numbers in Table 5.2 are the percentages of <u>victims</u> in each courtship stage who terminated the relationship or gave a specific reason for nontermination. The number of observations corresponding to the percentages is given in parentheses.

ence a combination of fear of further assault should they attempt to leave, contrition, and promises of reform if they will stay. While these may be significant factors in spousal abuse, they appear, from the present evidence, to have little bearing on courtship violence.

Precipitating Disagreements

It has already been shown that the rate of courtship violence is not consistent across stages. Therefore, courtship violence is not, sui generis, like spousal abuse and does not increase steadily across the courtship continuum. Indeed, "first is worst" is a more accurate assessment. The nature of the precipitating disagreements is another area of dissimilarity between spousal and courtship violence. Courtship violence does not become more like spousal abuse as relationships advance.

Straus, Gelles, and Steinmetz (1980) find that (1) the five issues of housekeeping, sex, social activities, money, and children are significantly related to spousal abuse; (2) housekeeping is the most frequent source of conflict; and (3) "conflict over children . . . is most likely to lead a couple to blows" (p. 171). There are two striking features of Table 5.3. First, the principal disagreements preceding the worst incidents of courtship violence have little similarity to those of marriage. Second, the issues common to spousal abuse do not appear *even*

Table 5.3
Courtship Stage by Type of Disagreement That Precipitated Courtship Violence among College Students[a]

	Courtship Stage					
	First Date	Casual Dating	Steady Dating	Eng'd	Living Tog'er	N
Jealousy	0.0 (0)	20.8 (5)	31.1 (37)	43.8 (7)	25.0 (7)	
Rejection	0.0 (0)	8.3 (2)	15.1 (18)	6.3 (1)	10.7 (3)	
Sex	33.3 (1)	37.5 (9)	9.2 (11)	6.3 (1)	17.9 (5)	
Alcohol/Drugs	33.3 (1)	16.7 (4)	10.1 (12)	6.3 (1)	7.1 (2)	
Family	0.0 (0)	4.2 (1)	2.5 (3)	6.3 (1)	10.7 (3)	
Date Activity	0.0 (0)	4.2 (1)	5.0 (6)	6.3 (1)	10.7 (3)	
Miscellaneous	33.3 (1)	8.3 (2)	26.9 (32)	25.0 (4)	17.9 (5)	
Totals	100.0 (3)	100.0 (24)	100.0 (119)	100.0 (16)	100.0 (28)	190

a. The numbers in Table 5.3 are the percentages of <u>victims</u> in each courtship stage whose disagreement was precipitated for the specified reason. The number of observations corresponding to the percentages is given in parentheses.

in engagement and living together, which are presumably more similar to marriage. To the extent that there are qualitative differences between stages, it appears that steady dating and engagement are more prone than the other stages to disagreements of an interpersonal nature (46.2 percent and 50.1 percent, respectively, of the worst incidents in these stages were precipitated by jealousy or rejection arguments). Sex and alcohol/drug use are the tough issues in the earlier (first and casual) dating stages.

Witnesses

The physical entrapment thesis would seem to imply that violence in the more advanced courtship stages, particularly living together, would be more likely to occur behind the closed doors of a residence and, as a result, be less frequently observed by witnesses. In the present data, however, the percentage of incidents witnessed in each stage was as follows: first date, 18.2 percent; casual dating, 43.3 percent; steady dating, 34.1 percent; engaged, 30.0 percent; and living together, 28.2 percent $(\chi^2 = 4.8, p = .44$, n.s.). In percentage terms, courtship violence was *most* likely to occur in a residence if the relationship was one of living together. However, the percentage of in-residence incidents among living together (58.3 percent) couples was not significantly greater than the percentage among steady dating or engaged couples (49.7 percent and 52.6 percent).

DISCUSSION

Courtship violence is not simply "just more patriarchal violence against women," or "spousal abuse without the legality of marriage," as the sui generis perspective assumes. There are differences, often significant, between stages in rates of occurrence, effects, breakup rates, precipitating disagreements, reasons for staying together, presence of witnesses, and places of occurrence.

Nor does courtship violence accrue steadily as relationships advance along the courtship continuum to marriage. Violence is not most common and most intense in advanced relationships (it is most intense on first dates), and it does not become more "like" marital violence in advanced relationships. In advanced relationships, violence is as likely to occur outside the home and to be witnessed as in the earlier dating stages. Further, in advanced relationships, the precipitating disagreements bear little similarity to marital conflict, and there is great similarity to the courtship violence that exists in earlier stages of dating.

The co-optation-seduction thesis appears to have some merit with respect to engagement in that the violence rate in that stage is quite low and couples do appear to tenaciously "hang in" when violence occurs. However, violence is relatively common and more severe in first-date and living together relationships, a fact that this thesis does not explain.

Instead of insisting on conceptualizing courtship violence with "borrowed" spousal abuse theories, it may be more helpful to interpret the violence in terms of the issues and stage-to-stage differences of courtship itself. An account that seems to fit the present results is that there are two distinct types of courtship violence, "predatory" and "relational," and these occur within a curvilinear continuum of intensity.

In early-stage relationships, especially first dates, there appears to be a predominance of the particularly intense violence labeled "predatory." It is emotionally and physically dangerous and is frequently coupled with sexual assault, often motivated precisely by sexual exploitation. These relationships usually break up. This is not surprising since first daters have invested relatively little in the relationship.

Predatory courtship violence has been neglected in the courtship literature. Because its victims simply terminate the relationship without reporting the violence to authorities, and thus neither victims nor assailants receive the help they need, it is particularly insidious. Further, this violence may be highly self-reinforcing and recidivistic, since the assailant achieves his goal without incurring any costs. The author advances this hypothesis not only because it fits the present data, but also because this pattern has been apparent in several in-depth interviews he has conducted.

Those relationships that advance to the intermediate stages of casual and steady dating gradually achieve some measure of understanding about the volatile issues of sex and alcohol/drug use—at least these are less often the hot issues that they were in the earlier stages. Couples now increasingly turn their attention to the less intense but still important and tough issues of with whom and how to socialize and the status of the relationship itself. While these are significant issues, the partners have not yet made a heavy investment in the permanency of their relationship; it is still primarily recreational. The violence that results from such disagreements tends to be less intense, less dangerous. At this stage, "walking away" may involve mainly a loss of pride and affection. It does not involve loss of a home, an intended spouse, an incipient network of kinship relationships, or a planned stable future. Violence at this stage, then, tends to be less physically and emotionally destructive, and more often results in breakup than does violence in more committed relationships.

In engagement and living together, violence continues to be precipitated by relationship issues, particularly jealousy and rejection. At this point, however, a substantial investment and a high public commitment to the relationship have often been made, and it is now much less easy to turn and walk away. The partners may, therefore, feel compelled to work through tough issues rather than flee from them, and this may involve some difficult times. Entrapment—primarily emotional/relational among the engaged, both relational and domestic (household obligations) among those living together—may now be quite real. The partners may feel and indeed, be, locked into an intimate and/or domestic bond from which secession is very difficult.

The failure of victims to leave violent relationships, to notify authorities, and to seek professional help has been viewed with some concern in the literature. But perhaps it would be prudent to refrain from too quick a condemnation. Certainly, many violent relationships have so much conflict that a breakup would be best. Yet, perhaps there are other relationships in which the difficulties arise from extraordinary temporary circumstances or in which the partners have sufficient redeeming qualities to justify an attempt to salvage the relationship. Indeed, the effort to do so may even result in considerable growth. No easy answers can be offered at this point. However, in view of the frequent seriousness of violence, particularly among those living together, a good deal of help often does seem indicated. Couples need to recognize this and to learn how to ask for help. And society, it would seem, needs to learn how to provide it.

From a more formal viewpoint, the social exchange perspective appears well-suited to accounting for the foregoing continuum. As advanced by Goode (1971) and applied to family violence by Gelles (1982), force is one of several major classes of resources that can be used to attain a goal; others include economic, affectional, and "prestige" resources. Generally, the exchange perspective presumes force to be a resource of last resort, that is, people prefer to deploy the more legitimate and normatively acceptable resources first, because they have been socialized to accept the most fundamental norm: "reciprocity," or "fairness of exchanges."

At each stage of a relationship, distinctly different reward/cost ratios pertain. The first stage is characterized by more predatory violence perpetrated by norm-disabiding individuals who do not subscribe to the fundamental norm of reciprocity, and who are inclined to rapidly deploy force in order to achieve goals, particularly sexual gratification, from an unwilling partner.

Partners in relationships that survive into the intermediate stages have more successfully learned to negotiate gratification of desires through socially acceptable exchanges. Subscribing to the basic norm of reciprocity—that is, preferring to engage in socially acceptable exchanges, and not yet having made the very heavy investment of resources in their relationships that characterize engagement and living together—they are disinclined to use force, or, more exactly, levels of force that exceed the socially acceptable; (that being, roughly, the level of minor violence popularly depicted as the "lover's quarrel"). The prospect of using force beyond this level would tend usually to be below the "comparison level" for the obvious alternative of walking away from the conflict or the relationship.

In advanced stages the relative reward/cost ratios of flight versus fight are dramatically altered by the heavy investments the partners have made in the relationship. Walking away now entails substantially increased losses compared to earlier stages, while the relative reward/cost ratio of employing more severe violence is much more "favorable," that is, there is an increased incentive to work out the problem, even if this means some nasty fighting. At the same time, there is less incentive to leave the relationship; and the probable costs that may accrue to those who resort to serious violence are significantly reduced by the social "veil of privacy" with which society surrounds advanced relationships and, in the case of living together, the physical enclosures within which the violence is more likely to occur.

IMPLICATIONS FOR POLICY AND PRACTICE

It now seems clear that courtship violence is a distinct phenomenon that cannot be adequately conceptualized by applying borrowed spousal abuse perspectives. An important implication of this is that treatment of courtship violence must be broadened beyond that which can be provided by spousal abuse agencies such as battered women's shelters or sexual assault centers. Such agencies have an important role to play because they have pioneered many of the strategies that are of help in treating those troubled by violence, and because they are the most likely agencies to which older individuals who become involved in couple violence will turn.

A second important implication is the specific kinds of assistance that might usefully be brought to bear on the problem. A great deal of difficulty in dealing with sex, alcohol/drug use, jealousy, and rejection is voiced among dating couples who experience violence. These are issues about which a great deal is known and for which many helpful treatment strategies have been developed. Since these issues often precipitate violence, violence may be substantially lessened if they can be ameliorated. They cannot be addressed, however, if they are not identified. At present there appear to be two primary obstacles to their identification. First, young people are not forthcoming about their problems, whether courtship violence or otherwise. There is, perhaps, an excessive "privatism" surrounding intimate relationships in our society that makes the young feel they have to work their problems out by themselves. The compulsive-masculinity theme which so many authors have noted as prevalent among young males and which idealizes the "strong, silent type" of character probably contributes to this as well. A second obstacle is that practitioners, for their part, do not ask about the problem. The author knows one practitioner in a drop-in center for troubled adolescents who had never come across a single case of courtship violence. Then, after reading one of the author's papers, she began asking about it in each intake interview. She was amazed to find that *most* of the youths she questioned had experience with courtship violence—sometimes brutal experiences with a number of partners.

Youths need to find ways to ask for help, professionals and adults need to develop ways to make it easier for youths to ask for help, and professionals dealing with young people presenting themselves for help with *other* problems should sensitively inquire about courtship violence as well.

Central to all of this, it seems, is the educational system. Courtship violence starts early—apparently in the earliest stages of dating. Most of these young people are still in school—indeed, most of courtship violence starts in high school. It is time for schools to recognize and face up to this problem. If the young are to feel comfortable in asking for help, they need to know that they are not the only ones in the world with the problem, and that confidential and effective help is available. This means, at the very least, that significant information about courtship violence should be incorporated into family-life educational materials in the schools. Practitioners, particularly school counselors, need to become knowledgeable about the problem. They must be able either to provide direct help or to refer clients to other sources of help with violence, its underlying emotional sources, such as dependency and anger, and related problem areas such as sex, drugs, interpersonal communication, and conflict resolution.

RECOMMENDATIONS FOR FURTHER STUDY

An enormous amount of work remains to be done in this field. This chapter provides information on violence in various courtship stages, but it is really a series of static portraits. Research that actually follows relationships through time would be enormously helpful in augmenting our understanding of the dynamic/processual nature of the phenomenon. One approach would be detailed in-depth interviews with a manageably small sample of couples who have experienced courtship violence. A more ambitious approach would be a longitudinal study of a cohort of students surveyed initially at the beginning of the dating years and then followed up annually through the first years of marriage. Such a case study of one cohort of a large high school would be extraordinarily revealing.

SUMMARY AND CONCLUSIONS

Courtship violence is not just spousal abuse before marriage. It is a distinct phenomenon with dynamics that can only be understood in terms of the issues and stages of courtship itself. There may be two fundamental types of courtship violence: a particularly brutal and often sexually motivated type, which is more prevalent in very early stage relationships, and a second type, which derives from the working out of relationship difficulties such as jealousy and rejection, and which becomes more injurious in the later stages of courtship, when the investment in the relationship is greater.

In general, prospects for improvement are better today than ever before, and there is considerable reason for optimism. Until very recently, interest in courtship violence was nonexistent. In the few years since the appearance of the first article in 1981, scores of studies have appeared. More is now known than ever before, and what we are learning suggests that much can be done for young people troubled by violence. Indeed, many of the therapies and resources are already available. The question at this point in history is not, "Can we help?" but "Will we help?" And our collective answer to that question will reveal, prima facie, how much we value our young and their physical safety.

REFERENCES

Cate, R., Henton, J., Koval, J., Christopher, F. Scott, & Lloyd, S. (1982). "Premarital abuse: A social psychological perspective." *Journal of Family Issues,* 3:79–90.

Dobash, R. E., & Dobash, R. (1979). *Violence Against Wives: A Case Against the Patriarchy.* New York: Free Press.

Gelles, R. J. (1982). "Applying research on family violence to clinical practice." *Journal of Marriage and the Family,* 44:9–20.

Glick, Paul C., & Spanier, Graham B. (1980). "Married and unmarried cohabitation in the United States." *Journal of Marriage and the Family,* 42:19–30.

Goode, W. J. (1971). "Force and violence in the family." *Journal of Marriage and the Family,* 33:624–36.

Henton, J., Cate, R., Koval, J., Lloyd, S. & Christopher, F. Scott (1983). "Romance and violence in dating relationships." *Journal of Family Issues,* 4:467–82.

Kanin, E. J. (1957). "Male aggression in dating-courtship relations." *American Journal of Sociology,* 63:197–204.

Laner, Mary R., & Thompson, Jeanine (1982). "Abuse and aggression in courting couples." *Deviant Behavior: An Interdisciplinary Journal,* 3:229–44.

Makepeace, J. M. (1981). "Courtship violence among college students." *Family Relations,* 30:97–102.

———. (1986). "Gender differences in courtship violence victimization." *Family Relations,* 35:383–88.

Roscoe, B., & Benaske, N. (1985). "Courtship violence experienced by abused wives: similarities in patterns of abuse." *Family Relations,* 34:419–24.

Sigelman, Carol K., Berry, Carol J. & Wiles, Katherine A. (1984). "Violence in college students' dating relationships." *Journal of Applied Social Psychology,* 5, 6:530–48.

Straus, M. A., Gelles, R. J., & Steinmetz, S. K. (1980). *Behind Closed Doors.* Garden City, NY: Anchor.

Walker, L. E. (1979) *The Battered Woman.* New York: Harper & Row.

Waller, W. (1937). "The rating and dating complex." *American Sociological Review,* 2:727–34.

Yllo, Kersti. (1978). "Non-marital Cohabitation: Beyond the College Campus." *Alternative Lifestyles,* 1:37–54.

Yllo, Kersti, & Straus, Murray A. (1981). "Interpersonal Violence Among Married and Cohabiting Couples." *Family Relations,* 30:339–47.

6 The Help-seeking Behavior of Physically and Sexually Abused College Students
Maureen A. Pirog-Good and Jan E. Stets

Estimates of physical and sexual abuse in dating relationships vary, but all estimates reveal that both types of aggression pose serious problems. Most research on dating violence has focused on estimating the incidence or determinants of abuse. Although researchers have documented the fact that many victims of marital violence do not seek help (Walker, 1984; Dobash & Dobash, 1979; Bowker, 1983) and that serious sexual assaults such as rapes are grossly underreported to criminal justice authorities (Estrich, 1987; Williams, 1984; Dukes & Mattley, 1977), the more general help-seeking patterns of abused men and women in dating relationships is an area which is largely unexplored.

We examine the extent to which victims of physical and sexual abuse report such incidents to their friends, parents, physicians, counselors, or criminal justice authorities. Limited evidence indicates that female victims are much more likely to report dating violence than their male counterparts (Henton et al., 1983; Stets & Pirog-Good, 1987b; Makepeace, 1981). Because women may be socialized to be more verbal about their experiences, the help-seeking behavior of male and female victims of physical or sexual abuse is examined separately. We examine whether or not help sought is related to the characteristics of the victim and the dating relationship, the seriousness of the physical and sexual abuse sustained, and the victim's perceptions regarding whether or not abuse is sustained.

PRIOR RESEARCH

Prior research on the help-seeking patterns of battered women typically focuses on marital abuse (Walker, 1984; Campbell, 1987; Dobash & Dobash, 1979; Bowker, 1983; Giles-Sims, 1983; Berk et al., 1984; Donato & Bowker,

1984; Wauchope, 1988). The incidence of help-seeking reported in this literature varies tremendously from study to study, ranging from a low of 5 percent
of battered women receiving counseling (Schulman, 1979) to a high of 97 percent seeking help (Giles-Sims, 1983). These differences in the rates of help-
seeking are not surprising, given that definitions of help-seeking have varied
widely from study to study as has the population of individuals studied. For
example, Wauchope (1988) considers help-seeking for any family or personal
problem from any of 15 possible sources of help including (to mention a few)
alcohol and drug treatment services, friends and neighbors, and battered wom-
en's shelters. In contrast, Berk et al. (1984) focus exclusively on domestic
violence incidents for which police are summoned. Similarly, some studies
have focused on very narrow groups of individuals, such as women who seek
help from shelters (Walker, 1984; Campbell, 1987), a rape crisis center (Williams, 1984) or volunteers recruited from newspaper and other advertisements
(Donato & Bowker, 1984).

In our research, we define help-seeking as having a discussion (at a mini-
mum) with one's friends, parents, counselor, physician, or criminal justice
authorities concerning one or more abusive incidents. We choose to examine
help-seeking from these sources because they are typically available to college
students. On the one hand, this definition of help-seeking is in some respects
more general than that of previous researchers who sometimes focus on help-
seeking from one specific agency such as the police (Berk et al., 1984; Williams, 1984). On the other hand, this definition is narrower than that of those
who include seeking help for any family or personal problem (Wauchope, 1988).
Nonetheless, with the measures used in this study, it is clear that respondents
are seeking help for dating violence experiences, not for school or other personal problems.

In addition to the conflicting evidence on the incidence of help-seeking in
the marital violence literature, many authors also disagree at a theoretical level.
On the one hand, Walker (1984), for example, argues for a theory of learned
helplessness in which recurring victimizations traumatize the victim and result
in depression, passivity, and indecision. Such a theory would suggest that as
the severity and frequency of violence increase, the depression, passivity, and
indecision would become increasingly acute and the victim would become less
and less likely to seek help. On the other hand, others have argued that as the
severity and frequency of battering increases, stress from the violence will ac-
cumulate and help-seeking will be more likely to occur (Wauchope, 1988). In
other words, when internal coping mechanisms are insufficient to deal with
serious or repeated abuse, victims will turn to external resources for help.

Our research departs from that discussed above in four key respects. First,
we focus on help-seeking by victims of dating, not marital, abuse. Second, we
look at victims of physical as well as sexual abuse. Third, the help-seeking
behaviors of men as well as women are examined. Finally, unlike most of our
predecessors in the marital violence literature, we estimate separate models for

seeking help from different sources. In other words, it is possible that different factors will predict from which sources—friends, parents, physicians, counselors, and criminal justice authorities—which categories of victims will seek help.

MODEL

As noted earlier, we examine whether help-seeking behavior is related to the characteristics of the respondent, the characteristics of the dating relationship, the seriousness of the abuse sustained, and the respondent's perceptions of the victimization.

First, we examine the influence of the respondent's age, self-esteem, and acceptance of violence. With regard to age, we anticipate that older individuals will be less likely to seek help from their parents and more likely to seek the help of friends, counselors, physicians, and criminal justice authorities. As individuals mature, we feel that they will be less likely to turn to their parents for assistance. As individuals grow older, they may also obtain the financial resources necessary to seek the assistance of counselors or physicians. They may also acquire the maturity needed to overcome any fear or apprehension about approaching the police.

Dating violence research reveals that low self-esteem influences violence (Deal & Wampler, 1986). If self-esteem influences the occurrence of violence, it may also affect the willingness of the victim to report the abuse. Individuals with high self-esteem may possess the confidence necessary to ask for assistance from all types of help providers.

Research also shows that acceptance of violence has a positive influence on dating violence (Cate et al., 1982; Henton et al., 1983). It is likely that those individuals who view violence as acceptable would be less likely to report such violence to criminal justice authorities, counselors, or physicians. However, individuals who view acts of violence as normal may be more likely to discuss these incidents with their friends or parents in the course of their everyday conversations.

Characteristics of the dating relationship are also examined. First, the effect of the number of dating partners over the past year on whether or not a victim will seek help is estimated. Individuals who date many partners may feel reluctant to confide incidents of physical and/or sexual abuse to help providers because they fear that they will be held responsible, in part, for their victimization. Alternatively, if individuals who date many partners are more gregarious and outgoing, it is also possible that they be more open to confiding abusive incidents to help providers.

The seriousness of the dating relationship is also examined. It is anticipated that as the relationship becomes more and more serious, the partners will have more invested in the relationship. Thus, in more serious relationships, victims of abuse may be more willing to seek help in order to maintain the relationship rather than simply terminating the relationship. In fact, prior research indicates that individuals who are abused on a first date or in a casual dating relationship are most likely to break off the relationship (Makepeace, this volume, Chapter 5). Having little invested in the relationship, these individuals are less likely to continue to take the abuse or seek help to resolve the problem.

The third characteristic of the dating relationship included in our model is whether or not the respondent is still dating the abuser. Confiding abusive experiences in friends, family, counselors, physicians, or criminal justice authorities may be more difficult when a relationship is ongoing. Victims of abuse may fear that others will respond to the abusive acts by asking why the respondent has not terminated the relationship. Thus, victims may feel that some of the abuse is their fault because they have not walked away from the abusive relationship. Additionally, if a relationship is still intact, the victim may fear retaliation from the abuser for having sought help. Finally, in some cases, the victim may not want to terminate the dating relationship and may fear offending the abuser by confiding the abuse to a help provider. Thus, for all sources of help providers, we anticipate that individuals who are still involved in a dating relationship will be less likely to seek help.

Turning to the seriousness of the physical and sexual abuse sustained, it has been argued that some victims learn helplessness with repeated and more serious abuse (Walker, 1984). If this is the case, then the seriousness of the abuse sustained should be negatively related to help-seeking behavior (Wauchope, 1988). Alternatively, if repeated abuse generates stress that accumulates, then internal coping mechanisms may become inadequate to deal with the stress and external sources of help may be sought. Thus, according to the stress theory, repeated and more serious abuse will be positively related to the likelihood that the victim will seek help.

Empirical evidence on help-seeking in the marital violence literature tends to support the stress models of help-seeking. Most researchers have found that victims are more (not less) likely to seek help as the frequency or seriousness of assaults increases (Bowker, 1983; Giles-Sims, 1983; Gelles, 1979; Berk et al., 1984).

Perceptions of abuse may also be related to the probability that a victim will seek help. Some individuals may view mild acts of physical or sexual aggression as normal and not abusive. If such acts of aggression are not viewed as abusive, then it is unlikely that an individual will seek aid from any help provider, for a problem of physical or sexual abuse. In fact, Ferraro and Johnson (1983) argue that rationalizations of abuse must give way to perceptions of victimization before battered women will seek help.

METHODS

Sample

Two random samples of upper-level classes were obtained from listings of courses at a large midwestern university during the spring of 1986 and 1987.

Letters were sent to the professors in the sampled classes asking them if they would agree to participate in a survey in class. The surveys covered four broad areas of information pertinent to this study: (1) whether or not the respondents told their friends, parents, a counselor or physician, or criminal justice authorities about having sustained abuse; (2) incidents of physical and sexual abuse sustained with up to four dating partners during the past year; (3) the perceptions of the respondents concerning whether or not they sustained an act of physical or sexual abuse; and (4) the characteristics of the respondent and their dating relationships. The response rates for the two surveys were approximately 80 percent. Those not participating were either married or not dating. When the samples were compared to the general population of upper-class students, no significant departures were found for age, sex, and area of study. Because of the very low frequency of nonwhite men and women in the data, observations for nonwhites were omitted from this study. The final sample included complete information on 714 female and 532 male dating relationships.

Measures

Help-seeking Behavior. Respondents were asked whether or not they told a friend about any incident of physical or sexual abuse. The question was repeated for parents, physician or counselor, and criminal justice authorities. We treated respondents who indicated that they told one or more persons about an incident of physical or sexual abuse as having sought help. Because the individuals were discussing abuse, not an innocuous dating experience, it was reasonable to assume that the discussions held were to seek advice or physical, therapeutic, or legal assistance.

Sustaining Physical and Sexual Abuse. The Conflict Tactics Scale (CTS) was used to measure physical violence in dating relationships (Straus, 1979). The scale is divided into three major types of conflict resolution tactics: reasoning, verbal, and violence tactics. The 19-item scale starts with less coercive items and gradually becomes more coercive toward the end of the scale.

Although the CTS does not incorporate the context in which violence arises or the injury that results (Ferraro & Johnson, 1983; Breines & Gordon, 1983), it is the most comprehensive index on the frequency and form of tactics used to resolve conflict. It has high reliability (Straus, Gelles & Steinmetz, 1980) and has been used in numerous studies on dating violence (Cate et al., 1980; Laner & Thompson, 1982; Henton et al., 1983; Makepeace, 1983; Sigelman, Berry & Wiles, 1984; Lane & Gwartney-Gibbs, 1985; Deal & Wampler, 1986; Stets & Pirog-Good, 1987a; Arias, Samios & O'Leary, 1987).

Respondents were asked to fill out the CTS with reference to how often they sustained the various tactics with up to four people they had been dating in the past year. The violence tactics of the CTS were used to determine if physical abuse was sustained. These items include the following: the partner threw something at me, pushed, grabbed or shoved me, slapped or spanked me, kicked, bit or hit me with a fist, hit or tried to hit me with something, beat me up, threatened me with a knife or gun, and used a knife or gun.

A separate survey was administered to 75 undergraduates in an upper-level class to determine their perceptions of the seriousness of these violence tactics when perpetrated against a man or a woman. Students were asked to rate the seriousness of the acts on a scale from zero to 10, where zero indicated that the act was not at all serious and 10 indicated that the act was extremely serious. The mean seriousness scores were different for men and women. Thus, the gender-specific seriousness scores were multiplied by the frequency with which each act occurred for a given dating partner to form a scale measuring the seriousness of physical abuse sustained for each dating partner.

To measure whether the respondents sustained acts of sexual aggression in the past year, they were asked how often they sustained each of seven sexual acts *against their will* with up to four partners they had been dating. These sexual acts included necking, breast/chest fondling, genital fondling, oral sex, attempted intercourse, intercourse without violence, and intercourse with violence. Thus, this scale covers a broad range of sexually abusive acts. This is desirable given that lesser intimate forms of sexual abuse are the most common (Kanin, 1957; Korman & Leslie, 1982; Stets & Pirog-Good, 1987b). Moreover, much of the research on sexual abuse in dating relationships has focused primarily on rape or attempted rape (Russell, 1982; Kilpatrick, Vernon & Best, 1984).

The frequency of each act of sexual aggression was multiplied by a gender-specific seriousness weight and then cumulated for each dating partner. The seriousness weights for sexual abuse inflicted against men and women were obtained in the same survey as the seriousness weights for physical abuse sustained.

Perceptions of Physical and Sexual Abuse

For each dating partner, respondents were asked if they had sustained one or more acts of physical abuse. The same question was repeated for sexual abuse. For both questions, 1 indicated that the respondent perceived abuse and zero indicated that abuse was not perceived.

Respondent and Relationship Characteristics

The self-esteem of respondents was measured using the Rosenberg self-esteem scale (Rosenberg, 1979). A high score on this ten-item scale reflects high self-esteem. The age of each respondent in years was also obtained.

Acceptance of violence against women was measured using the violence tactics of the Conflict Tactics Scale. Respondents were asked whether each tactic "always," "depends," or "never" was an act of violence. If the respondent answered "depends" or "never," a score of 1 was given. Otherwise, it was zero. The scores were summed across items with a higher score reflecting greater acceptance of violence against women.

Turning to the characteristics of the dating relationship, we captured the seriousness of each dating relationship with the variable, behavioral involvement. Two variables were combined to construct behavioral involvement: the number of months the respondent has been dating a partner and the number of dates per year that the respondent had with the dating partner. The correlations between these two variables was 0.6. Thus, these variables were each standardized (to zero mean and unit variance) and then summed to form behavioral involvement. Finally, a dummy variable was included to indicate whether the respondent was still dating each of his or her partners as well as a variable to indicate the number of dating partners over the past year.

RESULTS

Sample Characteristics

The means and standard deviations of all the variables other than the victim-reporting variables, are given for males and females in Table 6.1. The results reveal that male respondents were slightly older than the females, scored slightly higher on the self-esteem scale, and had a tendency to date more partners.

Approximately 7 percent of the females and 4 percent of the males felt that they had been physically victimized by a dating partner. Perceptions of sexual abuse were less common. About 5 percent of the women and 1 percent of the males felt that they had been sexually victimized. For women, at least, this result is somewhat surprising, given that the seriousness of the sexual abuse sustained by women was considerably greater than the seriousness of the physical abuse they sustained. While some of this seemingly contradictory result is due, in part, to the different seriousness weights for various types of physical and sexual aggression, the primary reason for this difference is that women reported more than four times as much sexual abuse as physical abuse (4.8 acts of sexual abuse in the prior year versus 1.1 acts of physical abuse). Given that most of the acts of sexual aggression were the less intimate forms of sexual behavior (necking, breast fondling, and genital fondling), this strongly suggests that many females view mild forms of sexual aggression as normal.

Males sustained an average of 1.2 acts of physical abuse each year. The frequency as well as the seriousness of this abuse is comparable to that sustained by female respondents. However, males sustained less than one-quarter of the number of sexually abusive incidents compared with women, averaging 1.1 acts of sexual aggression in the prior year. Because the seriousness-of-abuse scales incorporate both the frequency and seriousness of each act of aggression sustained, the lower frequency of sexual abuse sustained by males generates the males' considerably lower seriousness-of-sexual abuse scores.

Further examination of the t-tests in Table 6.1 indicates that while the actual

Table 6.1
Means and Standard Deviations, by Gender

	Females (N=714)	Males (N=532)
Age	21.513*	21.846*
	(2.053)	(2.080)
Self-Esteem	31.902*	32.758*
	(4.592)	(4.293)
Accept Violence	7.192	7.209
	(5.742)	5.624)
Number of Partners	2.409*	2.581*
	(1.107)	(1.120)
Behavioral Involvement	-.000	-.000
	(1.632)	(1.758)
Still Dating	.508	.489
	(.500)	(.500)
Perception of Physical Abuse	.073*	.038*
	(.260)	(.190)
Perception of Sexual Abuse	.052*	.013*
	(.222)	(.114)
Seriousness of Physical Abuse	8.184*	8.826*
	(63.843)	(60.166)
Seriousness of Sexual Abuse	38.564*	7.820*
	(239.540)	(55.519)

* Means are significantly different at the .01 level.

number of physically abusive incidents is very similar for males and females in dating relationships, more than twice as many women as men perceive that they were physically abused. The frequency, seriousness, and perceptions of sexual abuse are all approximately four times greater for females than for males.

Reporting Abuse

Table 6.2 presents the percentage of respondents who told friends, parents, counselors, physicians, or criminal justice authorities about abusive incidents. Examining the entire sample of female and male respondents, we see that more women than men told their friends and parents about abusive incidents. Nearly 14 percent of the women versus 6.4 percent of the men told their friends about physically and/or sexually abusive episodes. Parents were informed of abuse with a much lower frequency than friends. Overall, 3.4 percent of the women

Table 6.2

Percentage of Respondents Reporting Physical and Sexual Abuse, by Gender

	Females	Males
Total Sample	N=714	N=532
Tell Friends	.139**	.064**
Tell Parents	.034*	.015*
Tell Counselor/Physician	.004	0
Tell Criminal Justice Authorities	.011	.006
Physically Abused Only	N=48	N=37
Tell Friends	.479**	.216**
Tell Parents	.125	.081
Tell Counselor/Physician	.021	0
Tell Criminal Justice Authorities	.042	0
Sexually Abused Only	N=104	N=28
Tell Friends	.327	.286
Tell Parents	.077	.036
Tell Counselor/Physician	.019	0
Tell Criminal Justice Authorities	.048	.036
Physically and Sexually Abused	N=31	N=19
Tell Friends	.548	.474
Tell Parents	.097	.053
Tell Counselor/Physician	0	0
Tell Criminal Justice Authorities	.032	.053
Perceived to Be Physically Abused Only	N=44	N=20
Tell Friends	.545	.450
Tell Parents	.136	.200
Tell Counselor/Physician	.045	0
Tell Criminal Justice Authorities	.114	0
Perceived to Be Sexually Abused Only	N=29	N=7
Tell Friend	.345	0
Tell Parents	.034	0
Tell Counselor/Physician	0	0
Tell Criminal Justice Authorities	.034	0
Perceived to Be Physically and Sexually Abused	N=8	N=0
Tell Friends	.75	0
Tell Parents	.38	0
Tell Counselor/Physician	.13	0
Tell Criminal Justice Authorities	.25	0

* Means are significantly different at the .05 level.
** Means are significantly different at the .01 level.

told their parents about abuse versus 1.5 percent of the men. This may be due, in part, to the fact that most of the respondents were living away from home and did not have daily contact with their parents. Additionally, very few of the respondents may have been willing to venture beyond their immediate social network to discuss their victimization. Very few of the respondents sought the assistance of counselors, physicians, or criminal justice authorities.

The gender differences in the percentage of respondents reporting abuse to friends and parents may well be due to the fact that a significantly higher proportion of the females sustained sexual abuse in comparison to the males. Consequently, we examined the percentage of male and female respondents who sustained physical abuse only, sexual abuse only, and physical and sexual abuse.

The results for sustaining physical abuse only reveal that 47.9 percent of the women told their friends about physical abuse and 21.6 percent of the men also talked to their friends. Thus, even after controlling for an individual's having sustained physical abuse, more women than men discussed abuse when it occurred. Other gender differences in the percentages reporting physical abuse to parents, a physician or counselor or criminal justice authorities were not statistically significant.

For those sustaining only sexual abuse, we found that 32.7 percent of the women and 28.6 percent of the men told their friends about sexual abuse. These figures were markedly lower for all other categories of help providers listed. Among those respondents who sustained only sexual abuse, gender differences in reporting patterns were not evident.

Finally, we looked at the subgroup of respondents who sustained both physical and sexual abuse. For both men and women, those sustaining both types of abuse were most likely to discuss these incidents with their friends. However, it also appears that whenever sexual abuse constitutes part or the whole of an abusive episode, college students are even less likely to report discussing these incidents with their parents than students who sustain physical abuse alone. Thus, it appears that whenever the issue of sexuality arises, whether alone or in conjunction with other physical abuse, students are less likely to approach their parents. Embarrassment about being sexually active, generally poor communication about sex, or fear that parents will hold the victims partially responsible for the sexual abuse may all contribute to the lower rate of reporting sexual abuse to parents.

Because many individuals may view mild forms of physical or sexual abuse as normal, we also examined the percentage of respondents who perceived themselves to have been physically and/or sexually abused. Among the women, 54.5 percent reported physical abuse to their friends while among the men the figure was 45 percent. Again, both men and women confide physically abusive incidents to their parents less frequently than they do to their friends. Among women, 11.4 percent turned to criminal justice authorities whereas only 4.5 percent turned to a counselor or physician for advice. This clearly indicates that even among men and women who perceive themselves as having been physically abused, a very small percentage (11.4 percent of women and no men) turn to criminal justice authorities. Hence, the underreporting of domestic violence statistics discussed in the marital violence literature is also very apparent among the dating population.

When examining the group of respondents who perceived themselves as having sustained sexual but not physical abuse, we find that the number of men falling into this category is very small *(N = 7)*. Further, none of these men discussed the sexually abusive incidents with anyone. More women than men perceived themselves as having been sexually abused, but the percentage of women willing to talk to their friends, parents, counselors or physicians, or criminal justice authorities about sexual abuse is always lower than among women who perceive themselves as having sustained physical abuse alone. Thus, whenever an incident is sexually but not otherwise physically abusive, the probability that the incident will be reported is diminished.

Lastly, none of the men in the sample perceived themselves to have been both physically and sexually abused, and only a small number of women *(N = 8)* fell into this category. Among this very small group of women, however, reporting rates were typically higher than in any of the other categories discussed.

Predicting Help-seeking Behavior

Those factors that determine whether or not an individual reports abuse are considered in Table 6.3, where probit estimates for five equations predicting the probability of reporting abuse to friends, parents, or officials is given. Because of the very low frequency of reporting abuse to counselors, physicians, and criminal justice authorities, these categories are combined to form a new category: reporting to an "official." Thus, if an individual reported abuse to either a counselor, physician, or criminal justice authority, the value of "official" is 1; otherwise it is zero.

Females. The greater the number of dating partners of the victim, the more likely it is that friends will be told about the abuse. Individuals who date many partners may be more outgoing or gregarious and, hence, more likely to discuss such abuse with other friends.

The perception of having been physically abused has a large and positive effect on the likelihood of reporting abuse to friends, parents, and officials. It is interesting that the perception of physical abuse rather than the seriousness of the actual abuse sustained is important in predicting whether or not the victim will report the abuse.

A separate set of equations was estimated to see if the frequency of physical assaults exerted a different effect than the seriousness of the assaults sustained. In all cases, the probit estimates remained virtually identical, further indicating that it is a woman's perception of abuse rather than the number or seriousness of assaults that determines whether or not she seeks help for the abuse.

The results for the perceptions of having been sexually abused are somewhat less consistent. Women who feel that they have been sexually abused are more likely to tell their friends and officials about the abuse but not their parents. This suggests that the subject of sex or sexual abuse is taboo with many parents. In only one instance, telling friends, does the seriousness of the sexual abuse actually sustained exert an independent effect on the probability of reporting abuse.

Table 6.3
Probit Estimates, by Gender

| | Females (N=714) | | |
	Friends	Parents	Officials
Constant	-1.654*	-2.352	-7.078**
Age	.018	-.013	.139
Self-Esteem	-.013	.019	.062
Accept Violence	.015	-.026	-.069
Number of Partners	.145*	.106	-.256
Behavioral Involvement	.041	.023	.117
Still Dating	-.270	-.244	-.957
Perception of Physical Abuse	1.306**	.989**	2.158**
Perception of Sexual Abuse	.654**	.454	1.402**
Seriousness of Physical Abuse	.001	.001	.002
Seriousness of Sexual Abuse	.001*	-.0001	-.002
Chi-square	97.160	28.892	53.608
	(.001)	(.01)	(.001)

| | Males (N=532) | | |
	Friends	Parents	Officials
Constant	-.563	-1.695	
Age	.018	-.083	
Self-Esteem	-.052*	.036	
Accept Violence	.025	.001	
Number of Partners	-.028	.038	
Behavioral Involvement	.042	.078	
Still Dating	-.035	-.861	N/A
Perception of Physical Abuse	1.191**	1.468**	
Perception of Sexual Abuse	-3.732	-2.849	
Seriousness of Physical Abuse	.002*	.002	
Seriousness of Sexual Abuse	.003**	-.002	
Chi-square	47.130	26.507	
	(.001)	(.01)	

*p < .05
**p < .01

Males. Because so few men confided in physicians, counselors, or criminal justice authorities, the regression for officials was not estimated. With respect to the probabilities of confiding in friends and parents, we find that high self-esteem reduces the likelihood that men will tell their friends about abusive incidents. These men may be ashamed of the fact that they were abused and feel that it may reflect poorly on them with their friends.

For men, as for women, the perception of having been physically abused exerts a strong, positive effect on the probability of telling friends and parents about abuse. Additionally, the seriousness of the physical abuse actually sustained exerts an independent, positive, and significant effect on the probability of reporting abuse to friends. Thus, for men, perceptions as well as the seriousness of the physical abuse sustained are important in determining whether or not they will talk to friends about abusive incidents.

As the seriousness of the sexual abuse sustained increases, men are more willing to discuss the abuse with their friends but not with parents. Thus, for men, it is the actual seriousness of sexual abuse rather than their perceptions about this abuse that determines whether or not they will confide in their friends about the abuse.

IMPLICATIONS FOR POLICY AND PRACTICE

The findings from this study reveal that physical and sexual abuse in dating relationships is grossly underreported to officials. There are several reasons for this. First, many individuals who sustain mild forms of physical or sexual abuse may view these incidents as normal or not serious enough to be considered abusive. Regarding sexual abuse, we found that only 25.0 percent of the men and 27.9 percent of the women who sustained sexual abuse actually viewed these incidents as abusive. Clearly a message must be sent to those individuals whose partners force sexual acts on them that one need not also be hit with a bat for such an incident to be considered abusive. The figures regarding physical abuse are somewhat more encouraging. Nearly all of the women (91.6 percent) and more than half (54.1 percent) of the men who sustained physical abuse perceived these incidents to be abusive.

The fact that many men and women who sustain abuse do not view the incidents as abusive is only part of the explanation for the underreporting of official statistics. Even among those who feel that they have been physically or sexually abused, most do not report these incidents to criminal justice authorities. In many cases, the individuals may feel that the abuse is mild and that an official report of abuse is unwarranted. Some individuals may fear recriminations from the police and feel that they will be held partially responsible for the abuse, particularly if they are still dating the abusive partner. Additionally, some individuals may fear retaliation from their partners if abuse is reported to the police or may fear that such a report will end the relationship.

Our results also indicate that when abuse occurs, counselors and physicians are very unlikely to be approached. Victims typically turn first to their friends and parents. This is not surprising and is consistent with a host of research on help-seeking for many stressful life events (Gourash, 1978). Typically, most individuals accurately view their social network as a major source of help and turn to professionals only when assistance is not available within their network. Additionally, if friends are supportive of the abuse, assistance may be sought outside the immediate social network. If better use is to be made of counselors or physicians in a college setting, this suggests that those counselors and physicians will need to establish closer ties with students. Lectures or discussion groups in college dormitories or communal living quarters might be one method of achieving this goal.

Our research also reveals that an individual's perceptions of abuse are important to reporting the abuse. These perceptions are particularly relevant for women. In fact, it is a woman's perception of abuse rather that the seriousness of the abuse sustained that determines her reporting behavior. To a lesser extent, perceptions of physical abuse are also important in predicting the help-seeking behavior of men. Thus, it is apparent that both men and women will benefit from education concerning what constitutes abuse. It is not necessary to beat an individual for abuse to occur if aggressive acts are being inflicted against the will of an individual. Further, such education should stress that men need not conform to a sexually aggressive stereotype. If a young woman demands that her dating partner engage in sex acts against his will, then her partner need not feel ashamed and should feel free to discuss his feelings and reactions with his friends and family. Clearly, the notion that only women are physically or sexually abused must be dispelled.

A negative relationship between the seriousness of abuse sustained and the likelihood of reporting the abuse would tend to support a theory of learned helplessness. Our results provide no support for this theory as it relates to male or female victims or in reference to physical or sexual abuse. For men, our results provide reasonably direct support for the stress theory of help-seeking. The seriousness of their physical abuse affects the likelihood of their reporting abuse to friends. The seriousness of the sexual abuse sustained by men also has a direct and positive effect on the probability of their confiding in their friends. For women, however, the seriousness of the abuse sustained exerts a positive and significant effect in only one situation: The seriousness of the sexual abuse sustained increases the likelihood of telling friends about the abuse.

Nonetheless, the authors felt that even if the seriousness of an assault did not have a direct effect on the probability of reporting abuse after controlling for perceptions, the seriousness of the abuse sustained might have an indirect effect. Therefore, four additional equations were estimated that predicted whether or not men or women perceived a physically or sexually abusive incident in their dating relationship. As anticipated, for both men and women, the more serious the physical abuse sustained, the more likely the individual was to perceive that abuse occurred in the relationship. Thus, the seriousness of physical abuse sustained positively influences whether or not abuse is reported via its affect on one's perceptions of physical abuse. Again, this provides additional support for a stress theory of help-seeking.

With respect to sexual abuse, we felt that as the seriousness of the abuse increased, victims would also be more likely to perceive sexual abuse as having occurred. Somewhat surprisingly, for both men and women, this relationship was insignificant. This reaffirms some of the earlier findings that many individuals view mild forms of sexual abuse as normal. Thus, with respect to sexual abuse, we can lend only very modest support to a stress theory of help-seeking and no support to the theory of learned helplessness.

One final observation is that whenever sexual abuse occurs, men and women are reluctant to discuss the abuse with their parents. While the college dating population is more open to discussing physical abuse with their parents, sexual abuse appears to be a taboo topic. Evidence from many arenas indicates that this situation must change. The AIDS epidemic, the growth in the number of births to unmarried teenage girls, the spread of venereal diseases, and the very high incidence of sexual abuse in the dating population require open and honest communication between parents and their children about the latter's sexual behavior.

RECOMMENDATIONS FOR FURTHER STUDY

By modeling the reporting behavior of both men and women in dating relationships, this research breaks new ground in several areas. Nevertheless, much work on this subject remains to be done. Our study is limited, in part, by our small and geographically limited sample. Further research should be expanded to a larger dating population that would incorporate individuals who are dating but are not in college as well as individuals from all geographical regions.

We would also suggest that when individuals conduct research on the topic, respondents should be asked whether or not they sought help rather than whether or not they told someone about the abusive incidents. Discussions with friends may mean that abused individuals are trying to understand an abusive incident, are seeking the support of their friends, are bragging that their date tried to force sex with them, etc. The nature of such discussions must be clarified.

Third, as is apparent in this and a host of other research on help-seeking, very few individuals who are abused seek the assistance of counselors, physicians, or criminal justice authorities. Thus, to model this type of behavior, sample sizes, particularly those for men, must be very large. Even with 532 male dating relationships, we found that none of the men who perceived that they sustained any type of abuse reported it to a counselor, physician, or criminal justice authority.

SUMMARY AND CONCLUSIONS

This chapter has examined the extent to which victims of dating violence report the abuse to friends, parents, counselors, physicians, or criminal justice authorities. In general, we find that women are more likely to report abuse than men. Also, when an abusive incident is sex related, the probability of reporting the abuse markedly diminishes. Finally, the probability that abuse will be reported typically increases when the victim perceives an incident as abusive.

The second focus of this work is on predicting the help-seeking behavior of men and women in dating relationships. With the exception of the very strong, positive influence of perceiving oneself as physically abused on the likelihood of reporting abuse, we find that predictors of help-seeking are different for males and females. Interestingly, the seriousness of the abuse sustained is more important in predicting the help-seeking of males relative to females. For females, perceptions of abuse dominate the models. From these analyses, limited evidence was presented supporting a stress theory of help-seeking and no evidence could be put forward to support the hypothesis of learned helplessness.

This research has a variety of implications for policy and practitioners. First, physical and sexual abuse in dating is grossly underreported to criminal justice authorities. Second, if students are to seek help outside their immediate social networks, such help must be made more accessible. Third, education concerning abuse should be brought into our educational curriculum in the early teenage years when young people are beginning to date. Finally, more open and honest communications between parents and children about sex and sex abuse are absolutely essential.

ACKNOWLEDGMENTS

An earlier version of this chapter was presented at the 1988 meetings of the American Society of Criminology. This research was funded by a Summer Faculty Research Award to the first author from the School for Public and Environmental Affairs at Indiana University. It is a pleasure to acknowledge the university's support of this research.

REFERENCES

Arias, Ileana, Mary Samios & K. Daniel O'Leary. (1987). "Prevalence and Correlates of Physical Aggression During Courtship." *Journal of Interpersonal Violence* 2:82–90.
Berk, Richard A., Sarah F. Berk, Phyllis J. Newton & Donileen R. Loeske. (1984). "Cops on Call: Summoning the Police to the Scene of Spousal Violence." *Law and Society Review* 18:479–98.
Bowker, Lee H. (1983). *Beating Wife Beating*. Lexington, MA: Lexington Books.
Breines, Wini & Linda Gordon. (1983). "The New Scholarship on Family Violence." *Signs: Journal of Women in Culture and Society* 6:490–531.
Campbell, Jacquelyn C. (1987). "Making Sense of the Senseless: Women's Attributions About Battering." Paper presented at the Third National Family Violence Research Conference. Durham, NH.
Cate, Rodney, June Henton, James Koval, F. Scott Christopher & Sally Lloyd. (1982). "Premarital Abuse: A Social Psychological Perspective." *Journal of Family Issues* 3:79–90.
Deal, James E., & Karen Smith Wampler. (1986). "Dating Violence: The Primacy of Previous Experience." *Journal of Personal and Social Relationships* 3:457–71.

Dobash, R. Emerson & Russell Dobash. (1979). *Violence Against Wives: A Case Against the Patriarchy*. New York: Free Press.

Donato, Katherine M., & Lee H. Bowker. (1984). "Understanding the Helpseeking Behavior of Battered Women: A Comparison of Traditional Service Agencies and Women's Groups." *International Journal of Women's Studies* 7:99–109.

Dukes, Richard L., & Christine L. Mattley. (1977). "Predicting Rape Victim Reportage." *Sociology and Social Research* 62:63–84.

Estrich, Susan. (1987). *Real Rape*. Cambridge, MA: Harvard University Press.

Ferraro, Kathleen J., & John M. Johnson. (1983). "How Women Experience Battering: The Process of Victimization." *Social Problems* 30:325–28.

Gelles, Richard J. (1979). *Family Violence*. Beverly Hills, CA: Sage.

Giles-Sims, Jean. (1983). *Wife Battering: A Systems Theory Approach*. New York: Guilford.

Gourash, Nancy. (1978). "Help-Seeking: A Review of the Literature." *American Journal of Community Psychology* 6:413–23.

Henton, Judy, Rodney Cate, James Koval, Sally Lloyd & F. Scott Christopher. (1983). "Romance and Violence in Dating Relationships." *Journal of Family Issues* 4:467–82.

Kanin, E. J. (1957). "Male Aggression in Dating-Courting Relations." *American Journal of Sociology* 63:197–204.

Kilpatrick, D. G., L. J. Vernon & C. L. Best. (1984). "Factors Predicting Psychological Distress Among Rape Victims." In C. R. Figley (ed.), *Trauma and Its Wake: The Study of Treatment of Post-Traumatic Stress Disorder*, pp. 113–41. New York: Brunner/Mazel.

Korman, S. A., & Leslie, G. R. (1982). "The Relationships of Feminist Ideology and Date Expense Sharing to Perceptions of Sexual Aggression in Dating." *Journal of Sex Research* 18:114–29.

Lane, Katherine E., & Patricia Gwartney-Gibbs. (1985). "Violence in the Context of Dating and Sex." *Journal of Family Issues* 6:45–59.

Laner, Mary Riege, & Jeanine Thompson. (1982). "Abuse and Aggression in Courting Couples." *Deviant Behavior: An Interdisciplinary Journal* 3:229–44.

Makepeace, James M. (1981). "Courtship Violence Among College Students." *Family Relations* 30:97–102.

———. (1983). "Life Events Stress and Courtship Violence." *Family Relations* 32:101–9.

Rosenberg, Morris. (1979). *Conceiving the Self*. New York: Basic Books.

Russell, D. E. (1982). *Rape in Marriage*. New York: Macmillan.

Schulman, Mark A. (1979). *A Survey of Spousal Violence Against Women in Kentucky*. Lexington, KY: Kentucky Commission on Women.

Sigelman, Carol K., Carol J. Berry & Katherine A. Wiles. (1984). "Violence in College Students' Dating Relationships." *Journal of Applied Social Psychology* 5, 6:530–48.

Stets, Jan E., & Maureen A. Pirog-Good. (1987a). "Violence in Dating Relationships." *Social Psychology Quarterly* 50: 237–46.

———. (1989). "Patterns of Physical and Sexual Abuse in Dating Relationships." *Journal of Family Violence*.

Straus, Murray. (1979). "Measuring Intrafamily Conflict and Violence: The Conflict Tactics (CT) Scales." *Journal of Marriage and the Family* 41:75–88.

Straus, Murray, Richard J. Gelles, & Suzanne Steinmetz. (1980). *Behind Closed Doors: Violence in the American Family.* Garden City, NY: Anchor.
Walker, Lenore E. (1984). *The Battered Woman Syndrome.* New York: Springer.
Wauchope, Barbara A. (1988). "Help-Seeking Decisions of Battered Women: A Test of Learned Helplessness and Two Stress Theories." Paper presented at the Eastern Sociological Society meetings.
Williams, Linda S. (1984). "The Classic Rape: When Do Victims Report?" *Social Problems* 31:459–67.

7 Conflict and Violence in Dating Relationships
Sally A. Lloyd, James E. Koval, and Rodney M. Cate

Romance, love and commitment have become synonymous with dating in the United States. The romantic love model suggests that, no matter what the problem, love will conquer all and will sustain partners through times of difficulty. This typical "moonlight and roses" description of dating and courtship has recently come under serious scrutiny, however, by researchers studying premarital abusive behavior. Both conflict and violence are common features of courtship, and may be integral issues in the development and maintenance of premarital relationships (Cate et al., 1982; Lloyd, 1987). The impact of premarital conflict and violence is not limited to courtship development; both conflict and violence may carry over into the marital relationship and negatively influence satisfaction (Cate & Lloyd, 1988; Roscoe & Benaske, 1985).

Following the lead of Straus (1979) and Billingham and Sack (1986), we conceptualize violence as a conflict tactic. Under such a conceptualization, violence is inseparable from conflict (although the reverse is not necessarily true) and may be most fruitfully defined as a characteristic of interaction. Violence is thus viewed as a means of controlling the partner (Stets & Pirog-Good, 1987) or as a negotiating tactic (Billingham & Sack, 1986), rather than as a personality trait of individuals. This view represents a conscious shift in focus away from the traditional emphasis on characteristics of individuals toward an emphasis on interaction characteristics.

The purpose of the present chapter is to examine violence in dating relationships within a "conflict framework." While levels of premarital violence are admittedly high, it is evident that not all conflictual couples are violent toward each other. This chapter focuses on the factors associated with high conflict and the presence of violence versus high conflict and the absence of violence.

A CONFLICT FRAMEWORK

In examining the literature on violence, we have been surprised at the dearth of research on violence as a strategy of conflict negotiation. We do not mean to be tautological in our emphasis on conflict and violence in premarital relationships; rather, we wish to emphasize the utility of conflict theory as a conceptual base upon which to build further.

Conflict is a facet of any relationship, be it collegial or romantic (Coser, 1956; Simmel, 1955). Closely knit groups, such as the family, may be prone to particularly intense conflict (Coser, 1956). By virtue of the fact that close relationships are characterized by interdependence, high frequency of interaction, and the implicit right of influence, opportunities for disagreement abound (Peterson, 1983). These very characteristics may increase the likelihood of violence in relationships (Gelles & Straus, 1979; Goode, 1971).

Conflict is so woven into the fabric of family life that Sprey (1979) argues for a theory of the family as a system in conflict rather than a system in harmony. Within the family, there are frequent occasions for hostility to arise; however, such hostility is more often suppressed than expressed (Coser, 1956). As a result, when conflict does occur, it may cover accumulated grievances as well as the issue at hand (Jacobson & Margolin, 1979). The negative affect associated with a buildup of hostility may be particularly potent in maintaining relationship distress (Gottman, 1979) and, we would argue, aggression between partners. Recent evidence from Margolin, John, and Gleberman (1988) supports this assertion: physically aggressive husbands display greater negativism and defensiveness than nonaggressive husbands.

In a conflict framework, violence is viewed primarily as a negotiating strategy. Violence may be a particularly potent strategy for two reasons. First, it quickly brings the partner under one's control (Dobash & Dobash, 1979), and second, violence may be reinforced to the extent that it stops perceived aversive behavior on the part of the partner (Patterson, 1985). Indeed, Finkelhor (1983) emphasizes that violence is a response to perceived powerlessness and, therefore, a means of re-establishing power.

When is violence used in lieu of other negotiating strategies? The evidence accumulated thus far from studies of premarital and marital violence suggest that violence is used as an attempt to get one's partner to act according to one's own desires (Sprey, 1979) or, more succinctly, as an attempt to control the partner (Stets & Pirog-Good, 1987; Stets, 1988). Scanzoni (1979) argues that conflict is inseparable from issues of power and authority in the relationship; similarly, violence may be difficult to separate from issues of conflict and control (Stets, 1988).

Violence also appears to be a tactic that is used when other means of conflict negotiation break down (Gelles & Straus, 1979). Interestingly, the use of physical aggression in a relationship does not appear to preclude the use of more constructive tactics such as negotiation or reasoning (Billingham & Sack, 1986; Straus, Gelles & Steinmetz, 1980). Rather, the occurrence of violence may be an indication of faulty conflict management. In fact, Straus, Gelles & Steinmetz, (1980) conclude that ongoing, severe conflict is almost sure to end in violence. The conflict framework emphasizes that violence serves as a particularly powerful means of maintaining authority or getting what one wants when other methods fail (Straus & Steinmetz, 1974). Violence is, after all, the "ultimate resource" (Allen & Straus, 1980).

Still, not all couples who are experiencing high levels of conflict or difficulty in conflict management resort to violence as a negotiating strategy. The differences between conflictual-violent couples and conflictual-nonviolent couples may lie in the interplay of individual and relationship characteristics.

Individual Factors

Research on individual factors in relationship violence has emphasized the role of characteristics such as self-esteem, sex-role orientation, and social stress (Bernard, Bernard, & Bernard, 1985; Deal & Wampler, 1986; Makepeace, 1987). Unfortunately, these variables do not seem to explain very much of the variation in the experience of violence in a relationship. It is not that individual characteristics are irrelevant in the study of violence; rather, the factors studied to date may be too far removed from the experience of violence to be highly salient.

Under our conflict framework, the salient individual factors are those that emphasize an individual's beliefs about what interaction in relationships should be like. The emphasis here is on the role of learned patterns of interaction and expectations for self and partner behavior. These emphases can be found in investigations of the cycle of family violence and dysfunctional relationship beliefs.

The intergenerational transmission of violence has been examined in several studies as a factor in courtship violence. Individuals who have experienced violence in a premarital relationship are also more likely to have experienced and/or witnessed violence in their families of origin than are those with no dating violence history (Emery, 1983; Laner & Thompson, 1982; O'Keefe, Brockopp & Chew, 1986; Roscoe & Callahan, 1985). This cycle is often designated a "learned predisposition" to use violence (Straus, Gelles & Steinmetz, 1980).

Expectations, in the form of beliefs about relationships, may also play a key role in premarital violence. While expectations and beliefs have not yet been studied in relation to premarital violence, they do play a clear role in relationship formation (Surra, 1987), distress (Epstein & Eidelson, 1981; Fincham & Bradbury, 1987), and dissolution (Lloyd & Cate, 1985).

Epstein and Eidelson (1981) have specifically examined the role of dysfunctional relationship beliefs, and identify several beliefs that may lead to relationship distress. The belief that "disagreement is destructive" may prevent partners from bringing issues out in the open, leading to a state of accumulated grievances. The belief that "mind reading is okay" causes partners to assume that they know what the other is thinking, and the belief that "change is impossible" prevents partners from requesting constructive change and compromise.

These dysfunctional relationship beliefs may be related to the use of violence in relationships to the extent that violence is both a dysfunctional and distressing conflict-negotiating tactic. The relationship belief that "disagreement is destructive" or "mind reading is okay" may contribute to frustration, tension, and accumulated hostility. When interpersonal conflict does arise, it may erupt into aggression.

Relationship Factors

Less is known about the relationship factors that contribute to violence during courtship. Several researchers have found that violence is more likely to occur once a relationship has become serious, and that the occurrence of violence does not necessarily lead to termination of the relationship (Cate et al., 1982). Surprisingly, violence may be interpreted as a sign of positive relationship characteristics: In the study by Henton et al. (1983) nearly one-third of the respondents interpreted violent premarital behavior as a sign of love.

Viewing violence from a conflict framework points to several key variables to be included as relationship components of violent interaction. Patterns of conflict negotiation may be related to violence in premarital relationships. The use of negative negotiating strategies (such as manipulation) is related to a lack of resolution of conflict (Lloyd, 1987); if violence is viewed as a resolution technique (albeit a rather harsh one), then negotiation techniques that leave the situation unresolved may be related to the use or experience of premarital violence. In particular, strategies that entail pursuing the issue over and over (in the attempt to get one's goals met), versus strategies that emphasize compromise, may leave partners particularly vulnerable to violent episodes.

Exchange models complement the conflict framework in their delineation of the components of "give and take" in relationships. Social-exchange concepts such as alternatives and rewards (Thibaut & Kelley, 1959) may be particularly salient in the study of relationship violence. Individuals who remain in violent relationships, as compared to individuals who terminate their violent relationships, report a lower comparison level for alternatives (Cate et al., 1982). That is, those individuals feel they will be unable to find a new partner as "good" as the current partner. Similarly, the exchange concept of investment may explain why partners remain together despite dysfunctional interpersonal behavior: They may be unwilling to give up the investment of time, energy, and emotion already put into the relationship (Rusbult, 1983; Strube & Barbour, 1984). This may be especially true if there are few perceived alternatives (Levinger, 1979).

130   Lloyd, Koval, & Cate

SUMMARY AND PURPOSE OF STUDY

The purpose of the present study is to examine the occurrence of violence in premarital relationships within a conflict framework. This framework views violence as a conflict-negotiating strategy that may be enacted in an attempt to control the partner or when other strategies do not resolve the conflict.

Specifically, this project was designed to address the question of what differentiates violent from nonviolent relationships, given that both types of relationship are in conflict. Conflictual-violent relationships, as opposed to conflictual-nonviolent relationships, are hypothesized to be characteristic of individuals who hold more dysfunctional relationship beliefs, have a learned predisposition to use violence, use more negative conflict negotiating strategies, and have a greater investment in the relationship, a lower comparison level, and fewer alternatives.

Only currently dating partners are included in the analysis in order to avoid retrospection about a previous relationship. In addition, the stage of relationship is controlled by the exclusion of individuals who indicated a casual involvement in the relationship. Since violence appears more likely to happen in serious relationships (Cate et al., 1982), we wanted to avoid the comparison of serious violent relationships with casual nonviolent relationships. Finally, in order to address the question of differences between conflictual-violent and conflictual-nonviolent relationships, we have limited our analysis to individuals who indicated greater than average levels of conflict in their relationships.

METHOD

Procedure and Participants

Questionnaires were distributed to undergraduate students at two large western universities during the 1986–87 academic year. These questionnaires were administered in group sessions of approximately 20 students at a time. The questionnaires were anonymous and contained no identification numbers or markings whereby students could be matched with their responses. In addition, upon completion each questionnaire was placed by the respondent in a sealed envelope in order to ensure the privacy and confidentiality of the responses. A total of 1,274 students completed questionnaires. These students were representative of their respective universities in age, year in school, and income. They were not representative in terms of gender (an overabundance of females) and major (an overabundance of social science majors).

The sample consisted of nondating, casually dating, seriously dating, engaged, and married participants. For the purposes of the present study, the subsample analyzed was restricted according to the following criteria: (1) currently involved, (2) in a serious relationship (included seriously dating, engaged, or living together), (3) above average in conflict [defined as above the median score, 19, for this sample on Braiker & Kelley's (1979) conflict scale]. This group consisted of 243 individuals, 79 of whom were currently in a violent relationship.

The 243 participants had the following demographic characteristics. There were 61 males and 182 females. Average age of the participants was 21.34 (range of 17 to 43 years of age); average education was 15.00 years (range of 12 to 20 years of schooling); and the average length of the current relationship was 28.77 months (range of 5 months to 10 years).

Measures

Violence. The use of aggression in a premarital relationship was assessed with the violence subscale of the Conflict Tactics Scale (Straus, 1979). This scale asks respondents to report the frequency with which they have ever experienced and/or used the following behaviors in their current dating relationships: threw something at the other; kicked, bit, or hit with a fist; hit or tried to hit with something; beat up the other; threatened with a knife or gun; used a knife or gun. For the purposes of analysis, respondents were placed in the "violent" category if they indicated the occurrence of one or more of the above acts in their ongoing relationship. If no such acts were indicated, the respondent was placed into the "nonviolent" category.[1]

Conflictual Relationship. Conflict was assessed with the scale developed by Braiker and Kelley (1979). This five-item scale assesses the frequency of arguments and the seriousness of problems between partners. Each item is accompanied by a nine-point Likert scale; the higher the score, the greater the level of conflict in the relationship. Cronbach's alpha for this scale is 0.79. Individuals were considered to be in conflictual relationships if they scored above the median score of 19.

Individual Characteristics. Aggression in the family of origin was assessed using an adapted version of the Conflict Tactics Scale (Straus, 1979). Respondents first indicated whether they had ever observed their parents directing any of these behaviors at one another: pushing and shoving; slapping, other than face-slapping; face-slapping; kicking, biting or hitting with a fist; trying to hit with an object; beating; threatening with a knife or gun; using a knife or gun. Respondents then indicated whether these same behaviors had ever been directed toward them by their parents. For purposes of the analysis this variable was coded as a dummy variable; 1 indicated the respondent had reported observing parents acting violently and/or violence had been directed toward the respondent as a child; zero indicated neither observing nor receiving violence as a child.

Relationship beliefs were assessed with the Relationship Beliefs Inventory (Eidelson & Epstein, 1982). This scale is designed to assess the degree to which individuals hold unrealistic beliefs about relationships. The first three subscales of the inventory were used: Disagreement Is Destructive, Mind Reading Is Expected, and Partners Cannot Change. Each subscale consists of six items, which are each rated on six-point Likert scales of zero ("I strongly feel the statement is false") to 5 ("I strongly feel the statement is true"); the higher the score on the subscale, the more the individual holds the belief. In Epstein and Eidelson's (1981) development of the scales, Cronbach's alpha for the disagreement, mind-reading and change scales were 0.86, 0.83, and 0.80, respectively. With the present sample of premarital partners, Cronbach's alpha for disagreement, mind reading, and change are 0.78, 0.74 and 0.62.

Relationship Characteristics. Negotiating strategies were assessed using the scale developed by Cate, Koval, and Ponzetti (1984) based on the work of Falbo and Peplau (1980). The basic instrument asks respondents to indicate, on a scale of 1 (never) to 5 (always), how they go about getting what they want from their relationships. The original 13 items included in the Cate, Koval, Ponzetti (1984) study were factor analyzed to assess the underlying dimensions of the scale. Three internally consistent negotiating strategies emerged: persistence (I remind my partner of what I want until he/she gives in, I use persuasion, I pout or threaten to cry, I ask my partner to do what I want), logic (I reason with my partner, I state the importance of what I want, I state my needs), and compromise (we negotiate and compromise, we talk it over). The internal consistencies for persistence, logic, and compromise are 0.72, 0.60, and 0.54, respectively.

Social-exchange concepts were assessed using the scales developed by Rusbult (1983) for a test of the investment model. The original scales assessed rewards, costs, comparison level for alternatives, commitments, satisfaction, investment, and concrete investment. Due to problems of multicollinearity (12 of the intercorrelations for the scales were 0.50 or greater) and relatively poor internal consistency, the individual items used by Rusbult were factor analyzed in order to formulate a smaller set of unidimensional scales. The two items used to assess alternatives were not included in the factor analysis, as we were particularly interested in retaining alternatives as a separate dimension. The alternatives scale contains two items that assess the comparison of the current relationship to outside alternatives. Cronbach's alpha for this scale is 0.83; the higher the score, the more the individual perceives that alternative situations are superior in rewards to the current situation.

The factor analysis of the other 18 items yielded three factors. Factor one consisted mainly of items originally used to assess rewards, satisfaction, and commitment. This factor was named rewards; it includes eight items and has an internal consistency of 0.89. Factor two consisted of a reward item and a cost item, both of which assessed the comparison of the current relationship to an ideal. This factor was labeled comparison level, and it has an internal consistency of 0.73. The higher the comparison level score, the closer the current relationship is to an ideal relationship in terms of rewards and costs. The third factor consisted of five items from the investment and concrete investment scales; Cronbach's alpha for the investment scale is 0.83. The higher the score, the greater the investment the individual has in the relationship.

Since these scales were constructed from raw scores rather than factor scores, and since the alternative items were withheld from the factor analysis, correlations among the scales remain. Since the reward scale correlated above the level of 0.70 with both alternatives and investments, the reward scale was not used in the analysis in order to avoid multicollinearity problems.

RESULTS

Discriminant analysis was used to examine the ability of individual and relationship factors to differentiate between individuals currently involved in violent dating relationships versus individuals currently involved in nonviolent dating relationships. All relationships analyzed were high in levels of premarital conflict. Means, standard deviations, and univariate F ratios for the discriminating variables appear in Table 7.1.

Discriminant analysis chooses the set of independent variables that best discriminates between discrete groups (in this analysis, these groups consist of individuals in conflictual-violent versus conflictual-nonviolent relationships). The analysis constructs a discriminant function that maximizes the separation of these groups. This function is most easily interpreted by an examination of the structure coefficients, which are the correlations between the discriminant function and each variable. They indicate the degree of contribution of a particular variable to the discriminant function (Klecka, 1980). The last column of Table 7.1 presents the discriminant results. There is significant multivariate separation between the violent and nonviolent groups: Wilks λ = .836, χ^2 = 42.26, $p < .001$. The canonical correlation for this function is 0.405; this represents the correlation between the function derived from the set of predictor variables and group membership (that is, violent versus nonviolent relationship). The evaluation of the discriminant function at the group centroid is an assessment of the average score on the function across all members of each discriminating group, represented in standard deviations. The evaluation at group centroid indicates that the function is characteristic of individuals in violent relationships, for this group scores approximately two-thirds of a standard deviation above the mean on the function.

Eleven variables made a significant contribution to the discriminant function. The first four of these variables also evidenced univariate mean differences between the groups ($p < .05$ or lower). These four variables—persistence, length, change, and investment—will be emphasized in the discussion, as they made the clearest contribution to the discrimination of violent from nonviolent relationships. Persistence was the strongest contributor, indicating that violent relationships are characterized by greater use of persistence in conflict negotiation. Individuals in violent relationships are also characterized by having been in their relationships longer, and by a greater investment in the relationship as well as a greater belief that change is possible. Two additional factors, greater experience of violence in the family of origin and a lower comparison level, also characterized violent relationships. These two factors evidenced only marginally significant univariate differences ($p < .10$).

Table 7.1
Means, Standard Deviations, and Univariate *F* Ratios for the Discriminating Variables

	Mean (Standard Deviation) Nonviolent[a]	Violent	Univariate F Ratio	Structure Coefficient
Persistence	10.31 (2.71)	11.66 (2.74)	12.60 ***	.516[b]
Length	26.44 (18.47)	34.13 (22.19)	7.88 **	.408[b]
Investments	37.21 (5.48)	39.01 (3.80)	6.57 **	.372[b]
Change is Impossible	13.61 (4.57)	12.31 (4.00)	4.47 *	-.307[b]
Family Violence	0.35 (0.48)	0.47 (0.50)	3.35 +	.266[b]
Comparison Level	11.90 (3.34)	11.12 (3.48)	2.87 +	-.243[b]
Logic	11.37 (1.80)	11.79 (1.64)	2.66	.223[b]
Gender	0.73 (0.44)	0.82 (0.38)	2.33	.222[b]
Age	21.18 (2.51)	21.73 (3.70)	1.85	.198[b]
Mind Reading is Okay	11.27 (4.10)	10.64 (4.50)	1.14	-.155[b]
Alternatives	7.15 (3.77)	7.62 (3.84)	0.77	.128[b]
Education	15.06 (1.58)	14.89 (1.15)	0.67	-.119
Compromise	7.92 (1.36)	7.69 (1.29)	1.47	-.030
Disagreement is Destructive	10.20 (4.61)	10.12 (4.65)	0.02	.016

Chi-Square	42.26 ***
Wilks Lambda	.836
Canonical Correlation	.405
Evaluation at Group Centroid: Violent	.667
Nonviolent	-.292

a. Nonviolent, n = 174; Violent, n = 79.
b. Contributed significantly to the discriminant function.
+ p < .10   * p < .05   ** p < .01   *** p < .001

DISCUSSION

The purpose of this study was to differentiate conflictual-violent from conflictual-nonviolent premarital relationships. Using 14 individual, relationship, and background variables, these two types of relationships were successfully discriminated. Persistence, length of relationship, investment, and belief that change is possible were the strongest discriminating variables. These results should be interpreted with caution, however, for the final number of respondents used in the analysis was small (due to the limiting of the sample to ongoing, serious, conflictual relationships).

The picture of conflictual-violent relationships that emerges from this analysis is one of relationships characterized by repeated attempts to persuade the partner that one's own way is right, a belief that it is possible to change the partner, and a high investment in the relationship. It is almost as if the partners are "trapped" into staying in the current relationship (through their high investment in each other) despite the fact that the relationship is a costly one (due to the use of violence). Such an analysis is in keeping with social exchange conceptions of relationships, for investments that once served as attractions in the relationship may later serve as barriers to the termination of that pairing to the extent that partners view the loss of their invested time and emotion as a cost (Levinger, 1979). The finding that alternatives did not make a strong contribution to the discrimination of violent from nonviolent relationships may reflect the fact that alternatives are not salient until the point of consideration of termination (Leik & Leik, 1976).

The contribution of the relationship belief "change is possible" to the discriminant function is of particular interest. A greater belief that change is possible was associated with being in a conflictual-violent relationship. This finding makes sense in light of the fact that the use of persistence as a negotiating strategy was strongly associated with being in a conflictual-violent relationship. Individuals in violent relationships may believe they can change their partners (Ferraro & Johnson, 1983) and may use persistence and persuasion as techniques to bring about such change. Drawing on the conflict perspective, such persistence may increase frustration and tension in the relationship and thus create a breeding ground for aggressive behavior.

The positive association between "change is possible" and being in a conflictual-violent relationship may, however, reflect cognitive dissonance. Since the individuals analyzed were in ongoing relationships, part of the personal justification for remaining in a relationship that contains violence may be the hope that things will change and that the violent behavior will not recur. It may be very difficult to remain in such a relationship in the absence of the justification that the relationship can indeed be "saved." Such reasoning has been noted in battered women who return to their husbands (Ferraro & Johnson, 1983); the present findings lend preliminary support to the idea that trying to "save" the relationship and/or the partner is characteristic of premarital relationships as well. Since these data are cross-sectional, however, both the persistence and savior explanations are purely speculative, for the direction of causality cannot be determined. In addition, these results are limited to the extent that cross-sectional data do not really elucidate the dynamic nature of the use of violence in a premarital relationship.

This study found only a weak association between the cycle of family violence and being in a conflictual-violent dating relationship. It is interesting to speculate on the meaning of this. It could be that witnessing or experiencing violence in the family of origin is only one aspect of the intergenerational transmission of violence. In addition, individuals may learn other patterns of conflict negotiation which also increase the likelihood that violence may occur. For example, if an individual has witnessed the use of violence and the use of persistence as parental conflict negotiating strategies, then it seems plausible that both these factors contribute to the learned predisposition to behave violently (albeit the latter acts in an indirect manner). This can only be tenuously stated at the present time; yet there does seem to be some utility in a broader conceptualization of how intergenerational transmission occurs.

Finally, the conflict perspective on premarital violence appears to be supported by the results of the present study. Beliefs about conflict interaction as well as the use of persistent negotiation strategies helped to differentiate conflictual-violent from conflictual-nonviolent relationships. These results are consistent with earlier conceptualizations of violence as a means of control (Stets & Pirog-Good, 1987; Stets, 1988), as a conflict strategy (Billingham & Sack, 1986), and as an act of communication (Koval, Ponzetti & Cate, 1982).

IMPLICATIONS FOR POLICY AND PRACTICE

A number of researchers examining dating violence have identified the need for implementing conflict management and problem-solving skills programs for young adults (Laner, 1983; Yllo & Straus, 1981). The findings of this study certainly substantiate that suggestion. However, the findings of this study also suggest that dating partners need to be provided with skills for withdrawing from a conflict [both Jacobson & Margolin (1979) and O'Leary et al., (1985) emphasize this skill for violent married couples as well]. As Braiker and Kelley (1979) have noted, couples exhibit a powerful tendency to raise conflict to a point at which the precipitating issue is forgotten and the argument centers on the conflict process itself. Such a tendency would appear particularly problematic for dating individuals who not only persistently attempt to persuade or change their partners, but who also use violence during conflict situations. Teaching problem-solving skills, which tend to be very goal directed (for example, let's try to resolve the problem), without confronting individuals' beliefs surrounding conflict and change would seem to enhance the potential volatility of the conflict encounter. Given the high levels of conflict already noted in the relationships examined in this study, persistence on the part of one partner, regardless of the original argument or the otherwise admirable goal of "resolving the problem," would create a potentially dangerous situation.

Problem-solving approaches with violent and/or potentially violent dating partners need then to assess the processes underlying conflict management rather than simply emphasizing the resolution of the problem. In addition, the meaning behind the conflict process must be examined, for what is the pursuit of resolution to one partner may be viewed as rehashing the same old issue by the other (Lloyd, 1987).

The conflict perspective itself offers some guidelines for intervention. Viewing violence as a negotiating strategy or a power issue provides insight into the development of therapeutic and programmatic intervention strategies. If violence is viewed as an act of communication, client defensiveness about violent behavior may be reduced, for the emphasis is placed on changing interaction rather than dysfunctional personality (Koval, Ponzetti & Cate, 1982). In addition, the conflict perspective emphasizes the utility of helping clients change their patterns of interaction and conflict negotiation. This is especially important in light of the fact that violence is often reciprocal (Cate et al., 1982; Straus, Gelles & Steinmetz, 1980).

One critical issue confronting family violence interventionists has been accessing violent and at-risk families for treatment. Given that family violence typically occurs "behind closed doors" (Straus, Gelles & Steinmetz, 1980), identifying violent families is particularly problematic and, if contact is made, overcoming clients' denial and resistance is especially difficult. These concerns, however, are addressed to some degree by directing intervention efforts at individuals who are not yet married. Most specifically, the educational system, including high schools and universities, offers an excellent environment for working with the vast majority of individuals who eventually marry, become parents, and may repeat or develop violent family patterns. As Roark (1987) has noted in her review of violence prevention strategies for college students, a wide array of treatment methods is at the disposal of school administrators, counselors, and teachers. Intervention in violent premarital relationships is particularly important, given that patterns of conflict and violence may carry over into marriage (Cate & Lloyd, 1988; Roscoe & Benaske, 1985). The premarital period may be a key life stage in efforts targeted at "breaking the cycle" of family violence.

IMPLICATIONS FOR FURTHER STUDY

Based on the findings of this study, two critical areas for future research can be identified. First, there is a need for studies that further delineate the "conflict perspective" of premarital violence. Within this area, there are two methodological issues that must be addressed: the dyadic level of analysis and the identification of actual patterns of interaction. Technically, although the present study examined "relationship characteristics," the level of analysis was individual rather than dyadic. Gathering data from both members of the couple would allow a more "dyadic" view of the dynamics of violence. Couple data is important for several reasons. First, the dynamics of violence in a relationship are complicated by issues of whether there is a victim/aggressor pattern or a reciprocal pattern. Given that gender differences exist in the severity of violence tactics used and potential for serious harm, untangling the actual dynamics of violent episodes is a key component of a complete understanding of violence as a form of conflict negotiation. Second, males and females experience relationships and conflict differentially (Lloyd, 1987); there is every reason to suppose that violence has differential meanings and consequences as well. Third, reports of the frequency of violent acts vary according to which partner in a couple is queried (Szinovacz, 1983); such variation has important implications for the definition of a "violent" relationship in any research project.

Identifying patterns of conflict negotiation and how they differ among violent versus nonviolent couples may require the use of laboratory observational methods. Premarital partners who are in violent relationships may interact differently than those in nonviolent relationships; whether the differences center around more aversive behavior, lower base rates of positive behavior, or the reciprocity of negative behavior remains to be seen. Observational studies are integral to the further development of the conflict perspective of premarital violence.

The second critical area for future research is longitudinal study. Longitudinal studies may help to explicate the questions of the degree to which violent patterns are carried into marriage and why some violent premarital relationships terminate whereas others move toward deeper commitment. These questions are particularly important, for although the premarital period is the socially prescribed time for testing and evaluating relationship, it is clear that the presence of violence does not always hamper the continued development of the relationship (Henton et al., 1983). Violence may carry over from courtship to marriage for the very reason that partners have "too much invested to quit," thus maintaining the cycle of violence. The need to delineate how such carryover occurs is vitally important to "breaking the cycle."

SUMMARY AND CONCLUSIONS

The purpose in this chapter was to examine premarital violence within a "conflict framework." This framework emphasizes the inseparability of violence from interpersonal conflict; violence is thus seen as a conflict negotiating strategy. Specifically, we examined differences between relationships that were high in conflict and violent versus relationships that were high in conflict and nonviolent. The discriminating factors examined included relationship beliefs, the cycle of family violence, conflict negotiating strategies, investment in the relationship, alternatives, and comparison level.

Use of persistence as a negotiating strategy best discriminated conflictual-violent and conflictual-nonviolent relationships. Characteristically, individuals in a violent relationship were in the relationship longer and had a greater investment in the relationship as well as a greater belief that change was possible. These results are viewed within the conflict framework as indicating the importance of the interaction of individual and relationship factors to our understanding of dating violence. We conclude that it may be the interplay of the use of persistence and the hope of saving the relationship at any cost that helps to explain the coexistence of "romance and violence" during courtship.

ACKNOWLEDGMENTS

The authors wish to thank Joe F. Pittman for his helpful comments on an earlier draft of this chapter, and Gail S. Rapp for her help in preparing the manuscript. An earlier version of this chapter was presented at the 1988 Conference of the National Council on Family Relations.

NOTE

1. The issue of experience versus use of violence has not been entirely ignored in the analysis of these data. The majority (54 out of 79; 68 percent) of the violent relationships were reciprocally violent. Only 10 (13 percent) participants reported they experienced violence without using it, and only 15 (19 percent) reported they used violence without experiencing it. Thus, experience and use of violence are quite closely tied together. These data were analyzed once for individuals who had reported experiencing violence, and again for individuals who had reported using violence. The results of these two discriminant analyses were virtually identical, due to the large overlap between the groups (the reciprocal individuals fit into both groups). Given our emphasis on relationship characteristics and violence and the similarity of the separate analyses, we decided to combine individuals across the categories of experience, use, and reciprocal violence.

REFERENCES

Allen, Craig M., & Straus, Murray A. (1980). Resources, power and husband-wife violence. In M. A. Straus & G. Hotaling (eds.), *The social causes of husband-wife violence,* pp. 188–208. Minneapolis: University of Minnesota Press.
Bernard, J., Bernard, S., & Bernard, M. (1985). Courtship violence and sex-typing. *Family Relations,* 34:573–76.
Bernard, M., & Bernard J. (1983). Violent intimacy: The family as a model of love relationships. *Family Relations,* 32:283–286.
Billingham, R. E., & Sack, A. R. (1986). Courtship violence and the interactive status of the relationship. *Journal of Adolescent Research,* 20:37–44.
Braiker, H. B., & Kelley, H. H. (1979). Conflict in the development of close relationships. In R. L. Burgess & T. L. Huston (eds.), *Social exchange in developing relationships,* pp. 135–68. New York: Academic.
Cate, R. M., Henton, J. M., Koval, J. E., Christopher, F. S., & Lloyd, S. A. (1982). Premarital violence: A social psychological perspective. *Journal of Family Issues,* 3:79–90.
Cate, R. M., Koval, J. P., & Ponzetti, J. J. (1984). Power strategies in dual career and traditional couples. *Journal of Social Psychology,* 123:287–88.
Cate, R. M., & Lloyd, S. A. (1988). Courtship. Pp. 409–27. In S. Duck (ed.), *Handbook of personal relationships.* New York: Wiley.

Coser, L. A. (1956). *The functions of social conflict.* Glencoe, IL: Free Press.

Deal, J. E., & Wampler, K. (1986). Dating violence: The primacy of previous experience. *Journal of Social and Personal Relationships,* 3:457–71.

Dobash, R. E., & Dobash, R. (1979). *Violence against wives: A case against the patriarchy.* New York: Free Press.

Eidelson, R. J., & Epstein, N. (1982). Cognition and relationship maladjustment: Development of a measure of dysfunctional relationship beliefs. *Journal of Consulting and Clinical Psychology,* 50:715–20.

Emery, B. C. (1983). Factors contributing to violence in dating relationships. Master's thesis, Oregon State University.

Epstein, N., & Eidelson, R. J. (1981). Unrealistic beliefs of clinical couples: Their relationship to expectations, goals and satisfaction. *American Journal of Family Therapy,* 9:13–22.

Falbo, T., & Peplau, L. A. (1980). Power strategies in intimate relationships. *Journal of Personality and Social Psychology,* 38:618–28.

Ferraro, K. J., & Johnson, J. M. (1983). How women experience battering: The process of victimization. *Social Problems,* 30:325–39.

Fincham, F. D., & Bradbury, T. N. (1987). The impact of attributions in marriage: A longitudinal analysis. *Journal of Personality and Social Psychology,* 53:510–17.

Finkelhor, D. (1983). Common features of family abuse. In D. Finkelhor, R. J. Gelles, G. T. Hotaling & M. A. Straus (eds.), *The dark side of families,* pp. 17–28. Beverly Hills, CA: Sage.

Gelles, R., & Straus, M. A. (1979). Determinants of violence in the family: Toward a theoretical integration. In W. R. Burr, R. Hill, F. I. Nye & I. L. Reiss (eds.), *Contemporary theories about the family,* Vol. 1, pp. 549–81. New York: Free Press.

Goode, W. J. (1971). Force and violence in the family. *Journal of Marriage and the Family,* 33:624–36.

Gottman, J. M. (1979). *Marital interaction: Experimental investigations.* New York: Academic.

Henton, J. M., Cate, R. M., Koval, J. E., Lloyd, S. A. & Christopher, F. S. (1983). Romance and violence in dating relationships. *Journal of Family Issues,* 4:467–82.

Jacobson, N. S., & Margolin, G. (1979). *Marital therapy.* New York: Brunner/Mazel.

Klecka, W. R. (1980). *Discriminant analysis.* Beverly Hills, CA: Sage.

Koval, J. E., Ponzetti, J., & Cate, R. M. (1982). Programmatic intervention for men involved in conjugal violence. *Family Therapy,* 9:147–54.

Laner, M. R. (1983). Courtship abuse and aggression: Contextual aspects. *Sociological Spectrum,* 3:69–83.

Laner, M. R., & Thompson, J. (1982). Abuse and aggression in courtship couples. *Deviant Behavior,* 3:229–44.

Leik, R., & Leik, S. K. (1976). Transition to interpersonal commitment. In R. L. Kunkel & J. K. Kunkel (eds.), *Behavioral theory in sociology,* pp. 299–322. New Brunswick, NJ: Transaction.

Levinger, G. (1979). A social exchange view on the dissolution of pair relationships. In R. L. Burgess & T. L. Huston (eds.), *Social exchange in developing relationships,* pp. 169–93. New York: Academic.

Lloyd, S. A. (1987). Conflict in premarital relationships: Differential perceptions of males and females. *Family Relations,* 36:290–94.

Lloyd, S. A., & Cate, R. M. (1985). Attributions associated with significant turning points in premarital relationship dissolution. *Journal of Social and Personal Relationships,* 2:419–36.

Makepeace, J. M. (1981). Courtship violence among college students. *Family Relations,* 30:97–102.

———(1987). Social factor and victim-offender differences in courtship violence. *Family Relations,* 36:87–91.

Margolin, G., John, R. S., & Gleberman, L. (1988). "Affective Responses to Conflictual Discussions in Violent and Nonviolent Couples." *Journal of Consulting and Clinical Psychology,* 56:24–33.

O'Keefe, N. K., Brockopp, K., & Chew, E. (1986). Teen dating violence. *Social Work,* 31:465–68.

O'Leary, D. K., Curley, A., Rosenbaum, A., & Clarke, C. (1985). Assertion training for abused wives: A potentially hazardous treatment. *Journal of Consulting and Clinical Psychology,* 11:319–22.

Patterson, G. R. (1985). A microsocial analysis of anger and irritable behavior. In M. A. Chesney & R. H. Rosenman (eds.), *Anger and hostility behavioral and cardiovascular disorders,* pp. 83–100. Washington DC: Hemisphere.

Peterson, D. R. (1983). Conflict. In H. H. Kelley, E. Berscheid, A. Christensen, J. H. Harvey, T. L. Huston, G. Levinger, E. McClintock, L. A. Peplau & D. R. Peterson, (eds.), *Close relationships,* pp. 360–96. New York: Freeman.

Roark, M. L. (1987). Preventing violence on college campuses. *Journal of Counseling and Development,* 65:367–71.

Roscoe, B., & Benaske, N. (1985). Courtship violence experienced by abused wives: Similarities in patterns of abuse. *Family Relations,* 34:419–24.

Roscoe, B., & Callahan, J. E. (1985). Adolescents' self-report of violence in families and dating relations. *Adolescence,* 20:545–53.

Rusbult, C. E. (1983). A longitudinal test of the investment model: The development (and deterioration) of satisfaction and commitment in heterosexual involvements. *Journal of Personality and Social Psychology,* 45:101–17.

Scanzoni, J. (1979). Social processes and power in families. In W. R. Burr, R. Hill, F. I. Nye & I. L. Reiss (eds.), *Contemporary theories about the family,* Vol. 1. New York: Free Press.

Simmel, G. (1955). *Conflict and the web of group affiliations.* New York: Free Press.

Sprey, J. (1979). Conflict theory and the study of marriage and the family. In W. R. Burr, R. Hill, F. I. Nye & I. L. Reiss (eds.), *Contemporary theories about the family,* Vol. 2, pp. 130–59. New York: Free Press.

Stets, J. E. (1988). *Domestic violence and control.* New York: Springer-Verlag.

Stets, J. E., & Pirog-Good, M. A. (1987). Violence in dating relationships. *Social Psychology Quarterly,* 50:237–46.

Straus, M. A. (1979). Measuring intrafamily conflict and violence: The conflict tactics (CT) scales. *Journal of Marriage and the Family,* 41:75–90.

Straus, M. A., Gelles, R., & Steinmetz, S. (1980). *Behind closed doors.* Garden City, NY: Anchor.

Straus, M. A., & Steinmetz, S. K. (1974). Violence research, violence control and the good society. In S. K. Steinmetz & M. A. Straus (eds.), *Violence in the family*, pp. 321–24. New York: Harper & Row.

Strube, M. J., & Barbour, L. S. (1984). Factors related to the decision to leave an abusive relationship. *Journal of Marriage and the Family*, 46:837–44.

Surra, C. A. (1987). Reasons for changes in commitment: Variations by courtship type. *Journal of Social and Personal Relationships*, 4:17–34.

Szinovacz, M. E. (1983). Using couple data as a methodological tool: The case of marital violence. *Journal of Marriage and the Family*, 45:633–44.

Thibaut, J. W., & Kelley, H. H. (1959). *The social psychology of groups*. New York: Wiley.

Yllo, K., & Straus, M. A. (1981). Interpersonal violence among married and cohabiting couples. *Family Relations*, 30:339–47.

II Sexual Abuse in Dating Relationships

8   Hidden Rape: Sexual Aggression and Victimization in a National Sample of Students in Higher Education
Mary P. Koss

> You better not never tell nobody but God. It'd kill your mammy.
>
> (Walker, 1982: 1)

Officially, 87,340 rapes occurred in 1985 (FBI, 1986). However, this number greatly underestimates the true scope of rape, since it includes only instances that were reported to the police. Because many victims never tell even their closest friends and family about their rape (Koss, 1985), it is unrealistic to expect that they would report the crime to the police. Government estimates suggest that for every rape reported to police, 3–10 rapes are not reported (LEAA, 1975).

Victimization studies such as the annual National Crime Survey (NCS) are the major avenue through which the full extent of crime is estimated (for example, BJS, 1984). In these studies, the residents of a standard sampling area are asked to indicate those crimes of which they or any other household members have been victims during the previous six months. The survey results are then compared with the number of reported crimes in the area, and the rate of unreported crime is estimated. On the basis of such research, the authors of the NCS have observed rape is an infrequent crime (LEAA, 1974:12) and is the most rare of NCS-measured violent offenses (BJS, 1984:5). Women's chances of being raped have been described as a small fraction of 1 percent (Katz and Mazur, 1979).

However, the accuracy of these conclusions and the validity of the research on which they are based must be examined closely, as the perceived severity of rape influences the social and economic priority it is accorded.

Several features of the NCS approach (for example, BJS, 1984) may lead to the underreporting of rape, including the use of a screening question that requires the subject to infer the focus of inquiry, the use of questions about rape that are embedded in a context of violent crime, and the assumption that the term *rape* is used by victims of sexual assault to conceptualize their experiences.

In an effort to extend previous research on rape (for example, Koss and Oros, 1982; Koss, 1985) to a national sample, the *Ms.* Magazine Project on Campus Sexual Assault was undertaken. Because the FBI definition of rape (used in victimization studies such as the NCS) limits the crime to female victims (BJS, 1984) and because women represent virtually 100 percent of reported rape victims (LEAA, 1975), the project focused on women victims and male perpetrators.

PREVIOUS RESEARCH

Several recently reported estimates of the prevalence of sexual victimization have been reported that were based on studies designed specifically to gauge the extent of sexual assault. Kilpatrick and colleagues (Kilpatrick, Veronen & Best, 1984; Kilpatrick et al., 1985) conducted a victimization survey via telephone of 2,004 randomly selected female residents of Charleston County, South Carolina. In the sample, 14.5 percent of the women disclosed one or more attempted or completed sexual assault experiences, including 5 percent who had been victims of rape and 4 percent who had been victims of attempted rape. Of the women who had been raped, only 29 percent reported their assault to police. Russell found that 24 percent of a probability sample of 930 adult women residents of San Francisco described experiences that involved "forced intercourse or intercourse obtained by physical threat(s) or intercourse completed when the woman was drugged, unconscious, asleep, or otherwise totally helpless and unable to consent" (Russell, 1984:35). Only 9.5 percent of these women reported their experience to police.

Many studies of the prevalence of rape and lesser forms of sexual aggression have involved college students however. There are scientific as well as pragmatic reasons to study this group. College students are a high risk group for rape because they are in the same age range as the bulk of rape victims and offenders. The victimization rate for females peaks in the 16–19 year age group, and the second highest rate occurs in the 20–24 year age group. These rates are approximately four times higher than the mean for all women (BJS, 1984). In addition, 47 percent of all alleged rapists who are arrested are individuals under age 25 (FBI, 1986). Approximately 25 percent of all individuals aged 18–24 are attending school (U.S. Bureau of Census, 1980). Finally, a substantial proportion of rape prevention efforts take place under the auspices of educational institutions and are targeted at students.

Kanin and his associates (Kanin, 1957; Kilpatrick and Kanin, 1957; Kanin and Parcell, 1977) found that 20–25 percent of college women reported forceful attempts by their dates at sexual intercourse, during which the women ended up screaming, fighting, crying, or pleading and that 26 percent of college men reported making a forceful attempt at sexual intercourse that caused observable distress and offense in the women. Rapaport and Burkhart (1984) reported that 15 percent of a sample of college men acknowledged that they had obtained sexual intercourse against their dates' will. Koss and colleagues (Koss, 1985; Koss and Oros, 1982; Koss et al., 1985) administered the self-report sexual experiences survey to a sample of 2,016 female and 1,846 male midwestern university students. They found that 13 percent of the women experienced a victimization that involved sexual intercourse as a result of actual force or threat of harm, and 5 percent of the men admitted perpetrating an act of sexual aggression that met legal definitions of rape.

All of these prevalence studies suggest that rape is far more extensive than reported in official statistics. However, reported prevalence rates for rape vary from 5 percent (Kilpatrick et al., 1985) to 20–25 percent (Kanin, 1957; Russell, 1984). Unfortunately these different figures are not easy to reconcile, as the studies involved both relatively small and geographically diverse samples and different data collection techniques.

METHODS

The *Ms*. Magazine Project on Campus Sexual Assault involved administration of a self-report questionnaire to a sample of 6,159 students enrolled in 32 institutions of higher education across the United States. The following is an overview of the project's methodology, described more fully elsewhere (Koss, Gidycz, & Wisniewski, 1987).

Sampling Procedures

The sampling goals of the project were to represent the universe of the U.S. college student population. No sample design could be expected to result in a purely random or representative sample, as the subject of rape is sufficiently controversial that some schools targeted by a systematic sampling plan can be expected to refuse to participate.

On the basis of enrollment-characteristics data maintained by the U.S. Department of Education (Office of Civil Rights, 1980), the nation's 3,269 higher education institutions were sorted by location into ten regions (Alaska, Hawaii, New England, Mideast, Great Lakes, Plains states, Southeast, Southwest, Rocky Mountain, and West). Within each region, institutions were placed into homogeneous clusters according to five criteria: (1) location inside or outside a standard metropolitan statistical area (SMSA) of certain sizes; (2) enrollment of minority students above or below the national mean percentage; (3) control of the institution by private secular, private religious, or public authority; (4) type of institution, including university, other four-year college, two-year junior college, and technical/vocational institution; and (5) total enrollment within three levels. Every xth cluster was sampled according to the proportion of total enrollment accounted for by the region. Replacements were sought from among other schools in the homogeneous cluster if the original school proved uncooperative.

The amount of time required to obtain a sample of cooperating institutions was extended; some schools required 15 months to arrive at a final decision. During that period, 93 schools were contacted and 32 institutional participants were obtained. Of the institutions, 19 were first choices; the remaining 13 were solicitated from among 43 replacements. The institutional participants were guaranteed anonymity.

A random selection process based on each institution's catalogue of course offerings was used to choose target classes and alternates. The questionnaire was administered in classroom settings by one of eight postmaster's level psychologists: the two men and six women used a prepared script and were trained to handle potential untoward effects of participation. The anonymous questionnaire was accompanied by a cover sheet that contained all the elements of informed consent. Only 91 persons (1.5 percent) indicated that they did not wish to participate.

Subjects

The final sample consisted of 6,159 students: 3,187 females and 2,972 males. The female participants were characterized as follows: mean age = 21.4 years; 85 percent single, 11 percent married, 4 percent divorced; 86 percent white, 7 percent black, 3 percent Hispanic, 3 percent Asian, and 1 percent native American; 39 percent Catholic, 38 percent Protestant, 4 percent Jewish, 20 percent other or no religion. The male participants were characterized as follows: mean age = 21.0 years; 90 percent single, 9 percent married, 1 percent divorced; 86 percent white, 6 percent black, 3 percent Hispanic, 4 percent Asian, 1 percent native American; 40 percent Catholic, 34 percent Protestant, 5 percent Jewish, and 22 percent other or no religion.

Because of the assumptions on which the sampling plan was based and the hesitancy of many institutions to participate, the sample is not completely representative. Four variables were examined to determine the sample's representativeness: (1) institution location, (2) institution region, (3) subject ethnicity, and (4) subject income. Region in which the institutions were located was the only variable on which significant discrepancy was noted. The regional disproportion is unimportant in many respects, as even without extensive sampling in the West, the individual participants in the sample were still reflective of national enrollment in terms of ethnicity and family income. Nevertheless, for purposes of calculating prevalence data, weighting factors were used.

Survey Instrument

The data on the incidence and prevalence of sexual aggression were obtained through the use of the ten-item sexual experiences survey (Koss and Oros, 1982; Koss and Gidycz, 1985). This survey is a self-report instrument designed to reflect various degrees of sexual aggression and victimization. During survey administration, separate wordings were used for women and for men. The text of all ten items (female wording) can be found in Table 8.1. Descriptive data were obtained through the use of close-ended questions administered subsequent to the survey. The survey booklet instructed all respondents who described any level of experience with sexual aggression or victimization to turn to a section of questions about the characteristics of the most serious incident in which they were involved.

Many investigators have questioned the validity of self-reported sexual behavior. The accuracy and truthfulness of self-reports on the sexual experiences survey have been investigated (Koss and Gidycz, 1985), and significant correlations were found between a woman's level of victimization based on self-report and her level of victimization based responses related to an interviewer several months later ($r = .73$, $p < .001$). Most importantly, only 3 percent of the women (2/68) who reported experiences that met legal definitions of rape were judged to have misinterpreted questions or to have given answers that appeared to be false. Men's levels of aggression as described on self-report and reported to an interviewer were also significantly correlated ($r = .61$, $p < .001$).

A further validity study was conducted in conjunction with the *Ms.* project. Because previous work had raised more questions about the validity of males' responses than about females' responses, male students were selected as subjects. The sexual experiences survey items were administered both by self-report and by one-to-one interview on the same occasion and in one setting. The interviewer was a fully trained, licensed, and experienced male Ph.D. clinical psychologist. Subjects were 15 male volunteers, identified by first name only, recruited through newspaper advertisements on the campus of a major university. Participants gave their self-reports first and then were interviewed individually. The results indicated that 14 of the participants (93 percent) gave the same responses to the survey items on self-report and in the interviews.

Scoring Procedures

The groups labeled "rape" (yes responses to items 8, 9, and/or 10 and any lower-numbered items) and "attempted rape" (yes responses to items 4 and/or 5 but not to any higher-numbered items) included individuals whose experiences met broad legal definitions of these crimes. The legal definitions of rape

Table 8.1
Frequency of Individual Sexual Experiences Reported by Postsecondary Students: Prevalence since Age 14

Sexual Behavior	Women			Men		
	%	M	SD	%	M	SD
1. Have you given in to sex play (fondling, kissing, or petting, but not intercourse) when you didn't want to because you were overwhelmed by a man's continual arguments and pressure?	44	3.2	1.5	19	2.9	1.5
2. Have you had sex play (fondling, kissing, or petting, but not intercourse) when you didn't want to because a man used his position of authority (boss, teacher, camp counselor, supervisor) to make you?	5	2.7	1.7	1	2.5	1.5
3. Have you had sex play (fondling, kissing, or petting, but not intercourse) when you didn't want to because a man threatened or used some degree of physical force (twisting your arm, holding you down, etc.) to make you?	13	2.1	1.5	2	2.3	1.5
4. Have you had a man attempt sexual intercourse (get on top, attempt to insert his penis) when you didn't want to by threatening or using some degree of force (twisting your arm, holding you down, etc.) but intercourse did not occur?	15	2.0	1.4	2	2.0	1.2
5. Have you had a man attempt sexual intercourse (get on top, attempt to insert his penis) when you didn't want to by giving you alcohol or drugs, but intercourse did not occur?	12	2.0	1.4	5	2.2	1.4
6. Have you given into sexual intercourse when you didn't want to because you were overwhelmed by a man's continual arguments and pressure?	25	2.9	1.6	10	2.4	1.4
7. Have you had sexual intercourse when you didn't want to because a man used his position of authority (boss, teacher, camp counselor, supervisor) to make you?	2	2.5	1.7	1	2.0	1.4
8. Have you had sexual intercourse when you didn't want to because a man gave you alcohol or drugs?	8	2.2	1.5	4	2.5	1.5
9. Have you had sexual intercourse when you didn't want to because a man threatened or used some degree of physical force (twisting your arm, holding you down, etc.) to make you?	9	2.2	1.5	1	2.3	1.5
10. Have you had sexual acts (anal or oral intercourse or penetration by objects other than the penis) when you didn't want to because a man threatened or used some degree of physical force (twisting your arm, holding you down, etc.) to make you?	6	2.2	1.6	1	2.5	1.5

The sample size was 3,187 women and 2,972 men. All questions were prefaced with instructions to refer to experiences "from age 14 on." Sexual intercourse was defined as "penetration of a woman's vagina, no matter how slightly, by a man's penis. Ejaculation is not required."

in Ohio (*Ohio Revised Code*, 1980, 2907.01A, 2907.02), similar to that in many states, is the following:

Vaginal intercourse between male and female, and anal intercourse, fellatio, and cunnilingus between persons regardless of sex. Penetration, however slight, is sufficient to complete vaginal or anal intercourse. . . . No person shall engage in sexual conduct with another person . . . when any of the following apply: (1) the offender purposely compels the other person to submit by force or threat of force, (2) for the purpose of preventing resistance the offender substantially impairs the other person's judgment or control by administering any drug or intoxicant to the other person.

The group labeled "sexual coercion" (yes responses to items 6 and/or 7 but not to any higher-numbered items) included subjects who engaged in/experienced sexual intercourse subsequent to the use of menacing verbal pressure or misuse of authority. No threats of force or direct physical force were used. The group labeled "sexual contact" (yes responses to items 1, 2, and/or 3 but not to any higher-numbered items) consisted of individuals who had engaged in/experienced sexual behavior (such as fondling or kissing) that did not involve attempted penetration, subsequent to the use of menacing verbal pressure, misuse of authority, threats of harm, or actual physical force.

RESULTS

Prevalence of Sexual Aggression/Victimization

Prevalence rates indicate the total number of persons who report experiences with sexual aggression or victimization during a specified time period, which in this study was since the age of 14. The unweighted response frequencies for each item of the Sexual Experiences Survey are presented in Table 8.1. The frequencies of victimization ranged from 44 percent (women who reported having experienced unwanted sexual contact subsequent to coercion) to 2 percent (women who reported having experienced unwanted sexual intercourse subsequent to the offender's misuse of authority). The frequency with which men reported having perpetrated each form of sexual aggression ranged from the 19 percent who said that they had obtained sexual contact through the use of coercion to the 1 percent who indicated that they had obtained oral or anal penetration through the use of force. Those respondents who had engaged in/experienced sexually aggressive acts indicated that each act had occurred a mean of 2.0–3.2 times since age 14.

However, the data on the individual sexually aggressive acts are difficult to interpret, because persons may have engaged in/experienced several different sexually aggressive acts. Therefore, respondents were classified according to the highest degree of sexual victimization/aggression they reported (see Table 8.2). With weighted data correcting for regional disproportions, 46.3 percent of women respondents revealed no experiences whatsoever with sexual victim-

Table 8.2
Prevalence Rates for Five Levels of Sexual Aggression and Sexual Victimization

Sexual Aggression/Victimization (Highest Level Reported)	Women (%)		Men (%)	
	Weighted	Unweighted	Weighted	Unweighted
No sexual aggression/victimization	46.3	45.6	74.8	75.6
Sexual contact	14.4	14.9	10.2	9.8
Sexual coercion	11.9	11.6	7.2	6.9
Attempted rape	12.1	12.1	3.3	3.2
Rape	15.4	15.8	4.4	4.6

The sample size was 3,187 women and 2,972 men. Prevalence rates cover sexual experiences since age 14.

ization, while 53.7 percent of female respondents indicated some form of sexual victimization. The most serious sexual victimization ever experienced was sexual contact for 14.4 percent of the women, sexual coercion for 11.9 percent of the women, attempted rape for 12.1 percent of the women, and rape for 15.4 percent of the women. Weighted data for males indicated that 74.8 percent of men had engaged in no forms of sexual aggression, whereas 25.1 percent of the men revealed involvement in some form of sexual aggression. The most extreme level of sexual aggression perpetrated was sexual contact for 10.2 percent of the men, sexual coercion for 7.2 percent of the men, attempted rape for 3.3 percent of the men, and rape for 4.4 percent of the men. Examination of these figures reveals that the effect of weighting was minimal and tended to reduce slightly the prevalence of the most serious acts of sexual aggression.

The relationship of prevalence rates to the institutional parameters used to design the sample was examined via chi-square and analysis of variance (ANOVA). Due to the large sample size, differences that have no real practical significance could reach statistical significance. Therefore, effect sizes were calculated using Cohen's method (w for chi-square and f for F) to gauge the importance of any significant differences (1977). Cohen's guidelines for interpretation of effect sizes are the following: a w or f of 0.1 indicates a small effect, a w of 0.3 or an f of 0.25 indicates a medium effect, and a w of 0.5 and an f of 0.4 indicates a large effect. The prevalence of sexual victimization as reported by women did not differ according to the size of the city where the institution of higher education was located [X^2 (8, N = 2,728) = 5.55, p < .697, w = .05], the size of the institution [X^2 (8, N = 2,728) = 6.35, p < .608, w = .05], the type of institution [X^2 (8, N = 3,086) = 10.37, p < .240, w = .05], or whether the minority enrollment of the institution was above or below the national mean [X^2 (4, N = 2,728) = 4.03, p < .401, w = .04]. However, rates of sexual victimization did vary by region [X^2 (28, N = 3,086) = 63.00, p < .001, w = .14] and by the governance of the institution [X^2 (8, N = 3,086) = 22.93, p < .003, w = .09]. The rate at which women reported having been raped was twice as high in private colleges (14 percent) and major universities (17 percent) as it was at religiously affiliated institutions (7 percent). Victimization rates were also slightly higher in the Great Lakes and Plains states than in other regions.

The prevalence of reported sexual aggression by men also did not differ according to city size [X^2 (8, N = 2,641) = 6.41, p < .600, w = .05], institution size [X^2 (8, N = 2,641) = 3.76, p < .878, w = .04], minority enrollment [X^2 (4, N = 2,641) = 4.84, p < .303, w = .04], governance [X^2 (8, N = 2,875) = 13.66, p < .091, w = .07], and type of institution [X^2 (8, N = 2,875) = 3.99, p < .858, w = .04]. However, the percentage of men who admitted perpetrating sexual aggression did vary according to the region of the country in which they attended school [X^2(28, N = 2,875) = 56.25, p < .001, w = .14]. Men in the Southeast admitted rape twice as often (6 percent) as in the Plains states (3 percent) and three times as often as in the West (2 percent).

Finally, the relationships between the prevalence rates and individual subject demographic variables were also studies and included income, religion, and ethnicity. The rate at which women reported experiences of sexual victimization did not vary according to subject's family income [$F(4, 3,010) = .31$, $p < .871, f = .06$] or religion [$X^2(16, N = 3,077) = 17.86, p < .332, w = .08$]. The prevalence rates of victimization did vary according to ethnicity [$X^2(16, N = 3,075) = 37.05, p < .002, w = .11$]. For example, rape was reported by 16 percent of white women ($N = 2,655$), 10 percent of black women ($N = 215$), 12 percent of Hispanic women ($N = 106$), 7 percent of Asian women ($N = 79$), and 40 percent of Native American women ($N = 20$).

The number of men who admitted acts of sexual aggression did not vary according to subject's religion [$X^2 (16, N = 2,856) = 20.98, p < .179, w = .09$] or family income [$F(3, 2,821) = .08, p < .987$)]. However, the number of men who reported acts of sexual aggression did differ by ethnic group [$X^2(16, N = 2,861) = 55.55, p < .001, w = .14$]. For example, rape was reported by 4 percent of white men ($N = 2,484$), 10 percent of black men ($N = 162$), 7 percent of Hispanic men ($N = 93$), 2 percent of Asian men ($N = 106$), and 0 percent of native American men ($N = 16$).

Incidence of Sexual Aggression/Victimization

Incidence rates indicate how many new episodes of an event occurred during a specific time period. In this study, respondents were asked to indicate how many times during the previous year they had engaged in/experienced each item listed in the survey. To improve recall, the question referred to the previous academic year (from September to September), time boundaries that are meaningful to students. Some subjects reported multiple episodes of sexual aggression/victimization during the previous year. Therefore, the incidence of sexual aggression/victimization was calculated in two ways. First, the number of people who reported one or more episodes during the year was determined. Second, the total number of sexually aggressive incidents that were reported by women and by men was calculated.

The incidence rate for rape during a 12-month period was found to be 353 rapes involving 207 different women in a population of 3,187 women. Comparable figures for the other levels of sexual victimization were 533 attempted rapes (323 victims), 837 episodes of sexual coercion (366 victims), and 2,024 experiences of unwanted sexual contact (886 victims). The incidence data for the individual items used to calculate these rates are found in Table 8.3.

Incidence rates for the sexual aggression admitted by men also were calculated. Responses to the three items that characterize rape for the 12-month period preceding the survey indicate that 187 rapes were perpetrated by 96 different men. Comparable incidence rates during a 12-month period for the

Table 8.3
Frequency of Individual Sexual Experiences Reported by Postsecondary Students: One-Year's Incidence

Sexual Experience	Women		Men	
	Victims	Incidents	Perpetrators	Incidents
Sexual contact by verbal coercion	725	1716	321	732
Sexual contact by misuse of authority	50	97	23	55
Sexual contact by threat or force	111	211	30	67
Attempted intercourse by force	180	297	33	52
Attempted intercourse by alcohol/drugs	143	236	72	115
Intercourse by verbal coercion	353	816	156	291
Intercourse by misuse of authority	13	21	11	20
Intercourse by alcohol/drugs	91	159	57	103
Intercourse by threat or force	63	98	20	36
Oral/anal penetration by threat or force	53	96	19	48

The sample size was 3,187 women and 2,972 men.

other levels of sexual aggression were 167 attempted rapes (105 perpetrators), 854 episodes of unwanted sexual contact (374 perpetrators), and 311 situations of sexual coercion (167 perpetrators). The incidence data for the individual items that were used to calculate these rates also are presented in Table 8.3.

From these data, victimization rates can be calculated. If the total number of all the women who during the previous year reported a sexual experience that met legal definitions of rape and attempted rape is divided by two (to obtain a six-month basis) and set to a base number of 1,000 women (instead of the 3,187 women actually surveyed), the victimization rate for the surveyed population of women was 83/1,000 women during a six-month period. However, the FBI definition of rape (that is, forcible vaginal intercourse with a female against consent by force or threat of force, including attempts) on which the NCS is based, is narrower than the state laws (that is; oral, anal, or vaginal intercourse or penetration by objects against consent through threat, force, or intentional incapacitation of the victim via drugs), on which the groupings in this study were based (BJS, 1984). Therefore, the victimization rate was also calculated in conformance with the FBI definition. Elimination of all incidents except those that involved actual or attempted vaginal sexual intercourse through force or threat of harm resulted in a victimization rate of 38/1,000 women during a six-month period.

Perpetration rates were also determined using data from the male subjects. When all unwanted oral, anal, and vaginal intercourse attempts and completions were included in the calculations, a perpetration rate of 34/1,000 men was obtained. Use of the FBI definition resulted in a perpetration rate of 9/1,000 college men during a six-month period.

Descriptive Profile of Sexual Aggression/ Victimization

To develop a profile of the sexual aggression/victimization experiences that were reported by postsecondary students, researchers used inferential statistics descriptively.

Women's Vantage Point. Women were asked detailed questions about the most serious victimization, if any, that they had experienced since the age of 14. These criterion variables were analyzed by chi-square analysis for dichotomous data and ANOVA for continuous data by the five levels of the sexual victimization factor. The results of the ANOVAs with calculated effect sizes are reported in Table 8.4 and the results of the chi-square analyses with calculated effect sizes are reported in Table 8.5.

From the data in these tables, the following profile of the rapes reported by women students emerges. (All items were scored on a 1 [not at all] to 5 [very much] scale unless otherwise indicated.) The victimizations happened 1–2 years ago when the women were 18–19 years old ($M = 18.5$); 95 percent of the assaults involved one offender only; 84 percent involved an offender who was known to the victim; 57 percent of offenders were dates. The rapes happened primarily off campus (86 percent), equally as often in the man's house or car as in the woman's house or car. Most offenders (73 percent) were thought to be drinking or using drugs at the time of the assault, while the victim admitted using intoxicants in 55 percent of the episodes. Prior mutual intimacy had occurred with the offender to the level of petting above the waist ($M = 3.52$ on a 1–6 scale). However, the victims believed that they had made their nonconsent to have sexual intercourse "quite" clear ($M = 4.05$). Typically, the victim perceived that the offender used "quite a bit" of force ($M = 3.88$), which involved twisting her arm or holding her down. Only 9 percent of the rapes involved hitting or beating, and only 5 percent involved weapons. Women rated their amount of resistance as moderate ($M = 3.80$). Forms of resistance used by many rape victims included reasoning (84 percent) and physically struggling (70 percent). Many women (41 percent) were virgins at the time of their rape. During the rape, victims felt scared ($M = 3.66$), angry ($M = 3.97$), and depressed ($M = 3.93$). Rape victims felt somewhat responsible ($M = 2.80$) for what had happened, but believed that the man was much more responsible ($M = 4.29$).

Almost half of victimized women (42 percent) told no one about their assault. Just 8 percent of the victims who told anyone reported to police (equivalent to 5 percent of all rape victims), and only 8 percent of the victims who told anyone visited a crisis center (again equivalent to 5 percent of all rape victims). Those who reported to police rated the reaction they received as "not at all supportive" ($M = 1.02$). In contrast, family ($M = 3.70$) and campus agency ($M = 4.00$) reaction were seen as supportive.

Surprisingly, 42 percent of the women indicated that they had sex again with the offender on a later occasion, but it is not know if this was forced or voluntary; most relationships (87 percent) did eventually break up subsequent to the victimization. Many rape victims (41 percent) stated that they expected a similar assault to happen again in the future, and only 27 percent of the women whose experience met legal definitions of rape labeled themselves as rape victims.

Although these analyses demonstrated statistically significant differences between the situational characteristics of the rapes reported by women compared with the lesser degrees of sexual victimization, the effect sizes of these differences were generally small. Thus, the descriptive profile of the rapes reported by college women is applicable to a great extent to the lesser degrees of sexual victimization as well. With the effect sizes for guidance, the following large and important differences between rapes and other forms of sexual victimization can be noted. Rapes were less likely to involve dating partners than other forms of sexual victimization. While 70–86 percent of lesser forms of victimization involved dating couples, only 57 percent of the rapes did. Men who raped were perceived by the victims as more often drinking (73 percent) than men who engaged in lesser degrees of sexual aggression (35–64 percent). Rapes, as well as attempted rapes, were more violent. More than half of rape victims

Table 8.4
Descriptive Characteristics of Sexual Victimizations Reported by Women: Continuous Criterion Variables

Variable	Level of Sexual Victimization (Mean Response)				F	p	f
	Sexual Contact	Sexual Coercion	Attempted Rape	Rape			
How well known	3.40^a	3.88^{abc}	3.29^b	3.19^c	25.67	.000	.05
How many times	2.05^{ae}	2.50^{abc}	1.70^{bd}	2.02^{cde}	17.49	.000	.03
Age at assault	17.27^{ab}	19.00^{bc}	17.92^c	18.51^a	15.89	.000	.03
How long ago	3.79^a	3.87^b	3.81^c	4.28^{abc}	9.66	.000	.02
Prior intimacy	2.71^{ade}	4.06^{abc}	3.30^{bd}	3.52^{ce}	29.23	.000	.06
Clarity nonconsent	3.93^a	3.52^{abc}	4.07^b	4.05^c	16.15	.000	.03
Perceived violence	3.11^a	3.10^{ab}	3.31^c	3.88^{abc}	48.86	.000	.09
Degree of resistance	3.43^{ab}	3.12^{ace}	3.79^{bc}	3.80^{de}	31.49	.000	.06
Impact of resistance	2.06^{ad}	2.46^{bde}	1.86^{ce}	2.99^{abc}	108.98	.000	.19
Emotions: scared	2.80^{ac}	2.73^b	2.99^c	3.66^{abc}	40.01	.000	.08
angry	3.08^{ad}	3.17^{abe}	3.47^{cde}	3.97^{abc}	36.07	.000	.07
depressed	3.14^{ad}	3.33^{bd}	3.19^c	3.93^{abc}	36.49	.000	.07
Responsible: woman	2.76^a	3.27	2.78^b	2.80^c	14.75	.000	.03
man	3.86^a	3.90^b	4.03^c	4.29^{abc}	15.51	.000	.03
Family reaction	4.09^a	4.07	3.97	3.70^a	3.84	.010	.02
Police reaction	1.02	1.01	1.01	1.02	.37	.776	.00
Campus reaction	3.60	4.50	3.50	4.00	.34	.777	.05

Means are significantly different from any other means that share a common superscript (p<.05).

Table 8.5
Descriptive Characteristics of Sexual Victimizations Reported by Women: Dichotomous Variables

Variable	Sexual Contact	Sexual Coercion	Attempted Rape	Rape	v^2	N	df	p	w
			Level of Sexual Victimization % Responding "Yes"						
One man involved	99	99	97	95	19.95	1485	6	.003	.12
Perpetrator was date	71	86	70	57	132.42	1484	12	.000	.30
Party or group context	42	40	48	55	68.68	1475	9	.000	.22
Happened on male turf	52	52	53	50	35.50	1464	6	.001	.16
Happened off campus	84	86	82	86	3.33	1455	3	.344	.05
Man lives apt/home	53	64	54	73	100.59	3079	9	.000	.18
Man alcohol/drugs	35	64	54	73	138.56	1471	6	.000	.31
Woman alcohol/drugs	29	31	58	55	100.23	1476	6	.000	.26
Force used: held down	8	9	41	64	292.52	1449	3	.000	.45
hit	2	1	2	9	88.77	1407	3	.000	.25
weapon	1	0	1	5	29.56	1396	3	.000	.15
Resistance: reason	65	71	81	84	44.95	1378	3	.000	.18
struggle	33	26	52	70	162.50	1288	3	.000	.36
Woman was virgin	79	43	60	41	130.95	1466	3	.000	.30
Told anyone	47	42	58	58	28.49	1456	3	.000	.14
Visited a crisis center	1	2	3	8	18.05	800	3	.000	.15
Reported to police	2	1	3	8	17.68	794	3	.000	.15
Used a campus agency	2	0	1	2	3.49	1229	3	.000	.05
Sex with man since	37	48	35	42	13.77	1448	3	.003	.10
Ended relationship	79	73	82	87	24.87	1363	3	.000	.14
Expect it again	36	33	37	41	5.12	1415	3	.163	.06
It was definitely rape	1	3	3	27	285.00	1434	9	.000	.45

(64 percent) and attempted rape victims (41 percent) reported that the offender used actual violence, such as holding them down, while fewer than 10 percent of other victims reported actual force. Likewise, the use of physical resistance was reported by many more victims of rape (70 percent) and attempted rape (52 percent) than by victims of lesser degrees of sexual assault (26–33 percent). Finally, rape victims (27 percent) were much more likely than any other group (1–3 percent) to see their experience as rape.

Men's Vantage Point. Men were asked detailed questions about the most serious sexual aggression, if any, that they had perpetrated since the age of 14. These criterion variables also were analyzed by chi-square analysis for dichotomous data and ANOVA for continuous data by the five levels of the sexual aggression factor. The results of the ANOVAs with post hoc tests and calculated effect sizes are reported in Table 8.6, and the results of the chi-square analyses with calculated effect sizes are reported in Table 8.7.

With these data, characteristics of the rapes perpetrated by college men can be determined. The rapes happened 1–2 two years ago when the men were 18–19 years old ($M = 18.5$); 84 percent of the assaults involved one offender only; 84 percent involved an offender who was known to the victim; 61 percent of offenders were dates. The rapes happened primarily off campus (86 percent), equally as often in the man's house or car as in the woman's house or car. Most men who raped (74 percent) said they were drinking or using drugs at the time of the assault, and most (75 percent) perceived that their victims were using intoxicants as well. Men believed that mutual intimacy had occurred with the victim to the level of petting below the waist ($M = 4.37$), and they felt that the victim's nonconsent to have sexual intercourse was "not at all" clear ($M = 1.80$).

Typically, men who raped perceived that they were "somewhat" forceful ($M = 2.85$) and admitted twisting the victim's arm or holding her down. Only 3 percent of the perpetrators of rape said that they hit or beat the victim, and only 4 percent used weapons. They perceived victims' resistance as minimal ($M = 1.83$). Forms of resistance that assailants observed included reasoning, which was used by 36 percent of the rape victims, and physically struggling, which was used by 12 percent. Few men (12 percent) were virgins at the time they forced a woman to have sexual intercourse.

During the assault, offenders felt minimal negative emotions, including feeling scared ($M = 1.52$), angry ($M = 1.45$), or depressed ($M = 1.59$). Instead, perpetrators of rape were more likely to feel proud ($M = 2.27$). Although they felt mildly responsible ($M = 2.43$) for what had happened, rapists believed that the woman was equally or more responsible ($M = 2.85$). Half of the men who reported an act that met legal definitions of rape (54 percent) told no one at all about their assault, and only 2 percent of them were reported to police by the victim. Among the men, 55 percent indicated that after the assault they had had sex with the victim again, but it is not known if this was forced or voluntary. A substantial number of men who raped (47 percent) stated that they

Table 8.6
Descriptive Characteristics of Sexual Victimizations Reported by Men: Continuous Criterion Variables

Variable	Sexual Contact	Sexual Coercion	Attempted Rape	Rape	F	p	f
			Level of Sexual Victimization (Mean Response)				
How well known	3.67a	3.69b	3.27	3.20ab	7.03	.001	.17
How many times	2.20	2.29	1.90	2.29	1.54	.203	.10
Age at assault	17.87	18.70	18.36	18.49	2.50	.058	.10
How long ago	4.06	3.78	3.85	3.69	1.20	.310	.10
Prior intimacy	3.51a	4.18ab	3.56c	4.37bc	8.15	.000	.20
Clarity nonconsent	2.25a	2.15	2.06	1.80a	4.30	.005	.14
Perceived violence	2.45a	2.59	2.84	2.85a	4.52	.004	.14
Degree of resistance	2.01	1.87	2.11	1.83bc	2.17	.091	.10
Impact of resistance	2.21b	2.34a	1.92ac	2.59	7.93	.000	.20
Emotions: scared	1.56	1.51	1.44	1.52	.34	.794	.20
angry	1.40	1.39	1.53	1.45	.51	.673	.00
depressed	1.79	1.72	1.71	1.59	.78	.506	.00
proud	1.76a	1.83b	1.97	2.27ab	4.10	.007	.14
Responsible: woman	2.56	2.92	3.00	2.85	3.71	.012	.14
man	2.81	2.94a	2.76	2.43a	3.90	.009	.15
Partners since	1.56a	2.32b	2.01	2.53ab	10.24	.000	.23

Means are significantly different from any other means that share a common superscript (p<.05).

Table 8.7
Descriptive Characteristics of Sexual Aggressive Acts Reported by Men: Dichotomous Variables

Variable	Level of Sexual Victimization % Responding "Yes"				v^2	N	df	p	w
	Sexual Contact	Sexual Coercion	Attempted Rape	Rape					
One man involved	92	95	90	84	19.43	608	9	.022	.18
Victim was date	71	77	63	61	38.35	599	12	.001	.25
Party or group context	46	39	39	49	28.68	587	9	.000	.22
Happened on male turf	39	54	41	41	21.92	588	6	.039	.19
Happened off campus	86	86	77	86	4.41	580	3	.220	.09
Man lives apt/home	62	72	58	69	26.75	2868	9	.008	.10
Man alcohol/drugs	33	35	67	74	75.65	590	6	.000	.36
Woman alcohol/drugs	31	35	65	75	82.21	591	6	.000	.37
Force used: held down	7	1	12	17	27.86	582	3	.000	.22
hit	0	1	0	3	11.26	573	3	.000	.14
weapon	0	1	0	4	15.23	572	3	.000	.16
Resistance: reason	42	35	44	36	2.91	526	3	.405	.08
struggle	4	1	15	12	23.46	498	3	.000	.22
Man was virgin	48	24	33	12	34.01	588	3	.001	.24
Told anyone	34	37	47	46	6.78	588	3	.079	.11
Reported to police	2	1	1	2	.16	555	3	.983	.02
Sex with woman since	37	64	32	55	38.64	563	3	.000	.27
Expect it again	28	29	38	47	14.46	549	3	.002	.16
Definitely was not rape	96	94	90	88	15.04	566	9	.089	.16

expected to engage in a similar assault at some point. Most men (88 percent) who reported an assault that met legal definitions of rape were adamant that their behavior was definitely not rape.

Although these analyses demonstrated statistically significant differences between the assault characteristics reported by men who raped compared with men who perpetrated lesser degrees of sexual aggression, the effect sizes of these differences were generally small. Thus, the descriptive profile of the rapes reported by male college students generally is applicable to the lesser degrees of sexual aggression as well. With the effect sizes for guidance, the following large and important differences between rapes and other forms of sexual aggression can be noted. Men who raped were more often drinking (74 percent) than men who engaged in lesser degrees of sexual aggression (33–67%). They perceived that the victim was drinking (75 percent) more often than did men who perpetrated lesser degrees of sexual aggression (31–65 percent). Men who reported behavior that met legal definitions of rape were less likely to be virgins at the time of their assault (12 percent) than other sexually aggressive men (24–48 percent). Men who perpetrated rape and sexual coercion were more likely to have sex with the victim again (64 percent and 55 percent, respectively) than other perpetrators (32–37 percent). In addition, men who raped reported sexual intercourse with a larger number of partners since the assaultive episode than was reported by less sexually aggressive men.

DISCUSSION

In this study, behaviorally specific items regarding rape and lesser forms of sexual aggression/victimization were presented in a noncrime context to an approximately representative national sample of college students. The results indicate that 15.4 percent of women reported experiencing and 4.4 percent of men reported perpetrating since the age of 14, an act that met legal definitions of rape. Because virtually none of these victims or perpetrators had been involved in the criminal justice system, their experiences qualify as "hidden rape," which is not reflected in official crime statistics such as the *Uniform Crime Reports* (FBI, 1986).

As mentioned earlier, a victimization rate for women of 38/1,000 was calculated. This rate is 10–15 times greater than rates based on the NCS (BJS, 1984), which are 3.9/1,000 for women aged 16–19 and 2.5/1,000 for women aged 20–24. Even men's rate of admission to rape (9/1,000) is two to three times greater than NCS estimates of the high risk of rape for women between the ages of 16 and 24. At least among students in higher education, it appears that official surveys (such as the NCS) fail to describe the full extent of sexual victimization.

However, NCS rates are based on representative samples of all people in the United States who are 16–24 years old, whereas the present sample represents only the 25 percent of people aged 18–24 who attend college. Using other available data for guidance, one can speculate how the victimization rates among postsecondary students might compare with the rates among nonstudents in the same age group. Although the data do not suggest a direct relationship between level of education and rape victimization rates, the rates are related to family income. Thus, nonstudents, who are likely to come from poorer families than students enrolled in higher education, might show even higher incidence rates than those found in the study sample. However, only when empirical data on young persons not attending school become available can the victimization rates reported in the NCS for persons aged 18–24 be fully analyzed.

The characteristics of the rapes described by study respondents differ from the characteristics of rapes described by official statistics (such as BJS, 1984). For example, 60–75 percent of the rapes reported in the NCS by women age 16–24 involved strangers, and 27 percent involved multiple offenders (that is, group rapes). Study respondents, most of whom were between the ages of 18 and 24, did report stranger rapes (16 percent) and group rapes (5 percent), but the vast majority of incidents were individual assaults (95 percent) that involved close acquaintances or dates (84 percent).

The differences between the kinds of rape described in official reports and in this study suggest that it is episodes of intimate violence that differentiate between the results. Either the wording of screening questions or the overall crime context–questioning of the NCS may fail to elicit from respondents the large number of sexual victimizations that involve close acquaintances.

The findings of this study demonstrate that men do not admit enough sexual aggression to account for the number of victimizations reported by women. Specifically, 54 percent of women claimed to be sexually victimized, but only 25 percent of men admitted any degree of sexually aggressive behavior. However, the number of times that men admitted perpetrating each aggressive act is virtually identical to the number of times women reported experiencing each act. Thus, the results fail to support notions that a few sexually active men could account for the victimization of a sizable number of women. Clearly, some of the victimizations reported by college women occurred in earlier years and were not perpetrated by the men who were surveyed. In addition, some recent victimizations may have involved community members who were not attending college. Future research must determine the extent to which these explanations account for the sizable difference in rates.

The data on validity suggest that those sexual experiences reported by the women did, in fact, occur, while additional relevant sexual experiences may not have been reported by men. Men may not be intentionally withholding information, but, rather, may be perceiving and conceptualizing potentially relevant sexual experiences in a way that was not elicited by the wording of the sexual experiences survey. Scully and Marolla (1982) studied incarcerated rapists who denied that the incident for which they were convicted was a rape. Many of these men, although they used physical force and injured their victims, saw their behavior as congruent with consensual sexual activity. It may be that some men fail to perceive accurately the degree of force and coerciveness that was involved in a particular sexual encounter or to interpret correctly a woman's consent or resistance.

This hypothesis is supported by the descriptive differences between men's and women's perceptions of the rape incidents. Although there were many points of agreement between men and women (such as the proportion of incidents that involved alcohol and the relationship of victim and offender), victims saw their nonconsent as clearer and occurring after less consensual intimacy than offenders. Victims perceived their own resistance and the man's violence as much more extreme than the offenders did. Future research might compare consent, violence, and resistance attributions among sexually aggressive and sexually nonaggressive men. If differences were found, the line of inquiry would lead to a new focus for rape prevention programs; educating vulnerable men to perceive accurately and communicate clearly.

The results of the study have additional implications for clinical treatment and research. The extent of sexual victimization uncovered by the national survey suggests that clinicians should consider including questions about unwanted sexual activity in routine intake interviewing of women clients and that they should consider sexual victimization among the possible etiological factors that could be linked to presenting symptoms more frequently. Of course, the study sample consisted of students, whereas many psychotherapy seekers are adults. However, it is not unusual for symptoms of posttraumatic stress disorder, which victims of rape may experience, to emerge months or even years after the trauma (American Psychiatric Association, 1987).

For researchers, these results in combination with the work of others begin to describe the full extent of rape and suggest how reported statistics on rape reflect only those rapes reported to police (5 percent), rapes acknowledged as rape by the victim (27 percent), and those for which victim assistance services are sought (5 percent), rather than reflecting rapes that have not been revealed (42 percent). Future research must address the traumatic cognitive and symptomatic impact of rape on victims who do not report, confide in significant others, seek services, or even identify as victims. It is possible that the quality of many women's lives is reduced by the effects of encapsulated, hidden sexual victimization and the victims' subsequent accommodation to the experience through beliefs and behavior (Koss & Burkhart, in press).

Statistically significant regional and ethnic differences in the prevalence of sexual aggression/victimization were found. Unfortunately, the meaning of these results cannot be fully interpreted, as ethnicity and region were confounded (that is, minority students are not distributed randomly across the regions of the country). However, effect sizes calculated on the variables of region and ethnicity indicate that their impact on prevalence rates is small. In the future, researchers will need to analyze the effect of ethnicity by controlling for region (and vice versa). As a result, other data available on the subjects, including personality characteristics, values, beliefs, and current behavior, can be used to attempt to account for any remaining differences.

Overall, the prevalence rates for sexual victimization/aggression were robust and did not vary extensively from large to small schools; across types of institutions; or among urban areas, medium-sized cities, and rural areas. The ubiquity of sexual aggression and victimization supports Johnson's observation that "the locus of violence rests squarely in the middle of what our culture defines as 'normal' interaction between men and women" (Johnson, 1980: 146). As the editors of the *Morbidity and Mortality Weekly Report,* issued by the Centers for Disease Control (1985) in Atlanta, have noted, there is an ". . . increasing awareness in the public health community that violence is a serious public health problem and that nonfatal interpersonal violence has far-reaching consequences in terms of morbidity and quality of life" (p. 739). Future research needs to devote attention to the preconditions that foster sexual violence.

Within the rape epidemiology literature are studies that have differed in methodology and have reported varying prevalence rates. Although the *Ms.* project involved a set of self-report questions whose validity and reliability have been evaluated, each data-collection method has advantages and disadvantages and cannot be fully assessed without reference to the special requirements of the topic of inquiry, the target population, and practical and financial limitations. Future epidemiological research must define how much variation in rates is due to the method of data collection or the screening question format and how much is due to sample differences. Nevertheless, the most important conclusion suggested by this entire line of research is that rape is much more prevalent than official statistics suggest.

ACKNOWLEDGMENTS

This research was supported by a grant to the author from the Antisocial and Criminal Behavior Branch of the National Institute of Mental Health, MH-31618. To protect the anonymity of the participating institutions, the author cannot thank by name the people across the country who made the study possible; nevertheless, she expresses her appreciation. The author also acknowledges the assistance of Mary Harvey, who stimulated development of the study; Ellen Sweet, of the *MS.* Foundation for Education and Communication, who aided in the administration of the project and lent prestige to the work by allowing the use of the *Ms.* identity on survey materials; Hugh Clark, of Clark/Jones Inc., who supervised the sampling procedures; Ann Maney, of the National Institute of Mental Health, who gave technical advice; Thomas Dinero, who provided statistical consultation; and Chris Gidycz and Nancy Wisniewski, who performed data analyses.

REFERENCES

American Psychiatric Association. (1987). *Diagnostic and Statistical Manual of Mental Disorders.* 4th ed. Washington, DC: American Psychiatric Association.
BJS. Bureau of Justice Statistics. (1984). *Criminal Victimization in the United States, 1982.* Washington, DC: U.S. Department of Justice.

Centers for Disease Control. (1985). Adolescent Sex Offenders—Vermont, 1984. *Morbidity and Mortality Weekly Report* 34:738–741.

Cohen, J. (1977). *Statistical Power Analysis for the Behavioral Sciences*. Rev. ed. New York: Academic.

FBI. Federal Bureau of Investigation. (1986). *Uniform Crime Reports*. Washington, DC: US Department of Justice.

Johnson, A. G. (1980) "On the Prevalence of Rape in the United States." *Signs: Journal of Women in Culture and Society,* 6:136–46.

Kanin, E. J. (1957). "Male Aggression in Dating-Courtship Relations." *American Journal of Sociology* 63:197–204.

Kanin, E. J., and Parcell, S. R. (1977). "Sexual Aggression: A Second Look at the Offended Female." *Archives of Sexual Behavior* 6:67–76.

Katz, S., and Mazur, M. A. (1979). *Understanding the Rape Victim: A Synthesis of Research Findings*. New York: Wiley.

Kilpatrick, D. G., Best, C. L., Veronen, L. J., Amick, A. E., Villeponteaux, L. A., and Ruff, G. A. (1985). "Mental Health Correlates of Criminal Victimization: A Random Community Survey." *Journal of Consulting and Clinical Psychology* 53:866–73.

Kilpatrick, D. G., Veronen, L. J., and Best, C. L. (1984). "Factors Predicting Psychological Distress Among Rape Victims." In *Trauma and Its Wake: The Study and Treatment of Post-traumatic Stress Disorder,* ed. C. R. Figley, 113–41. New York: Brunner/Mazel.

Kirkpatrick, C., and Kanin, E. J. (1957). "Male Sexual Aggression on a University Campus. *American Sociological Review* 22:52–58.

Koss, M. P. (1985). "The Hidden Rape Victim: Personality, Attitudinal, and Situational Characteristics. *Psychology of Women Quarterly* 9:193–212.

Koss, M. P., and Burkhart, B. R. (In press). "The Long-term Impact of Rape: A Conceptual Model and Implications for Treatment." *Psychology of Women Quarterly.*

Koss, M. P., and Gidycz, C. A. (1985). "Sexual Experiences Survey: Reliability and Validity." *Journal of Consulting and Clinical Psychology* 53:422–23.

Koss, M. P., Gidycz, C. J., and Wisniewski, N. (1987). "The Scope of Rape: Incidence and Prevalence of Sexual Aggression and Victimization in a National Sample of Students in Higher Education." *Journal of Consulting and Clinical Psychology,* 55(2):162–70.

Koss, M. P., Leonard, K. E., Beezley, D. A., and Oros, C. J. (1985). "Nonstranger Sexual Aggression: A Discriminant Analysis of the Psychological Characteristics of Undetected Offenders." *Sex Roles,* 12:981–92.

Koss, M. P., and Oros, C. J. (1982). "Sexual Experiences Survey: A Research Instrument Investigating Sexual Aggression and Victimization." *Journal of Consulting and Clinical Psychology,* 50:455–57.

LEAA. Law Enforcement Assistance Administration. (1974). *Crimes and Victims: A Report on the Dayton-San Jose Pilot Survey of Victimization*. Washington, DC: National Criminal Justice Information and Statistics Service.

———. (1975). *Criminal Victimization Surveys in 13 American Cities*. Washington, DC: US Government Printing Office.

Office of Civil Rights. (1980). *Fall Enrollment and Compliance Report of Institutions of Higher Education*. Washington, DC: US Department of Education.

Ohio Revised Code. (1980). 2907.01A, 2907.02.

Rapaport, K., and Burkhart, B. R. (1984). Personality and Attitudinal Characteristics of Sexually Coercive College Males. *Journal of Abnormal Psychology,* 93:216–21.

Russell, D. E. H. (1984). *Sexual Exploitation: Rape, Child Sexual Abuse, and Sexual Harassment.* Beverly Hills, Calif: Sage.

Scully, D., and Marolla, J. (1982). "Convicted Rapists' Construction of Reality: The Denial of Rape." Paper presented at meeting of American Sociological Association, September, San Francisco.

US Bureau of Census. (1980). *Current population reports, 1980–1981.* Washington, DC: US Government Printing Office.

Walker, A. (1982). *The Color Purple.* New York: Harcourt Brace Jovanovich.

9 Date Rape: Prevalence, Risk Factors, and a Proposed Model
Paula Lundberg-Love and Robert Geffner

The primary purpose of this chapter is to discuss the prevalence, risk factors, and potential long-term consequences of date rape. A secondary purpose is to propose an additional risk factor for date rape: childhood or adolescent sexual abuse, particularly incestuous abuse. Finally, a theoretical model that integrates the risk-factor data for both date rape and child sexual abuse is proposed. The purpose of the model is to provide a framework for understanding the dynamics that appear to occur in date rape. When viewed from the proposed perspective, date rape is one step in a possible lifespan cycle of the sexual victimization of women that often begins in childhood.

PREVALENCE RATES OF DATE RAPE

Epidemiological studies of rape/attempted rape, in general, have differed in their methodologies and, not surprisingly, their prevalence rates. In interviews with 930 adult women in San Francisco, a prevalence rate of 44 percent was obtained (Russell, 1984). Results of a random-digit–dialing telephone survey of 2,000 adult women in South Carolina yielded a prevalence rate of 14.5 percent (Kilpatrick et al., 1985). More recently, the results of a study based upon self-reports of a national sample of students in higher education revealed a 27.5 percent rate (Koss, Gidycz, & Wisniewski, 1987). Thus, recent studies indicate that the prevalence rate of actual or attempted rape of women ranges between 15 percent and 44 percent. However, regardless of the precise magnitude, rape is much more prevalent than previously believed.

Historically, there has been a discrepancy in the literature regarding the prevalence of stranger rape versus acquaintance rape. For example, Resick et al., (1981) found that 5 percent of the victims they studied experienced acquaintance rape. However, Rabkin (1979) found that 50 percent of all rapes occur between acquaintances. Russell (1984) reported that 35 percent of the rape/attempted rape victims in her sample were victimized by an acquaintance.

Typically, prevalence data are derived from police reports, agency statistics, and/or the responses to questionnaires. However, inherent in the filing of a report or an affirmative response to a questionnaire regarding sexual victimization is the acknowledgment that one was victimized. Therein lies one possible explanation for discrepancies found in the literature. Additionally, when the victimizer is an acquaintance, a woman may be reluctant to label the event as victimization and/or she may be reluctant even to report the fact of her victimization. Hence, the discrepancies regarding the prevalence of date rape may occur as the result of sampling error (Koss, 1985). Data derived from police and agency statistics reflect only information that has been reported. Survey data can include information from individuals who reported their victimization as well as those who did not. Thus, prevalence data based upon police and agency reports might be expected to underestimate the prevalence of date rape. Survey data might be expected to estimate the prevalence of date rape better to the extent that nonreporting victims could be included. Face-to-face interviews using questions that do not necessarily require individuals to even acknowledge or label their experience as victimization might be expected to provide the best estimate of the prevalence of date rape.

The latter point is important because the prevalence of acquaintance rape among acknowledged victims may differ from the prevalence of acquaintance rape among victims who do not label the event as rape. Among those who do not recognize that a rape has occurred, the assailant is even more likely to be an acquaintance than among those who recognize a rape (Koss, 1985). Thus, much acquaintance rape is unreported and even unacknowledged.

Many victims who do not report rape may be romantically involved with their attackers. Koss (1985) found that this was true for 31 percent of acknowledged victims and 76 percent of unacknowledged victims. Additionally, Russell (1984) found that more women had been raped by dates and boyfriends than by strangers.

An early survey of college students found that 20–24 percent of college women reported experiencing forceful attempts at sexual intercourse while on a date during the year prior to administration of the survey (Kanin, 1957). Twenty years later, similar results were found (Kanin & Parcell, 1977). Kanin (1967) also indicated that 25 percent of the unmarried male undergraduates surveyed reported making forceful attempts to have sexual intercourse while on a date. Olday and Wesley (1983) found that 25 percent of the female college-age respondents in their sample and less than 3 percent of the male respondents indicated a forced sex act against their will.

Recently, Muehlenhard and Linton (1987) reported that date rape and other forms of sexual aggression appear to be common among college students. They found that 77 percent of the women and 57 percent of the men had been involved in rape. Dhaenens and Farrington (1987) obtained dissimilar data. In their study at a small liberal arts college, only 2 percent of the female students reported sexual aggression. However, Dhaenens and Farrington could not determine whether the students in their institution were actually less prone to date rape or merely less inclined to report such acts.

The prevalence of sexual aggression has also been investigated among adolescents. For example, Olday et al. (1985) found that 25 percent of the female respondents (ages 17–19) reported experiencing forced sexual contact, while about 2 percent of male and female respondents reported initiating forced sexual contact. Similarly, initial analysis of data from the Dating Violence Survey (Gubrud, 1987) administered by the Network Against Violence in rural North Dakota revealed that "forced sex by date" was a function of year of high school, with the younger students more likely to have experienced forced sex.

Clearly these data suggest that adolescent date rape occurs and that even high school dating has a dark side characterized by coercion and sexual violence at an early age. Koss, Gidycz & Wisniewski (1987) pointed out that the preponderance of rape victims and offenders span a range from 16 to 25 years of age. The victimization rate for women has its primary peak in the group aged 16–19 years and its secondary peak in the group aged 20–24 years. Forty-five percent of all alleged rapists who are arrested are individuals under age 25.

RISK FACTORS FOR DATE RAPE

A strategy to reduce date rape must be based on knowledge of the "risk factors" associated with date rape. Muehlenhard and Linton (1987) have identified variables that are risk factors for date rape. These include the male's initiating and taking a dominant role during the date, miscommunication regarding sex, heavy alcohol or drug use, "parking," and male acceptance of traditional sex roles, interpersonal violence, adversarial attitudes regarding relationships, and rape myths. Although Muehlenhard and Linton found that the length of time that dating partners were acquainted was unrelated to the risk of sexual aggression, Koss (1985) reported that some types of rape were more likely to occur within the context of a longer relationship.

Control Issues

Muehlenhard and Linton (1987) report that men who initiate the date, pay all expenses, and drive are more likely to be sexually aggressive. Muehlenhard and Linton discuss these results within the context of a disparity-of-power differential. Russell (1984), also suggests that rape is a consequence of the power disparity between women and men. The identity of the date initiator, the date financier, and the provider of transportation are all related to power (Peplau, 1984). The man's assumption of all these roles places him in a position

172 Lundberg-Love & Geffner

of power in that, for example, as the initiator of a date, he can plan activities conducive to sexual aggression (Muehlenhard & Linton, 1987).

It is interesting that when a woman assumes the role of date initiator (Muehlenhard, Friedman & Thomas, 1985; Muehlenhard, this volume, Chapter 13), she is judged by both sexes to be more likely to want sex. Also, if sex occurs against her will, it is judged as a likely "consequence" and, according to the authors, it is often viewed as "justifiable."

Turning to finances and dating, it has been suggested that in the U.S. dating system it is expected that money and sex will be exchanged (Korman & Leslie, 1982; McCormick & Jesser, 1983). If the man pays the dating expenses and the woman reneges on the implicit bargain, the man may feel that sexual aggression is warranted (Kanin, 1967; Muehlenhard et al., 1985). Among high school students, 12 percent of the girls and 39 percent of the boys indicate that it is acceptable for a boy to force sex on a girl if he spends a lot of money on her (Giarusso et al. 1979). College students indicate that if a woman permits a man to pay all dating expenses instead of splitting the cost with him, it is more likely that she wants to have sex and it is more justifiable for him to have sex with her against her will (Muehlenhard, this volume, Chapter 13; Muehlenhard et al., 1985).

In contrast, Korman and Leslie (1982) find that women who share dating expenses are more likely than other women to be victims of sexual aggression. However, it is possible that the women began sharing dating expenses after experiencing sexual aggression in an attempt to avoid further sexual exploitation. Paying for dating expenses could prove hazardous, however, if a man were to perceive his "manhood" as taken away by a woman who insisted on paying her way. He then might attempt to regain it via aggressive sexuality. Korman and Leslie (1982) also suggest that traditional males might expect traditional females to adhere to traditional dating rituals, and nontraditional females to break from this. Therefore, traditional males might view nontraditional women as candidates for sexual aggression.

Communication and Interpretation

Another risk factor for date rape is miscommunication about sex. Men tend to interpret behavior, particularly women's behavior, in a more sexualized manner than do women (Goodchilds & Zellman, 1984; Muehlenhard, this volume, Chapter 13). Misunderstanding can also occur when a woman wants to cuddle or "pet" and a man interprets this as a prelude to sexual intercourse. Such misinterpretation of a woman's intentions could facilitate sexual aggression. If the woman offers resistance in such a circumstance, it is probable that the man will view it as token resistance (Check & Malamuth, 1983). Even if the woman's resistance is believed, the man might feel led on and in such cases, many people believe rape is justifiable (Goodchilds & Zellman, 1984; Muehlenhard

& MacNaughton, in press). Alternatively, the man might become angry, which could also lower his inhibition against rape (Wydra et al., 1983).

Muehlenhard and Linton (1987) find that there is typically misinterpretation of behavioral cues on the part of both sexes during dates described as "sexually aggressive." Both college women and men report that the man often felt led on during sexually aggressive dates. The differences in behavioral interpretation between men and women cocurred with respect to the assessment of desire for sexual contact. Men report that the women they encounter on what became a sexually aggressive date wanted sexual contact *more* than the other women they had recently dated. In contrast, women who had experienced sexually aggressive dates reported that they had wanted sexual contact *less* on those dates as compared to their recent dates. These data suggest that college men are interpreting their dates' behavior as indicative of a desire for sexual contact when the women believe that they are indicating that they do *not* want sexual contact.

Alcohol Use

Another risk factor is alcohol use. A number of studies indicate that one-third to two-thirds of rapists and many rape victims ingest alcohol prior to the assault (Lott, Reilly & Howard, 1982; Wilson & Durrenberger, 1982; Wolfe & Baker, 1980). In addition to rendering women less able to defend themselves (Russell, 1984), alcohol ingestion operates as a risk factor in other ways. It reduces men's inhibitions against violence, including sexual violence (Richardson, 1981). Furthermore, when a rapist is intoxicated, college students, incarcerated rapists, and criminal statutes regard him as less responsible for his behavior (Rabkin, 1979; Richardson & Campbell, 1982; Wolfe & Baker, 1980). However, if the woman is intoxicated, people regard her as more responsible for the rape and degrade her character (Richardson & Campbell, 1982).

Even among high school students, 18 percent of the girls and 39 percent of the boys indicate that it is acceptable for a boy to force sex if the girl is "stoned" or drunk (Giarusso et al., 1979). In Muehlenhard and Linton's (1987) study of sexual aggression in dating situations, alcohol or drug ingestion was related to sexual aggression. However, only heavy usage of a substance was associated with sexually aggressive dates. This result lends additional support to the hypothesis that alcohol reduces men's inhibition against violence, provides a rationalization for sexual aggression, and renders a woman less able to resist rape.

Location and Activity

The location of the date and choice of dating activity are risk factors for date rape. A woman's willingness to go to certain places may be interpreted as a signal that she is interested in sex (Lott, Reilly & Howard, 1982). Subjects have rated visiting the man's house when nobody is home (Goodchilds & Zellman, 1984) or going to the man's apartment (Muehlenhard, this volume, Chapter 13) as indicative that the woman wants sex. Additionally, individuals, particularly traditional men, rate date rape as more justifiable if a couple goes to the man's apartment as opposed to a religious function or a movie. Muehlenhard and Linton (1987) report that the location or dating activity most strongly associated with sexual aggression is "parking." In general, the greater the sexual connotations of the dating activity, the greater the probability that men will interpret the situation in a more sexualized fashion than women.

The additional factors of privacy or seclusion also appear to enhance the sexual connotations of a dating location or activity. Both women and men reported that nearly twice as many sexually aggressive dates occurred at the man's apartment compared to the woman's apartment (Muehlenhard & Linton, 1987). This finding is consistent with the concept that the establishment of individual territory may lead to greater feelings of personal control (Pearson, 1985). Thus, a man may feel more in control in his own apartment, leading to a greater likelihood of inflicting sexual aggression.

Reports from college men and women differ with respect to the types of dating activities that are associated with sexual aggression. Women report that sexually aggressive dates are more likely to involve parties (Muehlenhard & Linton, 1987). Men, however, report that their sexually aggressive dates are more likely to involve attending a movie. Reports of rape often occur after a woman becomes intoxicated at a party. Similarly, movies that portray women as reacting positively to sexual violence significantly increase men's acceptance of violence toward women and may increase men's acceptance of rape myths. These factors could be disinhibiting with respect to date rape. Hence, it is interesting that the male participants in the Muehlenhard and Linton (1987) study reported that more sexually aggressive dates are associated with movie attendance.

Sex-Role Attitudes

The final risk factor for date rape as outlined by Muehlenhard and Linton (1987) involves attitudes, particularly adherence to traditional attitudes, adversarial attitudes toward women, and attitudes that accept violence toward women. People who accept rape myths, violence against women, adversarial sexual beliefs, and traditional sex-role attitudes tend to exhibit greater tolerance of rape, to blame rape victims more, and to report a greater likelihood of raping if they could be assured that no one would know (Acock & Ireland, 1983; Burt & Alkin, 1981; Check & Malamuth, 1983; Greendlinger & Byrne, 1987; Muehlenhard & MacNaughton, in press; Shotland & Goodstein, 1983). Sex-role stereotyping has recently been shown to have an effect on the attributions of responsibility for date rape, with traditional views being more associated with blame toward the victim (Coller & Resick, 1987). Moreover, some researchers report a relationship between these attitudes and actual experience with sexual aggression (Koss et al., 1985; Rapaport & Burkhart, 1984).

Traditional attitudes may influence the propensity to commit and to receive sexual aggression. Traditional people are more likely to believe the traditional sex scripts in which women are never to admit they want sex and men are to overcome this "token" resistance (Check & Malamuth, 1983). Traditional individuals are more likely to believe that "leading a man on" justifies force (Muehlenhard & MacNaughton, in press). With respect to the propensity for victimization, Russell (1984) suggests that the qualities typically ascribed to the traditional woman, such as kindness, compassion, patience, acceptance, and dependence, are the very qualities that put a woman at risk for rape. Perhaps most unsettling, however, is the observation that traditional women generally date traditional men (Peplau, 1984).

As Muehlenhard and Linton (1987) indicate, it is difficult to determine whether attitudes concerning sexual aggression are the cause or the consequence of sexual aggression. However, the relationship between attitudes and sexually aggressive behavior appears stronger among men than women. Men determine their victimizer status; however, victimization is a more random process, since any woman could become a victim (Burkhart & Stanton, 1985). Muehlenhard and Linton (1987) find that sexually aggressive men are more likely to accept traditional sex roles, violence toward women, and adversarial sexual beliefs. Men who report sexual aggression are more traditional than other men on the Attitudes Toward Women Scale, and score higher than others on the Acceptance of Interpersonal Violence Scale, the Adversarial Beliefs Scale and the Rape Myth Acceptance Scale. Moreover, women who experience sexual aggression exhibit adversarial sexual beliefs and greater acceptance of violence toward women. Perhaps a woman's adherence to traditional beliefs fosters the attitude that she is not entitled to stop unwanted sexual advances; or perhaps previous experience with sexual aggression and victimization has taught her that male-female relationships are indeed adversarial and violence is to be expected.

PRIOR SEXUAL ABUSE AND DATE RAPE

An important risk factor not studied by Muehlenhard and Linton (1987) but which other researchers reveal is important in predicting date rape is the experience of childhood or adolescent sexual abuse, particularly incest. Although long-term sequelae of childhood sexual abuse are numerous and varied, one of the most distressing problems is the tendency for a victim to be revictimized across the lifespan. The results of Russell's (1986) survey support this observation. Sixty-eight percent of incest victims were victims of rape or attempted rape (nonincestuous), as opposed to 36 percent of women who lacked a history of incest. Incest victimization also has been associated with subsequent marital rape, with 19 percent of incest victims experiencing marital rape as compared to a rate of 7 percent among women who were not victims of incest. Finally, 53 percent of the incest victims as compared to 26 percent of the nonincest victims reported at least one unwanted sexual advance by an authority figure (Russell, 1986). These data have prompted Russell to suggest that incestuous abuse is a contributing cause of the sexual revictimization of women.

From a theoretical perspective, Browne and Finkelhor (1986) outline four traumagenic dynamics that enable us to understand the impact of sexual abuse on the victim. These include traumatic sexualization, betrayal, powerlessness, and stigmatization. Traumatic sexualization refers to a process whereby a child's sexuality is shaped in a developmentally inappropriate and interpersonally dysfunctional fashion as a result of sexual abuse. Betrayal occurs when children discover that someone upon whom they are vitally dependent has caused them harm. Powerlessness refers to a process whereby the individual's will, desires, and sense of efficacy are continually contravened. Stigmatization refers to the negative connotations (shame, guilt, blame) that are communicated to the victim about the experience and subsequently incorporated into the individual's self-image.

Russell (1986) utilized the theoretical framework of Browne and Finkelhor to suggest explanations for the strong association found between incestuous abuse and revictimization. She proposed that some of the behavioral manifestations of traumatic sexualization exhibited by victims of incest may contribute to their sexual revictimization. For example, some sexually victimized children may exhibit age-inappropriate precocious sexual knowledge and interests, and as a result may attempt to engage others in sexualized behavior. Clearly such behavior or its derivatives, if continued in adolescence and adulthood, might place incest victims at greater risk for date rape. Studies have even suggested that some victims of child sexual abuse are at risk for becoming prostitutes (Browne & Finkelhor, 1986).

An alternative response to traumatic sexualization is the development of an aversion to sex in adolescence or adulthood. Sexual contact may be associated with fear, revulsion, anger, and powerlessness. These factors, especially the latter, may stimulate flashbacks of the molestation experience when the victim is in certain situations. Such flashbacks can "paralyze" her if she is in a sexually coercive situation (Lundberg, Sowell & Geffner, 1986).

Data derived from the recent reports of adult survivors of incest support this contention. Maltz and Holman (1987) and Lundberg, Sowell & Geffner (1986) report some of the sexual and/or relationship problems stated by adult incest survivors. Factors such as confusion regarding the normal sequence of dating and sexual behavior, aversion to particular sexual acts, difficulty setting limits, control and power issues surrounding sex, a propensity for sexual "acting out," and the use of sex to get attention, could operate to place an incest victim at greater risk for date rape. Because the incest victim typically has experienced the inappropriate pairing of love and attention with sexual exploitation and coercion, it is not surprising that she is rendered vulnerable to the exploitive manipulations of the date rapist. Nor should it be unexpected that for some individuals, appropriate dating and/or intimate relationships may be contravened.

Indeed, anecdotal data (Lundberg, Sowell & Geffner, 1986) from incest survivors reinforces Russell's findings regarding sexual revictimization. The incest survivors who have experienced date rape often report feeling uncomfortable at some point during the date. However, instead of acting upon their accurate perceptions of danger initially, and successfully extricating themselves from the situation, the incest survivors often discount their feelings. They tell themselves they are overreacting as a result of their early incestuous experience or they convince themselves that they are paranoid. In effect, the victim is placed in a double bind. While the potential victim conducts this internal dialogue, the potential rapist may interpret the victim's nonactive cognitive behavior as acquiescence. He continues his aggression. She becomes terrified, feels overwhelmed and powerless, and experiences a re-enactment of her early incestuous experience. This observation is consistent with the results of the Levine-Maccombie and Koss (1986) study, which suggests that compared to acquaintance rape victims, acquaintance rape avoiders are less likely to have experienced internalizing or passive emotions at the time of the assault and are more likely to have utilized active response strategies (running away, screaming).

Thus, incest victims, as a result of their traumagenic experience, may tend to perceive themselves as powerless and flawed. Moreover, they have difficulty trusting themselves, others, or the environment. These qualities, coupled with the victim's stigmatization, may coalesce to render her emotionally "less invested" in her survival. As a result, the female incest victim may be unknowingly less vigilant regarding her well-being and thereby be vulnerable to date rape. It is imperative, however, that this experience of revictimization not be construed as being the victim's "fault." The data do suggest, though, that prior conditioning and experience may have shaped her behavior to render her more vulnerable to sexually coercive situations.

The dynamics at work within an incestuous family system also may have the potential to render the incest victim vulnerable to date rape. Typically, the boundary disturbances that exist regarding sexuality in the sexually abusive family reveal a skewed or distorted family structure in which sex is a reflection of "dis-ease" (that is, lack of ease) and a vehicle for abusive, exploitive interaction (Trepper & Barrett, 1986). Incest victims are taught that sex equals love and that love equals sex. According to Maddock (1983), sexuality within the sexually abusive family involves a lack of respect for one or both genders and their sex-role associated behaviors, a negative view of sex and the body, a lack of appropriate interpersonal boundaries, a lack of effective communication, and a skewness in the power differential between partners.

After reviewing these characteristics of the sexually abusive family, particularly the victim's lack of self-respect, knowledge, power, and control, it is easy to conceptualize how these could operate to foster the types of attitudes and beliefs outlined as risk factors for date rape by Muehlenhard and Linton (1987).

While it is not implied that the factors operating in childhood sexual abuse and incest are identical to those operating in date rape, there may be some similarities. After all, childhood incestuous abuse is a subset of acquaintance rape and date rape, also, is a subset of acquaintance rape.

PROPOSED MODEL OF SEXUAL ABUSE AND DATE RAPE

Finkelhor (1986) has described a four-factor model of sexual abuse that incorporates some of the concepts derived from a family systems approach to the treatment of sexually abusive families. Finkelhor's model proposes that four preconditions must be fulfilled before sexual abuse can occur:

1. A potential offender needs to have some type of motivation to abuse sexually.
2. The potential offender has to overcome internal inhibitions against acting on that motivation.
3. The potential offender has to overcome external impediments to acting on that motivation.
4. The potential offender or some other factor has to undermine or overcome the potential victim's resistance to sexual abuse.

The "four-preconditions model of sexual abuse" is a good framework in which to consider how the experience of living in an incestuous family could enhance an individual's vulnerability to date rape.

Recall the risk factors for date rape outlined previously: (1) date initiated by male, (2) expenses paid by male, (3) transportation provided by male, (4) location of date, (5) miscommunication about sex, (6) heavy alcohol or drug use, (7) acceptance of traditional sex roles, (8) acceptance of violence toward women, (9) acceptance of rape myths, and (10) adversarial attitudes regarding male-female relationships (Muehlenhard & Linton, 1987). These risk factors can be integrated with the four-preconditions model. The net result of this operation is shown in Figure 9.1.

The proposed model suggests that when a potential offender has sufficient motivation, when his internal inhibitors are overcome, and when external inhibitors are absent or manipulated to aid and abet sexual exploitation, then date rape *can* occur. However, if the victim's resistance is *not* undermined or neutralized, date rape may be prevented. Furthermore, a block at any point along the stepwise path could theoretically deter date rape. Listed beneath each step in the progression are the factors that can operate to increase the likelihood that date rape may occur.

This model is neither immutable nor is it necessarily finite. It is offered as a heuristic framework with which to integrate the risk-factor data for date rape with a model of the dynamics involved in sexual abuse. This model can be examined from the perspective of a potential male offender as well as that of a potential victim in order to understand the dynamics of date rape and to suggest possibilities for its prevention.

Figure 9.1
Four-Preconditions Model of Date Rape

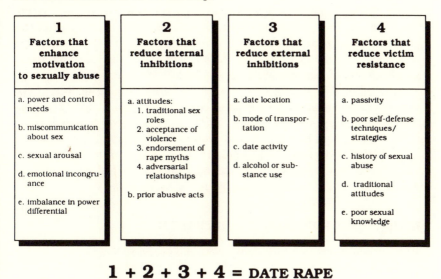

1 Factors that enhance motivation to sexually abuse	2 Factors that reduce internal inhibitions	3 Factors that reduce external inhibitions	4 Factors that reduce victim resistance
a. power and control needs	a. attitudes: 1. traditional sex roles 2. acceptance of violence 3. endorsement of rape myths 4. adversarial relationships	a. date location	a. passivity
b. miscommunication about sex		b. mode of transportation	b. poor self-defense techniques/ strategies
c. sexual arousal		c. date activity	c. history of sexual abuse
d. emotional incongruance	b. prior abusive acts	d. alcohol or substance use	d. traditional attitudes
e. imbalance in power differential			e. poor sexual knowledge

1 + 2 + 3 + 4 = DATE RAPE

Note: A block at any point may deter date rape.

Consider it first from the perspective of the potential offender. It reveals that if the male has strong needs for power and control, becomes sexually aroused, has difficulty with emotional congruence and communication about sex, and the power differential is in his favor, then the motivation for date rape may be present. However, date rape will occur only if the potential offender then overcomes his internal inhibitors (that is, his attitudes, a lowering of restraint due to a prior history of abusive acts, etc.) plus any remaining external inhibitors that were not previously manipulated (that is, date location, activity, transportation, substance use, etc.) and if he overcomes the resistance of the victim.

As the literature on date rape suggests, rape in this example is probable if the potential abuser is an individual who endorses traditional sex roles, rape myths, adversarial attitudes toward relationships, and violence toward women. Endorsement of these attitudes weakens internal inhibitions against rape. The presence of external impediments to date rape are often minimal because the male may have organized these to his advantage at the outset of the date or during the course of the evening. Unless the victim is somehow able to exert sufficient resistance, date rape may occur. Thus, the burden of resistance is inequitably placed upon the victim.

Other factors that increase a potential victim's risk for date rape include (1) difficulty communicating about sex, (2) choosing traditional males as dates, (3) allowing the power differential to be strongly skewed in favor of the male, (4) engaging in significant alcohol or drug use, (5) being unassertive, (6) having minimal knowledge of self-defense strategy and techniques, (7) having minimal appropriate sexual education, and (8) endorsement of traditional attitudes, rape myths, and violence against women. Additionally, since date rape and incest are both subsets of acquaintance rape it is highly probable that the long-term consequences of date rape may bear some similarity to those of incest. The consequences of untreated sexual abuse continue to be exhibited in a cycle throughout the lifespan. Results from clinical data (Lundberg, Sowell & Geffner, 1986; Lundberg-Love, Crawford & Geffner, 1987) suggest that incest victims are indeed at risk for several problems many years after the initial victimization. When the abuse is severe and traumatic, the actual events can be completely blocked out and repressed by the victim for many years.

IMPLICATIONS FOR POLICY AND PRACTICE

Examination of the proposed model also suggests possible strategies for intervention to prevent date rape. Clearly, a focus on methods to increase the internal inhibitions of the potential abuser is one possible strategy. As feminist scholars have suggested (such as Bograd, 1982; Schecter, 1982), changes in our adherence to traditional sex-role stereotypes, rape myths, and adversarial attitudes, as well as a refusal to tolerate violence against all individuals, would be predicted to increase the internal inhibitions against date rape. Ways to increase and reinforce cooperation, reciprocity, empathy, and compassion between the sexes might also reduce the prevalence of date rape. However, this is a societal problem that may take years to alter.

Educational programs would appear to have the potential to reduce the motivation factors, increase the inhibition factors, and increase victim resistance factors in order to prevent date rape. Educational programs designed to enhance the self-defense strategies of women may reduce date rape also. Dissemination of the Levine-MacCombie and Koss (1986) data on rape victims and rape avoiders in conjunction with physical and cognitive strategies for rape self-defense could enhance victim resistance. Teaching women assertiveness has been recommended (Muehlenhard & Linton, 1987). Consciousness-raising regarding the prevalence of acquaintance rape and the sexual rights of women as well as cognitive modification and stress inoculation procedures have also been suggested (Levine-MacCombie & Koss, 1986).

Sex-education programs are critical to help reduce the amount of sexual miscommunication that occurs among adolescents. If appropriate educational programs were implemented early in development, avoidance or better reporting of date rape might be facilitated. Some of the sexual abuse prevention programs may be effective in this respect, although more rigorous, comprehensive programs may be required. Role playing to learn and practice alternative responses may be very helpful for adolescents. In addition, enhancing awareness of potentially dangerous situations may help women better recognize the signals that predict date rape so that certain situations can be avoided. This could psychologically increase a woman's self-confidence and resistance, as well as maintain or erect external inhibitors with respect to the date itself.

Finally, effective treatment of incestuous families may reduce the prevalence of date rape for both sexes. It can enable the potential victim to resolve some of the traumagenic dynamics operating as a result of the sexual abuse so that her resistance to date rape is not determined or contravened at a later time. It can also alter the dysfunctional dynamics of incestuous families that fosters the attitudes which enable and promote sexual abuse. It appears that being raised in abusive families is a very strong predictor for both sexes of subsequent abusive behavior or victimization (Finkelhor, 1986).

Raising the issue of treatment for incestuous families generates additional policy implications. One is the need for allocation of funds to enable the development, implementation, and evaluation of treatment programs for incestuous families as well as rape victims. Acknowledging the seriousness of this problem and the enormous numbers of women that have been victims of this type of sexual abuse is the first step. Then, perhaps, adequate identification and treatment can occur. Again, financial resources and legislative and judicial changes would be necessary so that attitudes toward these crimes of assault and their victims could be changed.

RECOMMENDATIONS FOR FURTHER STUDY

Funds are needed to support research concerning the effectiveness of identification and treatment programs for sexual abuse, both when it occurs on a date and in the family. Additional research concerning the long-term behavioral sequelae of victimization is needed so that more appropriate treatment programs can be developed. Increasing numbers of women are seeking therapy to resolve the trauma of sexual abuse/assault. Yet data are scarce that describe the most effective methods for treating such trauma. It would also be worthwhile to determine whether different types of treatment programs are necessary for different types and ages of victims.

It appears that research is also needed to determine better methods for the identification of victims of sexual abuse, especially during childhood. Longitudinal research is lacking in this area. Therefore, prospective research to determine the long-term consequences of date rape as well as incestuous abuse and the impact of treatment is needed. Finally, research to test the proposed model of date rape risk factors presented above is needed. If this theoretical model is appropriate, then interventions can be planned accordingly.

SUMMARY

This chapter has described current research concerning the prevalence of and risk factors involved in date rape. The possible relationship of prior incestuous abuse as a risk factor in date rape was suggested. Finally, the integration of the date rape risk factors of Muehlenhard and her colleagues (for example, Muehlenhard & Linton, 1987) with the expanded four-preconditions model of sexual abuse (Finkelhor, 1986) was proposed as a possible model. This can provide a valuable framework within which to understand and to propose strategies for reducing date rape. This model is not necessarily the definitive one. However, its consideration raises important theoretical and practical issues for future research in the areas of date rape and sexual abuse. As Russell (1984) has so aptly written: "A great deal of work must be undertaken to bring about the changes necessary to begin to solve the ubiquitous, painful and destructive problem of sexual exploitation. The first step is to realize the importance of this. The second step is to do it" (p. 290).

REFERENCES

Acock, A. C., & Ireland, N. K. (1983). "Attribution of Blame in Rape Cases: The Impact of Norm Violation, Gender, and Sex-role Attitude." *Sex Roles,* 9:179–93.

Bograd, M. (1982). "Battered Women, Cultural Myths and Clinical Interventions: A Feminist Analysis." In New England Association for Women in Psychology (eds.), *Current Feminist Issues in Psychotherapy.* New York: Haworth.

Browne, A., & Finkelhor, D. (1986). "The Impact of Child Sexual Abuse: A Review of the Research. *Psychological Bulletin,* 99:66–77.

Burkhart, B. R., & Stanton, A. L. (1985). "Sexual Aggression in Acquaintance Relationships." In G. Russell (ed.), *Violence in Intimate Relationships.* Englewood Cliffs, NJ: Spectrum.

Burt, M. R., & Alkin, R. S. (1981). "Rape Myths, Rape Definitions, and Probability of Conviction." *Journal of Applied Social Psychology,* 11:212–30.

Check, J. V. P., & Malamuth, N. M. (1983). "Sex Role Stereotyping and Reactions to Depictions of Stranger Versus Acquaintance Rape." *Journal of Personality and Social Psychology,* 45:344–56.

Coller, S. A. & Resick, P. A. (1987). "Women's Attributions of Responsibility for Date Rape: The Influence of Empathy and Sex-Role Stereotyping." *Violence and Victims,* 2:115–25.

Dhaenens, R. A. P., & Farrington, K. (1987). *A Study of Stereotyped Attitudes Toward Rape.* Paper presented at Third National Family Violence Research Conference, Durham, NH.

Finkelhor, D. (1986). "Sexual Abuse: Beyond the Family Systems Approach." In T. S. Trepper & M. J. Barrett (eds.), *Treating Incest: A Multimodal Systems Perspective,* 53–65. New York: Haworth.

Giarusso, R., Johnson, P., Goodchilds, J., & Zellman, G. (1979). "Adolescents' Cues and Signals: Sex and Assault." Paper presented at the Western Psychological Association meetings.

Goodchilds, J. D., & Zellman, G. L. (1984). "Sexual Signaling and Sexual Aggression in Adolescent Relationships." In N. M. Malamuth & E. Donnerstein (eds.), *Pornography and Sexual Aggression*, 233–43, Orlando, FL: Academic.

Greendlinger, V., & Byrne, D. (1987). "Coercive Sexual Fantasies of College Males as Predictors of Self-reported Likelihood to Rape and Overt Sexual Aggression." *Journal of Sex Research*, 23:1–11.

Gubrud, J. (1987). "Network Against Teenage Violence: Dating Violence Survey." Williston, ND. Unpublished.

Kanin, E. J. (1957). "Male Aggression in Dating-Courtship Relations." *American Journal of Sociology*, 63:197–204.

———. (1967). "Reference Groups and Sex Conduct Norms." *Sociological Quarterly*, 8:495–504.

Kanin, E. J., & Parcell, S. R. (1977). "Sexual Aggression: A Second Look at the Offended Female." *Archives of Sexual Behavior*, 6:67–76.

Kilpatrick, D. G., Best, C. L., Verona, L. J., Amick, A. E., Villeponteaux, L. A., & Ruff, G. A. (1985). "Mental Health Correlates of Criminal Victimization: A Random Community Survey." *Journal of Consulting and Clinical Psychology*, 53:866–73.

Korman, S. K., & Leslie, G. R. (1982). "The Relationship of Feminist Ideology and Date Expense Sharing to Perceptions of Sexual Aggression in Dating." *Journal of Sex Research*, 18:114–20.

Koss, M. P. (1985). "The Hidden Rape Victim: Personality, Attitudinal, and Situational Characteristics." *Psychology of Women Quarterly*, 9:193–212.

Koss, M. P., Gidycz, C. A., & Wisniewski, N. (1987). "The Scope of Rape: Incidence and Prevalence of Sexual Aggression and Victimization in a National Sample of Higher Education Students." *Journal of Consulting and Clinical Psychology*, 55:162–70.

Koss, M. P., Leonard, K. E., Beezley, D. A., & Oros, C. J. (1985). "Nonstranger Sexual Aggression: A Discriminant Analysis of the Psychological Characteristics of Undetected Offenders." *Sex Roles*, 12:981–92.

Levine-MacCombie, J., & Koss, M. P. (1986). "Acquaintance Rape: Effective Avoidance Strategies." *Psychology of Women Quarterly*, 10:311–20.

Lott, B., Reilly, M. E., & Howard, D. R. (1982). "Sexual Assault and Harassment: A Campus Community Case Study." *Signs: Journal of Women in Culture and Society*, 8:296–319.

Lundberg-Love, P. K., Crawford, C. M., & Geffner, R. A. (1987). "Personality Characteristics of Adult Incest Survivors." Paper presented at the Southwestern Psychological Association meetings.

Lundberg, P. K., Sowell, C. B., & Geffner, R. (1986). *Behavioral Characteristics of Adult Incest Survivors*. Paper presented at the second biennial Midwest Society for Research in Lifespan Development.

Maddock, J. W. (1983). "Human Sexuality in the Life Cycle of the Family System." In J. D. Woody & R. H. Woody (eds.), *Sexual Issues in Family Therapy*. Rockville, MD: Aspen Systems.

Maltz, W., & Holman, B. (1987). *Incest and Sexuality: A Guide to Understanding and Healing*. Lexington, MA: Lexington Books.

McCormick, N. B., & Jesser, C. J. (1983). "The Courtship Game: Power in the Sexual

Encounter." In E. R. Allgeier & N. B. McCormick (eds.), *Changing Boundaries: Gender Roles and Sexual Behavior*, 64–86. Palo Alto, CA: Mayfield.

Muehlenhard, C. L., Friedman, D. E., & Thomas, C. M. (1985). "Is Date Rape Justifiable? The Effects of Dating Activity, Who Initiated, Who Paid, and Men's Attitudes Toward Women." *Psychology of Women Quarterly*, 9:297–309.

Muehlenhard, C. L., & Linton, M. A. (1987). "Date Rape and Sexual Aggression in Dating Situations: Incidence and Risk Factors." *Journal of Counseling Psychology*, 34:186–96.

Muehlenhard, C. L., & MacNaughton, J. S. (in press). "Women's Beliefs About Women Who 'Lead Men On.' " *Journal of Social and Clinical Psychology*.

Olday, D., & Wesley, B. (1983). "Premarital Courtship Violence: A Summary Report." Moorhead, KY. Moorhead State University. Unpublished.

Olday, D., Wesley, B., Keating, B., & Bowman, D. (1985). *High School Age Dating Violence: A Preliminary Report*. Moorehead, KY. Moorehead State University. Unpublished.

Pearson, J. C. (1985). *Gender and Communication*. Dubuque, IA: Brown.

Peplau, L. A. (1984). "Power in Dating Relationships." In J. Freeman (ed.), *Women: A Feminist Perspective*, 100–112, Palo Alto, CA: Mayfield.

Rabkin, J. G. (1979). "The Epidemiology of Forcible Rape." *American Journal of Orthopsychiatry*, 49:634–47.

Rapaport, K., & Burkhart, B. R. (1984). "Personality and Attitudinal Characteristics of Sexually Coercive College Males." *Journal of Abnormal Psychology*, 93:216–21.

Resick, P. A., Calhoun, K. S., Atkeson, B. M., & Ellis, E. M. (1981). "Social Adjustment in Victims of Sexual Assault." *Journal of Consulting and Clinical Psychology*, 49:705–12.

Richardson, D. (1981). "The Effect of Alcohol on Male Aggression Toward Female Targets." *Motivation and Emotion*, 5:333–44.

Richardson, D., & Campbell, J. L. (1982). "The Effect of Alcohol on Attributions of Blame for Rape." *Personality and Social Psychology Bulletin*, 8:468–76.

Russell, D. E. H. (1984). *Sexual Exploitation: Rape, Child Sexual Abuse and Workplace Harassment*. Beverly Hills, CA: Sage.

———. (1986). *The Secret Trauma: Incest in the Lives of Girls and Women*. New York: Basic Books.

Schecter, S. (1982). *Women and Male Violence*. Boston: South End.

Shotland, R. L., & Goodstein, L. (1983). "Just Because She Doesn't Want to Doesn't Mean it's Rape: An Experimentally Based Causal Model of the Perception of Rape in a Dating Situation." *Social Psychology Quarterly*, 46:220–32.

Trepper, T. S., & Barrett, M. J. (1986). "Conceptual Framework for the Assessment of Intrafamily Sexual Abuse." In T. S. Trepper & M. J. Barrett (eds.), *Targeting Incest: A Multimodal Systems Perspective*, 13–25. New York: Haworth.

Wilson, W., & Durrenberger, R. (1982). "Comparison of Rape and Attempted Rape Victims." *Psychological Reports*, 50:198.

Wolfe, J., & Baker, V. (1980). "Characteristics of Imprisoned Rapists and Circumstances of the Rape." In C. G. Warner (ed.), *Rape and Sexual Assault*, 265–78. Germantown, MD: Aspen.

Wydra, A., Marshall, W. L., Earls, C. M., & Barbaree, H. E. (1983). "Identification of Cues and Control of Sexual Arousal by Rapists." *Behavior Research and Therapy*, 21:469–76.

10   Courtship Aggression and Mixed-Sex Peer Groups
Patricia Gwartney-Gibbs and Jean Stockard

Peer groups may provide a context or environment in which courtship aggression is learned (or tolerated) and legitimized. Consider, for example, the following true case study: The "red ox" party is a three-day event sponsored by a local college fraternity. It begins on Thursday night, when the members of the fraternity go over to the house of their "sister" sorority. The key event of the evening involves "tapping." The women stand in a circle; each man paces around the group, and eventually taps the shoulder of the woman he wants to date for the weekend. Each man pushes his date slowly to the floor, places his foot upon her, and reads aloud a poem he has written on her behalf. The poem is at once praiseworthy, yet somewhat lewd and mocking in tone. The women say that not to be tapped is an embarrassment, a social disgrace; to be chosen is an honor. The next major event of the weekend is a formal dinner at the fraternity on Friday night. All the guests show their best clothes and their best behavior. The meal is large, slow, delicious, and obviously very expensive. The women again feel honored but also indebted to the men for their generosity and graciousness. The next afternoon the couples board a bus for a party in a rented barn in the countryside 10 miles away. There is live music for dancing, good food, and alcohol; drugs are not as obvious, but available. The event that everyone watches for is "ox" wrestling. Two or three steers are hired for the event. The men take turns tussling the steers in the stalls of the barn. Then they wrestle their women companions in the stalls of the barn. Informants report that the peer pressure to engage in sex is enormous.[1]

As this case study suggests, sexual aggression and victimization may be a part of peer group culture. That is, the friendship networks from which individuals draw their dating partners may allow, or even encourage, male sexual aggression and female victimization in different degrees. Previous research provides some support for this speculation. Males who have sexually aggressive male friends, for example, are more likely to be aggressive themselves (Ageton, 1983; Alder, 1982; Kanin, 1957, 1985; Polk et al., 1981). For mixed-sex peer groups, individuals who have sexually aggressive male friends and sexually victimized female friends are more likely to be involved in various forms of courtship aggression themselves, as aggressors and as victims (Ageton, 1983; Schwendinger & Schwendinger, 1985). These findings indicate that young adults who have frequent and close association with friends who engage in, and thus seemingly endorse, sexually aggressive behavior appear to accept and engage in such behavior more often themselves.

Little is known, however, about the nature of sexually aggressive peer groups, particularly those that involve both females and males. Previous research on this topic (Gwartney-Gibbs, Stockard & Bohmer, 1987) found, quite unexpectedly, that it was possible to distinguish three distinct subgroups of college students on the basis of their reports of their friends' involvement in sexually aggressive courtship relations: (1) a nonaggressive peer group, in which female friends had not been sexually victimized and male friends had not been sexually aggressive; (2) a female victimization peer group, which included female friends who had been sexually victimized, but no male friends who had been sexually aggressive; and (3) a sexually aggressive peer group, which included both males who had been sexually aggressive and females who had been sexually victimized. Although a fourth peer group is logically possible—one with sexually aggressive male friends and no sexually victimized female friends—only three people (1.3 percent of the total) reported these characteristics. In other words, having male friends who had been sexually aggressive was sufficient to assure that individuals also had female friends who had been sexually victimized.

The purpose of this paper is to replicate the original study to see if these distinctive peer groups appear in another sample and to explore the correlates of membership in these three groups in both samples. Specifically, three research questions are addressed: (1) Does the distribution of sexually aggressive mixed-sex peer groups found in the first study appear in the second sample? (2) To what extent do members of these different peer groups report different personal experiences with courtship violence? (3) What demographic, attitudinal, and behavioral characteristics distinguish members of the three groups?

RELATED LITERATURE

Because of a paucity of prior research on the topic, this research is necessarily exploratory and descriptive. Even though previous research documents the importance of peer groups in adolescent socialization and delinquent behavior (Colvin & Pauly, 1983; Schwendinger & Schwendinger, 1985), no prior research specifically examines the sexually aggressive experiences of mixed-sex peer groups or finds the three distinctive peer groupings described above. Similarly, even though several studies have found that males with sexually aggressive male friends are more likely to be involved in such aggression themselves, as noted above, little research has examined the influence of mixed-sex peer groups on both males' and females' experiences with sexual aggression and victimization. Such research seems particularly important given that young people are likely to draw their dating partners from their mixed-sex peer groups.

Theoretical work on victimization suggests that individuals' lifestyles and routine activities influence their chances of being victimized (Hindelang, Gottfredsom & Garofalo, 1978). Simply put, this perspective predicts that people are likely to be victimized if their everyday activities involve contact with those who are likely to commit crimes. A recent large-scale empirical test of this theory failed to establish a linkage between lifestyle and violent crime victimization (Miethe, Stafford & Long, 1987), but the link between lifestyle and courtship aggression or sexual aggression apparently remains untested. It is possible that peer-group membership, a more specific indicator of lifestyle, may yield a stronger relationship.

Previous research also provides no clear expectations regarding other correlates of membership in the three sexually aggressive peer groups, although it points toward some potentially important areas. The literature on delinquency, for instance, suggests that violence and sexual promiscuity are related to other types of delinquent behavior (Ageton, 1983; Hindelang, 1971). If parallels exist among college age persons, those in the more aggressive peer groups may be more likely to engage in other deviant behaviors, such as heavy drug and alcohol use.

The subculture of violence literature (such as Wolfgang & Ferracutti, 1967) suggests that people who engage in violent behavior have different values and attitudes than those in the general population. Although empirical evidence has produced only limited support for this view when large, representative samples have been studied (such as Ball-Rokeach, 1973), this theory implies that it might be worthwhile to examine the attitudes and values of members of the three peer groups.

Finally, literature on adolescent friendship patterns suggests that friendship choices are homogeneous with respect to attitudes and behaviors (Cohen, 1977; Kandel, 1978), including sexuality (DeLamater & MacCorquodale, 1979), although the strength of this relationship may vary by race and sex (Billy, Rodgers & Udry, 1984; Billy & Udry, 1985). Similarly, research on college students' attitudes and behaviors has noted the presence of different subcultures within college communities. Of potential interest to the present paper is Astin's (1977) finding, based on a large sample of students in a wide range of settings, that students become more hedonistic over time, and that certain subgroups are more likely to exhibit hedonistic values and behaviors, such as excessive alcohol and drug use, particularly those more involved in college life through dormitories and the Greek system. This in turn suggests that students in different living situations might have different chances of having friends with hedonistic attitudes and behaviors.

METHODS

Data and Samples

The data used in this investigation come from self-administered mail-out/ mail-back questionnaires sent to random samples of undergraduates at a large public university on the West Coast in 1982 and 1987. The response rates were 56 percent in 1982 and 72 percent in 1987, with 224 and 485 students, respectively, returning questionnaires with complete data on the variables of interest. Excluded from the analysis were students from abroad because their peer group experiences involve different cultures, and students aged 24 or more, because their experiences may reflect different epochs or generations than those of the younger students. Thus, the two samples of students represent two different college-age generations or cohorts: The 1982 sample includes students born between 1959 and 1964; the 1987 sample includes students born between 1964 and 1969.

Variables

The dependent variable in the analysis, peer group membership, involves responses to the following questions:

It has been noted that in the course of men's and women's sexual lives together, some men on occasion make physically forceful attempts at sexual activity which are disagreeable enough to cause the woman to respond in an offended manner, such as by crying, fighting, screaming, or pleading.

A. Roughly speaking, how many of your male friends would you estimate have been in such situations?[2]
B. Roughly speaking, how many of your female friends would you estimate have been in such situations?

Answer categories were (1) none, (2) a few, (3) some, and (4) a great many. When answers to these two questions were cross-tabulated, three groups emerged: (1) a nonaggressive peer group (answers "none" to questions A and B above); (2) a female victimization peer group (answers "none" to question A, but "a few," "some," or "many" to question B); and (3) a sexually aggressive peer group (answers that "a few" or more male friends had been sexually aggressive and "a few" or more female friends had been sexually victimized). The few students who did not fit into these groups were omitted from this analysis (3 in 1982 and 7 in 1987). For purposes of this research, respondents' answers about their male and female friends are assumed to represent peer groups, networks of interacting friends.

The independent variables include students' experiences with courtship violence (1982 sample only), demographic and college characteristics (both 1982 and 1987 samples), and several indicators of values, attitudes, and behaviors (some in both samples and some not).

Measures of the students' experiences with courtship violence were derived from modified versions of the Conflict Tactics Scale (Straus, 1979) and Koss and Oros's (1982) Sexual Experiences Survey. Two separate scales measure the extent to which students have ever sustained courtship aggression and the extent to which they have ever inflicted courtship aggression on others since they began dating. The "inflicted" and "sustained" scales each have four categories: (1) no experiences with courtship aggression, (2) abusive acts only (such as insults, threats), (3) violent behavior, and (4) violent behavior combined with sexual aggression (sexual intercourse by aggressive means). An additional scale, also based on the CTS, measures the extent to which respondents witnessed their parents in aggressive acts while they were growing up. It includes three categories: (1) never observed parents engage in abuse or violence, (2) saw parents in abusive interactions only, and (3) saw parents in violent interactions. These three scales are available for the 1982 data set only. (See Gwartney-Gibbs, Stockard & Bohmer, 1987, for details on construction of these variables.)

Both the 1982 and 1987 data sets include variables on students' demographic background [sex, race, age, marital status, number of children, employment status, spending money, parents' education, and parents' occupation and employment (1987 only)]; religious affiliation and the strength of religious beliefs; and college characteristics (year in school, grade point average, number of credits enrolled for [1987 only], living arrangements, and major). For analysis, living arrangements were grouped into four categories: fraternities and sororities, dormitories, at home with parents, and other (such as off-campus apartments, student family housing). Students' majors were grouped in two ways: MAJOR1 reflects four broad subject areas—business, physical and biological sciences, social sciences, and other (such as humanities, music, journalism, physical education). MAJOR2 is a proxy for six model personality orientations: realistic, artistic, intellectual, social, conventional, and enterprising (Astin & Holland, 1961).

Students' behaviors, values, and attitudes are reflected to some extent in their choices of living arrangements and major. More direct measures of behaviors, values, and attitudes include students' reported drinking behavior and drug use, measured by the average number of alcoholic drinks and illegal drugs consumed each day in the previous month. The 1987 survey also queried students' educational values and orientations. For multivariate analysis, answers to these questions were combined into a "serious student" scale (which indexes students' commitment to finishing their bachelors' degrees, and their perceptions of the importance of career preparation, occupational training, in-depth knowledge of an area of study, and higher education in general) and a "social student" scale (which measures students' social motivations for going to college, including to have a good time, to meet people, because their friends were going, and to find a spouse.)[3] The latter scale may serve as a proxy for the hedonistic orientation described by Astin (1977). Students scoring high on this scale also are more likely to believe that a college education should develop individual creativity and provide a critical awareness of society (as opposed to obtaining knowledge for its own sake).

Analysis

The data are analyzed initially with tables of percentages, crosstabulations, and one-way analyses of variance. Following the three research questions outlined earlier, the analysis first compares the distribution of the 1987 survey respondents among the three peer groups to that found in the 1982 survey. Then, for each year, the bivariate relationship between peer group membership and each of the independent variables described above is examined, both for each sample and within each sex group in each sample. Finally, discriminant analysis, a multivariate technique, is used to describe the differences between the three peer groups in each year. Variables that helped distinguish the peer groups in the bivariate analysis are used as the predictors or independent variables in the discriminant analyses.

RESULTS

Peer Groups in 1982 and 1987

The distinct peer groups found in the 1982 sample appeared again with the 1987 sample. In 1982, 34 percent of the sample fell into the nonaggressive peer group (had neither male friends who had been sexually aggressive nor female friends who had been sexually victimized), 26 percent fell into the female victimization peer group (had female friends who had been sexually victimized, but no sexually aggressive male friends), and 39 percent fell into the aggressive peer group (had both male friends who had been sexually aggressive and female friends who had been sexually victimized). In 1987, the figures were 37 percent, 36 percent, and 26 percent, respectively. In both years only 1 percent of the student respondents fell into the null category (having male friends who were sexually aggressive but no female friends who had been sexually victimized). This is significantly fewer than would have been expected by chance (14 percent in 1982 and 10 percent in 1987), and the results are highly significant ($\chi^2 = 65.6$, df $= 1$, $p < .0001$ in 1982; $\chi^2 = 83.24$, df $= 1$, $p < .0001$ in 1987). Thus, in both years, students who had male friends who had been sexually aggressive also had female friends who had been sexually victimized.

Although the proportion of students in the null category and in the nonaggressive peer group were very similar for the two college cohorts, the proportion of students in the other two peer groups varied significantly between the two years. There were approximately 10 percent more students in the female victimization group and 13 percent fewer students in the sexually aggressive peer group in 1987 than in 1982. These cohort differences are statistically significant ($\chi^2 = 14.1$, df = 2, $p < .001$). In other words, the structure of the peer groups remained unchanged over time, but the distribution of students in them changed, so that fewer students in 1987 than in 1982 reported they had sexually aggressive male friends.

Correlates of Peer Group Membership

How does peer group membership vary by students' own experiences with courtship aggression and with witnessing parental aggression? Table 10.1 answers this question separately for females and males in the 1982 sample. Females in the sexually aggressive peer group were somewhat more likely to report inflicting both violence and sexual violence, and were much more likely to report sustaining sexual violence, than females in the other two groups. Both of these associations are statistically significant. In contrast, even though the percentages in the table indicate that males in the sexually aggressive group were somewhat more likely than those in the other groups to report inflicting sexual violence, and that males in the female victimization group were less likely than those in either of the other two groups to report sustaining sexual violence, these differences were not statistically significant. In addition, peer group membership has no association with students' reports of parental aggression for either males or females in 1982.

Table 10.2 summarizes the results of crosstabulating peer group membership with the independent variables related to demographic background, college characteristics, and an array of values, attitudes, and behaviors. Significant differences by sex are also noted in Table 10.2 and discussed below. Overall, few statistically significant differences appear in students' demographic background or college characteristics, but the three peer groups show significant differences in their educational orientations and use of alcohol and drugs.

In both years, members of the three peer groups had a similar distribution of males and females, similar age distributions, similar marital and family situations, and similar employment and socioeconomic-status characteristics (although in 1987 those in the nonaggressive group tended to have less spending money). There are also no significant differences among the three groups in religious affiliation or the strength of religious beliefs, although in 1987 members of the sexually aggressive group were somewhat less likely to have a religious affiliation. The peer groups had a similar racial composition in 1982, but the 1987 sample exhibited significant differences, particularly for females. Asian-Americans, the largest minority group on campus, were significantly overrepresented in the nonaggressive peer group compared to whites.

Turning to college characteristics, members of the three peer groups had similar grade point averages, carried similar study loads, and in 1982 were equally likely to be upper division students and choose majors in the four sub-

Table 10.1
Cross-Tabulations of Peer Groups[a] by Courtship and Parental Aggression, for Males and Females, 1982

Scaled Independent[b] Variables	Male Peer Groups:			Female Peer Groups:		
	1	2	3	1	2	3
	Inflicted Courtship Aggression			Inflicted Courtship Aggression		
None	28%	10%	18%	45%	41%	21%
Abuse	41	52	46	30	32	27
Violence	25	33	24	25	24	38
Sex & Violence	6	5	12	0	3	14
	100%	100%	100%	100%	100%	100%
N	32	21	33	40	34	52
	x^2=4.21; df=6; p=.65; γ=.13			x^2=14.00; df=6; p=.03; γ=.37		
	Sustained Courtship Aggression			Sustained Courtship Aggression		
None	19%	19%	13%	29%	21%	10%
Abuse	23	29	34	39	17	18
Violence	35	52	28	20	41	28
Sex & Violence	23	0	25	12	21	44
	100%	100%	100%	100%	100%	100%
N	31	21	32	41	34	50
	x^2=8.41; df=6; p=.21; γ=.01			x^2=21.56; df=6; p=.002; γ=.44		
	Witnessed Parental Aggression			Witnessed Parental Aggression		
None	53%	45%	54%	55%	47%	45%
Abuse	21	23	19	24	28	30
Violence	26	32	27	21	25	25
	100%	100%	100%	100%	100%	100%
N	34	22	37	42	36	53
	x^2=0.47; df=4; p=.98; γ=.1			x^2=0.94; df=4; p=.92; γ=.09		

a   Peer groups are defined as 1. Nonaggressive - neither males peers sexually aggressed nor female peers sexually victimized; 2. Female Victimization - males peers did not sexually aggress, but female peers had been victimized; 3. Aggressive - male peers sexually aggressed and female peers victimized.

b   See text for information on scale construction.

Table 10.2
Selected[a] Descriptive Statistics from Cross-Tabulations and Analyses of Variance of Peer Groups, by Independent Variables, 1982 and 1987 Samples

	1982 Peer Groups[b]			1987 Peer Groups[b]		
	1(n= 76)	2(n= 58)	3(n= 87)	1(n=177)	2(n=175)	3(n=126)
Demographic Characteristics						
% Female	55.3	62.1	58.9	55.9	59.4	54.8
Average age	20.5	20.3	20.4	20.9	21.0	20.6
Race: % White	92.1	87.9	93.3	86.4	93.1	95.2*#
% Asian	3.9	8.6	6.7	10.7	3.4	3.2
% Unmarried	93.5	100.0	95.5	96.0	94.3	96.8
% Childless	100.0	100.0	100.0	98.8	99.4	100.0
% Employed	33.3	40.4	40.4	39.5	39.7	37.3
Average hours/week	15.9	11.4	15.2	17.7	18.3	14.8
Religion: % Protestant	46.4	34.7	39.1	32.0	30.6	29.6
% Catholic	13.0	10.2	20.7	20.6	20.2	17.6
% No religion	39.7	55.1	40.2	42.3	44.9	50.4
Religiosity: % Strong	26.3	22.2	17.8	18.8	24.7	24.2
Monthly spending money:						
% $0 - $50	43.2	45.6	48.9	52.8	45.2	46.4
% $51 - $100	36.5	35.1	35.6	26.7	27.5	28.8
% $101 - $200	14.9	14.1	12.2	13.7	23.4	20.0
Parents' Education						
% Father's college degree	68.0	66.0	60.2	60.0	66.2	60.5
% Mother's college degree	42.4	46.5	40.4	36.9	43.5	42.4
College Characteristics						
% Upper division	64.8	58.9	63.3	49.7	53.7	58.0
Average G.P.A.	3.04	3.07	3.10	2.96	3.02	3.04
Average # credit hour	[not asked in 1982]			14.9	15.0	15.4
Living arrangements:						
% Sorority/fraternity	11.7	6.9	10.0*	4.8	14.4	19.8*#
% Dormitory	22.1	37.9	34.4	30.5	29.3	25.4
% Home with parents	18.2	6.9	6.7	10.2	2.9	8.7
Major1: % Business	19.7	13.8	12.2	22.6	20.5	14.2
% Hard sciences	14.5	12.1	16.7	10.4	6.2	6.7
% Social sciences	30.3	22.4	26.7	20.1	28.0	30.8
Major2: % "Enterprising"	23.8	9:1	12.3*#	10.3	15.9	14.0
% "Realistic"	2.6	1.8	8.9	3.6	4.3	4.1
Alcohol and Drug Use						
Average # drinks/day	.659	.780	1.15*#	.661	.928	.881*#
Average # drugs/day	.091	.210	.184	.221	.208	.188
Educational Orientations						
% wanting to go to						
graduate school	[not asked in 1982]			45.1	67.4	60.3*#
"Social student" scale[c]				11.5	11.9	12.3*#
"Serious student" scale[c]				13.6	13.6	13.4

a. To conserve space, figures were selected from cross-tabulations of peer groups with the independent variables to illustrate differences among significant categories; most percentages add to 100 only with the excluded categories in mind.
b. Peer groups are defined as follows 1. Nonaggressive; 2. Female Victimization; 3. Aggressive.
c. See text and footnote 3 for details on these scales.
* Chi-square or F ratio significant at p<.05
# Significant for one sex group, but not the other; see text for details.

ject areas. In 1987 members of the sexually aggressive group tended to be upper division students and to be social science majors. In both years, significant differences between the groups appeared to be in their living arrangements, with members of the nonaggressive peer group more likely to live at home with parents. Members of the sexually aggressive and female victimization groups were more likely to live on campus in dormitories in 1982 and in fraternities and sororities in 1987. In addition, males in the sexually aggressive group in 1982 were overrepresented in majors with model personality traits classified as "realistic." Students in these majors were described by Astin and Holland (1961) as "physically strong, unsociable and aggressive" and included those studying physical education and recreation. Nonaggressive males in 1982 were overrepresented in "enterprising majors," described by Astin and Holland (1961) as having verbal skills for dominating, selling, and leading others and including political science, history, industrial relations, and public administration majors.

Significant differences between the three groups appear in measures of behaviors which may be considered hedonistic: alcohol and drug use. In both 1982 and 1987, males in the nonaggressive group were much less likely to report heavy drinking, but in 1987, contrary to expectations, females in the nonaggressive group reported significantly greater alcohol consumption than those in the other groups. In 1982, but not in 1987, students in the nonaggressive peer group reported significantly lower use of illegal drugs than students in the other two peer groups.[4]

The three peer groups in 1987 also differed in educational orientations. Males (but not females) in the nonaggressive peer group were least likely, and those in the sexually aggressive group were most likely, to score high on items that comprise the social-student scale; they were especially likely to report that it was "very important" to meet people and have a good time at the university. Those in the female victimization group, particularly females, had the highest educational aspirations, that is, they were most likely to say that they wanted to go to graduate school.

Discriminant Analysis of Peer-Group Membership

Discriminant function analysis attempts to locate groups in a multidimensional space and assess which factors define the dimensions. Function means for each group describe where in the multidimensional space the groups are located. In the discriminant function analyses performed here, the function means for the nonaggressive groups are all negative; the function means for the sexually aggressive peer groups are all positive; with one exception (males in 1982), the function means for the female victimization group fall in between.

Standardized discriminant function coefficients reported for each model indicate by their signs and sizes how much each predictor variable independently contributes to the discriminating dimension. The coefficients are analogous to standardized regression coefficients used in multiple regression. Large negative coefficients in these examples indicate that a high score on an independent variable is associated with the end of the dimension along which members of the nonaggressive peer group cluster and a low score is associated with the end of the dimension along which members of the sexually aggressive group cluster, when the effects of other independent variables are controlled. Conversely, large positive coefficients indicate that a high score on an independent variable is associated with the end of the dimension along which members of the sexually aggressive peer group cluster and a low score is associated with the end along which members of the nonaggressive group cluster. Chi-square statistics and the proportion of each group correctly classified by its discriminant function scores are used to assess the extent to which the functions can accurately predict group membership.

The discriminant function analyses presented here continue, in a multivariate context, the largely exploratory analyses in the previous section. Variables that helped distinguish between the three peer groups in the bivariate analyses are used as independent variables in this multivariate framework. Since different sets of indicators are available in each year for males and females, each of the four models presented in Table 10.3 is different. Missing data reduced the size of each sample somewhat. Each of the four functions presented is statistically significant at the 0.05 level or beyond, and over half of each sample is correctly classified by the functions. As expected from the bivariate results, the discriminant functions vary substantially by sex.

For males in 1982 the strongest predictors of group membership are experiences with courtship aggression, in contrast to the bivariate results. Having inflicted courtship aggression is associated with the end of the dimension along which members of the female victimization and sexually aggressive groups tend to cluster. Having sustained but not inflicted courtship aggression is associated with the end of the dimension along which members of the nonaggressive group tend to fall. Alcohol and drug use, living arrangements, and academic majors have moderate influences on the function. As in the bivariate analysis, high alcohol and drug use, living in a dormitory, and "realistic" majors are associated with the end of the dimension along which members of the aggressive and female victimization groups cluster. Living at home with parents associates with the end of the dimension along which those in the nonaggressive group tend to fall.

Examination of the correlations among the predictor variables suggests that some of these results may be due to a suppressor effect. Among males in 1982, several bivariate correlations of alcohol and drug use with inflicting courtship aggression were negative; that is, males with lower levels of alcohol and drug use were more likely to report that they had inflicted courtship aggression. Thus, when levels of drug and alcohol use were held constant in the multivariate analysis, the association between peer group membership and inflicting courtship aggression was enhanced. Similarly, the bivariate correlation between alcohol and sustaining courtship aggression was negative for males in the female victimization group. As noted above and in Table 10.1, members of this group were also less likely than others to report that they had sustained sexual violence. Thus, when levels of alcohol use are controlled in the multivariate

Table 10.3
Results of Peer-Group Discriminant Analyses, by Sex, 1982 and 1987[a]

	1982 Sample (N=197)				1987 Sample (N=372)			
Function means for peer groups:	Males	(n)	Females	(n)	Males	(n)	Females	(n)
1. Nonaggressive	-.75	(31)	-.46	(33)	-.50	(68)	-.38	(92)
2. Female Victimization	.55	(19)	-.31	(31)	.26	(59)	.09	(86)
3. Aggressive	.46	(28)	.55	(45)	.60	(31)	.77	(36)

	Standardized Discriminant Function Coefficients				Standardized Discriminant Function Coefficients	
Independent Variables	Males	Females	Independent Variables	Males	Females	
Alcohol consumption	.25	b	Alcohol consumption	.32	-.33	
Drug use	.43	-.23	Drug consumption	.22	b	
Inflict aggression scale	.54	.29	Social Student Scale	.58	.06	
Sustain aggression scale	-.50	.69	Serious Student Scale	-.05	-.29	
Live in sorority/fraternity	-.08	-.21	Want to go to graduate school	.32	.13	
Live in on-campus dorm	.35	.12	Social science major	.35	-.01	
Live at home with parents	-.20	-.54	Business major	.22	-.39	
"Realistic" major	.45	b	College junior or senior	.22	.46	
"Enterprising" major	-.42	b	Live in sorority/fraternity	.27	.58	
			Live in on-campus dorm	-.23	.53	
			Live at home with parents	.05	.02	
			No religion	-.15	.44	
			Race (1=White)	b	.44	
			Spending money	-.09	-.07	
Chi-square (df)	33.7(18)	25.4(12)	Chi-square (df)	41.1(26)	40.0(26)	
probability	.01	.01	probability	.03	.04	
Percent correctly classified:			Percent correctly classified:			
1. Nonaggressive	65%	52%	1. Nonaggressive	62%	60%	
2. Female Victimization	63%	42%	2. Female Victimization	51%	38%	
3. Aggressive	43%	69%	3. Aggressive	55%	58%	
TOTAL	56%	56%	TOTAL	56%	51%	

a. Each analysis also produced a second, nonsignificant function; details on these are available from the authors on request.

b. Not included in the discriminant analysis.

analysis, the association between peer-group membership and sustaining court-ship aggression was enhanced.[5]

For females in 1982 the strongest predictor of peer group membership is having sustained courtship aggression; living arrangements and drug use have somewhat smaller effects. Having sustained courtship aggression is associated with the sexually aggressive group's end of the discriminant function, while living with one's parents and, to lesser extents, living in a sorority and, in contrast to the bivariate results, high drug use are associated with the end of the continuum along which members of the nonaggressive and female victimi-zation groups tend to cluster. The association of high drug use with member-ship in the nonaggressive group appears in this multivariate analysis with fe-males (but not with males). High drug use is associated with higher reports of both inflicting and sustaining courtship aggression. Once experiences with courtship aggression were statistically controlled, the association of peer group membership with drug use actually reversed.[6]

In 1987 for males the social student scale is the best predictor of peer group membership, with alcohol and drug use, educational aspirations, major, year in school, and living arrangements having smaller influences. A high score on the social student scale, greater drug and alcohol consumption, living in a fraternity but not in a dormitory, majoring in the social sciences and business, being an upper division student, and having high educational aspirations are all associated with the end of the discriminant function along which members of the sexually aggressive and female victimization groups tend to cluster.

Finally, for females in 1987 the strongest predictors of peer group member-ship are living arrangements, year in school, race/ethnicity, and religious affil-iation; moderately influencing peer group membership are alcohol consump-tion, the serious student scale, and academic major. Living in a sorority or dormitory, being an upper division student, being white, reporting no religious affiliation, lower alcohol consumption, not being a business major, and lower scores on the serious student scale are all associated with the end of the dis-criminant function along which members of the sexually aggressive group tend to cluster.

SUMMARY

The results described above confirm the presence of the three types of mixed-sex peer groups in two different samples and indicate that the representation of individuals in these groups shifted somewhat over time. The multivariate anal-yses show that in the 1982 sample females who belonged to the sexually ag-gressive peer group were more likely than other students to have sustained courtship aggression, while males were more likely to have inflicted courtship aggression on others. Neither males nor females in this sexually aggressive peer group were more likely to have witnessed parental violence. In both 1982 and 1987, the three peer groups varied little in most of their demographic, family background, and college characteristics. As expected, however, they varied significantly in a few key dimensions, notably living arrangements, alcohol and drug use, and educational aspirations and values.

DISCUSSION

The finding of these three mixed-sex peer groups with their distinctly varying involvements in sexual aggression, and replicating this finding in two different college cohorts, is striking and noteworthy. As noted above and in Table 10.2, the peer groups were truly mixed-sex; the relative representation of females and males did not vary from one peer group to another, and none of the three groups was small. In both cohorts only 1 percent of the students had male friends who had been sexually aggressive but no female friends who had been sexually victimized. In other words, if college students had male friends who had been sexually aggressive, they almost always also had female friends who had been sexually victimized. The sexual aggression of males within a mixed-sex peer group appears to be an important determinant of the probability that females within the group will be sexually victimized.

The pivotal role of males in determining the sexual victimization of female peers is probably related to the overall system of male dominance within society and, especially, the centrality of this pattern to sexual relations (Stockard & Johnson, 1980; Johnson, 1988). Studies of peer culture suggest that interactions within peer groups lead to the legitimation of certain behaviors and actions. Schwendinger and Schwendinger (1985:148–49) suggest that patterns of discourse in peer groups help assuage anxiety and achieve cooperation from peers who feel morally uneasy. If, given the system of male dominance, especially in sexual relations, the views of males are accorded more credence than those of females, it is understandable that the peer groups described in this paper would develop. In social groups that include males who have inflicted sexual aggression, interactions would be more likely to occur that legitimize such actions. Assuming that students acquire many of their dating partners from their group of male and female friends, those with male friends who have inflicted sexual aggression would also have female friends who had experienced sexual aggression.

The results of this research support such an interpretation. The findings presented above suggest that living groups on campuses, as well as students encountered regularly in classes in one's major, may offer networks of friends and potential dating partners. These friendship networks vary significantly in their attitudes and values toward college, in their patterns of drug and alcohol use, and in the extent to which they tolerate or condone sexual aggression and victimization. The peer culture of sororities and fraternities in particular emerged significantly in the analyses of 1987 data; in 1982 it did not.

The case study presented at the beginning of this chapter may not be typical, but it illustrates how the peer culture in fraternities and sororities can create and sustain male sexual aggression and female victimization in college. The three-day party described earlier was essentially a systematic process of honoring the female guests, degrading them, honoring them again, creating indebtedness, and eventually obtaining sex from them. The institutional auspices of such events—tradition-laden fraternities and sororities and the college itself—lend the activities credibility, while the peer culture rationalizes activities that might be questioned in other circumstances. Thus, within these organizations and friendship networks, a multistage process of sexual aggression and victimization gains legitimation; indeed, for members of. the peer culture to question the process is to invite contempt.

While the case study and the statistical results of this research may imply that the resurgence of sororities and fraternities in the mid-1980s is associated with increased sexual aggression and victimization, such an interpretation is open to question. In the analyses reported here, the sexually aggressive peer group actually declined in size between 1982 and 1987, while the female victimization peer group grew substantially. Why this occurred is unclear, but there are three possible explanations. Between 1982 and 1987 the saliency of courtship violence as a social issue increased. This may have increased on-campus discourse on the issues and resulted in more women's sharing their experiences, and therefore more students knowing women who had sustained sexual aggression in dating in 1987 than in 1982. Such discourse also may have undermined the legitimacy of sexual aggression among men, so that it occurred less often in 1987 than in 1982. A final possible explanation is methodological: In the 1982 survey, the questions on peers followed a long series of questions on many facets of courtship aggression; in the 1987 survey, the questions on peers followed questions on unrelated topics. Thus, heightened sensitivity to the topic in 1982 through prior survey questions may have resulted in more respondents' remembering sexually aggressive male peers than in 1987. The data in this study provide no opportunity to disentangle these possible explanations for the growth of the female victimization peer group and the decline of the sexually aggressive peer group over time.

It is important to stress that peer group membership was largely unassociated with a wide variety of demographic and collegiate variables. In other words, members of the sexually aggressive peer group, at least in the samples studied here, were similar to their less violent peers. Variables that distinguish peer group members tended to involve living arrangements, behaviors, and attitudes, with the sexually aggressive and victimized students more likely to live in sororities, fraternities, and dormitories, to report alcohol and drug use, and to value the social aspects of college life. This general pattern suggests some support for Astin's (1977) findings on the relative hedonism of different college subgroups, for Hindelang's (1971) and Ageton's (1983) research on the association of various deviant behaviors with each other, and for the subculture of violence theories. The major exception is the association, once other variables were controlled, of females' lower drug and alcohol use with membership in the sexually aggressive group. Given the unexpected nature of this finding, replications seem crucial.

Perhaps the most important associations found in this research were between peer group membership and courtship aggression. The results of the multivariate analyses demonstrated the strong association between membership in the sexually aggressive peer group and women's sustaining and men's inflicting courtship aggression. This finding may provide some support for Schwendinger and Schwendinger's (1985) notions of the legitimation of deviant activity that occurs in peer groups (see also Chin et al., 1986). Students in the sexually aggressive peer group may perceive courtship aggression as a regularized part of the courtship process, and thus are more likely to experience it.

Finally, it is important to note that the strong association between peer group membership and women's sexual victimization seems to support the theoretical work of Hindelang, Gottfredson, and Garofalo (1978), who hypothesize that personal lifestyle is a determinant of crime victimization. Although a previous empirical test provided little support for the relationship between lifestyle and violent crime (Miethe, Stafford & Long, 1987), this may have been due to the global measures of lifestyle that were used. Insofar as peer group membership reflects the behaviors, values, and attitudes of friendship networks, it may be a more precise measure of the lifestyle characteristics associated with sexual victimization for adolescents and young adults. This suggests that studies of sexual victimization should not dismiss theories regarding lifestyles, but should employ more precise measures of the phenomenon.

IMPLICATIONS FOR POLICY AND PRACTICE

Practitioners must remember that peer groups are an extremely important part of college students' lives. Peer groups are a much more salient part of adolescents' and young adults' lives than professors, counselors, or parents (Davis, 1974; Walsh, Farrel, & Tolone, 1976). Our findings suggest that peer group membership, and especially the actions of males in peer groups, are related to the probability that females will be sexually victimized. Thus, practitioners need to be aware, and they need to make students aware, that mixed-sex peer groups vary in the extent to which they participate in and seemingly legitimize courtship aggression.

Practitioners also need to realize that the role of the males in these groups appears to be pivotal. In the two samples studied here, having male friends who are sexually aggressive is sufficient to guarantee that students, both males and females, will have female friends who have been sexually victimized. In addition, females who belong to such sexually aggressive groups are much more likely to be victims of courtship violence. In helping students to minimize the probability of sexual victimization, it thus seems very important to have them consider the characteristics of their own networks of friends and acquaintances.

RECOMMENDATIONS FOR FURTHER STUDY

The research presented here has been largely exploratory, and it is limited by geographic location, the nature of the survey questions asked, and the relatively few correlates of peer group membership that were statistically significant. Future research could pursue several directions. First, it is important to determine if the three peer groups found in this research appear in samples drawn from different types of schools, in noncollege populations, in other age groups and cohorts, and in samples that are broader in socioeconomic status, race, and geographic region. In addition, it is important to know if peer groups that seem to foster or tolerate courtship aggression can be identified in ways that may be more precise than the survey questions used here.

The inability of the many measures used in this study to distinguish peer group membership, but the promising nature of the findings on living arrangements and certain behaviors, values, and attitudes, suggests that additional measures should be employed in examining correlates of peer group membership. Specifically recommended are measures of attitudes toward the legitimacy of courtship violence (cf. Rapaport & Burkhart, 1984; Koss et al., 1985; Garrett-Gooding & Senter, 1987) and more specific measures of the friends who comprise these peer groups. Of particular interest is the nature of friends' experiences with courtship violence and the nature of the subjects' relationships with these friends (cf. Giordano, Cernkovich & Pugh, 1986).

The decline in the representation of students in the sexually aggressive peer group in the 1987 sample as compared with the 1982 sample raises additional questions. Did students in the 1982 cohort retain their greater degree of male sexual aggression in 1987? Given that violent acts in general tend to decline with age, what are the age, period, and cohort differences in the preponderance of sexually aggressive peer groups?

Most importantly, future research needs to employ different research designs than the cross-sectional surveys typically used in research on courtship aggression. Longitudinal studies of young people would help explain the development of peer group norms and help separate age, period, and cohort effects. Intervention studies would help scholars and practitioners understand whether peer-group norms can be altered to prevent courtship aggression and, perhaps, future marital and family violence. Studies that use peer groups as the unit of analysis are important, with specific attention given to the way peer groups legitimize sexual aggression and to the roles of males and females in these interactions. Finally, given the results obtained in the present analysis, it seems essential for future researchers to continue employing multivariate statistical procedures.

SUMMARY AND CONCLUSIONS

This research has replicated the finding of three mixed-sex peer groups with distinctly different patterns of sexual aggression and victimization in two randomly sampled college cohorts in 1982 and 1987. Although the structure of the peer groups changed somewhat in the five-year period, in both years a student's having male friends who had been sexually aggressive guaranteed that the student also had female friends who had been sexually victimized. This finding was discussed within the context of theory regarding the centrality of male dominance in sexual relations.

Both bivariate and multivariate analyses were used to explore the correlates of membership in the three peer groups. Members of the peer groups were usually similar in their demographic, family background, and collegiate characteristics. However, males who had no friends who inflicted sexual aggression were less likely to have inflicted courtship aggression themselves and to have a "social" orientation toward college, and they consumed less alcohol and drugs than other males. Females in this nonaggressive peer group were less likely than other females to have sustained courtship aggression or to live in on-campus housing, but they were more likely to live at home with parents and to consume somewhat more alcohol and drugs. Theories and empirical literature regarding the linkage between lifestyles and crime victimization, homogamy in friendship choices, and correlates of delinquency and violent behavior were used to explain the differences between members of the three peer groups.

Overall, this research has offered an exploratory window on the nature of sexually aggressive peer groups and courtship relations—a topic that until now has remained largely unexamined by either researchers or practitioners. Several specific suggestions for future research on this topic were proffered, and clinicians who treat young persons involved in courtship aggression were reminded to consider the importance of peer group membership.

ACKNOWLEDGMENTS

Authorship for this chapter is shared equally. This research was supported in part by the Center for the Study of Women in Society at the University of Oregon. We are grateful to S. Bohmer, J. DeGidio, M. M. Johnson, C. S. Kirkpatrick, S. S. Simpson, and the editors for comments, and to L. Cogswell, M. Newby, and K. Olson for word processing and research assistance.

NOTES

1. This vignette is based upon in-depth interviews. Some details of the event have been changed to protect the identities of informants.

2. The wording for the question regarding male friends was based on the questionnaire of Polk et al., 1981 and Adler, 1982.

3. The items listed in the text as comprising the scales had three categories each: $1 = $ not important, $2 = $ somewhat important, $3 = $ very important. The Serious Student scale is the sum of five items and ranges from 5 to 15, while the Social Student scale is the sum of six items and ranges from 6 to 18. Cronbach's alpha, which was used to test the internal reliability of the scales, resulted in coefficients of 0.47 and 0.61, respec-

tively. Details on the construction of all scales and indexes are available upon request from the authors.

4. As shown in Table 10.2, the F-ratio testing the hypothesis that the three group means were equal was not significant. However, t tests comparing the means of the nonaggressive group with those in the other two groups were significant. Comparison of the nonaggressive group with the female victimization group yielded $t = 2.2$, $p = .03$, and with the aggressive group yielded $t = 2.0$, $p = .05$.)

5. The Pearson product moment correlations between alcohol use and inflicting and sustaining (respectively) courtship aggression for men in 1982 are: -0.01 and 0.05 for those in the nonaggressive group; -0.22 and -0.38 for those in the female victimization group; and 0.04 and 0.04 for those in the sexually aggressive group. The parallel correlations for drug use are: -0.22 and 0.00 for those in the nonaggressive group; 0.05 and -0.07 for those in the female victimization group; and -0.19 and 0.08 for those in the sexually aggressive group.

6. The pooled within-group correlations for females in 1982 between drug use and inflicting and sustaining courtship aggression are both 0.25.

REFERENCES

Ageton, S. S. (1983). *Sexual Assault Among Adolescents*. Lexington, MA: Heath.

Alder, C. (1982). "An Exploration of Self-reported Sexual Aggression." Doctoral diss., Department of Sociology, University of Oregon, Eugene.

Astin, A. W. (1977). *Four Critical Years: Effects of College on Beliefs, Attitudes, and Knowledge*. San Francisco: Jossey-Bass.

Astin, A. W. & Holland, J. L. (1961). "The Environmental Assessment Technique: A Way to Measure College Environments." *Journal of Educational Psychology*, 52:308–16.

Ball-Rokeach, S. J. (1973). "Values and Violence: A Test of the Subculture of Violence Thesis. *American Sociological Review*, 38:736–49.

Billy, J. O. G., Rodgers, J. L., & Udry, J. R. (1984). "Adolescent Sexual Behavior and Friendship Choice." *Social Forces*, 62:653–78.

Billy, J. O. G, & Udry, J. R. (1985). "Patterns of Adolescent Friendship and Effects on Sexual Behavior." *Social Psychology Quarterly*, 48:27–41.

Chin, J., Snyder, C., McClure, B. & Forrestal, M. (1986). "Courtship Violence Among College Students." Paper presented at the American Psychological Association meetings.

Cohen, J. (1977). "Sources of Peer Group Homogeneity." *Sociology of Education*, 30:241–77.

Colvin, M., & Pauly, J. (1983). "A Critique of Criminology: Toward an Integrated Structural-Marxist Theory of Delinquency Production." *American Journal of Sociology*, 89:543–51.

Davis, P. (1974). "Contextual Sex Saliency and Sexual Activity: The Relative Effects of Family and Peer Group in the Sexual Socialization Process." *Journal of Marriage and the Family*, 36:196–202.

DeLamater, J., & MacCorquodale, P. (1979). *Premarital Sexuality: Attitudes, Relationships, Behavior*. Madison, WI: University of Wisconsin Press.

Garrett-Gooding, J. & Senter, R. (1987). "Attitudes and Acts of Aggression on a University Campus. *Sociological Inquiry*, 57:348–72.

Giordano, P. C., Cernkovich, S. A., & Pugh, M. D. (1986). "Friendships and Delinquency." *American Journal of Sociology*, 91:1170–202.

Gwartney-Gibbs, P. A., Stockard, J., & Bohmer, S. (1987). "Learning Courtship Aggression: The Influence of Parents, Peers, and Personal Experiences. *Family Relations*, 36:276–82.

Hindelang, M. J. (1971). "Age, Sex, and the Versatility of Delinquent Involvements." *Social Problems*, 18:522–35.

Hindelang, M. J., Gottfredson, M. R., & Garofalo, J. (1978). *Victims of Personal Crime: An Empirical Foundation for a Theory of Personal Victimization.* Cambridge, MA: Ballinger.

Johnson, M. M. (1988). *Strong Mothers, Weak Wives: The Search for Gender Equality.* Berkeley, CA: University of California Press.

Kandel, D. B. (1978). "Homophyly, Selection, and Socialization in Adolescent Friendships. *American Journal of Sociology*, 84:427–36.

Kanin, E. J. (1957). "Male Aggression in Dating-Courting Relations." *American Journal of Sociology*, 63:197–204.

———. (1985). "Date Rapists: Differential Sexual Socialization and Relative Deprivation." *Archives of Sexual Behavior*, 14:219–31.

Koss, M. P., Leonard, K. E., Beezley, D. A., & Oros, C. J. (1985). "Nonstranger Sexual Aggression: A Discriminant Analysis of the Psychological Characteristics of Undetected Offenders." *Sex Roles*, 12:981–92.

Koss, M. P., & Oros, C. J. (1982). "Sexual Experiences Survey: A Research Instrument Investigating Sexual Aggression and Victimization." *Journal of Consulting and Clinical Psychology*, 50:455–57.

Miethe, T. D., Stafford, M. C., & Long, J. S. (1987). "Social Differentiation in Criminal Victimization: A Test of Routine Activities/Lifestyle Theories." *American Sociological Review*, 52:184–94.

Polk, K., Alder, C., Bazemore, G., Blake, G., Cordray, S., Coventry, G., Galvin, J., & Temple, M. (1981). "Becoming Adult: An Analysis of Maturational Development From Age 16 to 30 of a Cohort of Young Men." Final report of the Marion County Youth Study. Eugene, OR: University of Oregon.

Rapaport, K., & Burkhart, B. R. (1984). "Personality and Attitudinal Characteristics of Sexually Coercive College Males." *Journal of Abnormal Psychology*, 93:216–21.

Schwendinger, H., & Schwendinger, J. S. (1985). *Adolescent Subcultures and Delinquency: Research Edition.* New York: Praeger.

Stockard, J., & Johnson, M. (1980). *Sex Roles: Sex Inequality and Sex Role Development.* Englewood Cliffs, NJ: Prentice-Hall.

Straus, M. A. (1979). "Measuring Intrafamily Conflict and Violence: The Conflict Tactics Scales." *Journal of Marriage and the Family*, 44:75–88.

Walsh, R., Farrel, M. Z., & Tolone, W. L. (1976). "Selection of Reference Group, Perceived Reference Group Permissiveness, and Personal Permissiveness Attitudes and Behavior: A Study of Two Consecutive Panels." *Journal of Marriage and the Family*, 38:495–507.

Wolfgang, M., & Ferracutti, F. (1967). *The Subculture of Violence: Towards an Integrated Theory in Criminology.* New York: Tavistock.

11   The Sexual Victimization of Unmarried Women by Nonrelative Acquaintances
Joanne Belknap

HISTORICAL AND THEORETICAL ISSUES

The labeling of a phenomenon by the media or social scientists as a "social problem," does not necessarily mean that the phenomenon has only recently become a social problem. This appears to be particularly true for issues that feminists have uncovered in the last two decades, such as stranger rape, child sexual abuse (including incest), sexual harassment, and woman battering. These various forms of abuse against women have all occurred in what some have referred to as epidemic proportions, probably for centuries. However, it is only within the past two decades that these victimizations have been acknowledged to occur in proportions so large as to be labeled social problems.

A particularly important concern that recently has been labeled a social problem is acquaintance rape. While the uncovering of the large proportions of women who have experienced stranger rapes shocked many people in the 1970s, more recently has been the acceptance that many women are commonly sexually victimized by males whom they know, and often know quite well. One category or subset of acquaintance rape has been that of "date rape." *Ms.* magazine is largely credited with uncovering date rape in a 1982 article entitled "Date Rape: A Campus Epidemic." This article made a successful attempt to acknowledge the significant degree to which young women were being raped on dates.

However, it is interesting to note that a similar finding had already been published much earlier (Kanin, 1957). Kanin was primarily concerned with aggression at five levels of what he referred to as "erotic intimacy": necking, petting above the waist, petting below the waist, attempted sexual intercourse, and attempted sexual intercourse accompanied by violence. He found that approximately 62 percent of college freshmen women had experienced some level of sexual victimization during the year prior to university entrance. Almost half of these victimizations occurred in relationships in which the couple had some form of a permanent dating relationship. Approximately 18 percent had experienced attempted or completed intercourse as one aspect of their sexual victimization.[1] This article appears to have made little or no impact, and "date rape" continued as a hidden social problem until the early 1980s. Explanations for the lack of impact of Kanin's article are hypothetical at this point, but it is possible that the laying of the groundwork for similar feminist issues had not yet begun.

Russell (1984) states that the identification of the rape of women by strangers preceded the identification of the social problem of nonsexual wife abuse. Since the early and mid-1970s, there has been an increased awareness that wife battering is not restricted to wives, but also occurs to girlfriends and lovers. Hence, some have chosen to refer to this phenomenon as "woman battering," in order to define the situation more realistically. Furthermore, one aspect of wife abuse is marital rape (Finkelhor & Yllo, 1983, 1985; Russell, 1982). Since battering occurs in intimate relationships outside of marriage, and since one form of wife abuse is marital rape, it should not be surprising to find that unmarried women involved in intimate relationships experience a great deal of sexual victimization.

While Makepeace's (1981) study of college students' experiences in courtship violence did not directly address rape or sexual victimization, it is interesting to note that the most common reasons for courtship violence were (1) jealousy over a real or perceived third party, (2) drinking behavior, and (3) anger over sexual desire. Jealousy and anger over sexual desires are related to the sexual intimacy between the couple. Similarly, Lane and Gwartney-Gibbs's (1985) study of college student courtship violence claimed that the major source of conflict between dating couples was probably sexual. Korman and Leslie (1982:114) attempt to explain the source of sexual victimization in dating couples, and state that the dating situation itself is structured in such a way that there are "expectations of erotically tinged experimentation and participation" and that there is the potential for this to lead to the sexual exploitation of women.

Koss and Oros (1982) conducted a study on college students' ($N = 3,862$) sexual experiences and found that approximately 70 percent of the women claimed a man had misinterpreted the degree of sexual intimacy they desired, 6 percent had been orally or anally raped, and 6 percent had been vaginally raped by force or the threat of force. Koss, Gidycz, and Wisniewski's (1987) study of 6,159 college students in 32 institutions of higher learning found that 54 percent of the women had experienced some form of sexual victimization (25 percent of the men reported committing some form of sexual aggression). Twelve percent of the women had experienced attempted rape, and 15 percent had experienced oral, anal, or vaginal rape by force or threat of force or under the influence of alcohol or drugs. Muehlenhard and Linton (1987) also studied university students, and found proportions similar to those in the above study: 78 percent of the women reported experiencing sexual victimization by a male, while 58 percent of the men reported using sexual aggression against a female. Fifteen percent of the women and 7 percent of the men reported being involved in sexual intercourse against the woman's will. Similarly, Rapaport and Burkhart (1984) found in their study of college males that 15 percent admitted forcing intercourse at least once, and 12 percent admitted physically restraining a woman in order to commit a sexual act. Over one-third admitted to ignoring the woman's protests.

What is clear from the above findings is that young women are at a high risk of experiencing sexual victimization by men whom they are acquainted with, including dates. Research in this area has uncovered two patterns: Women are not as likely to identify their experiences as "rapes" when the perpetrators are acquaintances, and men are less likely to report committing sexual aggression than women are to report experiencing it. The first pattern is probably largely due to our media and culture, which mistakenly emphasize rape as something that occurs between strangers. There are two possible explanations for the second pattern: Either men are simply less likely to define the situation as rape; for instance, they may believe that the women really wanted to have sex even if they resisted verbally or even physically, or the men being surveyed are different (perhaps younger) than the men whom the women report are victimizing them. At any rate, date and other forms of acquaintance rapes have finally been identified as a serious social problem.

In order to understand sexual victimization, it is useful to draw upon prior literature concerning categories of rapes and rapists. For instance, Groth (1979) developed three types of rape: anger, power, and sadistic rape. *Anger rape* occurs where physical force is used in excess of what would be necessary to simply overpower the victim to achieve sex. Thus, *anger rapes* are extremely brutal, with physical assaults in addition to sexual assaults. Groth found that *anger rape* described 40 percent of convicted rapists. *Power rapes* are characterized by a motivation to sexually possess and dominate the victim, with use of no more than the amount of force necessary to do so. Thus, if the rapist is able to secure sexual submission by the threat of violence, he will not resort to the actual use of violence. When physical force is used, it is in order to overpower the victim in order to secure sexual submission, and the rapist will only use that amount of force necessary to do so. *Power rapes* described 55 percent of Groth's convicted rapists. *Sadistic rape* occurs when sexuality and aggression are fused, so that aggression itself becomes erotic. Only 5 percent of Groth's rapists were involved in sadistic rape.

Finkelhor and Yllo (1985) have developed three types of marital rape: battering, force only, and obsessive rapes. *Battering rapes* were those in which the victim experienced both marital rape and nonsexual physical violence within the marital relationship. These rapes are comparable to Groth's (1979) *anger rapes. Force only rape* is similar to Groth's *power rape* in that only the force necessary to coerce the victim into sexual submission is used by the husbands. In *obsessive rape* husbands were willing to use force in order to achieve sexual experiences with their wives that the authors described as "strange," "perverse," and "bizarre"; this is similar to Groth's sadistic rapes. Finkelhor and Yllo (1985) found that obsessive rapes were the least frequent of their three categories, thus paralleling Groth's finding.

THE FOCUS OF THIS STUDY

Most research on date rape has been conducted on college students. Clearly, these are not the only persons who date. The present research analyses the sexual victimization of unmarried (including divorced, separated, widowed, and never married) women who are 12 years old or older and who have experienced attempted rape or rape by persons known to them.[2] Data from the National Crime Survey for the years 1973 through 1982 are examined. These data are advantageous because they are collected nationally and over time. Additionally, they include information on a wide variety of characteristics about the offender, the victim, and the offense.

The major shortcoming of these data is that it is likely that much rape is still highly unreported, even to the National Crime Survey. While the self-report victimization method of the National Crime Survey data collection makes them preferable to the Uniform Crime Reports (which collect information only on rapes reported to the police), the National Crime Survey has been criticized for failing to directly ask whether the respondent has been a victim of rape. (For a more extensive critique of the National Crime Survey, refer to Russell, 1984.) Another shortcoming to using the National Crime Survey data in the present study is that the victim-offender relationship is only coded into a few major categories, and a dating relationship is not one of them.

The research on date rape tends to use one of two approaches. The first is to report the frequencies of various sexual assaults women experience or men admit to perpetrating. The second is to describe which characteristics determine whether college students will identify a situation as rape. In the latter case, for instance, various vignettes may be used and features of the situation are varied, including the place of the date, the amount of money the man spends on the woman, and who initiates the date, in order to determine the respondent's assessment of the victim's culpability when these features are manipulated. However, most of these studies do not include descriptions (with the exception of race) of the victims, they are usually limited to a fairly narrow age group (18–22 years old), they describe little about the assault except what sexual violation occurred, and they fail to address reactions of the victim to the assault. These omissions are to a large degree a result of date rape's being a recently identified social problem.

However, such characteristics as resistance by the offender and the amount of injury have been addressed more thoroughly with respect to marital rapes. For example, Finkelhor and Yllo's (1985) research on marital rape examined such factors as brutality, injury, and victim resistance.

This chapter will address some of the neglected issues mentioned above as they apply to unmarried women who are victims of nonrelative acquaintance rapes. Specifically, descriptions of the victims, the offenders, the offense, the response of the victim, and the degree of injury are addressed. It is believed that this information will add to our und 'standing of date rape.

The analysts divide the victims into .aree groups: Those who have experienced attempted rape or rape by an acquaintance, by a well-known person, or both. For simplification, the combination of the groups "acquaintance" and "well-known" will be referred to as "total acquaintance."

The National Crime Survey categorizes the victim-offender relationships as (1) stranger, (2) known by sight only, (3) casual acquaintance, and (4) well-known. Those victims whose assailants are "well-known" are further categorized according to whether or not the offender was a relative. The following analysis excludes stranger rapes and rapes that were perpetrated by relatives of the victim (such as marital rape or incest). Those instances in which the offenders were recognized by sight only or were casual acquaintances were classified as acquaintance rapes. Nonrelative rapes in which the offender was well-known were categorized as well-known rapes. Finally, all victims who reported rapes and attempted rapes by nonrelative acquaintances were placed in the third category, "total acquaintances." The resulting sample is composed of 212 women of whom 95 (44.8 percent) knew their offenders well ("well-known"), while 117 (55.2 percent) described their offenders as "casual acquaintances" or as known by "sight only."

THE FINDINGS

The analysis of women 12 and older who experienced sexual victimization in the form of attempted or completed rape by men who were known but not related to them is summarized in Tables 11.1, 11.2, and 11.3. Each table contains three subheadings: total acquaintance, acquaintance only, and well-known only.

Demographic Characteristics of the Victims

Table 11.1 reports the demographic characteristics of the victims. The risk of rape victimization by a person known to the victim appear to be greatest for women who are of typical dating age. Over half of the total acquaintance victimizations occur to women who are between 16 and 24 years old, and almost 80 percent of the total acquaintance rapes happen to women between the ages of 16 and 34. Twelve- to 15-year-olds are more likely to experience acquain-

Table 11.1
Demographic Characteristics of the Victims

	Total Acquaintance		Acquaintance (only)		Well-Known (only)		Chi-Square
	%	(n)	%	(n)	%	(n)	
Age							
12-15	15.6	(33)	22.2	(26)	7.4	(7)	
16-19	29.2	(62)	26.5	(31)	32.6	(31)	
20-24	24.5	(52)	20.5	(24)	29.5	(28)	
25-34	24.1	(51)	24.8	(29)	23.2	(22)	
35+	6.6	(14)	6.0	(7)	7.4	(7)	10.03*
Race							
white	81.6	(173)	86.3	(101)	75.8	(72)	
black	17.0	(36)	12.8	(15)	22.1	(21)	
other	1.4	(3)	0.9	(1)	2.1	(2)	3.95[a]
Family Income							
< $3,999	26.8	(53)	26.9	(29)	26.7	(24)	
$4,000-9,999	32.3	(64)	25.0	(27)	41.1	(37)	
$10,000-19,999	31.3	(62)	37.0	(40)	24.4	(22)	
$20,000+	9.6	(19)	11.1	(12)	7.8	(7)	7.00

[a]The expected cell frequency was less than 5 for 2 of the 9 cells.
*p≤.05.

tance rapes rather than well-known rapes. A likely explanation for this significant difference is that younger women are probably less likely to be involved in intimate relationships.

While there appears to be a tendency for black women to be somewhat more at risk of total acquaintance rapes than white women or other women of color, this relationship was not quite significant ($p \leq .07$). Other findings regarding race were not significant.

Table 11.1's report on family income shows that most of the victims are from the lower economic strata. Only about 10 percent of the victims are from families in which the yearly income is $20,000 or more. However, family income does not distinguish acquaintance only victims from well-known victims.

Characteristics of the Offense

Table 11.2 presents characteristics of the offense. "Well-known" attempts at rape were more likely to result in completed rapes (55.8 percent) than were the "acquaintance" attempts at rape (40.2 percent). This is consistent with prior research (Russell, 1984).

Total acquaintance rapes were least likely to occur in the winter. The riskiest time of day for total acquaintance rapes was between 6:00 P.M. and midnight.

Table 11.2
Characteristics of the Offense

	Total Acquaintance		Acquaintance (only)		Well-Known (only)		Chi-Square
	%	(n)	%	(n)	%	(n)	
Attempted Rape Completed?							
yes	47.2	(100)	40.2	(47)	55.8	(53)	
no	52.8	(112)	59.8	(70)	44.2	(42)	4.52*
Occurred in Victim's Home?							
yes	42.5	(90)	37.6	(44)	48.4	(46)	
no	57.5	(122)	62.4	(73)	51.6	(49)	2.09
Season							
winter	15.2	(32)	15.4	(18)	14.9	(14)	
spring	28.0	(59)	29.9	(35)	25.5	(24)	
summer	31.3	(66)	29.1	(34)	34.0	(32)	
autumn	25.6	(54)	25.6	(30)	25.5	(24)	0.78
Time							
6 a.m.- 6 p.m.	26.4	(55)	20.7	(24)	33.7	(31)	
6 p.m.-midnight	41.3	(86)	47.4	(55)	33.7	(31)	
midnight-6 a.m.	32.2	(67)	31.9	(37)	32.6	(30)	5.63
Offender's Race							
white	66.0	(140)	62.2	(74)	69.5	(66)	
black	28.8	(61)	31.6	(37)	25.3	(24)	
other	5.2	(11)	5.1	(6)	5.3	(5)	1.05[a]
Weapon							
none	87.9	(175)	86.7	(98)	89.5	(77)	
gun	5.5	(11)	8.0	(9)	2.3	(2)	
knife	2.5	(5)	1.8	(2)	3.5	(3)	
other	4.0	(8)	3.5	(4)	4.7	(4)	3.58[b]
Police Informed?							
yes	41.0	(86)	40.0	(46)	42.1	(40)	
no	59.0	(124)	60.0	(69)	57.9	(55)	0.03
Reason Police Not Told?[c]							
can't do anything	16.1	(20)	15.9	(11)	16.4	(9)	0.00
not important	9.7	(12)	11.6	(8)	7.3	(4)	0.25
police not bother	8.1	(10)	11.6	(8)	3.6	(2)	1.65
priv./personal	40.3	(50)	34.8	(24)	47.3	(26)	1.50
fear reprisal	26.6	(33)	26.1	(18)	27.3	(15)	0.00

[a]Expected cell frequency was less than 5 for one cell.
[b]Expected cell frequency was less than 5 for five cells.
[c]The victims could report more than one of these categories; thus only those reporting "yes" to each category are reported in the table.
*p$\leq$.05

Most instances of acquaintance rape did not involve a gun. However, 12 percent of the total acquaintance rapes involved a weapon. This finding tends to contradict our societal belief that acquaintance rapes are not likely to be very forceful or threatening.

It is not very surprising that less than half (41.0 percent) of the total acquaintance rape victims reported their victimizations to the police. Rape victims are known to be skeptical about treatment by the police, and this is particularly problematic in acquaintance rapes, where the victim herself may be unwilling to define the act as a rape, and is also less likely to feel that others, particularly the police, will define the act as criminal. What is surprising is that there is no significant difference between the acquaintance and well-known rapes in the percentage who reported the occurrence to the police. We would expect the acquaintance rape victims to be more likely to report the occurrence to the police, because of their having less of a bond to the offender.

The victims were to indicate why they did not notify the police. The most frequent response was that they viewed it as a "private or personal matter." The next most frequent response was "fear of reprisal." The third most frequent response was the belief that "nothing could be done," possibly due to a lack of proof.

Description of Injuries and Self-Defense Reported

In Table 11.3 a description of the injuries and types of self-defense are presented. Three-fourths of the total acquaintance victims reported one or more injuries. This challenges stereotypes that date rapes and acquaintance rapes are not violent. Victims of well-known rape were more likely to experience injuries than victims of acquaintance rape.

At least half of the victims of total acquaintance rape reported receiving bruises, cuts, or black eyes. Once again, this is inconsistent with views of acquaintance rapes being less violent. A full 7 percent of the sample received internal injuries, or were knocked unconscious (K.U.). Forty percent of the total acquaintance victims reported requiring medical attention.

In addition to sexual victimization, many victims reported further attacks. The most common forms of further attacks included being "grabbed, held, tripped, jumped, or pushed." Almost half of the women experienced this. One-third of the victims were "hit, slapped, or knocked down."

A large percentage of total acquaintance victims attempted to resist the rape or fight back. For example, over half of the victims used or tried to use physical force. Forty-three percent of the victims attempted to reason with the offender.

IMPLICATIONS FOR PRACTICE AND POLICY

Previous research has established the widespread occurrence of date rape. However, most of this research has been conducted on college students. The

Table 11.3
Description of Injuries and Self-Defense Reported

	Total %	Acquaintance (n)	Acquaintance (only) %	Acquaintance (only) (n)	Well-Known (only) %	Well-Known (only) (n)	Chi-Square
No. Injuries							
none	25.0	(53)	32.5	(38)	15.8	(15)	
one	37.7	(80)	33.3	(39)	43.2	(41)	
two	28.3	(60)	27.4	(32)	29.5	(28)	
three-four	9.0	(19)	6.8	(8)	11.6)	(11)	8.58*
Injury Type (% who answered "yes")[a]							
intern inj./ku[b]	7.3	(13)	4.3	(4)	10.6	(9)	1.75
bruises/cuts	53.4	(95)	52.7	(49)	54.1	(46)	0.00
Req. med'l attention							
yes	40.3	(64)	36.7	(29)	43.8	(35)	
no	59.7	(95)	63.3	(50)	56.2	(45)	0.55
Attacks in Addition to the Rape (% who answered "yes")[a]							
shot/knifed/hit with object	6.1	(13)	3.4	(4)	9.5	(9)	2.37
hit/slapped/ knocked down	32.5	(69)	30.8	(36)	34.7	(33)	0.22
grabbed/held/ tripped	47.2	(100)	48.7	(57)	45.3	(43)	0.13
Attempts to Protect Self[a]							
use/try force	55.1	(103)	53.3	(56)	57.3	(47)	0.16
reason w/him	43.3	(81)	41.9	(44)	45.1	(37)	0.09
screamed/yelled	54.5	(102)	55.2	(58)	53.7	(44)	0.00
left scene/ran	26.7	(50)	27.6	(29)	25.6	(21)	0.02

[a]The victims could report more than one of these categories, thus only those reporting "yes" to each category are reported in the table.
[b]ku: knocked unconscious.
*p≤.05

research in this chapter examined unmarried women 12 years old and older who reported an attempted or completed acquaintance rape in the National Crime Survey data for the years 1973 through 1982.

The findings of the present study have numerous implications for practice and policy. First, there are very few differences between acquaintance and well-known rapes. Thus, the two have strikingly similar characteristics. The differences that do exist reveal that a rape is more likely to be completed if the offender is well-known rather than an "acquaintance," and the victim is more likely to suffer injuries if the offender is well-known rather than an acquaintance. Given the serious nature of well-known rapes, women should become more aware of self-defense methods, men should become more educated in acknowledging that "no means no," and the criminal justice system should take more responsive action in arresting and prosecuting well-known rape offenders.

Second, young women of dating age (16 to 24) are more at risk of rape victimization whether the offender is casually acquainted or well-known to them. However, it is important to acknowledge that roughly 30 percent of rapes occur to women 25 or older, and 16 percent occur to females under 16. Thus, it is important that all women be educated about the risks of being raped. Also, it appears that it may be necessary to educate men of all ages as to what rape is in order to decrease myths about what "justifies" forcing a female to have sex against her will.

There were no significant differences regarding race (of both the victims and offenders) and family income (although it appears that lower income women may be most at risk). This implies the importance of implementing planning to educate potential victims and offenders of all races and incomes as to the risk of rape and what constitutes rape.

A large proportion of sexual victimizations is not reported to the police. It is necessary that programs be developed to educate the police about the reality of date rape and other forms of acquaintance rapes, so that they will respond. Only through communicating to potential victims and offenders that the police indeed view date and acquaintance rapes as crimes will we be able to increase the reporting rates of these frequent and very serious victimizations.

The present study found that the greatest inhibitor to reporting rapes to the police was the view that it was a "private or personal matter." While it is indeed a personal matter, labeling the act and punishing the offender are necessary in order to deter the occurrence of acquaintance forms of rape.

Over one-quarter of the victims in this study stated a "fear of reprisal" as inhibiting their decision to contact the police. We need to develop policies to help protect victims once they have made reports. While their safety is often extremely difficult to achieve, it is a useful goal of the criminal justice system.

A victim's feeling of helplessness, and/or her belief that the police don't want to be bothered, and/or her feeling that her experience is not important enough to warrant attention also deter her from reporting the occurrence to the police. These findings are consistent with the messages many girls in our culture receive while growing up: that it is their "duty" to take care of others and minimize or deny their own problems. Rape victims frequently feel a sense of not wanting to do anything to harm their offenders despite the devastation they feel from the assault. It is therefore necessary that victims be perceived as worthwhile, that they be treated with respect, and that the offenders suffer retribution for the pain they have caused their victims.

Finally, this research revealed that force and violence do occur in acquaintance rapes. Twelve percent of the victimizations involved some sort of weapon.

Three-fourths of the victims reported one or more injuries. Seven percent of the sample experienced internal injuries or were knocked unconscious, and 53 percent experienced bruises, cuts, and/or black eyes. Forty percent of the sample required medical attention. Six percent were shot, knifed, or hit with an object; one-third were hit, slapped, or knocked down; and 47 percent were grabbed, held, or tripped. Thus, these findings indicate that not all acquaintance rapes are nonviolent. This information is useful for potential victims as well as for criminal justice and health professionals dealing with the victims.

RECOMMENDATIONS FOR FURTHER STUDY

This study broadens our understanding of the sexual victimization of unmarried women by nonrelatives who are known to the victims. Unlike previous research on the topic of sexual violence experienced by unmarried persons, this research did not limit itself to college students. This does not mean that studies of college students are unwarranted. However, we need to look at the experiences of sexual victimization of noncollege individuals.

While some research has posed attitudinal questions to youths regarding what they perceive as rape or when they believe forced sex may be justifiable, we know very little about the acquaintance, nonrelative sexual victimization experiences of precollege youth (for an exception see Giarrusso et al., 1979). There is no information on the occurrence of date rapes of noncollege women who are of typical college age and older. The National Crime Survey data used in this study provided a good description of the sexual victimization of unmarried women of all ages. The next step is to conduct research on women of all ages, whether they are divorced, separated, widowed, or never married. Additionally, it is also likely that sexual violence occurs in extramarital affairs and relationships. A study needs to be developed to address these victimizations.

Future research on date rape (and other nonrelative acquaintance rapes) should also include the levels of injury and attacks in addition to the rape. The present research points out how prevalent this is in acquaintance rapes. It is also of extreme importance to continue to determine not only how many of these acquaintance forms of rape remain unreported to the police, but additionally, *why* they are unreported. Only through this approach will we be better equipped to address shortcomings of our criminal justice system in dealing with and deterring date (and other forms of acquaintance) rapes.

SUMMARY AND CONCLUSIONS

This research has addressed the labeling of date rapes as a social problem. It adds to the existing literature by analyzing unmarried women 12 years old and older who experienced nonrelative acquaintance rapes. The inclusion of a wider age group helps further our understanding of sexual victimization by nonrelative intimates.

The findings concerning demographic characteristics indicated that the victims are most at risk between the ages of 16 and 24. Twelve- to 15-year-olds were more likely to experience acquaintance than well-known rapes.

Almost half of the total acquaintance attempts at rape resulted in completed rapes. Well-known attempts at rape were significantly more likely to be completed than were acquaintance attempts. Potential victims seem most at risk during summer, spring, and autumn. They are also most at risk between 6:00 P.M. and midnight.

Twelve percent of the rapes involved weapons, and 59 percent of the victims did not report the event to the police. The rationales for not reporting to the police were, in decreasing order, viewing the crime as a private or personal matter, fearing reprisal, feeling nothing could be done, viewing the crime as not important enough, or feeling the police would not want to be bothered with it. These findings suggest the need to improve relations between potential date and other types of acquaintance rape victims and the police.

That these victimizations were violent may be evidenced by the fact that 12 percent of the rapes involved weapons, three-fourths involved injuries, and two-fifths required medical attention. In addition to the rape, it was not uncommon for the victims to be hit, slapped, knocked down, grabbed, held, or tripped. In 6 percent of the rapes, the victim was shot, knifed, or hit with an object.

The most popular means victims used in attempting to protect themselves were, in decreasing order, using or trying physical force, screaming or yelling, reasoning with the offender, and leaving the scene or running away.

The only significant differences between acquaintance and well-known victims were in age (12- to 15-year-olds were less at risk of well-known than of acquaintance rapes, and 16- to 24-year-olds were more at risk of well-known than of acquaintance rapes). Also, well-known rape victims were more likely to be victims of completed rapes (as opposed to attempted rapes) than were acquaintance victims, and well-known victims were more likely to be injured. Thus, there appear to be few differences in the characteristics of the rape offense that relate to the degree to which the victim and offender were acquainted.

In closing, this chapter supports the emerging definition of date rape as a social problem, and encourages broadening the span of the population to be researched. College students are not the only people at risk for acquaintance rapes by nonrelatives. We need to further our knowledge of the occurrence of these types of rapes among adolescents, noncollege women in their twenties, and women beyond their twenties.

All women are at risk of nonrelative acquaintance rapes, and a better understanding of this issue is required through further research. The time is overdue for criminologists to address the need for assessing this phenomenon, and for criminal justice and health professionals to become more aware of the problem in order to better address the needs of the victims and in order to deter potential offenders. Both potential offenders and potential victims need education in the right of all women, whether they are young or old, married, divorced, separated, widowed, or never married, to be able to say "no" and to have it be heard and respected when they do not desire to have sex.

ACKNOWLEDGMENTS

The National Crime Survey data used in this chapter were made available through the Inter-University Consortium for Political and Social Research, Ann Arbor, MI.

NOTES

1. Kanin (1957) did not indicate whether the attempts at sexual intercourse were "completed" or remained "attempted" rapes. I only note this in passing, not that I believe it is particularly germane, since most research suggests that the effects of sexual victimization, whether they are attempted or completed, appear to be fairly equally devastating.

2. Most of the research on sexual violence examines heterosexual couples. Battering is known to exist in lesbian and gay relationships, but it is not known to what degree, although it is believed to be significantly lower than that occurring in heterosexual relationships. In particular, heterosexual relationships contain the gender inequalities of power, which are manifested in our society, as well as the frequent physical and financial gender disparities that function to the woman's disadvantage.

REFERENCES

Barrett, K. (1982). "Date Rape: A Campus Epidemic?" *MS.*, September, 49–51, 130.

Finkelhor, D. & Yllo, K. (1983). "Rape in Marriage: A Sociological View." In *The Dark Side of Families*, ed. D. Finkelhor, R. J. Gelles, G. T. Hotaling & M. A. Straus, pp. 119–30. Beverly Hills, CA: Sage.

———. (1985). *License to Rape: Sexual Abuse of Wives*. New York: Free Press.

Giarrusso, R. Johnson, P., Goodchilds, J., & Zellman, G. (1979). "Adolescents' Cues and Signals: Sex and Assault." Paper presented at the Western Psychological Association meetings.

Groth, A. N. (1979). *Men Who Rape: The Psychology of the Offender*. New York: Plenum.

Kanin, E. J. (1957). "Male Aggression in Dating-Courtship Relations." *American Journal of Sociology*, 63:197–204.

Korman, S. K., & Leslie, G. R. (1982). "The Relationship of Feminist Ideology and Date Expense Sharing to Perceptions of Sexual Aggression in Dating." *Journal of Sex Research*, 18 (2):114–29.

Koss, M. P., Gidycz, C. A., & Wisniewski, N. (1987). "The Scope of Rape: Incidence and Prevalence of Sexual Aggression and Victimization in a National Sample of Higher Education Students." *Journal of Consulting and Clinical Psychology*, 55 (2):162–70.

Koss, M. P., & Oros, C. J. (1982). "Sexual Experiences Survey: A Research Instrument Investigating Sexual Aggression and Victimization." *Journal of Consulting and Clinical Psychology* 50 (3):455–57.

Lane, K. E., & Gwartney-Gibbs, P. A. (1985). "Violence in the Context of Dating and Sex." *Journal of Family Issues* 6 (1):45–49.

Makepeace, J. M. (1981). "Courtship Violence Among College Students." *Family Relations,* 30:97–102.

Muehlenhard, C. L., & Linton, M. A. (1987). "Date Rape and Sexual Aggression in Dating Situations: Incidence and Risk Factors." *Journal of Counseling Psychology* 34 (2):186–96.

Rapaport, K., & B. R. Burkhart (1984). "Personality and Attitudinal Characteristics of Sexually Coercive College Males." *Journal of Abnormal Psychology,* 93 (2):216–21.

Russell, D. E. H. (1982). *Rape in Marriage.* New York: Macmillan.

————. (1984). *Sexual Exploitation: Rape, Child Sexual Abuse, and Workplace Harassment.* Beverly Hills, CA: Sage.

12   Predictors of Naturalistic Sexual Aggression
Neil M. Malamuth

Within the last decade, there has been increasing research on the causes of male sexual aggression against women, particularly rape. As described later, most of this research attempted to identify individual factors that may predict such aggression. More recently, however, there has been growing recognition of the need for multifactorial models.

The theoretical guidance for the present research was provided at the general level by Bandura's social learning theory of aggression (1973, 1978) and by various applications of it to sexual aggression (for example, Earls, 1983; Malamuth, 1983b; Marshall & Barbaree, 1984). Also providing theoretical guidance was a recent model of the causes of child sexual abuse (Finkelhor, 1984; Finkelhor & Araji, 1983) and its extension by Russell (1984) to sexual aggression. These theories have several features in common. Most important, they emphasize that to understand the causes of sexual aggression it is essential to consider the role of multiple factors, such as those creating the motivation to commit the act, those reducing internal and external inhibitions that might prevent it from being carried out, and those providing the opportunity for the act to occur. Some of these multifactorial models propose additive (for example, Earls, 1983) and others propose interactive (for example, Bandura, 1978; Finkelhor, 1984; Malamuth, 1983b) combinations of the causal factors.

The research reported here compared empirically three alternative theoretical models regarding the causes of sexual aggression: The single factor model, which suggests that sexual aggression results from a single factor (such as hos-

This chapter is reprinted from the *Journal of Personality and Social Psychology* 50:6(1986): 953–62. Copyright © 1986 by the American Psychological Association. Reprinted by permission of the author and publisher.

tility); the additive model, which posits multiple factors combining in an additive manner (Earls, 1983); and the interactive model, which asserts that multiple factors (such as motivation, disinhibitory, and opportunity) interact to produce sexual aggression, particularly at high levels. Although the dependent measure used here primarily assesses sexual aggression among acquaintances, as noted later, I suggest that considerable similarity may exist among the causes of such aggression and that committed against nonacquaintances.

In studying self-reported naturalistic sexual aggression, six predictors were used in the present study.[1] Three were intended to assess the motivation to commit sexual aggression. These were sexual arousal in response to aggression, the desire to be sexually dominant or powerful, and hostility toward women. In addition, two variables were included primarily to measure factors that may overcome internal and external inhibitions. These consisted of attitudes that condone sexual aggression and of antisocial personality characteristics. Finally, sexual experience was assessed because if a person did not engage in sexual acts generally, then the "opportunity" to carry out sexually aggressive acts would not exist. As discussed later, an additional reason for including this dimension relates to differences in the degree and nature of sexual experiences between relatively sexually aggressive and nonaggressive men. The following discussion expands on the rationale for the selection of the various predictors and describes previous research pertaining to each.

SEXUAL RESPONSIVENESS TO RAPE

The most widely studied response designed to differentiate rapists from nonrapists has been the penile tumescence rape index, a ratio of sexual arousal to rape portrayals compared with arousal to consenting sex portrayals (Abel et al., 1977). With this index, a man whose penile tumescence to rape is similar to or greater than his tumescence to consenting depictions is considered to have some inclination to rape (see Quinsey, in press, for a review).

DOMINANCE

The view has been widely expressed that the desire to dominate women is an important motive of sexual aggression both at the cultural (Brownmiller, 1975; Sanday, 1981) and individual (for example, Scully & Marolla, 1985) levels. Based on clinical interviews with convicted rapists, Groth (1979) concluded that in all cases of forcible rape, three components are present: power, anger, and sexuality. Groth (1979) distinguished among several types of rapists depending on the primary element characterizing their motivation: the power rapist, the anger rapist, and the sadistic rapist. The most common type among the convicted rapists studied by Groth (that is, 55 percent) was the power rapist. Here he suggests the offender's desire is to conquer and sexually dominate his victim.

HOSTILITY TOWARD WOMEN

The second most frequent type of rapist, according to Groth (1979) (that is, about 40 percent of those he studied) is the "anger" rapist, characterized by his hostility to women. In the present research, hostility toward women was studied primarily for its possible motivating functions. However, it may also discriminate between men who would and those who would not be inhibited by a women's suffering from and resistance to sexual aggression. Research on the consequences of victims' reactions to nonsexual aggression indicates that the aggressors' hostile feelings may be a very important determinant. For those feeling relatively low hostility, the victim's suffering and resistance is likely to be unpleasant and therefore inhibit aggression (Geen, 1970; Rule & Leger, 1976). In contrast, for those with relatively high hostility, the victim's suffering may actually be reinforcing and thereby encourage further aggression in the face of resistance (Baron, 1974, 1977; Feshbach, Stiles & Bitter, 1967; Hartmann, 1969).

ATTITUDES FACILITATING AGGRESSION

Burt (1978, 1980) theorized that certain attitudes that are widely accepted in Western culture but are particularly held by rapists and potential rapists play an important role in contributing to sexual violence by acting as "psychological releases or neutralizers, allowing potential rapists to turn off social prohibitions against injuring or using others" (1978:282). She developed several scales to measure attitudes that directly and indirectly support aggression against women. Data consistent with Burt's theorizing indicate that male college students' levels of sexual aggression are correlated with attitudes condoning violence against women (for example, Koss et al., 1985). In addition, it has been found that convicted rapists have relatively high acceptance of violence against women (for example, Scully & Marolla, 1984).

ANTISOCIAL PERSONALITY CHARACTERISTICS/ PSYCHOTICISM

Rapaport and Burkhart (1984) recently suggested that, although certain factors may provide a context for coercive sexual behavior, the actual expression of aggression occurs only if the subject also has certain personality or characterological deficits. Although these investigators did not directly test this proposition, convicted rapists do sometimes show elevated scores on measures of psychopathic/antisocial characteristics (Armentrout & Hauer, 1978; Rada, 1977). Koss and Leonard (1984) point out, however, that a major problem in these studies has been the failure to control for demographic variables that could cause spurious elevation. Koss and Leonard (1984) found only very weak and/ or nonsignificant relations in various studies assessing possible links between measures of psychopathy and sexual aggression among men from the general population.

SEXUAL EXPERIENCE

As noted earlier, assessment of sexual experience may be useful to include in the prediction of sexual aggression due to *opportunity* or access. If powerful factors (such as religious convictions) prevented a person from participating in sexual relationships generally, he might not be sexually aggressive even if he has a high proclivity for such behavior. Particularly in the case of nonstranger sexual aggression, it is likely that the willingness and opportunity to engage in sexuality per se is an important factor distinguishing those who will and those who will not express an inclination to sexually aggress in actual behavior.

In addition to the opportunity function, an assessment of sexual experience was included in the present research in light of Kanin's (1957, 1983, 1984) studies of college males who have engaged in various degrees of sexual aggression. He found that more sexually aggressive men were more likely to view sexuality as a means of establishing their self-worth and as an arena for "conquest." They were also found to be more sexually experienced at younger ages, but also less likely to view these experiences as satisfactory. Similar data with convicted rapists were recently reported by Langevin, Paitich, and Russon (1985).

PREDICTING LABORATORY AGGRESSION

Malamuth (1983a) assessed the extent to which two of the factors described earlier predicted males' laboratory aggression against women. Males' penile tumescence to rape portrayals as compared with mutually consenting depictions and their attitudes condoning violent acts such as rape and wife battering were assessed in one session. About a week later, subjects participated in what they believed was a totally unrelated experiment. In it they were first angered by a female confederate of the experimenter. Later, they could choose to aggress against her via the administration of aversive noise and other responses. It was found that both the degree of men's attitudes facilitating aggression and of their sexual arousal to rape predicted significantly the amount of their laboratory aggression against the woman. In assessing one aspect of these findings, Malamuth and Check (1982) successfully replicated the relations between attitudes condoning aggression against women and laboratory aggression measured several days later in an ostensibly unrelated context.

THE PRESENT RESEARCH

The present study assessed empirically the prediction of sexual aggression in naturalistic settings using the factors described earlier. Sexual aggression was measured by a self-report inventory developed by Koss and Oros (1982). This measure asks male subjects whether they have engaged in a wide range of coercive sexual activities, from trying to get intercourse by "threatening" to end the relationship to actually using physical force, such as twisting a woman's arm, to coerce her into intercourse.

It is important to note that the two types of aggression measures used in our research program complement each other well, having opposite advantages and disadvantages. The advantage of the laboratory assessment of aggression (Malamuth, 1983a, 1984b; Malamuth & Check, 1982) is that it is an "objective" measure that does not rely on subjects' self-reports. However, it assesses behavior in a setting that some argue is artificial and low in ecological validity (for example, Kaplan, 1983). The measure of naturalistic aggression has the advantage of assessing behavior occurring in nonartificial settings. Its disadvantage is in being a self-report measure. Consequently, considerable confidence in the validity of the relations would be gained if the predictors related to both of these aggression measures. Of course, while some similarity may be expected, conceptually there are also important differences between aggression in the laboratory, which does not contain any overt sexual elements (such as administering aversive noise to a person in the next room), and aggression in natural settings, which occurs within a sexual context.

The factors studied in the present investigation are based on theory and research conducted either with convicted rapists or with subjects from the general population, particularly college students. One of the issues the current data pertain to is the assertion (see Russell, 1984; Scully & Marolla, 1985) that similar factors contribute to both the type of sexual aggression committed by incarcerated rapists (usually against nonacquaintances) and the type that does not receive legal attention, particularly that against acquaintances. If variables derived from work with convicted rapists and with sexual aggressors in the general population can be integrated within a unified empirical and theoretical framework, the findings will provide a firmer basis for understanding the causes of sexual aggression in both populations.

Based on the theory and research described, three interrelated questions were investigated in the present research:

1. Would the predictor factors relate significantly to naturalistic aggression against women?
2. If the factors related to sexual aggression against women, would they provide "redundant prediction" or would a combination of factors predict better than each alone?
3. If a combination of factors were superior, would the additive or the interactive models provide the best prediction of naturalistic aggression?

METHOD

Overview of Design

A total of 155 males participated in the first phase of the research. In this phase subjects completed various scales, including all the predictors except the sexual arousal measure, as well as the dependent measure of sexual aggression.

The second phase consisted of the assessment of sexual arousal in response to rape portrayals and to consenting depictions. A total of 95 of those participating in Phase 1 also participated in Phase 2.

Subjects

Subjects were recruited from various sources: several university courses, announcements displayed on university campuses and at a city summer employment center, and via newspaper ads.

The initial descriptions of the research indicated that applicants at or over the age of 18 were needed to participate in various unrelated experiments. They were told that they may sign up for a general subject pool. Experimenters would then select subjects from this list and invite them to participate in specific experiments. Participants were paid about $5.50 per hour.

When contacted by the different experimenters conducting each phase (presented to subjects as independent experiments), potential subjects were given general descriptions of the procedures and measures used. For example, in Phase 2 they were informed that genital measures of sexual arousal would be used. It was emphasized in each phase that subjects could leave at any time and that there would be no penalty whatsoever nor would any explanation be required. Subjects were paid upon arrival at each study and were told that they could keep the money irrespective of whether they completed the experiment or not. As an additional safeguard, an ombudsman, who was a professor of law, was hired for the project. All subjects were given his name and phone number upon signing up for the subject pool. They were told that he was completely independent of the staff conducting the research and that they could voice any complaints to him. No complaints were ever made.

At the end of Phase 2 subjects were given debriefings, including segments emphasizing the horror of rape and presenting several points designed to dispel rape myths. The effectiveness of such debriefings in counteracting some potential negative effects of exposure to sexually violent stimuli has been demonstrated in several studies (Check & Malamuth, 1984; Donnerstein & Berkowitz, 1981; Linz, 1985; Malamuth & Check, 1984).

Although subjects' names were not obtained, various background information that was gathered (such as date of birth) enabled an exact match of responses across the two research phases. The purpose of leading subjects to believe that these were independent studies was to reduce "demand characteristics" (Orne, 1962) and/or undue self-consciousness that might have affected honest responding. Similar procedures have been used successfully in other studies (for example, Malamuth, 1983a; Malamuth & Check, 1981). The two research phases were completed within two months for virtually all subjects.

Obtaining background information enabled a general description of the sample. Subjects were asked about their age, their marital status, whether they were students, their major, their religious affiliation, and their frequency of attendance at church or other religious institution. These variables were selected on the basis of previous research (for example, Koss et al., 1985; Schulz et al., 1977) showing that factors such as religiousness and age may affect college students' sexual and sexually aggressive behavior. If the regression analyses reported later are computed by first partialing out the background factors, the relations are at least as strong as those reported without such partialing.

The average age of the 155 subjects was 23, with a range of 18 to 47 years; 66 percent of the sample were between the ages of 18 to 22, 24 percent between the ages of 23 to 30, and the remaining 10 percent were above the age of 30. Eighty-seven percent of the sample were single, 8 percent were married, and the remaining 5 percent were separated or divorced. Eighty percent were university students, 20 percent were not. Of the students, 21 percent majored in the "pure" sciences, 13 percent in engineering, and 23 percent in the humanities and the social sciences (including psychology). The remainder were distributed over a wide range of majors or as yet undeclared. Twenty percent were Catholics, 32 percent Protestants, 8 percent Jewish, and the remaining 40 percent listed no specific religious affiliation. Fifteen percent indicated that they visit a religious institution (for example church) at least once a week, 11 percent at least once a month, 8 percent approximately every two months, and the remaining 56 percent seldom or never.

Phase 1: Procedure and Materials

In the first phase, subjects completed a questionnaire administered by a male experimenter. While filling out this measure they were seated sufficiently apart to insure confidentiality of responses. Embedded within other items on this questionnaire were the following measures:

Dominance as Sexual Motive. Part of a measure developed by Nelson (1979) assessed the function of or motivations for engaging in sexual acts. This measure asks respondents the degree to which various feelings and sensations are important to them as motives for sexual behavior. Nelson (1979) presented data concerning the reliability and validity of this scale, which yields scores on several functions of sexuality. The present study used the dominance segment (8 items) of the power function (composed of the dominance and submissiveness segments). This dominance component refers to the degree to which feelings of control over one's partner motivate sexuality (for example, "I enjoy the feeling of having someone in my grasp"; "I enjoy the conquest"). It yielded an alpha coefficient of 0.78.

Hostility. The Hostility Toward Women (HTW) scale (30 items) was recently developed by Check and Malamuth, 1983 (see also Check et al., 1985). Data concerning its reliability and validity were presented by Check (1985). Examples of items are "Women irritate me a great deal more than they are aware of," and "When I look back at what's happened to me, I don't feel at all resentful toward the women in my life.'' In the present study it had an alpha coefficient of 0.89.

Attitudes Facilitating Violence. The attitude measure used in this study was the Acceptance of Interpersonal Violence (AIV) against women scale developed by Burt (1980). Five of its six items measure attitudes supporting violence against women; the sixth concerns revenge. An example of an item is ''Sometimes the only way a man can get a cold woman turned on is to use force.'' This scale was selected because it measures attitudes that *directly* condone the use of force in sexual relationships. Two other scales developed by Burt (1980) assessing attitudes *indirectly* supportive of sexual aggression, the Rape Myth Acceptance and the Adversarial Sexual Beliefs scales, were also assessed. The findings with these measures were very similar to those with the AIV, but, as expected, the relations with sexual aggression were somewhat weaker. The results presented in this article are for the AIV scale only. It had an alpha coefficient of 0.61, which is similar to that originally reported by Burt (1980).

Antisocial Characteristics/Psychoticism. The Psychoticism (P) scale of the Eysenck Personality Questionnaire (EPQ) was used (Eysenck, 1978). As Eysenck makes abundantly clear, this scale purports to reflect a variable that stretches through the normal, nonpsychiatric population.

There were three reasons for selecting this particular measure to assess antisocial tendencies. First, Eysenck (1978) hypothesized that psychoticism may be particularly associated with interest in impersonal sex and in sexual aggression. He also reports the findings of an unpublished study that sex offenders are relatively high P scorers. Second, reviews of the literature pertaining to this measure (for example, Claridge, 1983) concluded that rather than being a measure of psychoticism in the clinical sense, this scale primarily assesses antisocial traits that may relate to aggression. Third, recent research (Barnes, Malamuth & Check, 1984; Linz, 1985) suggests that this measure may be particularly useful in predicting some sexually aggressive responses.

The alpha coefficient obtained herein was 0.49. Although Eysenck (1978) had originally reported relatively high alpha coefficients, other researchers have recently reported similar relatively low levels of internal consistency, as found here (for example, McCrae & Costa, 1985). Nevertheless, this measure was retained in the current analyses with the recognition that relatively low levels of internal consistency reduce the likelihood of obtaining statistically significant relations with other variables (Cohen & Cohen, 1983).

Sexual Experience. The Sexual Behavior Inventory (SBI: Bentler, 1968) was used to assess sexual experience in conventional heterosexual acts. Subjects indicated whether they had engaged in various sexual behaviors including kissing, fondling of breasts, intercourse, and oral sex. The alpha coefficient for this scale was 0.97.

Naturalistic Sexual Aggression. As noted earlier, the self-report instrument used to measure sexual aggression was developed by Koss and Oros (1982). It assesses a continuum of sexual aggression including psychological pressure, physical coercion, attempted rape, and rape. Subjects are asked to respond to a sexual experience survey consisting of nine circumstances pertaining to the use of aggression in the context of sexuality (for example sexual, oral, or anal intercourse).[2] An example of an item is "I have had sexual intercourse with a woman when she didn't want it because I used some degree of physical force (twisting her arm, holding her down, etc.)." Respondents reply on a *true* versus *false* scale. Koss and Oros (1982) and Koss and Gidycz (1985) presented data regarding the reliability and validity of this scale. In the present study, it had an alpha coefficient of 0.83.

Phase 2: Materials and Procedure

In the second research phase, sexual arousal in response to rape and to mutually consenting depictions was assessed. In keeping with the accepted methodology and empirical data in this area (for example, Abel et al., 1977; Earls & Marshall, 1983), the primary assessment was direct genital arousal measured by penile tumescence. Subjects were seated in a comfortable chair located in a sound attenuated and electrically shielded room equipped with an intercom. Penile tumescence was measured by a mercury-in-rubber strain gauge (Davis Inc., New York City), a device recommended in analyses of various instruments (Laws, 1977; Rosen & Keffe, 1978). Changes in penile diameter that resulted in resistance changes in the mercury column of this strain gauge were amplified through a Wheatstone Bridge and recorded on a polygraph.

For comparison of consistency with the physiological measure, self-reported sexual arousal was assessed on an 11-point scale ranging from 0 percent (not at all) to 100 percent (very) in units of ten percent. Subjects indicated their arousal immediately after reading each story.

Upon arrival at the laboratory, the subject was greeted by a male experimenter. He then was given a sheet reiterating the information provided on the phone regarding the sexual content of some stimuli and the use of genital arousal measures. After signing a consent form, which emphasized that the subject was free to leave at any time without any penalty and without having to provide any reason to the experimenter, he was escorted to the sound attenuated room. Further instructions were taped, although an intercom was available if communication between the subject and the experimenter were necessary.

The subject was instructed to put on the penile gauge. Following a baseline period, he was told to open a numbered envelope and read the story. Arousal to the stories was monitored by the polygraph in the adjoining room. After the subject read each story and indicated his sexual arousal on a scale, a resting period was interposed to insure that arousal returned to baseline levels before proceeding to the next story.

Three depictions were read in order. The first described a woman masturbating. Its primary purpose was to generate some initial level of sexual arousal in light of data (Kolarsky & Madlafousek, 1977) suggesting that arousal levels are better differentiated if presented following the elicitation of some sexual arousal rather than immediately following the first baseline period. Additionally, this story was intended to strengthen the credibility of the experimental instructions that the research concerned responses to various types of stimuli. The second and third written stories depicted rape and mutually consenting sex, respectively. They were virtually identical to those used by Abel et al. (1977).

Rape indexes were computed for each subject following Abel et al. (1977) by dividing maximum arousal to rape by maximum arousal to consenting sex for the tumescence data and for self-reported arousal.[3]

RESULTS

Volunteers versus Nonvolunteers

Comparisons were made between the 95 volunteers for the second research phase and the 60 who did not volunteer. These comparisons used the five predictors assessed in the first phase and the measure of sexual aggression. No significant differences or effects approaching significance were obtained in either a multivariate analysis of variance or in univariate analyses of variance (ANOVAS).

Intercorrelations among Predictors

Simple Pearson correlations among the predictors are presented in Table 12.1. In general, these data are highly consistent with previous findings (for example Malamuth, 1983a; 1984a; Malamuth & Check, 1983), as well as revealing relations not examined in earlier studies. The tumescence index of sexual arousal (that is, arousal to rape contrasted with arousal to nonrape) was highly correlated with the similar index based on self-reported arousal. To a large degree, these two sexual arousal indexes showed similar relations with the other variables: Both indexes were significantly associated with the dominance motive and neither related significantly to psychoticism or to sexual experience. Although the reported arousal index significantly correlated with hostility toward women and with AIV, the tumescence index showed a marginally significant effect with hostility and no significant correlation with AIV.

The dominance motive related significantly to all of the other predictors, except for sex experience, for which a marginally significant correlation occurred. Hostility toward women correlated with AIV and revealed a marginally significant relation with psychoticism. Hostility showed a nonsignificant inverse relation with sexual experience. AIV did not relate to either psychoticism or to sexual experience, nor were these two variables related to each other.

Naturalistic Aggression

The last column of Table 12.1 shows simple correlations between the predictors and self-reported naturalistic sexual aggression. All the predictors related

Table 12.1

Simple Correlations among the Predictor Variables and Sexual Aggression

Predictors and Dependent Variable	1	2	3	4	5	6	7	8
Motivation predictors								
1. TUMRAPE	--	.66****	.25***	.19*	.13	.07	.06	.43****
2. REPRAPE		—	.23**	.26***	.22**	.06	.15	.33***
3. DOM			—	.37****	.36****	.19**	.15*	.38****
4. HTW				—	.37****	.16*	-.11	.30****
Disinhibiting predictors								
5. AIV					—	.08	-.08	.38***
6. PSYCH						—	-.03	.15*
Opportunity predictor								
7. SEXEXP							—	.32****
Dependent variable								
8. SEXAGG								—

Note: TUMRAPE = tumescence arousal to rape index; REPRAPE = reported arousal
     to rape index; DOM = dominance motive; HTW = hostility toward women scale;
     AIV = acceptance of interpersonal violence (against women) scale; PSYCH =
     psychoticism scale; SEXEXP = sexual experience measure; SEXAGG = sexual
     aggression.
a.   n = 155, except with sexual arousal measures, where n = 95.

* p < .10   ** p < .05   *** p < .02   **** p < .001.

significantly to sexual aggression, except for psychoticism which showed a marginally significant correlation.

Multiple regression analyses were conducted to address the issue of the combined success of the predictors to relate to sexual aggression. As recommended by Cohen and Cohen (1983), all the predictors were centered at their mean, a linear transformation that reduces multicollinearity that may occur with products such as interaction terms. In this analysis, I sought to compare the single Factor, Additive, and Interactive models. For the 155 participants in Phase 1, this regression analysis included dominance, hostility toward women, AIV, psychoticism, and sexual experience. For the 95 participants in both research phases, analyses were conducted with the addition of the tumescence rape index.

The regression analyses were performed in the following way: To test the single factor model versus the additive model, each predictor was "forced entered" as a main effect and its unique contribution (that is, that not shared with any other predictors) to the dependent variable was assessed by squared semi-partial correlations (Cohen & Cohen, 1983). The results clearly showed that the predictors did not, in general, provide redundant information, but that their combined prediction was considerably greater than that achieved by any variable alone. More specifically, when the entire sample was used (n = 155) the HTW, AIV, and sex experience variables all had significant unique contributions to the regression equation, whereas the unique contribution of dominance was marginally significant (see first two data columns of Table 12.2). The psychoticism variable did not make a significant unique contribution. As indicated in the first two data columns of Table 12.2, the Multiple R yielded by this equation assessing additive effects was 0.547.

When the regression analysis assessing additive effects was performed on the 95 participants in both research phases, the Multiple R was 0.619 (see first two data columns of Table 12.3). As indicated in this table, the tumescence rape index, AIV, HTW, and sex experience contributed significant, unique variance, whereas the dominance and psychoticism predictors did not.

Although these data show that a combination of predictor variables is superior to individual ones, an additional regression analysis compared the interactive and the additive models for combining predictors. Although the Interactive model contends that several factors must interact for relatively high levels of sexual aggression to occur, the use of more than one variable within a given

Table 12.2
Multiple Regression Analyses on Index of Sexual Aggression without Tumescence

Predictor	Without interactions		With interactions	
	Beta[a]	sr^{2b}	Beta[a]	sr^{2b}
DOM	.153	.017*	.078	.005
HTW	.198	.030**	.147	.017**
AIV	.205	.033***	.210	.032***
PSYCH	.073	.005	.102	.010
SEXEXP	.340	.109****	.257	.058****
HTW X PSYCH	—	—	.150	.022**
HTW X AIV X SEXEXP	—	—	.334	.092****
HTW X DOM X AIV X SEXEXP	—	—	.313	.078****
Multiple				
R		.547****		.673****
R^2		.300		.453

Note: DOM — dominance motive; HTW — hostility toward women scale; AIV — acceptance of interpersonal violence (against women) scale; PSYCH — psychoticism scale; SEXEXP — sexual experience measure.
a. Standardized regression coefficient.
b. Squared semipartial correlation coefficient indicating unique contribution of predictor variable to dependent variable.

* p < .06   ** p < .05   *** p < .01   **** p < .0001; n — 155.

Table 12.3
Multiple Regression Analyses on Index of Sexual Aggression with Tumescence

Predictor	Without interactions		With interactions	
	Beta[a]	sr^{2b}	Beta	sr^{2b}
TUMRAPE	.329	.100***	.206	.026**
DOM	.085	.006	.170	.017*
HTW	.209	.032*	.037	.001
AIV	.207	.035*	.168	.022*
PSYCH	.027	.001	.016	.000
SEXEXP	.267	.066**	.111	.010
AIV X SEXEXP	—	—	.166	.025**
TUMRAPE x DOM x AIV x PSYCH	—	—	.200	.029**
TUMRAPE x DOM x HTW x AIV	—	—	.493	.151****
TUMRAPE x DOM x HTW x AIV x SEXEXP	—	—	.445	.158****
Multiple R	.169****		.865****	
R^2	.383		.748	

Note: TUMRAPE - tumescence arousal to rape index; DOM - dominance motive;
HTW - hostility toward women scale; AIV - acceptance of interpersonal
violence (against women) scale; PSYCH - psychoticism scale; SEXEXP -
sexual experience measure.
a.   Standardized regression coefficient.
b.   Squared semi-partial correlation coefficient indicating unique contribution of variable.

* $p < .05$ ** $p < .005$ *** $p < .001$ **** $p < .0001$.

theoretical category (for example, sexual arousal in response to aggression and
hostility toward women variables were included as motivational factors) did not
enable precise specification of the interaction set that would best test this model.
Rather than preferring a particular interaction, all possible interactions (that is,
the cross-products) were allowed "free entry" in a stepwise process after the
"forced entry" of the main effects.[4]

The resulting equation for the 155 subjects yielded a Multiple R of 0.673
(see last two columns of Table 12.2). Contributing significant unique variance
were a two-way interaction between the HTW and psychoticism, a three-way
interaction among HTW, AIV, and sex experience and a four-way interaction
that contained these three variables as well as dominance (see Table 12.2). A
hierarchical comparison of the model with the interactions ($R^2 = .453$) versus
the model with the main effects only ($R^2 = .300$) yielded a significant effect:
$F(3, 146) = 9.99$; $p < .001$.

With the 95 subjects participating in both research phases, the regression
equation including interactions yielded a Multiple R of 0.865 (last two columns
of Table 12.3). The squared semipartial correlation coefficients indicated that

contributing unique variance were a two-way interaction between AIV and sex experience, a four-way interaction among the tumescence index, dominance, AIV, and psychoticism, a four-way interaction among the tumescence index, dominance, HTW, and sex experience, as well as a five-way interaction containing these four variables and AIV (see last two columns of Table 12.3). A comparison of the models with and without the interactions yielded a highly significant difference: $F(4, 84) = 12.86; p < .001$. The results for both samples, therefore, indicate that a regression model containing interactive relations among the predictors is preferable to a model containing additive relations only.

To directly assess whether the tumescence rape index provides additional predictive information, it was necessary to compare regression models with and without this variable for the same 95 subjects. This comparison indicated that the regression model with this variable (Multiple $R = .865$) was significantly better than without it: (Multiple $R = .600$), $F (3, 85) = 16.45, p < .001$.

To illustrate and further examine the data, the following analysis was performed: For each predictor, a relatively high score was defined as above the median of its distribution. Subjects were then divided according to the number of predictors for which they scored high and low. This approach is analogous to classifying a characteristic as present or not by defining presence as a relatively high score. A person scoring above the median on all the variables would be considered as possessing all the characteristics. In keeping with the regression results, for the 155 subjects the dominance, HTW, AIV, psychoticism, and sex experience predictors were used for this classification, whereas for the 95 subjects, these variables as well as the tumescence rape index were used.

Figure 12.1 shows the average level of sexual aggression according to this classification scheme, with the top graph showing the results for the entire sample of 155 subjects and the bottom graph showing the results for the 95 participants in the two research phases. In both instances, ANOVAs performed on these data yielded highly significant ($p < .0001$) effects. Comparisons among means were performed using the Scheffé test (Scheffé, 1953) for groups differing substantially in size and the Tukey test (Tukey, 1953) for those of similar size. These comparisons indicated that the highest levels in both graphs were significantly different ($p < .05$) from all others and that the second highest levels differed significantly from some of the lowest levels. Trend analyses showed that a cubic term fitted the curve within statistical error for the sample of 155 subjects whereas a quintic term fitted the curve for the 95 participants in both research phases. Analyses of variance (ANOVAs) comparing average sexual aggression within each level of this classification scheme (for example, those scoring high on one set of four predictors vs. those scoring high on a different set of four predictors) supported the rationale of classifying subjects according to the number of predictors on which they scored relatively high: For both samples, no significant differences were found within each classification level. It should be noted, however, that the relatively small numbers in each cell reduced the likelihood of finding such differences.

Figure 12.1
Mean Level of Sexual Aggression as a Function of Number of Factors on Which Subjects Scored above Median

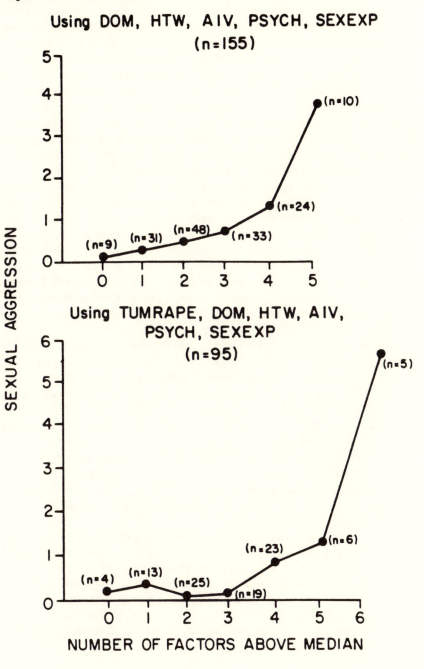

Using DOM, HTW, AIV, PSYCH, SEXEXP
(n=155)

Using TUMRAPE, DOM, HTW, AIV, PSYCH, SEXEXP
(n=95)

SEXUAL AGGRESSION

NUMBER OF FACTORS ABOVE MEDIAN

Note: See Table 12.1 for meaning of abbreviations.

DISCUSSION

The data provided the following answers to the three questions posed earlier: First, in the simple correlation analyses all the predictors except psychoticism were significantly related to naturalistic aggression, and psychoticism showed a marginally significant relation. Second, the predictors did not, on the whole, provide "redundant information," in that a combination of them was superior to any individual ones for predicting levels of sexual aggressiveness. Third, the data were more consistent with the interactive than with the additive model of combining the predictors. Regression equations containing interactive effects accounted for a significantly greater percentage of the variance (45 percent for the 155 subjects and 75 percent for the 95 subjects) than equations containing additive effects only (30 percent and 45 percent, respectively). However, it may be that a modified version of the interactive model that also incorporates additive effects would best account for the data. Multifactorial models in other areas of research (for example, Faraone & Tsuang, 1985) may provide useful guides in the development of such a model.

Additional analyses were conducted classifying subjects according to the number of predictors on which they scored relatively high (that is, above the median). A curve was found indicating that with an increasing number of predictors with high scores, greater levels of sexual aggression occurred. The data pattern appeared to show a synergistic process whereby the combined action of several variables yielded considerably higher levels of sexual aggression than would be expected by their additive combination.

Malamuth and Check (1985b) very recently attempted a partial replication of the research reported here. They administered to 297 males the same measures used here, except for the sexual arousal indexes and for psychoticism. The results replicated very successfully the present conclusions: The predictors related significantly to sexual aggression, a combination of predictors was superior to individual ones, and an equation including interactions was preferable to an additive one only. Further, classifying subjects according to the number of predictors on which they scored relatively high showed the same general relations reported here, although the slope of the line was somewhat less steep. This appeared to be due, at least in part, to a lower proportion of subjects in that study at the very high levels of sexual aggression as compared with the present or earlier studies.

Malamuth (1984b) recently assessed the ability of a number of the predictors used in the present research (that is, tumescence rape index, self-reported arousal to rape index, dominance, AIV, and psychoticism) to predict laboratory aggression against female and against male targets. Laboratory aggression was measured in a procedure similar to that used by Malamuth (1983a). The results showed that except for the penile tumescence measure (which was in the expected direction but not statistically significant), all the predictors significantly related to aggression against females. The data for male targets were more ambiguous, suggesting no or possibly weak relations with the predictors. On the basis of this study and earlier work (Malamuth, 1983a; Malamuth & Check, 1982), it is apparent that the same predictors found here to relate to self-reported naturalistic sexual aggression also relate in similar ways to laboratory aggression against women.[5]

The present findings suggest a high degree of similarity between some factors contributing to stranger and to acquaintance rape. Although we did not specifically ask subjects whether they knew their victims, based on earlier studies using the same measure (see Koss & Leonard, 1984), it seems very likely that the vast majority of the sexually aggressive acts reported were in acquaintance situations. Yet, some of the same factors theorized and/or found to contribute to stranger rape (for example, sexual arousal in response to aggression, dominance motivation, hostility toward women) related to sexual aggression among the subjects studied here.

The results suggest that the presence of any predictor alone is unlikely to result in high levels of sexual aggression. This conclusion may be particularly relevant to research focusing on sexual arousal in response to aggression. Although measures assessing such arousal (that is, the tumescence rape index) have been used in the diagnosis and treatment of rapists (Quinsey, in press), there are considerable data showing that within the general population a substantial percentage of men show arousal patterns similar to those of known rapists (for example, Malamuth, Check & Briere, 1986). The present results are supportive of the view that sexual arousal in response to aggression is one of the factors that may create an inclination to aggress against women. They also indicate clearly that other factors must be present before such an arousal pattern will lead to aggressive behavior. The findings point to the types of variables that should be included in clinical and research assessments.

The data also provide important information pertaining to recent research on the effects of sexually aggressive mass media stimuli. In several studies (for example, Linz, 1985; Malamuth & Check, 1981, 1985a) exposure to certain types of media stimuli changed men's attitudes about aggression against women, including rape. Some (for example, Vance, 1985) have downplayed the social significance of such findings by asserting that attitudes of this type have not been shown to actually relate to aggressive behavior. The present data extend earlier laboratory findings (Malamuth, 1983a; 1984b; Malamuth & Check, 1982) in showing that the same scales used to measure the impact of media exposure on attitudes (for example, the AIV scale) are useful predictors, in combination with other factors, of actual aggression in naturalistic and in laboratory settings. Although causal relations cannot be inferred on the basis of such correlational data alone, the findings are consistent with a theoretical model hypothesizing that media depictions contribute to changes in attitudes and that these may, under certain conditions, be one of the contributing factors affecting actual aggressive behavior (see Malamuth & Briere, in press).

An important goal for future research is to further develop and empirically test varied multifactorial models regarding the causes of sexual aggression. These models should attempt to define the causal links among the predictor variables in addition to their influences on sexual aggression. Structural equation modeling with latent variables (for example, Bentler & Bonett, 1980; Kenny & Judd, 1984) may be particularly suited for this purpose. Also, such models should incorporate two conceptual elements suggested by the present data in combination with earlier work (for example, Malamuth, 1984a). First, rather than adopting an "all or none" approach, sexual aggressiveness should be conceptualized along a continuum encompassing both differing degrees of inclinations to aggress and differing levels of actual aggressive behavior. Second, in attempting to understand the causes of relatively high levels of this continuum, emphasis should be placed on analyzing crucial configurations of multiple interacting factors (that is, motivational, disinhibitory, and opportunity) rather than on searching for the single or even the primary causal factor.

ACKNOWLEDGMENTS

This research was facilitated by grants from the Social Science and Humanities Research Council (SSHRC) of Canada. Portions of this research were presented at the 1985 meeting of the International Society for research on Aggression, in Parma, Italy. The author is particularly grateful to L. Rowell Huesmann for constructive suggestions. Thanks are also expressed to Daniel Linz, Steven Penrod, and James V. P. Check for their helpful suggestions.

NOTES

1. The term *predictor* is used here in the statistical sense and does not necessarily imply temporal or causal relations with the criterion (or dependent) variable.

2. Although the scale used by Koss and Oros (1982) contains ten items, one item judged ambiguous was not used in the analyses here. It asks whether the subject ever became so sexually aroused that he could not stop himself even though the woman did not want to continue. The ambiguity is in the lack of information regarding what sexual acts occurred and what type of coercion may have been used.

3. In some previous research (for example, Malamuth, 1983a) a difference rather than a ratio score was used. The ratio was used here in keeping with the commonly accepted procedure. The findings are very similar if the difference score is used.

4. Some statisticians might test the Interaction model by a fully hierarchical approach in which regression models with higher order interactions are assessed only in comparison to nested models including all the lower-order interactions. The difference in such an approach as contrasted to that used here (that is, allowing "free entry" to all the interactions) concerns only which interactions are most appropriate to include in the model and not whether some interactions account for additional variance.

5. Some subjects in the research measuring laboratory aggressiveness also participated in the present research. This enabled assessment of the relations between laboratory aggression and a composite of six items from the measure of naturalistic sexual aggression that concern the use of force or aggression. (The other three items refer to

psychological tactics such as "saying something you don't mean"). Reported naturalistic aggression correlated significantly with both laboratory aggression against male targets [r (47) = .25, p < .04, one-tailed] and against female targets [r (38) = .31, p < .025, one-tailed].

REFERENCES

Abel, G. G., Barlow, D. H., Blanchard, E., & Guild, D. (1977). "The Components of Rapists' Sexual Arousal." *Archives of General Psychiatry,* 34:895–903.

Armentrout, J. A., & Hauer, A. L. (1978). "MMPIs of Rapists of Adults, Rapists of Children, and Nonrapist Sex Offenders." *Journal of Clinical Psychology,* 34:330–32.

Bandura, A. (1973). *Social Learning Theory.* Englewood Cliffs, NJ: Prentice-Hall.

————. (1978) "Social Learning Theory of Aggression." *Journal of Communication,* 3:12–19.

Barnes, G., Malamuth, N. M., & Check, J. V. P. (1984). "Personality and Sexuality." *Personality and Individual Differences,* 5:159–72.

Baron, R. A. (1974). "Aggression as a Function of Victim's Pain Cues, Level of Prior Anger Arousal, and Exposure to an Aggressive Model." *Journal of Personality and Social Psychology,* 29:117–24.

————. (1977). *Human Aggression.* New York: Plenum.

Bentler, P. M. (1968). "Heterosexual Behavior Assessment—1: Males." *Behaviour Research and Therapy,* 6:21–25.

Bentler, P. M., & Bonett, D. G. (1980). "Significance Tests and Goodness of Fit in the Analysis of Covariance Structures." *Psychological Bulletin,* 88:588–606.

Brownmiller, S. (1975). *Against Our Will: Men, Women and Rape.* New York: Simon & Schuster.

Burt, M. R. (1978). "Attitudes Supportive of Rape in American Culture." In Hearing of the 95th Cong., 2nd Sess., House Committee on Science and Technology, Subcommittee on Domestic and International Scientific Planning Analysis and Cooperation, *Research into Violence Behavior: Sexual Assaults,* pp. 277–322. Washington, DC: U.S. Government Printing Office.

————. (1980). "Cultural Myths and Supports for Rape." *Journal of Personality and Social Psychology,* 38:217–30.

Check, J. V. P. (1985). "The Hostility Toward Women Scale." Doctoral diss., University of Manitoba, Winnipeg, Canada.

Check, J. V. P., & Malamuth, N. M. (1983, June). "The Hostility Toward Women Scale." Paper presented at Western meetings of the International Society for Research on Aggression, Victoria, Canada.

————. (1984). "Can Participation in Pornography Experiments Have Positive Effects?" *Journal of Sex Research,* 20:14–31.

Check, J. V. P., Malamuth, N. M., Elias, B., & Barton, S. (1985). "On Hostile Ground." *Psychology Today,* 19:56–61.

Claridge, G. (1983). "The Eysenck Psychoticism Scale." In J. N. Butcher & C. D. Spielberger (eds.), *Advances in Personality Assessment,* vol. 2, pp. 71–114. Hillsdale, NJ: Erlbaum.

Cohen, J., & Cohen, P. (1983). *Applied Multiple Regression/Correlation for the Behavioral Sciences.* Hillsdale, NJ: Erlbaum.

Donnerstein, E., & Berkowitz, L. (1981). "Victim Reactions in Aggressive-Erotic Films as a Factor in Violence Against Women. *Journal of Personality and Social Psychology*, 41:710–24.

Earls, C. M. (1983). "Some Issues in the Assessment of Sexual Deviance." *International Journal of Law and Psychiatry*, 6:431–41.

Earls, C. M., & Marshall, W. L. (1983). "The Current State of Technology in the Laboratory Assessment of Sexual Arousal Patterns." In J. G. Greer & I. R. Stuart (eds.), *The Sexual Aggressor: Current Perspectives on Treatment*, pp. 336–62. New York: Van Nostrand Reinhold.

Eysenck, H. J. (1978). *Sex and Personality*. London: Open Books.

Faraone, S. V., & Tsuang, M. T. (1985). "Quantitative Models of the Genetic Transmission of Schizophrenia." *Psychological Bulletin*, 98:41–66.

Feshbach, S., Stiles, W. B., & Bitter, E. (1967). "The Reinforcing Effect of Witnessing Aggression." *Journal of Experimental Research in Personality*, 2, 133–39.

Finkelhor, D. (1984). *Child Sexual Abuse: New Theory and Research*. New York: Free Press.

Finkelhor, D., & Araji, S. (1983). *Explanations of Pedophilia: A Four Factor Model*. Durham, NH: University of New Hampshire.

Geen, R. G. (1970). "Perceived Suffering of the Victim as an Inhibitor of Attack-induced Aggression." *Journal of Social Psychology*, 81:209–15.

Groth, A. N. (1979). *Men Who Rape: The Psychology of the Offender*. New York: Plenum.

Hartmann, D. P. (1969). "Influence of Symbolically Modeled Instrumental Aggression and Pain Cues on Aggressive Behavior." *Journal of Personality and Social Psychology*, 11:280–88.

Kanin, E. J. (1957). "Male Aggression in Dating—Courtship Relations." *American Journal of Sociology*, 63:197–204.

———. (1983). "Rape as a Function of Relative Sexual Frustration." *Psychological Reports*, 52:133–34.

———. (1984). "Date Rape: Unofficial Criminals and Victims." *Victimology: An International Journal*, 1:95–108.

Kaplan, R. (1983). "The Measurement of Human Aggression." In R. Kaplan, V. Konecni, & R. Novaco (eds.), *Aggression in Children and Youth*, pp. 44–72. The Hague, Netherlands: Sijthoff & Noordhuff.

Kenny, D. A., & Judd, C. M. (1984). "Estimating the Nonlinear and Interactive Effects of Latent Variables." *Psychological Bulletin*, 96:201–10.

Kolarsky, A., & Madlafousek, J. (1977). "Variability of Stimulus Effect in the Course of Phallametric Testing." *Archives of Sexual Behavior*, 6:135–41.

Koss, M. P., & Gidycz C. A. (1985). "Sexual Experiences Survey: Reliability and Validity." *Journal of Consulting and Clinical Psychology*, 53:422–23.

Koss, M. P., & Leonard, K. E. (1984). "Sexually Aggressive Men: Empirical Findings and Theoretical Implications." In N. M. Malamuth & E. Donnerstein (eds.), *Pornography and Sexual Aggression*, pp. 213–32. New York: Academic.

Koss, M. P., Leonard, K. E., Beezley, D. A., & Oros, C. J. (1985). "Nonstranger Sexual Aggression: A Discriminant Analysis of Psychological Characteristics of Nondetected Offenders." *Sex Roles*, 12:981–92.

Koss, M. P., & Oros, C. J. (1982). "Sexual Experiences Survey: A Research Instrument Investigating Sexual Aggression and Victimization." *Journal of Consulting and Clinical Psychology*, 50:455–57.

Langevin, R., Paitich, D., & Russon, A. E. (1985). "Are Rapists Sexually Anomalous, Aggressive or Both?" In R. Langevin (ed.), *Erotic Preference, Gender Identity, and Aggression in Men: New Research Studies*, pp. 17–38. Hillsdale, NJ: Erlbaum.

Laws, D. R. (1977). "A Comparison of the Measurement Characteristics of Two Circumferential Penile Transducers." *Archives of Sexual Behavior*, 6:45–51.

Linz, D. (1985). "Sexual Violence in the Media: Effects on Male Viewers and Implications for Society." Doctoral diss., University of Wisconsin, Madison.

Malamuth, N. M. (1983a). "Factors Associated With Rape as Predictors of Laboratory Aggression Against Women." *Journal of Personality and Social Psychology*, 45:432–42.

———. (1983b, June). "Mediators of Aggression: Personality, Attitudinal, Cognitive and Emotional." Paper presented at Western meetings of the International Society for Research on Aggression, Victoria, Canada.

———. (1984a). "Aggression against Women: Cultural and Individual causes." In N. M. Malamuth & E. Donnerstein (eds.), *Pornography and sexual aggression*, pp. 19–52. New York: Academic.

———. (1984b, August). "Violence Against Women: Cultural, Individual and Inhibitory-Disinhibitory Causes." Paper presented at the annual meeting of the American Psychological Association, Toronto, Canada.

Malamuth, N. M., & Briere, J. (in press). "Sexually Violent Media: Indirect Effects of Aggression Against Women." *Journal of Social Issues*.

Malamuth, N. M., & Check, J. V. P. (1981). "The Effects of Mass Media Exposure on Acceptance of Violence Against Women: A Field Experiment. *Journal of Research in Personality*, 15:436–46.

———. (1982, June). "Factors Related to Aggression Against Women." Paper presented at annual meeting of the Canadian Psychological Association, Montreal, Canada.

———. (1983). "Sexual Arousal to Rape Depictions: Individual Differences." *Journal of Abnormal Psychology*, 92:35–67.

———. (1984). "Debriefing Effectiveness Following Exposure to Pornographic Rape Depictions." *Journal of Sex Research*, 20:1–13.

———. (1985a). "The Effects of Aggressive Pornography on Beliefs in Rape Myths: Individual Differences." *Journal of Research in Personality*, 19:299–320.

———. (1985b). "Predicting Naturalistic Sexual Aggression: A Replication." University of California, Los Angeles. Unpublished.

Malamuth, N. M., Check, J. V. P., & Briere, J. (1986). "Sexual Arousal in Response to Aggression: Ideological, Aggressive and Sexual Correlates." *Journal of Personality and Social Psychology*, 50:330–40.

Marshall, W. L., & Barbaree, H. E. (1984). "A Behavioral View of Rape." *International Journal of Law and Psychiatry*, 7:51–77.

McCrae, R. R., & Costa, P. T. (1985). "Comparison of EPI and Psychoticism Scales with Measures of the Five Factor Model of Personality." *Personality and Individual Differences*, 6:587–97.

Nelson, P. A. (1979). *A Sexual Functions Inventory*. Doctoral diss., University of Florida.

Orne, M. (1962). "On the Social Psychology of the Psychological Experiment: With Particular Reference to Demand Characteristics and Their Implications." *American Psychologist*, 17:776–83.

Quinsey, V. L. (in press). "Sexual Aggression: Studies of Offenders Against Women." *International Yearbook on Law and Mental Health.*

Rada, C. M. (1977). "MMPI Profile Types of Exposers, Rapists, and Assaulters in a Court Services Population." *Journal of Consulting and Clinical Psychology,* 45:61–69.

Rapaport, K., & Burkhart, B. R. (1984). "Personality and Attitudinal Characteristics of Sexually Coercive College Males." *Journal of Abnormal Psychology,* 93:216–21.

Rosen, R. C., & Keefe, F. J. (1978). "The Measurement of Human Penile Tumescence." *Psychophysiology,* 15:366–76.

Rule, B. G., & Leger, G. H. (1976). "Pain Cues and Differing Functions of Aggression." *Canadian Journal of Behavioural Science,* 8:213–22.

Russell, D. E. H. (1984). *Sexual Exploitation: Rape, Child Sexual Abuse and Workplace Harassment.* Beverly Hills, CA: Sage.

Sanday, P. (1981). "The Socio-cultural Context of Rape: A Cross-Cultural Study." *Journal of Social Issues,* 37:5–27.

Scheffe, H. A. (1953). "A Method for Judging all Possible Contrasts in the Analysis of Variance." *Biometrika* 40:87–104.

Schulz, B., Bohrnstedt, G. W., Borgatta, E. F., & Evans, R. R. (1977). "Explaining Premarital Sexual Intercourse Among College Students." *Social Forces,* 56:148–65.

Scully, D., & Marolla, J. (1984). "Convicted Rapists' Vocabulary of Motive: Excuses and Justifications." *Social Problems,* 31:530–44.

———. (1985). " 'Riding the Bull at Gilleys': Convicted Rapists Describe the Rewards of Rape." *Social Problems,* 32:251–63.

Tukey, J. W. (1953). "The Problem of Multiple Comparisons." Princeton University. Unpublished.

Vance, C. S. (1985, April). "What Does the Research Prove?" *Ms,* 40.

13   Misinterpreted Dating Behaviors and the Risk of Date Rape

Charlene L. Muehlenhard

There have long been social skills training programs to teach men how to initiate dates (for example, McGovern, Arkowitz & Gilmore, 1975; Twentyman & McFall, 1975). Women, however, have even more trouble than men do in making contact with prospective dates (Klaus, Hersen & Bellack, 1977); thus, it would seem useful also to have dating initiation programs for women. Previous studies have found that if a woman asks out a man who likes her, he will probably accept (Muehlenhard & McFall, 1981; Muehlenhard & Miller, 1988). This result has led to the conclusion that a woman has "virtually nothing to lose by taking the initiative" (Muehlenhard & McFall, 1981: 691). There may be other consequences of initiation, however, besides whether the woman gets a date with the man.

PARALLELS BETWEEN WOMEN'S DATING INITIATION AND ASSERTION

Consider the parallels between women's dating initiation and assertion. Early research on assertion looked at how to teach people to be assertive (for example, McFall & Marston, 1970). Later research began to look at some of the consequences of assertion; for example, assertive persons were perceived to be effective but not very nice (Hull & Schroeder, 1979; Kelly et al., 1980; Woolfolk & Dever, 1979). It was suggested that assertiveness training needs to be concerned not only with the effectiveness of the response, but also with the consequences for the assertive person's relationships (Hull & Schroeder, 1979).

Similarly, dating skills training needs to be concerned not only with the effectiveness of a woman's behavior, but also with other consequences. One

This chapter is reprinted with permission from the *Journal of Social and Clinical Psychology, 6*, 20–37, 1988.

consequence may be that men will misinterpret her behavior and think that she wants sex more than she actually does, and will subsequently feel that she has "led them on," which may increase the risk of date rape.

MISINTERPRETATION AND THE RISK OF DATE RAPE

A previous study found that men interpret who initiates a date, where the couple goes, and who pays the dating expenses as cues indicative of how much a woman wants sex (Muehlenhard, Friedman & Thomas, 1985). Men are more likely to think the woman wants sex if the couple goes to the man's apartment to talk than if they go to a religious function; going to a movie is intermediate. Men are more likely to think the woman wants sex if she asks the man out rather than if he asks her out, unless they go to a religious function. Men are more likely to think the woman wants sex if she allows the man to pay all the dating expenses than if she pays her own expenses.

This previous study did not, however, investigate how women interpret these dating behaviors. Abbey (1982) found that men view the world more sexually than do women, and men are likely to interpret women's friendliness as seductiveness. If women and men interpret dating behaviors differently, there may be serious repercussions. A woman may ask a man out, meaning only that she wants to go out with him, or she may go to his apartment "to talk," meaning only that she wants to talk to him. If the man interprets such activities as a sign that she wants sex, he may feel led on if he finds that she does not want sex. Unfortunately, many males regard being led on as justification for having sex with the woman against her will—in other words, as justification for rape (Giarrusso et al., 1979; Kanin, 1967b).

The tendency toward rape justification may be a particular problem for men with traditional attitudes toward women. A traditional person is more likely than a nontraditional person to regard rape as being the woman's fault (Feild, 1978) or to endorse rape myths (Burt, 1980). Check and Malamuth (1983) found that traditional persons are more accepting of rape than are nontraditional persons, especially if the rape occurs during a date. Such findings suggest that a woman may be in even greater jeopardy if the man she asks out is traditional in his attitudes toward women.

The present study compared women's and men's interpretations of who initiated a date, where a couple went, and who paid in hypothetical dating scenarios in order to identify discrepancies in the meanings the women and men attributed to these behaviors. Such discrepancies would highlight possible sources of misunderstanding that might result in some men's feeling they had been "led on." This study also compared women's and men's ratings of the justifiability of date rape in these dating situations. Finally, it compared traditional and nontraditional persons' ratings of how much the woman wanted sex and how justifiable rape was in each case. The results have implications for heterosocial skills training programs for women as well as for better understanding of attitudes toward rape.

METHOD

Subjects

Participants were 272 female and 268 male introductory psychology students. Their mean age was 19. They received course credit for their participation.

Questionnaires

The dating-scenarios questionnaire presented 11 brief scenarios describing hypothetical persons, John and Mary, who went on a date. These scenarios manipulated who initiated the date, where the couple went, and who paid the dating expenses. Three levels of dating initiation (he asked, she hinted, or she asked) were crossed with three dating activities (going to a religious function, going to a movie, or going to his apartment to talk), resulting in nine scenarios in 3×3 within-subjects design.

Two additional scenarios manipulated who paid the dating expenses (the man paid or they split the expenses). These were added as two separate scenarios, rather than crossed with the other nine scenarios in a $3 \times 3 \times 2$ design, because it makes no sense to specify who pays the dating expenses if the dating activity is a religious function or going to the man's apartment (neither of which involve expenses).

The dating scenarios were very brief, each consisting of only two or three sentences. The scenarios that manipulated who asked and where they went began: "John and Mary are in a psychology class together and they talk with each other occasionally." This statement established their relationship as casual acquaintances. The second sentence described who initiated the date: either "After class one day, he asked her out for Saturday night" or "After class one day, she mentioned to him that she had no plans for the weekend, and he asked her out for Saturday night" (that is, she hinted) or "After class one day, she asked him out for Saturday night." The third sentence described the dating activity: either "They went to a religious function," or "They went to a movie on campus," or "They went to his apartment to talk." These three activities were selected because, in a previous study, men had interpreted them as increasingly indicative that the woman would want sex (Muehlenhard, Friedmen & Thomas, 1985).

The two scenarios manipulating who paid the dating expenses both began, "Suppose that John and Mary go to a rock concert together." The second sentence was either "John pays for both tickets himself," or "They each pay for their own tickets."

To control for order effects, these scenarios were counterbalanced. There were 12 different versions of the questionnaire, with the scenarios presented in 12 different orders.

Each scenario was followed by two questions, which were rated on 7-point scales ranging from "definitely not" (1) to "definitely" (7). These questions were: "Given this information, do you think that Mary wants to have sexual intercourse with John?" (sex-willingness ratings), and "If it turned out that Mary did not want to have intercourse with John, would John be justified in doing it against her wishes?" (rape-justifiability ratings).

Participants also completed the attitudes toward women scale (AWS: Spence & Helmreich, 1972), which measures traditional versus nontraditional attitudes toward women and sex roles. Using a four-point scale, respondents indicate their level of agreement with 55 statements about the rights of women in vocational, educational, social, sexual, and marital situations. Total scores can range from zero for the most traditional responses to 165 for the most nontraditional responses. Several studies have provided information on the reliability and validity of the AWS; for example, a test-retest reliability coefficient of 0.94 over a two-week period (Muehlenhard & Scardino, 1985) and a coefficient alpha of 0.91 (Muehlenhard & Miller, 1988) have been reported. Compared with those who scored as traditional on the AWS, nontraditional mothers were more likely to have worked when their children were small and to have attained greater occupational achievement (Slevin & Wingrove, 1983); nontraditional fathers were more likely to take sole responsibility for some child care activities (Baruch & Barnett, 1981); and nontraditional parents were more likely to grant independence to their daughters at an early age (Barnett, 1981). Benson and Vincent (1980) reported that the AWS correlated positively with Tavris's (1973) Women's Liberation Movement Scale and self-rated desire to subscribe to *Ms.* magazine; the AWS correlated negatively with Benson and Vincent's (1980) Sexist Attitudes toward Women Scale and humor rating of sexist jokes.

Procedure

Participants met in large groups of about 50 and filled out questionnaires anonymously.

RESULTS

Most participants (77.5 percent) said that it was never justifiable for John to have sex with Mary against her will. This result also means, however, that 22.5 percent thought it was sometimes justifiable. Under what circumstances was date rape regarded as most justifiable?

Effects of Dating Activity and Who Initiated

Two four-factor analyses of variance (ANOVAs) were performed, using dating activity and who initiated as the within-subject factors and the participant's sex and traditionality as between-subjects factors. Sex-willingness ratings and rape-justifiability ratings were treated as two separate dependent variables.

Figure 13.1
Who Initiated the Date

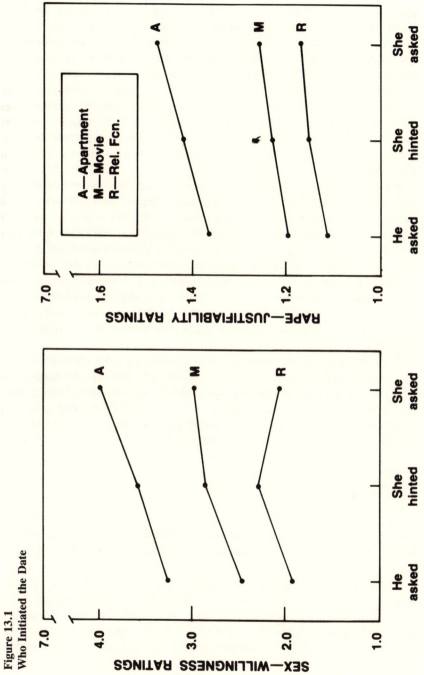

Dating activity had a highly significant effect on both sex-willingness ratings, [$F(2, 1036) = 691.27$, $p = .0000$] and rape-justifiability ratings [$F(2, 1036) = 47.72$, $p = .0000$]. The participants thought that Mary was more likely to want sex and that rape was more justifiable when the couple went to John's apartment rather than to a religious function; ratings for the movie were intermediate (see Figure 13.1). Post hoc ANOVAs showed significant differences between ratings for the religious function and the movie: For sex-willingness ratings, $F(1, 518) = 407.11$, $p = .0000$; for rape-justifiability ratings, $F(1, 518) = 16.83$, $p = .0000$. They also showed significant differences between ratings for the movie and the apartment: For sex-willingness ratings, $F(1, 518) = 562.58$, $p = .0000$; for rape-justifiability ratings, $F(1, 518) = 55.94$, $p = .0000$.

Who initiated the date also significantly affected both sex-willingness ratings, [$F(2, 1036) = 106.83$, $p = .0000$], and rape-justifiability ratings, [$F(2, 1036) = 7.94$, $p = .0004$]. Participants thought that Mary was more likely to want sex and that rape was more justifiable when Mary rather than John initiated the date (see Figure 13.1); ratings for Mary's hinting were intermediate. Post hoc ANOVAs showed significant differences between ratings for Mary's waiting versus hinting: For sex-willingness ratings, $F(1, 518) = 143.51$, $p = .0000$; for rape-justifiability ratings, $F(1, 518) = 6.74$, $p = .0097$. Sex-willingness ratings were significantly different for Mary's hinting versus asking [$F(1, 518) = 12.68$, $p = .0004$], but rape-justifiability ratings were not [$F(1, 518) = 2.13$, $p = .1450$].

There was a significant interaction between dating activity and who initiated for sex-willingness ratings, $F(4, 2072) = 65.78$, $p = .0000$. If the couple had gone to John's apartment, participants' estimates of how much Mary wanted sex increased when she had initiated the date. If the couple had gone to a religious function, however, their estimates of how much Mary wanted sex decreased if she had initiated (see Figure 13.1).

Effects of Who Paid

Two three-factor ANOVAs were performed, using who paid as the within-subject factor and the participants' sex and traditionality as between-subjects factors. Dependent variables were sex-willingness and rape-justifiability ratings.

Participants thought that Mary was significantly more likely to want sex when John rather than Mary paid for Mary's ticket: $F(1, 513) = 58.49$, $p = .0000$ (M's $= 2.80$ and 2.50, respectively). They also thought that rape was significantly more justifiable when John paid all the dating expenses rather than splitting the expenses, $F(1, 513) = 4.67$, $p = .03$ (M's $= 1.28$ and 1.22, respectively).

Effects of Participants' Sex

Sex-Willingness Ratings. Across all situations, men's ratings of how much Mary wanted sex were higher than women's ratings. This sex difference was found in the four-factor ANOVA in which the dating activity and who initiated were manipulated; $F(1, 518) = 78.16$, $p = .0000$ (see Figure 13.2). Notice that in Figure 13.2, men's ratings of how much Mary wanted sex when the couple went to a religious function almost coincided with women's ratings for when the couple went to a movie, and men's ratings for when the couple went to a movie almost coincided with women's ratings for when the couple went to John's apartment. There was a significant sex × dating activity interaction, [$F(2, 1036) = 7.61$, $p = .0005$]; the difference between men's and women's sex-willingness ratings was smaller when the dating activity was a religious function rather than a movie or going to John's apartment. A sex difference in sex-willingness ratings was also found in the three-factor ANOVA in which who paid was manipulated: $F(1, 513) = 90.73$, $p = .0000$ (see Figure 13.3). Again, men's ratings were higher than women's.

Rape-Justifiability Ratings. Men also thought that rape was more justifiable than did women. This sex difference was found in the situations involving who initiated and where the couple went, [$F(1, 518) = 6.46$, $p = .0113$] (see Figure 13.4), and in the situations involving who paid [$F(1, 513) = 10.89$, $p = .0010$] (see Figure 13.3). Rape was rated as being at least somewhat justifiable by 27.5 percent of the men and 17.5 percent of the women.

Effects of Participants' Traditionality

Participants were divided into traditional and nontraditional groups based on median split of the AWS scores. Scores ranged from 35 to 92 for the traditional group and from 93 to 150 for the nontraditional group. Most of the men (68.28 percent) were traditional; most of the women (63.60 percent) were nontraditional. There were 183 traditional and 85 nontraditional men, and 99 traditional and 173 nontraditional women.

Sex-Willingness Ratings. The traditionality of participants' attitudes toward women yielded no main effects on their ratings of how much Mary wanted sex: For situations involving who initiated and where the couple went, $F(1, 518) = .85$, $p = .3570$ (see Figure 13.2); for situations involving who paid, $F(1, 513) = 2.37$, $p = .1246$ (see Figure 13.3). There was a significant interaction between traditionality and who initiated: $F(2, 1036) = 4.35$, $p = .0132$. Traditional and nontraditional persons' ratings of how much Mary wanted sex were almost equal when John asked Mary out, but diverged as Mary took a more active role; when Mary asked John out, traditional persons rated Mary as more willing to have sex than did nontraditional persons.

Figure 13.2
Who Initiated the Date

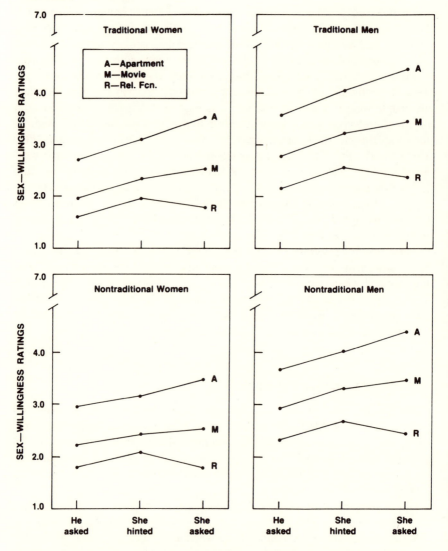

Rape-Justifiability Ratings. In contrast to sex-willingness ratings, rape-justi-fiability ratings were consistently influenced by traditionality. Across all situa-tions, traditional persons thought rape was more justifiable than did nontradi-tional persons: for the four-factor ANOVA involving who initiated and where the couple went, $F(1, 518) = 11.22$, $p = .0009$ (see Figure 13.4); for the three-factor ANOVA involving who paid, $F(1, 513) = 9.41$, $p = .0023$ (see Figure 13.3). There were also several interactions involving traditionality. There were

Figure 13.3
Who Paid the Dating Expenses

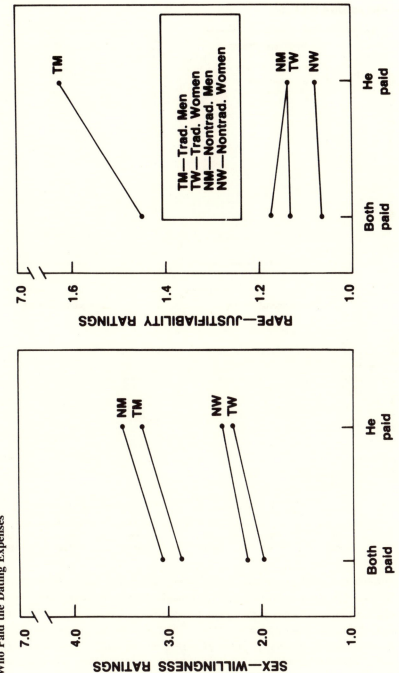

Figure 13.4
Who Initiated the Date

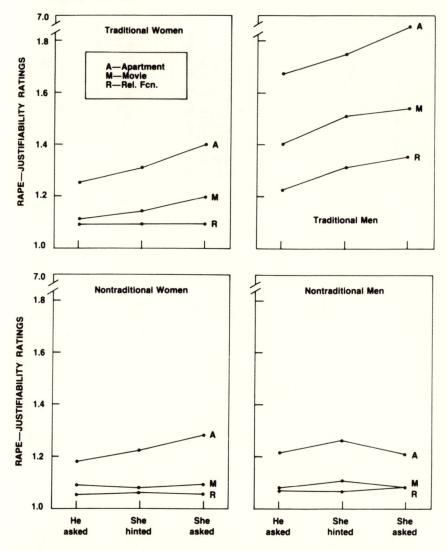

significant sex × traditionality interactions in the four-factor ANOVA, [$F(1$, $518) = 5.62$, $p = .018$] (see Figure 13.4) and in the three-factor ANOVA, [$F(1$, $513) = 4.84$, $p = .0283$] (see Figure 13.3), with traditional men rating rape as more justifiable than any other group. There was an interaction between who initiated and traditionality, [$F(2$, $1036) = 3.86$, $p = .0213$] (see Figure 13.4), with traditional persons' rape-justifiability ratings increasing more than those of nontraditional persons as Mary took an increasingly active role in initiating the date. There was a dating-activity × traditionality interaction, $[F(2, 1036) = 5.20, p = .0056]$ (see Figure 13.4); the tendency for traditional persons to view rape as more justifiable than nontraditional persons was weakest when the couple went to a religious function and strongest when the couple went to John's apartment. There was an interaction between traditionality and who paid, $[F(1, 513) = 5.32, p = .0215]$ (see Figure 13.3), in which the rape-justifiability ratings of traditional persons, but not nontraditional persons, increased when John rather than Mary paid for Mary's ticket. Finally, there was a sex × traditionality × who paid interaction, $[F(1, 513) = 6.04, p = .0143]$ (see Figure 13.3), in which traditional men's rape-justifiability ratings were higher than those of any other group, especially when John paid for both concert tickets.

Rape was rated as at least somewhat justifiable by 29.7 percent of the traditional persons and 14.7 percent of the nontraditional persons. Analyzed by sex, rape was rated as at least somewhat justifiable by 32.8 percent of the traditional men, 24.0 percent of the traditional women, 16.5 percent of the nontraditional men, and 13.9 percent of the nontraditional women.

Correlations Between Sex-Willingness and Rape-Justifiability Ratings

Because rape-justifiability ratings were positively skewed rather than normally distributed, correlations between sex-willingness ratings and rape-justifiability ratings were assessed using a nonparametric statistic, the Spearman rank-correlation coefficient (r_s). Traditional persons showed higher correlations than did nontraditional persons. For the scenario in which rape was rated as most justifiable—that is, when Mary asked John out and they went to his apartment—correlations were 0.450 $(p < .0001)$ for traditional men, 0.466 $(p < .0001)$ for traditional women, 0.097 $(p = .3783)$ for nontraditional men, and 0.2570 $(p = .0006)$ for nontraditional women. Median correlations for all 11 scenarios were 0.327 $(p < .0001)$ and 0.269 $(p = .0072)$ for traditional men and women, respectively, and 0.175 $(p = .1102)$ and 0.209 $(p = .0058)$ for nontraditional men and women, respectively.

DISCUSSION

Theoretical Issues

No matter who initiated the date, who paid, or where the couple went, men were always more likely than women to interpret the behavior as a sign that the women wanted sex. This discrepancy could cause some men to feel "led on" if they thought that a woman was acting as if she wanted sex more than she really did, and some men regard being led on as justification for rape (Giarrusso et al., 1979; Kanin, 1967b). In fact, the situations that were rated as most indicative that the woman wanted sex—when the woman asked the man out, went to his apartment, or let him pay the dating expenses—were the same situations in which rape was rated as most justifiable if she did not want sex.

Rape-justifiability ratings cannot be explained solely by how much participants had thought the woman had wanted sex, however. Traditional and nontraditional persons made similar sex-willingness ratings, but traditional persons—especially traditional men—rated rape as significantly more justifiable than did nontraditional persons.

If differences in sex-willingness ratings cannot account for the difference in rape-justifiability ratings between traditional and nontraditional persons, what can? There are several hypotheses. Perhaps traditional and nontraditional persons do not differ in their estimates of how much the woman wants sex before she says no, but they do differ after she says no. Check and Malamuth (1983) suggested that traditional persons accept the traditional sexual script, which holds that ''women are not supposed to indicate directly their sexual interest or to engage freely in sexuality. Men, on the other hand, are taught to take the initiative even when a woman indicates verbally that she is unwilling to have sex (presumably because of the male belief that a woman's initial resistance is only token)'' (p. 344). Thus, while both traditional and nontraditional men may initially misinterpret a woman's behavior to mean she wants sex more than she really does, traditional men may be more likely to continue in this belief even after she says no. If so, traditional men may find it more justifiable to have sex with a woman even after she resists.

While this explanation is appealing, it cannot entirely explain the results of the present study. The rape-justifiability question in this study explicitly told participants that Mary did not want sex: ''If it turned out that Mary did not want to have intercourse with John, would John be justified in doing it against her wishes?'' The phrasing of the question made it less plausible that traditional men would assume that Mary really wanted sex and was merely offering token resistance. Thus, while this explanation may account for the differences between traditional and nontraditional men in some cases, it probably does not account for the differences found in the present study.

Another hypothesis may be entertained but can be rejected: Perhaps traditional men think women who defy tradition (for example, by initiating dates) deserve what they get, whereas women who conform to traditional stereotypes (for example, by waiting to be asked out) deserve to be protected and not raped. This hypothesis is not supported by the present results, because traditional men thought it was more justifiable to rape a woman who allowed the man to pay the dating expenses (which is traditional) than to rape a woman who paid her own dating expenses (which is less traditional).

Another hypothesis is that, even though they may make similar assumptions about how much a woman wants sex, traditional men may be more likely than nontraditional men to feel led on, and thus to feel that rape is justifiable. Or perhaps traditional and nontraditional men are equally likely to feel led on, but traditional men are more likely than nontraditional men to think that women who "lead men on" deserve to be raped. Both these hypotheses are consistent with the fact that correlations between sex-willingness and rape-justifiability ratings were larger for traditional persons than for nontraditional persons. More research is needed to evaluate these and related hypotheses about differences between traditional and nontraditional persons' attitudes toward rape.

Check and Malamuth (1983) found that nontraditional persons evaluated date rape more negatively than did traditional persons, but they found no interaction between subject sex and traditionality. The present study did find such an interaction, however: Traditional men rated date rape as significantly more justifiable than did traditional women or nontraditional women or men. Thus, the conclusion that "traditional sex roles socialize both men and women—men to be offenders and women to be victims" (Check and Malamuth, 1983: 354) should perhaps be re-evaluated. Women are not necessarily as accepting of date rape as are men, even if they are as traditional.

It should be noted that the questionnaire used in this study did not use the word "rape." If it had asked how justified John would be in "raping" Mary, participants' ratings probably would have been lower. For example, when Koss and Oros (1982) asked women whether they had ever had sexual intercourse with a man when they did not want to because he used some degree of physical force, 8.2 percent said yes; when they asked these same women whether they had ever been raped, only 6.0 percent said yes. The other 2.2 percent apparently did not consider unwanted, forced sex to be rape. Forced intercourse is rape, however. It seems likely that if people do not construe this behavior as rape when filling out a questionnaire, they will not construe it as rape when it actually happens. Regardless of what it is called, it is problematic if people see this behavior as justifiable.

Implications for Social Skills Training

Rape between acquaintances—including rape between dating couples—is both common and serious. In a recent study of 703 undergraduates, 14.7 percent of the women and 7.1 percent of the men reported dates in which the male had sexual intercourse with the female against her wishes (Muehlenhard & Linton, 1987). Kanin and his associates, in studies spanning 20 years, found that 20.9 percent to 23.8 percent of college women reported experiencing forceful attempts at sexual intercourse while on dates during the past year (Kanin, 1957; Kanin & Parcell, 1977; Kirkpatrick & Kanin, 1957). Kanin (1967a) also found that 25.5 percent of the unmarried male undergraduates surveyed reported making forceful attempts at sexual intercourse while on a date. McCahill, Meyer, and Fischman (1979) found that women who had been raped by casual acquaintances had more severe adjustment problems than women who had been raped by strangers, friends, or family members. They speculated that this effect is because a woman does not know a casual acquaintance who rapes her well enough to distinguish between his motives and those of other casual acquaintances, so she begins to fear all casual acquaintances. It is likely that most men with whom she must interact will be casual acquaintances, so that fearing all casual acquaintances will lead to serious adjustment problems.

What implications does this research have for social skills training? Do possible negative consequences of women's dating initiation mean that therapists should encourage their female clients to avoid asking men for dates? I think not, just as possible negative consequences of assertion do not mean that therapists should encourage their clients to avoid being assertive.

Any behavior has many types of consequences that must be weighed against each other. Linehan (1984) distinguishes among three types of consequences for assertive behavior: (1) objectives effectiveness—whether the goals of the behavior are achieved; (2) relationship effectiveness—how the behavior affects one's relationship with the other person; and (3) self-respect effectiveness—how the behavior affects "one's sense of integrity, morality, mastery, and self-esteem" (p. 152). This conceptualization is also applicable to dating behaviors, such as women's dating initiation.

The objectives effectiveness of women's dating initiation is positive. Asking a man out is more likely to result in a date than either hinting or merely waiting to be asked out (Muehlenhard & Miller, in press).

The relationship effectiveness of women's dating initiation is also positive. When men rated videotapes of a woman who did versus a woman who did not ask a man for a date, the woman who asked was rated as kinder, warmer, more thoughtful, and less selfish than the woman who did not ask (Muehlenhard & Scardino, 1985).

The self-respect effectiveness of women's dating initiation also seems positive. Instead of waiting passively for the phone to ring, a woman can take action for herself and can take control of her social life. Women can have the freedom to do what they want, unfettered by narrow gender-role stereotypes. Such freedom would seem to enhance women's feelings of mastery and self-esteem. Thus, women's dating initiation has many positive consequences, which must be weighed against the potential consequence of sexual aggression.

There may be ways to allow women to have the advantages of asking for dates while minimizing the disadvantages. To continue the comparison with assertion, solutions have been found that allow persons to have the advantages of being assertive while minimizing the disadvantages. For example, persons who combine assertion with a statement of empathy for the other person, when compared with persons who use assertion without an empathy statement, are rated as being just as effective but kinder (Woolfolk & Dever, 1979). Similarly, solutions are needed that allow women the freedom to ask for dates or to go where they want, while minimizing the risk of rape. We are currently investigating a way to reduce the risk of date rape by facilitating more open communication between the sexes, which could reduce misinterpretations of dating behaviors and perhaps cause males to feel less "led on" (Muehlenhard & Andrews, 1985). Preliminary results look promising, but more research is clearly needed. Research is also needed on ways to change the attitude that date rape is ever justifiable under any circumstances.

REFERENCES

Abbey, A. (1982). "Sex Differences in Attributions for Friendly Behavior: Do Males Misperceive Females' Friendliness?" *Journal of Personality and Social Psychology*, 42:830–38.

Barnett, R. C. (1981). "Parental Sex-Role Attitudes and Child-Rearing Values." *Sex Roles*, 7:837–46.

Baruch, G. K., & Barnett, R. C. (1981). "Fathers' Participation in the Care of Their Preschool Children." *Sex Roles*, 7:1043–55.

Benson, P. L., & Vincent, S. (1980). "Development and Validation of the Sexist Attitudes Toward Women Scale (SATWS)." *Psychology of Women Quarterly*, 5:276–91.

Burt, M. R. (1980). "Cultural Myths and Supports for Rape." *Journal of Personality and Social Psychology*, 38:217–30.

Check, J. V. P., & Malamuth, N. M. (1983). "Sex Role Stereotyping and Reactions to Depictions of Stranger Versus Acquaintance Rape." *Journal of Personality and Social Psychology*, 45:344–56.

Field, H. S. (1978). "Attitudes Toward Rape: A Comparative Analysis of Police, Rapists, Crisis Counselors, and Citizens." *Journal of Personality and Social Psychology*, 36:156–79.

Giarrusso, R., Johnson, P., Goodchilds, J., & Zellman, G. (1979, April). "Adolescents' Cues and Signals: Sex and Assault." In P. Johnson (chair), "Acquaintance Rape and Adolescent Sexuality." Symposium conducted at meeting of the Western Psychological Association, San Diego.

Hull, D. B., & Schroeder, H. E. (1979). "Some Interpersonal Effects of Assertion, Non-Assertion, and Aggression." *Behavior Therapy*, 10:20–28.

Kanin, E. J. (1957). "Male Aggression in Dating-Courtship Relations." *American Journal of Sociology*, 63:197–204.

———. (1967a). "An Examination of Sexual Aggression as a Response to Sexual Frustration." *Journal of Marriage and Family*, 29:428–33.

———. (1967b). "Reference Groups and Sex Conduct Norm Violations." *Sociological Quarterly*, 8:495–504.

Kanin, E. J., & Parcell, S. R. (1977). "Sexual Aggression: A Second Look at the Offended Female." *Archives of Sexual Behavior*, 6:67–76.

Kelly, J. A., Kern, J. M., Kirkley, B. G., Patterson, J. N., & Keane, T. M. (1980). "Reactions to Assertive Versus Unassertive Behavior: Differential Effects for Males and Females and Implications for Assertiveness Training." *Behavior Therapy*, 11:670–82.

Kirkpatrick, C., & Kanin, E. (1957). "Male Sexual Aggression on a University Campus." *American Sociological Review*, 22:52–58.

Klaus, D., Hersen, M., & Bellack, A. S. (1977). "Survey of Dating Habits of Male and Female College Students: A Necessary Precursor to Measurement and Modification." *Journal of Clinical Psychology*, 33:369–75.

Koss, M. P., & Oros, C. J. (1982). "Sexual Experiences Survey: A Research Instrument Investigating Sexual Aggression and Victimization." *Journal of Consulting and Clinical Psychology,* 50:455–57.

Linehan, M. M. (1984). "Interpersonal Effectiveness in Assertive Situations." In E. A. Blechman (ed.), *Behavior Modification with Women,* (143–69). New York: Guilford.

McCahill, T. W., Meyer, L. C., & Fischman, R. M. (1979). *The Aftermath of Rape.* Lexington, MA: Lexington.

McFall, R. M., & Marston, A. R. (1970). "Experimental Investigation of Behavior Rehearsal in Assertive Training." *Journal of Abnormal Psychology,* 76:295–303.

McGovern, K. B., Arkowitz, H., & Gilmore, S. K. (1975). "Evaluation of Social Skills Training Programs for College Dating Inhibitions." *Journal of Counseling Psychology,* 22:505–12.

Muehlenhard, C. L., & Andrews, S. L. (1985, November). "Open Communication About Sex: Will It Reduce Risk Factors Related to Date Rape?" Paper presented at annual meeting of the Association for Advancement of Behavior Therapy, Houston, TX.

Muehlenhard, C. L., Friedman, D. E., & Thomas, C. M. (1985). "Is Date Rape Justifiable? The Effects of Dating Activity, Who Initiated, Who Paid, and Men's Attitudes Toward Women." *Psychology of Women Quarterly,* 9:297–310.

Muehlenhard, C. L., & Linton, M. A. (1987). "Date Rape and Sexual Aggression in Dating Situations: Incidence and Risk Factors." *Journal of Counseling Psychology,* 34:186–96.

Muehlenhard, C. L., & McFall, R. M. (1981). "Dating Initiation from a Woman's Perspective." *Behavior Therapy,* 12:682–91.

Muehlenhard, C. L., & Miller, E. N. (1988). "Traditional and Nontraditional Men's Responses to Women's Dating Initiation." *Behavior Modification* 12:385–403.

Muehlenhard, C. L., & Scardino, T. J. (1985). "What Will He Think? Men's Impressions of Women Who Initiate Dates and Achieve Academically." *Journal of Counseling Psychology,* 32:560–69.

Slevin, K. F., & Wingrove, C. R. (1983). "Similarities and Differences Among Three Generations of Women in Attitudes Toward the Female Role in Contemporary Society." *Sex Roles,* 9:609–24.

Spence, J. T., & Helmreich, R. (1972). "The Attitudes Toward Women Scale: An Objective Instrument to Measure Attitudes Toward the Rights and Roles of Women in Contemporary Society." *JSAS Catalog of Selected Documents in Psychology,* 2:66.

Tavris, C. (1973). "Who Likes Women's Liberation—and Why: The Case of the Unliberated Liberals." *Journal of Social Issues,* 29:175–98.

Twentyman, C. T., & McFall, R. M. (1975). "Behavioral Training of Social Skills in Shy Males." *Journal of Consulting and Clinical Psychology,* 43:384–95.

Woolfolk, R. L., & Dever, S. (1979). "Perceptions of Assertion: An Empirical Analysis." *Behavior Therapy,* 10:404–11.

14 Acquaintance Rape on Campus: Responsibility and Attributions of Crime
Sarah Fenstermaker

The furor over an allegation that a young women had been raped by three acquaintances at the Berkeley campus of the University of California (*Los Angeles Times*, 1986) represents only one of the now mounting number of incidents referred to as "date rape." The lighthearted, diminutive sound of the term belies a serious problem for educators and those who serve the needs of women on high school and college campuses (Meyer, 1984; Association of American Colleges, 1986). The more that is learned about the prevalence, incidence, and dynamics of sexual coercion between "friends," the more changes are implied in the ways in which rape prevention, student conduct codes, and administrative intervention are conceived and organized.

To date, the primary scholarly emphasis has been on estimating the incidence and prevalence of sexual coercion between acquaintances. College populations have been a primary focus for such studies, with estimates varying, depending upon operational definitions and method, from 25 to 51 percent of the females reporting some sexually coercive experiences during a single academic year (Kanin & Parcell, 1977; Korman & Leslie, 1982; Koss & Oros, 1982). Self-reported data from potential assailants are more suspect, but the best estimates from male students suggest that from 4 percent to 15 percent have engaged in behavior that would be legally defined as rape. Moreover, the vast majority of these acts involved men and women who were acquainted (Rapaport & Burkhart, 1984; Koss et al., 1985). Thus, whatever the exact figures, both systematic study and student grapevines support the notion that acquaintance sexual assault and coercion are very real facts of campus life.

The circumstantial dynamics of acquaintance rape have yet to receive concerted sociological attention. Byers et al. (1977) studied some of the circumstances surrounding campus sexual assault and found that the majority of assailants had seen their victims socially at least once before and typically chose their own homes, cars, or the outdoors for the assault. In their survey of perpetrators, Koss and Oros (1982) found that victims were romantically involved with their assailants prior to the assault and had previously engaged in some sexual activity with that partner and that the sexual coercion required a moderate, rather than high, degree of force. Lane and Gwartney-Gibbs (1985) reported that students from high income households were more likely to both victimize and be victimized through the ploy of getting the other person intoxicated in order to gain sexual favors.

Perceptions of sexual coercion, whether involving attributions of "blame" (Thorton, Robbins & Johnson, 1981), responsibility (Wiener & Rhinehart, 1986), or some legal definition of rape (Wiener & Vodanovich, 1986), have been examined primarily through the use of "vignettes" in which respondents are asked to interpret scenarios involving sexual coercion. (Further examples include Giarusso et al., 1979; Shotland & Goodstein, 1983; Fischer, 1985.) Most result in the identification of a variety of zero-order correlates of attributions of rape, or responsibility, centering on circumstance and/or individual biography. These correlational studies are marked by methodological flaws and unwarranted statistical assumptions, but nevertheless suggest that there are intriguing dynamics operating among coercive sexual experiences, attributions of responsibility, and conceptions of rape and criminality.

Thus, for example, Shotland and Goodstein (1983) found that both men and women were less likely to attribute the term "rape" to the behavior or to attribute responsibility to the male in a situation in which low force was employed. Similarly, Fischer (1985) found that those more tentative in their definitions of rape were also more traditional in their attitudes toward women, less knowledgeable about sex, and more likely to blame the situation rather than the assailant. Giarusso and colleagues (1979) found that the degree to which victims portrayed in vignettes intimated consensus or quid pro quo sexual bargains had significant effects on the attribution of blame. Finally, Wiener and Rhinehart (1986) found that both *initial* intention and *subsequent* remorse were significant to the attribution of responsibility.

It is slowly becoming clear that sexual coercion among acquaintances poses unique dynamics that the study of stranger rape does not. In particular, the degree of underreporting linked to acquaintance rape reminds us again of how many hidden crimes of sexual coercion there may be. The degree of psychological trauma, disillusion, and self-blame resulting to the victim can only compound the effects of assault when it follows a conscious decision to trust another. Lastly, much more than stranger rape, acquaintance rape challenges individuals and institutions to acknowledge the depth and degree to which we daily ratify male entitlement and dominance in our culture.[1]

This chapter will explore the relationship between women's experiences with sexual coercion, their perceptions of responsibility in coercive situations, and their attributions of sexually coercive acts as crimes. Data are drawn from a survey of 481 female students at a medium-sized public university in the West. Respondents were asked about their most recent sexually coercive experiences and their reaction to a series of vignettes in which the circumstances of a sexually coercive situation were systematically varied. Conclusions will be drawn about the complicated dynamics of acquaintance rape and its implications for institutional policies.

DESIGN, SAMPLE, AND INSTRUMENTS

This small study was intended to establish, for one university campus, the incidence and prevalence of sexual coercion among undergraduates and to analyze the factors that influence respondent interpretations of sexually coercive situations. To those ends, a two-part questionnaire was mailed to a random probability sample of 15 percent of the female and male undergraduate population (1,115 females and 939 males).

As was expected, the return rate for females was much greater (43 percent) than for males (31 percent), but both samples proved statistically indistinguishable from the larger student populations from which they were drawn.[2] Thus, the campus population and the sample had the same characteristics: 81 percent white, 80 percent not primarily residing in campus owned dorms or apartments, 96 percent not active in intercollegiate or club sports, 90 percent not active in a fraternity or sorority; the same distribution among classes (freshman, sophomore, etc.) and with respect to a religious preference; and a mean grade point average (GPA) of 2.75 (B−). For the present analysis, only questionnaires of female respondents are considered.

Sexual Coercion Vignettes

The utilization of vignettes, or scenarios, to which respondents react has found frequent use in psychological as well as sociological research (Reilly et al., 1982; Rossi & Nock, 1982; Fischer, 1985). The most ambitious use of the vignette, has been to construct what are in essence systematically varied experimental "conditions" represented by variations in the dimensions of the vignettes. This provides the power of a fully crossed design in which the effect of each condition can be isolated and treated as orthogonal to the others (for discussion see Rossi & Nock, 1982).

This is obviously the ideal method of employing vignettes. However, less sophisticated uses may nevertheless generate compelling findings. In the present analysis, an initial scenario was presented to respondents, as follows:

Imagine a male and female student on a study date at the female student's apartment. The two have known each other through classes for the better part of a school year, but have never dated. Well into the evening, the male student makes some suggestive remarks, which the female student ignores. A short time later, he sits down next to her and tries to kiss her. She tries to push him away and explicitly says "No," but he becomes more aggressive. He then pushes her to the floor, pins her down, and in the next 10 minutes manages over her pleadings to complete an act of sexual intercourse.

Seven subsequent variations on that scenario followed. For *each,* respondents were asked to: (1) employ an eleven-point (0–10) scale to attribute responsibility for actions to the man and (2) the woman; (3) decide whether a crime had been committed; and (4) decide whether the female student should report the incident to the police.

Appendix A to this chapter reproduces the first vignette above and the seven variations on it. In the first two variations (vignettes 2 and 3), the departures from the initial scenario involve first a change in the location of the date (from female to male apartment) and then a change in the type of date (from study date to first date).

The next three variations (vignettes 4, 5, and 6) involve changes in the history of the relationship and level of intimacy that has been defined as acceptable in the relationship. Vignette 4 gives the hypothetical students a short history of dating and some sexual intimacy (kissing, petting, necking). Vignette 5 extends the level of intimacy to include a single, recent act of intercourse. Finally, vignette 6 portrays the students as having been dating and sleeping together regularly, and has the female student "encouraging" initial advances by the male. The next variation simply adds alcohol use by both partners to the prior scenario. The last variation introduces physical violence into the already sexually coercive situation. The stark differences associated with this dimension will be noted throughout the analysis.

Measuring Sexually Coercive Experiences

This questionnaire asked about any experience with specific types of coercion while the respondent was enrolled as a student and the number of occasions on which undesirable experiences occurred. "Coercion" was defined for respondents as "against your will and without your consent." Respondents were asked to note a variety of characteristics about the *most recent* coercive incident.

The number victimized proved to be small, and this insufficient sample size precluded a separate analysis of victims. Hence, the actual experiences of respondents is presented first. Next, the relationship between the attributions of responsibility and perceptions of criminality are discussed.

RESULTS AND DISCUSSION

Campus Sexual Coercion

Table 14.1 shows the types of coercive sexual behaviors that women students experienced. It is clear from this table that the vast majority of undergraduates

Table 14.1
Sexually Coercive Behaviors Reported by College Women

	(N = 481)	
Type of Behavior	f	%
Kiss	74	15.4
Breasts Touched	56	11.6
Genitals Touched	36	7.5
Another's Genitals Touched	17	3.5
Oral Sex	3	.6
Oral Sex on Another	3	.6
Vaginal Sex	3	.6
Other (including pinch/grab)	20	4.2
None Experienced	356	74.2

f: number of reported occurrences.

(74.2 percent) have not experienced any sexual coercion in their dating relationships. Moreover, the largest single group (15.4 percent) of those who reported a sexually coercive experience said that they were kissed without their consent, while a smaller percentage (11.6%) said that the incident ended with their breasts being touched, and the coercion ended there.

There is a hint that the longer a female student is on campus, the more likely it is that she will experience coercion, with senior-class women reporting the most (27 percent), followed by juniors (24 percent), sophomores (23 percent), and freshmen (22 percent). However, the differences between the percentages are not statistically significant at conventional levels. The absence of steep increases between class levels suggests a more subtle dynamic in the data that is consistent with other research (Koss et al., 1982); it may be that freshmen are the true at-risk group for sexual coercion in dating.

Based on the respondents' description of the "most recent incident," we find that in nearly all cases (92 percent) a single male assailant was involved, and that the incident usually occurred in his apartment or dorm room (25 percent). Over three-fourths of the incidents happened at night (77 percent) and mostly during the week (60 percent).

Whatever the type of coercion, or the circumstance, it can be safely concluded that more than one-quarter of the female students had felt coerced at least once in their campus career, and over half of those coerced (56 percent) had experienced coercion on more than one occasion. The most conservative interpretation of these data would suggest that in 7 percent of the instances of coercion a felony sex offense was committed (oral sex act, vaginal penetration). A slight extrapolation of the sample data to the campus's 8,000 female undergraduates suggests it is likely that such offenses occur at least once a day.

To reiterate a point made earlier, the vignette data complement the experientials data well enough to permit exploring the relationship between responsibility, and attributions of crime.

Attribution of Responsibility

Recall that after each vignette variation, respondents were to assign the degree of responsibility attributable to the male and female depicted on a scale of 0 to 10.[3] Table 14.2 presents the means and standard deviations for the attribution-of-responsibility scores. For ease of presentation, the vignettes are also clustered by the pertinent feature that they introduce into the scenario.

It is clear from these simple marginals that the degree of responsibility attributed to males changes markedly as vignettes change.[4] Specifically, each change in the scenario also implies either a change in the implied consent of the female or her lack of foresight in avoiding trouble. The change in scores for the first two vignettes represents a shift in the location of the date (from her apartment to his) and a shift in type of date and thus the implied relationship from study date to regular date). In both cases, what begins as almost total responsibility attributed to the male drops slightly (from 9.29 in vignette 1 to 8.96 in vignette 3).

In the next three vignettes, this process continues, as more features are altered in the vignettes, thus appearing to muddy the issues of consent and encouragement on the part of the female. In vignettes 4–6, the female participates in sexual activity with the male (necking, petting), and the relationship is given a history of sexual activity (prior intercourse). This appears to precipitate a major drop in the degree to which the male is granted responsibility, since there is an average of two full points' difference between the responsibility attributed to the male on the "first regular date" (vignette 3) and the male whose initial advances were "encouraged" (vignette 6).

In vignette 7, the use of alcohol is added for both students and is associated with another drop in male responsibility (mean of 6.58). It is instructive to note that even with the alcohol use of vignette 7, when *battery* of the female is introduced ("the male student hit the female student several times as he pinned her down"), mean male responsibility jumps back up two levels to 8.7 (standard deviation = 1.65).

Given the strong temptation to blame herself that acquaintance rape always presents, it is not surprising that female respondents did assign progressively more and more responsibility to the female as the vignettes depicted greater implied female complicity or greater ambiguity surrounding consent, unless explicit violence was depicted. Despite this clear progression, it should also be

Table 14.2
Respondent Attribution of Responsibility to Males in Sexual Coercion Vignettes

Vignette		X Attribution to Male	SD
		(N = 481)	
1		9.29	1.26
2	*	9.13	1.36
3		8.96	1.43
4		8.23	1.77
5	**	7.70	1.95
6		6.96	2.22
7	***	6.58	1.95
8	****	8.70	1.65

* Location of Date   X: average score.
  Type of Date   SD: standard deviation.

** Past Level of Intimacy

*** Alcohol Use

**** Battery

noted that males retain much of the responsibility, even when the situation is complicated by the use of alcohol.

Attribution of a Crime

The next question addressed is how that sense of responsibility and blame may translate to an assessment of criminality. If respondents employed a purely legal definition of whether a crime had been committed, we would expect no relationship between blame and attribution of crime. However, our sense of what is criminal is often confounded with normative notions of intention, responsibility, and circumstance. Table 14.3 illustrates how the respondents reacted to each vignette on the question of whether a crime had been committed.

Table 14.3 shows the extent to which a sense of male responsibility and the attribution of crime are associated. Just as in Table 14.2, as the vignettes pro-

Table 14.3

Respondent Designation of Behavior in Sexual Coercion Vignettes as a Crime

Vignette		(N = 481) Crime Committed?	
		f	% yes
1		470	97.5
2	*	467	96.9
3		464	96.3
4		402	83.4
5	**	340	70.5
6		296	61.4
7	***	271	56.2
8	****	457	94.8

* Location of Date   f: numbers answering yes.
  Type of Date

** Past Level of Intimacy

*** Alcohol Use

**** Battery

gressively complicate matters, and male responsibility drops, so too does the normative sense that crimes are committed.[5] Particularly stark is the drop in the percentage of respondents who think a crime has been committed once they confront the vignettes that imply at least initial consent by the female student (vignettes 4–8). Moreover, there is an especially precipitous drop (from 83.4 percent to 61.4 percent) overall, and from vignettes 4 to 6, as first some history of sexual activity, followed by female encouragement of initial advances, is introduced. In fact, by the time alcohol is introduced into the scenario, the percentage of respondents attributing a crime to the situation has already dropped over 35 percent. Alcohol contributes an additional drop of only 5 percent in those who say a crime has been committed.[6]

The marginals presented above indicate that when respondents conclude that a situation involves the commission of a crime, they are not thinking of "law breaking" per se. Also involved may be some assessment of (1) the responsibility rightly attributable to the lawbreaker, (2) the responsibility rightly attributable to the victim, and even (3) the practicalities of legally calling someone to account for his actions.[7] Each of these separately, and then together, are determined by the complicated dynamics that present themselves with a "gendered" normative order that establishes the ways in which we conceive and practice our social judgments of men and women.

A Final Note on Responsibility

As a complement to the earlier examination, an ordinal logit analysis was also undertaken to determine the relationship between the attribution of male responsibility for sexual coercion depicted in the vignettes, and actual respondent experience with sexual coercion. The results are hardly conclusive, but do confirm the complicated dynamics surrounding acquaintance sexual coercion and rape.[8]

For each vignette, the level of attributed responsibility served as the dependent variable, and variables reflecting any actual experience with coercion served as the exogenous terms. Respondents' own victimization seemed to have the greatest (and significant) effect on the attribution of responsibility, *given* a certain context depicted in the vignettes. In these data specifically, prior experience exerted no effect on respondents' judgments for any but the sixth and seventh scenarios. For those vignettes, the presence of prior experience with sexual coercion—of any variety—significantly increases the blame attributed to the male. So, for example, for vignette 7, if the respondent experienced any prior victimization of this sort, she was one and one-half times more likely to increase her attribution of responsibility to males by one level than were respondents without that experience.

The experiential measures are not sensitive enough to reflect any more subtle effects nor sustain much more analysis, but these findings at least suggest an interesting connection between experience and perceptions of responsibility. Recall that vignettes 6 and 7 are the scenarios depicting the greatest degree of initial female complicity and most complicated history for the relationship. In both, the couple has a continuing relationship and the female encourages initial advances; in vignette 7, both students are "drinking heavily."

Earlier findings suggested a general tendency on the part of female students to allocate more and more responsibility to females as the context implied their more willing participation. Respondents did not absolve males, but they certainly allocated responsibility more evenly to both parties.[9] Given that tendency, those respondents who have actually experienced sexual coercion may distinguish themselves from this pattern. They may, instead, be more reluctant to attribute responsibility to females, regardless of the complicity implied. And, it is in vignettes 6 and 7—in which complicity is the most obvious—that the effect of experience on the attribution of responsibility reveals itself.

The respondent who has experienced coercion may bring something different to her judgments than does the naive respondent. The respondent who can do more than simply *imagine* sexual coercion can draw on a more sophisticated sense of how it is that sexual coercion can shift the initial interactional terrain from one of trust to physical threat and dominance. She may thus be more reluctant to blame the coerced female, despite the depiction of a long-term relationship, active complicity, or the use of alcohol.[10]

IMPLICATIONS FOR POLICY AND PRACTICE

To varying degrees, rape prevention educators, campus police authorities, and college administrators are aware that rape and sexual assault are not confined to the deserted beach or the unlocked dorm. Yet, it is the rare campus rape prevention program or the even rarer police department whose policies, procedures, or educational programs reflect that fact. Similarly, campus administrators may find it increasingly difficult to ignore the reality that campus "security" may imply the control of most ordinary crime and criminals, but hardly renders the campus a safe place for students at risk of sexual victimization.

The difficulties posed to educators by sexual coercion among students raises questions about the ways in which the movement away from *in loco parentis* policies 20 years ago put female students at risk, even as they were told they were safe. One would be hard pressed to argue that the removal of strict controls on the comings and goings of women students was a mistake, but it nevertheless meant that campus administrators abdicated any real responsibility for the safety of women students and left them to fend for themselves in an environment that was perceived to be a safe haven but was sometimes downright dangerous.

The challenge posed to campus personnel by acquaintance sexual coercion is a legitimately daunting one. Just as some earnest district attorneys' offices and police departments convey the message to batterers that "hitting is not ok," so too must campus police and service providers attempt to deter those who coerce others. In the short run, students face a situation in which their own good sense, well-considered choices, and determination to keep *themselves* safe must prevail.

The obvious obstacles to the development of workable, effective policy also present compelling research questions that have not yet been addressed.

RECOMMENDATIONS FOR FURTHER RESEARCH

The vignette method of studying how potentially problematic encounters are interpreted directs attention to the *context* in which sexual coercion and dating occur. The data show that both in *interpretations* of coercion in dating and in individual experience, what understandings one brings to the particular situation vary widely but are significantly affected by the context in which actions occur. The situated nature of acquaintance coercion and rape poses a variety of unanswered research questions centering on the *individual* biographic history, awareness of the problem, and actual experience. But, other compelling questions could focus on the effects of *campus* climate.

The visible and sometimes vocal presence of student groups organized to challenge the traditional attitudes and practices of some campus communities may provide a future opportunity to study the larger context in which campus sexual coercion occurs. The generation of a hospitable campus climate for women, whether in the classroom or the student dorm, may bring with it discernably different student views of what constitutes "appropriate" dating behavior. If even a few campuses become places where women feel entitled to their own safety and where men and women presume that they share equal responsibility for their behavior, then researchers might do well to study how a campus climate can affect individual dating behavior. Yet, at present, we see little variation in how campuses and student bodies view their women students and the women's responsibility for insuring their own safety.

SUMMARY AND CONCLUSION

Acquaintance rape—perhaps even more than spousal abuse or, certainly, stranger rape—so muddies the normative waters that our very different sense of what is sexually appropriate for women and what is sexually appropriate for men is brought to bear not only on our judgments of differential responsibility for actions, but on our judgments of presumably factual matters like the commission of a crime. What is illustrated here is that the only "facts" of acquaintance rape are its ambiguity and the ambivalent ways we respond to it.

Nevertheless, such sexual coercion rests firmly on a foundation that higher education embraces, namely, the token presence of women in the production and dissemination of knowledge and the at least tacit approval of many forms of female domination, including sexual harassment and highly stylized, "gendered" relationships between female staff and male bosses.

Thus, the context of male dominance that so pervades social and academic life on the campus leads us all to wonder how the problem of acquaintance rape can be seriously addressed or ameliorated. As we have found with some programs directed at the problem of spousal battery (Sherman & Berk, 1984), an aggressive "shock" to the system in the form of a well-monitored, well-funded social program can undermine the support that the general cultural milieu of male dominance provides the particular problem. Regrettably, it may be the case that *only* a concerted, authentic, and perhaps long-term investment in procedural, policy, and educational change would begin to deter the undergraduate who perceives a female acquaintance as fair game for criminal assault.

ACKNOWLEDGMENTS

Support and encouragement for this project came from the University of California at Santa Barbara Chancellor's Office, and the Office of Student Affairs. Thanks to Sharman Badgett, Richard Berk, Farfalla Borah, Cheri Gurse, Chris Klukkert, and especially, Scott Whiteley for their assistance.

APPENDIX A: SEXUAL COERCION VIGNETTES

1. Imagine a male and female student on a study date at the female student's apartment. The two have known each other through classes for the better part of a school year, but have never dated. Well into the evening, the male student makes some suggestive remarks, which the female student ignores. A short time later, he sits down next to her and attempts to kiss her. She tries to push him away and explicitly says, "No," but he becomes more aggressive. He then pushes her to the floor, pins her down, and in the next 10 minutes manages over her pleadings to complete an act of sexual intercourse.

2. Imagine the same scene, but at the male student's apartment rather than the female's.

3. Now imagine that intercourse occurred as in the first scene, but the two were at the male student's apartment. They were on their first regular date together, not a study date.

4. Now imagine that intercourse occurred as in the first scene but the two were at the male student's apartment and had been dating for a short while. In the past they had kissed, necked, and petted regularly but had never slept together.

5. Now imagine that intercourse occurred as in the first scene, but the two were at the male student's apartment. They had been dating for a while, and had slept together recently.

6. Now imagine that the two were at the male student's apartment, had been dating and regularly sleeping together, and the female student had encouraged his initial advances. However, when it was clear that he wanted sexual intercourse, she did not, and said no.

7. Now imagine all the events were as just described in number 6, but both the students had been drinking heavily.

8. Now imagine that all of the events were as just described in numbers 6 and 7, but that the male student hit the female student several times as he pinned her down.

NOTES

1. For an enlightening personal discussion of stranger rape, see Estrich, 1987.
2. While the final sample differed in no discernible respect from the initial male sample (and thus the larger population), it is nevertheless possible that there were biases on unmeasured variables. For example, the sample may have underrepresented the experiences and views of women who had never been victimized and/or had no friends who had been victimized.
3. Respondents were asked, "On a scale of 0 to 10, how much responsibility for these events falls to each individual?" Unfortunately, an untoward decision in questionnaire construction forced respondents to allocate responsibility so that total male and female responsibility added to 10. There is clearly no sufficient argument to justify the notion that responsibility for behavior is conceived by respondents to be some sort of

"pie" to be sliced up and apportioned. The practical outcome of this decision, of course, is that when one knows the response for males, they necessarily know the response for females, since the two always add to 10. Therefore, only male responsibility is presented.

4. The reader new to questions of statistical significance between groups might imagine that an F-test for Table 14.2 followed by paired comparisons is appropriate here. Of course, an F-test only indicates whether means are different by more than chance would suggest; it says nothing about *how* they are different—exactly the issue at hand. Moreover, over 30 paired comparisons would follow from this indiscriminate approach. Instead, a priori, it was hypothesized that the first seven means in Table 14.2 would decline monotonically. Perhaps the most simple and reasonable statistical test assumes a straight line as one monotonic functional form, and then tests the null hypothesis that the slope is zero or positive. Using ordinary least squares for the first seven means listed in Table 14.2, the slope was 0.49, and the associated t-value was -11.21. Since the adjusted R-square was 0.95, there seemed to be no need to attempt other monotonic forms. Finally, there is a strong suggestion that the substantive difference between the first seven scenarios and the last is a significant one; the difference between the eighth mean and the adjacent mean of 6.58 is significant at $p<.01$.

5. Just as in Table 14.2, a declining monotonic relationship was postulated a priori and, as with Table 14.2, a linear regression was used to test the null hypothesis. Again, the null hypothesis was easily rejected at conventional levels, although a slightly better fit was obtained with a quadratic rather than linear form. For the quadratic form, the regression coefficient was 16.26, and the associated t-value was 21.36. It may also be worth noting that the means in Table 14.3 are correlated well over 0.90 with the means in Table 14.2.

6. Yet again, and notably, once battery is introduced into the scenario, respondents view things very differently. In this instance, and with all other features remaining the same, if the male hits the female, fully 95 percent of the respondents think a crime has been committed. In hindsight, one might have wished that we had asked *what* crime had been committed, since it may not be forcible rape, but battery that respondents are classifying as criminal.

7. An ordinal logit analysis was undertaken to explore the relationship between respondents' prior experience of sexual coercion and the attribution of criminality to each vignette. An ordinal scale measuring the increasing reluctance by the respondent to attribute the commission of a crime to a scenario served as the dependent variable. The independent variable simply reflected whether or not the respondent ever experienced sexual coercion while a student. No significant relationship emerged.

8. Ordinal procedures were chosen because there was no reason to assume that the ratings of responsibility were derived from an equal-interval scale. Moreover, even if an equal-interval scale were assumed, the scale was clearly bounded at 0 and 10. Hence, a nonlinear functional form was required (asymptotic at 0 and 10), coupled with adjustments for heteroscedasticity (since the variance of the disturbances was necessarily largest for values in the middle ranges). The ordinal procedures are therefore, conservative and bypass a good deal of unnecessary econometrics.

An analysis was undertaken for each vignette. Tables have not been included since in five of the analyses, the null hypothesis of no effect (of victimization on attribution of responsibility) could not be rejected with symptotic t-tests. Thus, the reader is not being kept from anything of substantive interest.

9. The argument that female respondents are, as they proceed through the vignettes, "learning" to remove responsibility from the male is not supported by the data. This argument would maintain that something about the vignette *process* (and not the vignettes themselves) affects the attribution of responsibility to males. If this were the case, however, the sharp increase in responsibility attributed to males when they engage in battery (as in vignette 8) is certainly hard to explain.

10. This does, however, raise the question of whether the generalization of the findings is jeopardized by, for example, the inadvertent oversampling of victims or victims' friends, that is, the greater the number of victims in the sample the more frequent the attributions of male responsibility. Luckily, the ordinal logit results are unaffected by this since sample selection bias only pertains to sampling on an endogenous variable, and of course here victimization is treated as exogenous.

REFERENCES

Association of American Colleges. (1986). *Campus Gang Rape: Party Games?* Washington, D.C.: Project on the Status and Education of Women.

Byers, E. S., Eastman, A. M., Nilson, B. G., & Roehl, C. E. (1977). "Relationships Between Degree of Sexual Assault Antecedent Conditions, and Victim Offender Relationship." Paper presented at meeting of American Psychological Association, San Francisco.

Estrich, S. (1987). *Real Rape.* Cambridge: Harvard University Press.

Fischer, G. J. (1985). "College Student Attitudes Toward Forcible Date Rape: Cognitive Predictors." Paper presented at the Society for the Scientific Study of Sexuality meetings.

Giarusso, R., Johnson, P., Goodchilds, J., & Zellman, G. (1979). "Adolescent Cues and Signals: Sex and Assault." Paper presented at the Western Psychological Association meetings.

Kanin, E., & Parcell, S. (1977). "Sexual Aggression: A Second Look at the Offended Female." *Archives of Sexual Behavior,* 6:67–76.

Korman, S., & Leslie, G. (1982). "The Relationship of Feminist Ideology and Expense Sharing to Perceptions of Sexual Aggression in Dating." *Journal of Sex Research,* 18:114–29.

Koss, M. P., Leonard, K. E., Beezley, D. A., & Oros, C. J. (1985). "Nonstranger Sexual Aggression: A Discriminant Analysis of the Psychological Characteristics of Undetected Offenders." *Sex Roles,* 12:981–92.

Koss, M. P., & Oros, C. J. (1982). "Sexual Experiences Survey: A Research Instrument Investigating Sexual Aggression and Victimization. *Journal of Consulting and Clinical Psychology,* 50:455–57.

———. (1986). "Hidden Rape: A Survey of the Incidence of Sexual Aggression and Victimization on a University Campus." Paper presented at the Midwestern Psychological Association meetings.

Lane, K. E., & Gwartney-Gibbs, P. A. (1985). "Violence in the Context of Dating and Sex." *Journal of Family Issues,* 6:45–59.

Los Angeles Times. (1986). "UC Women Object to Settlement of Group Rape Case." November 28.

Meyer, T. J. (1984). " 'Date Rape': A Serious Campus Problem That Few Talk About." *Chronicle of Higher Education,* December 5.

Rapaport, K., & Burkhart, B. R. (1984). Personality and Attitudinal Characteristics of Sexually Coercive College Males." *Journal of Abnormal Psychology,* 13:216–21.

Reilly, T. S., Carpenter, S., Dull, V. & Bartlett, K. (1982). "The Factorial Survey Technique: An Approach to Defining Sexual Harassment on Campus. *Journal of Social Issues,* 38:99–109.

Rossi, P. H., & Nock, S. L. (eds.). (1982). *Measuring Social Judgments: The Factorial Survey Approach.* Beverly Hills, CA: Sage.

Sherman, L. W., & Berk, R. A. (1984). "The Specific Deterrent Effects of Arrest for Domestic Assault." *American Sociological Review,* 49:261–71.

Shotland, R. L., & Goodstein, L. (1983). "Just Because She Doesn't Want to Doesn't Mean Its Rape: An Experimentally Based Causal Model of the Perception of Rape in a Dating Situation. *Social Psychology Quarterly,* 46:220–32.

Thornton, B. L., Robbins, M. A., & Johnson, J. A. (1981). "Social Perceptions of the Rape Victims Culpability: The Influence of Respondents' Personal-Environmental Causal Attribution Tendencies." *Human Relations,* 34(3):225–37.

Wiener, R. L., & Rinehart, N. (1986). "Psychological Causality in the Attribution of Responsibility for Rape. *Sex Roles,* 14 (7/8):369–82.

Wiener, R. L., & Vodanovich, S. J. (1986). "The Evaluation of Culpability for Rape: A Model of Legal Decision Making." Unpublished.

Selected Bibliography

Abbey, A. (1982). "Sex differences in attributions for friendly behavior: Do males misperceive females' friendliness?" *Journal of Personality and Social Psychology*, 42, 830–38.

Acock, A. C., & Ireland, N. K. (1983). "Attribution of blame in rape cases: The impact of norm violation, gender, and sex-role attitude." *Sex Roles*, 9, 179–93.

Ageton, S. S. (1983). *Sexual assault among adolescents*. Lexington, MA: Heath.

Allen, Craig M., & Straus, Murray A. (1980). "Resources, power and husband-wife violence." In M. A. Straus & G. T. Hotaling (eds.), *The social causes of husband-wife violence*, pp. 188–208. Minneapolis, MN: University of Minnesota Press.

Arias, Ileana, Samios, Mary, & O'Leary, K. Daniel. (1987). "Prevalence and correlates of physical aggression during courtship." *Journal of Interpersonal Violence*, 2, 82–90.

Armentrout, J. A., & Hauer, A. L. (1978). "MMPIs of rapists of adults, rapists of children, and nonrapist sex offenders." *Journal of Clinical Psychology*, 34, 330–32.

Association of American Colleges. (1986). "Campus gang rape: party games?" Washington, DC: Project on the Status and Education of Women.

Astin, A. W. (1977). *Four critical years: Effects of college on beliefs, attitudes, and knowledge*. San Francisco, CA: Jossey-Bass.

Ball-Rokeach, S. J. (1973). Values and violence: A test of the subculture of violence thesis. *American Sociological Review*, 38, 736–49.

Bandura, Albert. (1973). *Aggression: A social learning analysis*. Englewood Cliffs, NJ: Prentice-Hall.

———. (1978). "Social learning theory of aggression." *Journal of Communication*, 3, 12–19.

Barnes, G., Malamuth, N. M., & Check, J. V. P. (1984). "Personality and sexuality." *Personality and Individual Differences*, 5, 159–72.

Barnett, R. C. (1981). "Parental sex-role attitudes and child-rearing values." *Sex Roles,* 7, 837–46.

Bell, R. R. (1966). *Premarital sex in a changing society.* Englewood Cliffs, NJ: Prentice-Hall.

Berk, Richard A., Berk, Sarah Fenstermaker, Loeske, Donileen R., & Rauma, David. (1983). "Mutual combat and other family violence myths." In D. Finkelhor, R. J. Gelles, G. T. Hotaling, & M. A. Straus (eds.), *The dark side of families: Current family violence research,* pp. 197–212. Beverly Hills, CA: Sage.

Berk, Richard A., Berk, Sarah F., Newton, Phyllis J., & Loeske, Donileen R. (1984). "Cops on call: Summoning the police to the scene of spousal violence." *Law and Society Review,* 18, 479–98.

Berkowitz, Leonard. (1965). "The concept of aggressive drive: Some additional considerations." In L. Berkowitz (ed.), *Advances in Experimental Social Psychology,* volume 2, pp. 301–29. New York: Academic.

———. (1983). "The goals of aggression." In D. Finkelhor, R. J. Gelles, G. T. Hotaling, & M. A. Straus (eds.), *The dark side of families: Current family violence research,* pp. 166–81. Beverly Hills, CA: Sage.

Bernard, J. L., Bernard, S., & Bernard, M. L. (1985). "Courtship violence and sextyping." *Family Relations,* 34, 573–76.

Bernard, J. L., & Bernard, M. L. (1984). The abusive male seeking treatment: Jekyll and Hyde. *Family Relations,* 33, 543–47.

———. (1983). "Violent intimacy: The family as a model of love relationships." *Family Relations,* 32, 283–86.

Billingham, Robert E. (1987). "Courtship violence: The patterns of conflict resolution strategies across seven levels of emotional commitment." *Family Relations,* 36, 283–89.

Billingham, R. E., & Sack, A. R. (1986). "Courtship violence and the interactive status of the relationship." *Journal of Adolescent Research,* 20, 37–44.

———. (1987). "Conflict resolution tactics and the level of emotional commitment among unmarrieds." *Human Relations,* 40, 59–74.

Billings, A. (1979). "Conflict resolution in distressed and nondistressed married couples." *Journal of Counseling and Clinical Psychology,* 47, 368–76.

Billy, J. O. G., Rodgers, J. L., & Udry, J. R. (1984). "Adolescent sexual behavior and friendship choice." *Social Forces,* 62, 653–78.

Billy, J. O. G., & Udry, J. R. (1985). "Patterns of adolescent friendship and effects on sexual behavior." *Social Psychology Quarterly,* 48, 27–41.

Bogal-Allbritten, R. B., & Allbritten, W. (1985). "The hidden victims: Courtship violence among college students." *Journal of Student Personnel,* 19, 201–4.

Bowker, Lee H. (1983). *Beating wife beating.* Lexington, MA: Lexington Books.

Braiker, H. B., & Kelly, H. H. (1979). "Conflict in the development of close relationships." In R. L. Burgess & T. L. Huston (eds.), *Social exchange in developing relationships,* pp. 135–68. New York: Academic.

Breines, Wini, & Gordon, Linda. (1983). The new scholarship on family violence. *Signs: Journal of Women in Culture and Society,* 8, 490–531.

Browne, Angela, & Finkelhor, David. (1986). "The impact of child sexual abuse: A review of the research." *Psychological Bulletin,* 99, 66–77.

Brownmiller, S. (1975). *Against our will: Men, women and rape.* New York: Simon and Schuster.

Burkhart, B. R., & Stanton, A. L. (1985). "Sexual aggression in acquaintance relationships." In G. Russell (ed.), *Violence in intimate relationships*. Englewood Cliffs, NJ: Spectrum.

Burt, Martha R. (1980). "Cultural myths and support for rape." *Journal of Personality and Social Psychology*, 38, 217–30.

Burt, M. R., & Alkin, R. S. (1981). "Rape myths, rape definitions, and probability of conviction." *Journal of Applied Social Psychology*, 11, 212–30.

Carlson, B. (1987). Dating violence: A research review and comparison with spouse abuse." *Social Casework*, 68, 16–23.

Cate, Rodney M., Henton, June M., Koval, James E., Christopher, F. Scott, & Lloyd, Sally A. (1982). "Premarital violence: A social psychological perspective." *Journal of Family Issues*, 3, 79–90.

Cate, Rodney M., & Lloyd, Sally A. (1988). "Courtship." In S. Duck (ed.), *Handbook of personal relationships*, pp. 809–27. New York: Wiley.

Cazenave, Noel A., & Straus, Murray A. (1979). "Race, class, network embeddedness and family violence: A search for potent support systems." *Journal of Comparative Family Studies*, 10, 280–99.

Check, J. V. P., & Malamuth, N. M. (1983). "Sex role stereotyping and reactions to depictions of stranger versus acquaintance rape." *Journal of Personality and Social Psychology*, 45, 344–56.

Cohen, J. (1977). "Sources of peer group homogeneity. "*Sociology of Education*, 30, 241–77.

Coleman, K. Howes. (1980). "Conjugal violence: What 33 men report." *Journal of Marital and Family Therapy*, 6, 207–13.

Coller, S. A., & Resick, P. A. (1987). "Women's attributions of responsibility for date rape: The influence of empathy and sex-role stereotyping." *Violence and Victims*, 2, 115–25.

Coser, Lewis A. (1956). *The functions of social conflict*. Glencoe, IL: Free Press.

Davis, P. (1974). "Contextual sex saliency and sexual activity: The relative effects of family and peer group in the sexual socialization process." *Journal of Marriage and the Family*, 36, 196–202.

Deal, James E., & Wampler, Karen S. (1986). "Dating violence: The primacy of previous experience." *Journal of Social and Personal Relationships*, 3, 457–71.

DeLamater, John. (1987). "Gender differences in sexual scenarios." In K. Kelley (ed.), *Females, males and sexuality: Theories and research*, pp. 127–38. Albany, NY: State University of New York.

DeLamater, J., & MacCorquodale, P. (1979). *Premarital sexuality: Attitudes, relationships, behavior*. Madison, WI: University of Wisconsin Press.

DeMaris, A. (1987). "The efficacy of a spouse abuse model in accounting for courtship violence." *Journal of Family Issues*, 8, 291–305.

Dobash, R. E., & Dobash, R. P. (1978). "Wives: The 'appropriate' victims of marital violence." *Victimology*, 2, 426–42.

———. (1979). *Violence against wives: A case against the patriarchy*. New York: Free Press.

Donato, Katherine M., & Bowker, Lee H. (1984). "Understanding the helpseeking behavior of battered women: A comparison of traditional service agencies and women's groups." *International Journal of Women's Studies*, 7, 99–109.

Donnerstein, E., & Berkowitz, L. (1981). "Victim reactions in aggressive-erotic films as a factor in violence against women." *Journal of Personality and Social Psychology*, 41, 710–724.

Dukes, Richard L., & Mattley, Christine L. (1977). "Predicting rape victim reportage." *Sociology and Social Research*, 62, 63–84.

Edleson, J. L., & Brygger, M. P. (1986). "Gender differences in reporting of battering incidences." *Family Relations*, 35, 377–82.

Ehrmann, W. (1959). *Premarital dating behavior*. New York: Holt.

Ellis, A. (1962). *The American sexual tragedy*. New York: Grove.

Erez, E. (1986). Intimacy, violence and the police. *Human Relations*, 39, 265–81.

Estrich, Susan. (1987). *Real rape*. Cambridge: Harvard University Press.

Falbo, T., & Peplau, L. A. (1980). "Power strategies in intimate relationships." *Journal of Personality and Social Psychology*, 38, 528–618.

Feinstein, S. C., & Ardon, M. S. (1973). "Trends in dating patterns and adolescent development." *Journal of Youth and Adolescence*, 2, 157–66.

Ferraro, Kathleen J., & Johnson, John M. (1983). "How women experience battering: The process of victimization." *Social Problems*, 30, 325–39.

Feshbach, S. (1970). Aggression. In P. H. Mussen (ed.), *Carmichael's manual of child psychology*, volume 2, pp. 159–260. New York: Wiley.

Field, H. S. (1978). "Attitudes toward rape: A comparative analysis of police, rapists, crisis counselors, and citizens." *Journal of Personality and Social Psychology*, 36, 156–79.

Finkelhor, David. (1979). *Sexually victimized children*. New York: Free Press.

———. (1983). "Common features of family abuse." In D. Finkelhor, R. J. Gelles, G. T. Hotaling, & M. A. Straus (eds.), *The dark side of families: Current family violence research*, pp. 17–28. Beverly Hills, CA: Sage.

———. (1984). *Child sexual abuse: New theory and research*. New York: Free Press.

———. (1986). "Sexual abuse: Beyond the family systems approach." In T. S. Trepper & M. J. Barrett (eds.), *Treating incest: A multimodal systems perspective*, pp. 53–65. New York: Haworth.

Finkelhor, David, & Yllo, Kersti. (1983). "Rape in marriage: A sociological view." In D. Finkelhor, R. J. Gelles, G. T. Hotaling, & M. A. Straus (eds.), *The dark side of families*, pp. 119–30. Beverly Hills, CA: Sage.

———. (1985). *License to rape: sexual abuse of wives*. New York: Holt, Rinehart & Winston.

Fletcher, G., Fincham, F., Cramer, V., & Hernon, N. (1987). "The role of attributions in the development of dating relationships." *Journal of Personality and Social Psychology*, 53, 481–89.

Flynn, C. P. (1987). "Relationship violence: A model for family professional." *Family Relations*, 36, 295–99.

Garrett-Gooding, Joy, & Senter, Richard (1987). "Attitudes and acts of aggression on a university campus." *Sociological Inquiry*, 57, 348–72.

Gayford, J. J. (1975). "Wife battering: A preliminary survey of 100 cases." *British Medical Journal*, 1, 194–97.

Gelles, Richard J. (1972). *The violent home*. Beverly Hills, CA: Sage.

———. (1979). *Family violence*. Beverly Hills, CA: Sage.

———. (1982). "Applying research on family violence to clinical practice." *Journal of Marriage and the Family*, 44, 9–20.

Gelles, Richard J., & Straus, Murray A. (1979). "Determinants of violence in the family: Toward a theoretical integration." In W. R. Burr, R. Hill, F. I. Nye, & I. L. Reiss (eds.), *Contemporary theories about the family*, volume 1, pp. 549–81. New York: Free Press.

———. (1988). *Intimate violence*. New York: Simon and Schuster.

Giles-Sims, Jean. (1983). *Wife-battering: A systems theory approach*. New York: Guilford.

Glick, Paul C., & Spainer, Graham B. (1980). "Married and unmarried cohabitation in the United States." *Journal of Marriage and the Family*, 42, 19–30.

Goldstein, Diane, & Rosenbaum, Alan. (1985). "An evaluation of the self-esteem of maritally violent men." *Family Relations*, 34, 425–28.

Goodchilds, J. D., & Zellman, G. L. (1984). "Sexual signaling and sexual aggression in adolescent relationships." In N. M. Malamuth & E. Donnerstein (eds.), *Pornography and sexual aggression*, pp. 233–43. Orlando, FL: Academic.

Goode, W. J. (1971). "Force and violence in the family." *Journal of Marriage and the Family*, 33, 624–36.

Greenblat, C. S. (1988). "A hit is a hit is a hit, or is it? Approval and tolerance of the use of physical force by spouses." In D. Finkelhor, R. J. Gelles, G. T. Hotaling, & M. A. Straus (eds.), *The dark side of families: Current family violence research*, pp. 235–60. Beverly Hills, CA: Sage.

Greendlinger, V., & Byrne, D. (1987). "Coercive sexual fantasies of college males as predictors of self-reported likelihood to rape and overt sexual aggression." *Journal of Sex Research*, 23, 1–11.

Groth, A. N. (1979). *Men who rape: The psychology of the offender*. New York: Plenum.

Gwartney-Gibbs, Patricia A., Stockard, Jean, & Bohmer, Susanne. (1987). "Learning courtship aggression: The influence of parents, peers, and personal experiences." *Family Relations*, 36, 276–82.

Henton, June M., Cate, Rodney M., Koval, James E., Lloyd, Sally A., & Christopher, F. Scott. (1983). "Romance and violence in dating relationships." *Journal of Family Issues*, 4, 467–82.

Hotaling, Gerald T., & Sugarman, David B. (1986). "An analysis of risk markers in husband to wife violence: The current state of knowledge." *Violence and Victims*, 1, 101–24.

Johnson, A. G. (1980). "On the prevalence of rape in the United States." *Signs: Journal of Women in Culture and Society*, 6, 136–46.

Jouriles, E. N., & O'Leary, K. D. (1985). "Interspousal reliability of reports of marital violence." *Journal of Consulting and Clinical Psychology*, 53, 419–21.

Jouriles, E., Barling, J., & O'Leary, K. D. (1987). "Predicting child behavior problems in maritally violent families." *Journal of Abnormal Child Psychology*, 15, 165–73.

Kanin, Eugene J. (1957). "Male aggression in dating-courting relations." *American Journal of Sociology*, 63, 197–204.

———. (1967). "An examination of sexual aggression as a response to sexual frustration." *Journal of Marriage and the Family*, 29, 428–33.

———. (1967). "Reference groups and sex conduct norms." *Sociology Quarterly*, 8, 495–504.

———. (1969). "Selected dyadic aspects of male sexual aggression." *Journal of Sex Research*, 5.

———. (1983). "Rape as a function of relative sexual frustration." *Psychological Reports*, 52, 133–34.

————. (1984). "Date rape: Unofficial criminals and victims." *Victimology: An International Journal,* 1, 95–108.

————. (1985). "Date rapists: Differential sexual socialization and relative deprivation." *Archives of Sexual Behavior,* 14, 219–31.

Kanin, Eugene J., & Parcell, Stanley R. (1977). "Sexual aggression: A second look at the offended female." *Archives of Sexual Behavior,* 6, 67–76.

Kantor, Glenda Kaufman, & Straus, Murray A. (1987). "The drunken bum theory of wife abuse." *Social Problems,* 34, 213–30.

Katz, S., & Mazur, M. A. (1979). *Understanding the rape victim: A synthesis of research findings.* New York: Wiley.

Kilpatrick, D. G., Veronen, L. J., & Best, C. L. (1984). "Factors predicting psychological distress among rape victims." In C. R. Figley (ed.), *Trauma and its wake: The study and treatment of post-traumatic stress disorder,* pp. 113–41. New York: Brunner/Mazel.

Kirkpatrick, C., & Kanin, E. J. (1957). "Male sexual aggression on a university campus." *American Sociological Review,* 22, 52–58.

Klaus, D., Hersen, M., & Bellack, A. S. (1977). "Survey of dating habits of male and female college students: A necessary precursor to measurement and modification." *Journal of Clinical Psychology,* 33, 369–75.

Korman, Sheila A., & Leslie, Gerald R. (1982). "The relationship of feminist ideology and date expense sharing to perceptions of sexual aggression in dating." *Journal of Sex Research,* 18, 114–29.

Koss, Mary P. (1985). "The hidden rape victim: Personality, attitudinal, and situational characteristics." *Psychology of Women Quarterly,* 9, 193–212.

Koss, M. P., & Burkhart, B. R. (In press). "The long-term impact of rape: A conceptual model and implications for treatment." *Psychology of Women Quarterly.*

Koss, M. P., & Gidycz, C. A. (1985). "Sexual experiences survey: reliability and validity." *Journal of Consulting and Clinical Psychology,* 53, 422–23.

Koss, M. P., Gidycz, C. A., & Wisniewski, N. (1987). "The scope of rape: Incidence and prevalence of sexual aggression and victimization in a national sample of higher education students." *Journal of Consulting and Clinical Psychology,* 55(2)162–70.

Koss, M. P., & Leonard, K. E. (1984). "Sexually aggressive men: Empirical findings and theoretical implications." In N. M. Malamuth & E. Donnerstein (eds.), *Pornography and sexual aggression,* pp. 213–32. New York: Academic.

Koss, Mary P., Leonard, Kenneth E., Beezley, Dana A., & Oros, Cheryl J. (1985). "Nonstranger sexual aggression: A discriminant analysis of the psychological characteristics of undetected offenders." *Sex Roles,* 12, 981–92.

Koss, Mary P., & Oros, Cheryl, J. (1982). "Sexual experiences survey: A research instrument investigating sexual aggression and victimization." *Journal of Consulting and Clinical Psychology,* 50, 455–57.

Koval, J. E., Ponzetti, J., & Cate, R. M. (1982). "Programmatic intervention for men involved in conjugal violence." *Family Therapy,* 9, 147–54.

Lane, Katherine E., & Gwartney-Gibbs, Patricia A. (1985). "Violence in the context of dating and sex." *Journal of Family Issues,* 6(1), 45–9.

Laner, Mary Riege. (1983). "Courtship abuse and aggression: Contextual aspects." *Sociological Spectrum,* 3, 69–83.

Laner, Mary Riege, & Thompson, Jeanine. (1982). "Abuse and aggression in courtship couples." *Deviant Behavior,* 3, 229–44.

Langevin, R., Paitich, D., & Russon, A. E. (1985). "Are rapists sexually anomalous, aggressive or both?." In R. Langevin (ed.), *Erotic preference, gender identity, and aggression in men: New research studies,* pp. 17–38. Hillsdale, NJ: Erlbaum.

Levine-MacCombie, J., & Koss, M. P. (1986). "Acquaintance rape: effective avoidance strategies." *Psychology of Women Quarterly,* 10, 311–20.

Levinger, G. (1979). "A social exchange view on the dissolution of pair relationships." In R. L. Burgess & T. L. Huston (eds.), *Social exchange in developing relationships,* pp. 169–93. New York: Academic.

Lloyd, Sally A. (1987). "Conflict in premarital relationships: Differential perceptions of males and females." *Family Relations,* 36, 290–94.

Lloyd, Sally A., & Cate, Rodney M. (1985). "Attributions associated with significant turning points in premarital relationship dissolution." *Journal of Social and Personal Relationships,* 2, 419–36.

Lott, B., Reilly, M. E., & Howard, D. R. (1982). "Sexual assault and harassment: A campus community case study." *Signs: Journal of Women in Culture and Society,* 8, 296–319.

Makepeace, James M. (1983). "Life events, stress and courtship violence." *Family Relations,* 32, 101–9.

———. (1981). "Courtship violence among college students." *Family Relations,* 30, 97–102.

———. (1986). "Gender differences in courtship violence victimization." *Family Relations,* 35, 383–88.

———. (1987). "Social factor and victim-offender differences in courtship violence." *Family Relations,* 36, 87–91.

Malamuth, N. M. (1983). "Factors associated with rape as predictors of laboratory aggression against women." *Journal of Personality and Social Psychology,* 45, 432–44.

———. (1984). "Aggression against women: Cultural and individual causes." In N. M. Malamuth & E. Donnerstein (eds.), *Pornography and sexual aggression,* pp. 19–52. New York: Academic.

Malamuth, N. M., & Briere, J. (In press). "Sexual violence in the media: Indirect effects on aggression against women." *Journal of Social Issues.*

Malamuth, N. M., & Check, J. V. P. (1981). "The effects of mass media exposure on acceptance of violence against women: A field experiment." *Journal of Research in Personality,* 15, 436–46.

———. (1985). "The effects of aggressive pornography on beliefs in rape myths: Individual differences." *Journal of Research in Personality,* 19, 299–320.

Malamuth, N. M., Check, J. V. P., & Briere, J. (1986). "Sexual arousal in response to aggression: Ideological, aggressive and sexual correlates." *Journal of Personality and Social Psychology,* 50, 330–40.

Maltz, W., & Holman, B. (1987). *Incest and sexuality: A guide to understanding and healing.* Lexington, MA: Lexington Books.

Margolin, G., John, R. S., & Gleberman, L. (1988). "Affective responses to conflictual discussions in violent and nonviolent couples." *Journal of Consulting and Clinical Psychology,* 56, 24–33.

Marshall, L. L., & Rose, P. (1987). "Gender, stress and violence in adult relationships of a sample of college students." *Journal of Social and Personal Relationship,* 4, 299–316.

————. (1988). "Family of origin and courtship violence." *Journal of Counseling and Development,* 66, 414–18.

Marshall, W. L., & Barbaree, H. E. (1984). "A behavioral view of rape." *International Journal of Law and Psychiatry,* 7, 51–77.

Mathews, W. J. (1984). "Violence in college couples." *College Student Journal* 18, 150–58.

May, M. (1978). "Violence in the family: An historical perspective." In J. P. Martin (ed.), *Violence and the family,* pp. 135–68. New York: Wiley.

McCabe, M. P. (1984). "Toward a theory of adolescent dating." *Adolescence,* 19, 159–70.

McCahill, T. W., Meyer, L. C., & Fischman, R. M. (1979). *The aftermath of rape.* Lexington, MA: Lexington Books.

McCormick, N. B., & Jesser, C. J. (1983). "The courtship game: Power in the sexual encounter." In E. R. Allgeier & N.B. McCormick (eds.), *Changing boundaries: Gender roles and sexual behavior,* pp. 64–86. Palo Alto, CA: Mayfield.

McDaniel, C. O. (1969). "Dating roles and reasons for dating." *Journal of Marriage and the Family,* 31, 97–107.

McGovern, K. B., Arkowitz, H., & Gilmore, S. K. (1975). "Evaluation of social skills training programs for college dating inhibitions." *Journal of Counseling Psychology,* 22, 505–12.

McKinney, K. (1986). "Measures of verbal, physical and sexual dating violence by gender." *Free Inquiry into Creative Sociology,* 14, 55–60.

————. (1986). "Perceptions of courtship violence: Gender difference and involvement." *Free Inquiry into Creative Sociology,* 14, 61–66.

Meyer, T. J. (1984). " 'Date rape': A serious campus problem that few talk about." *Chronicle of Higher Education,* December 5.

Muehlenhard, C. L., Friedman, D. E., & Thomas, C. M. (1985). "Is date rape justifiable? The effects of dating activity, who initiated, who paid, and men's attitudes toward women." *Psychology of Women Quarterly,* 9, 297–309.

Muehlenhard, C. L., & Linton, M. A. (1987). "Date rape and sexual aggression in dating situations: Incidence and risk factors." *Journal of Counseling Psychology,* 34(2), 186–96.

Muehlenhard, C. L., & MacNaughton, J. S. (In press). "Women's beliefs about women who 'lead men on.' " *Journal of Social and Clinical Psychology.*

Muehlenhard, C. L., & McFall, R. M. (1981). "Dating initiation from a woman's perspective." *Behavior Therapy,* 12, 682–91.

Muehlenhard, C. L., & Miller, E. N. (1988). "Traditional and nontraditional men's responses to women's dating initiation." *Behavior Modification,* 12, 385–403.

Muehlenhard, C. L., & Scardino, T. J. (1985). "What will he think? Men's impressions of women who initiate dates and achieve academically." *Journal of Counseling Psychology,* 32, 560–69.

Murstein, B. I. (1980). "Mate selection in the 1970s." *Journal of Marriage and the Family,* 42, 51–66.

Nisonoff, L., & Bitman, I. (1979). "Spouse abuse: Incidence and relationship to selected demographic variables." *Victimology,* 4, 131–40.

O'Keefe, N. K., Brockopp, K., & Chew, E. (1986). "Teen dating violence." *Social Work,* 31, 465–68.

O'Leary, D. K., Curley, A., Rosenbaum, A., & Clarke, C. (1985). "Assertion training for abused wives: A potentially hazardous treatment." *Journal of Consulting and Clinical Psychology*, 11, 319–22.

————. (1988). Physical aggression between spouses: A social learning theory perspective. In V. B. Van Hasselt, R. L. Morrison, A. S. Bellack, & M. Hersen (eds.), *Handbook of family violence*, pp. 31–55. New York: Plenum Press.

O'Leary, K. D., & Arias, I. (1987). Prevalence, correlates and development of spouse abuse. In R. deV. Peters & R. J. McMahon (eds.), *Marriage and family: treatments and processes*. New York: Brunner/Mazel.

Pagelow, Mildred Daley. (1981). *Woman-battering: Victims and their experiences*. Beverly Hills, CA: Sage.

Peplau, L. A. (1984). "Power in dating relationships." In J. Freeman (ed.), *Women: A feminist perspective*, pp. 100–112. Palo Alto, CA: Mayfield.

Peterson, D. R. (1983). "Conflict." In H. H. Kelley, E. Berscheid, A. Christensen, J. H. Harvey, T. L. Huston, G. Levinger, E. McClintock, L. A. Peplau, & jD. R. Peterson (eds.), *Close relationships*, pp. 360–96. New York: Freeman.

Plass, M. S., & Gessner, J. C. (1983). "Violence in courtship relations: A Southern example." *Free Inquiry into Creative Sociology*, 11, 198–202.

Pleck, E., Pleck, J., Grossman, M., & Bart, P. (1978). "The battered data syndrome: A comment on Steinmetz' article." *Victimology*, 2, 680–83.

Ponzette, J. J., Cate, R. M., & Koval, J. E. (1982). "Violence between couples: Profiling the male abuser." *The Personnel and Guidance Journal*, 61, 222–24.

Puig, A. (1984). "Predomestic strife: A growing college counseling concern." *Journal of College Student Personnel*, 25, 268–69.

Rapaport, K. and Burkhart, B. R. (1984). "Personality and attitudinal characteristics of sexually coercive college males." *Journal of Abnormal Psychology*, 93, 216–21.

Reilly, T. S., Carpenter, S., Dull, V., & Bartlett, K. (1982). "The factorial survey technique: An approach to defining sexual harassment on campus." *Journal of Social Issues*, 38, 99–109.

Resick, P. A., Calhoun, K. S., Atkeson, B. M., & Ellis, E. M. (1981). "Social adjustment in victims of sexual assault." *Journal of Consulting and Clinical Psychology*, 49, 705–12.

Richardson, D. (1981). "The effect of alcohol on male aggression toward female targets." *Motivation and Emotion*, 5, 333–44.

Richardson, D., & Campbell, J. L. (1982). "The effect of alcohol on attributions of blame for rape." *Personality and Social Psychology Bulletin*, 8, 468–76.

Roark, M. L. (1987). "Preventing violence on college campuses." *Journal of Counseling and Development*, 65, 367–71.

Roche, J. P. (1986). "Premarital sex: Attitudes and behavior by dating stage." *Adolescence*, 21, 107–21.

Roscoe, Bruce, & Benaske, Nancy (1985). "Courtship violence experienced by abused wives: Similarities in patterns of abuse." *Family Relations*, 34, 419–24.

Roscoe, B., & Callahan, J. E. (1985). "Adolescents' self-report of violence in families and dating relations." *Adolescence*, 20, 545–53.

Roscoe, B., Diana, M. S., & Brooks, R. H., II (1987). "Early, middle, and late adolescents' views on dating and factors influencing partner selection." *Adolescence*, 22, 59–68.

Rosenbaum, Alan. (1986). "Of men, macho, and marital violence." *Journal of Family Violence*, 1, 121–29.

Rosenbaum, A., & O'Leary, K. D. (1981). "Marital violence: Characteristics of abusive couples." *Journal of Consulting and Clinical Psychology*, 49, 63–71.

Rounsaville, B. J. (1978). Theories of marital violence: Evidence from a study of battered women. *Victimology*, 3, 11–31.

Roy, M. (1982). "Four thousand partners in violence: A trend analysis." In M. Roy (ed.), *The abusive partner*, pp. 17–38. New York: Van Nostrand Reinhold.

Rubin, Zick. (1970). "Measurement of romantic love." *Journal of Personality and Social Psychology*, 16, 265–73.

Russell, Diana E. H. (1982). *Rape in marriage*. New York: Macmillan.

———. (1984). *Sexual exploitation: Rape, child sexual abuse and workplace harassment*. Beverly Hills, CA: Sage.

———. (1986). *The secret trauma: Incest in the lives of girls and women*. New York: Basic Books.

Sack, A. R., Keller, J. F., & Howard, R. D. (1982). "Conflict tactics and violence in dating situations." *International Journal of the Sociology of the Family*, 12, 89–100.

Sanday, P. (1981). "The socio-cultural context of rape: A cross-cultural study." *Journal of Social Issues*, 37, 5–27.

Saunders, D. G. (1986). "When battered women use violence: Husband-abuse of self-defense." *Violence and Victims*, 1, 47–60.

Scanzoni, J. (1979). "Social processes and power in families." In W. R. Burr, R. Hills, F. I. Nye, & I. L. Reiss (eds.), *Contemporary theories about the family*, volume 1, pp. 295–316. New York: Free Press.

Schultz, B. Bohrnstedt, G. W., Borgatta, E. F., & Evans, R. R. (1977). "Explaining premarital sexual intercourse among college students." *Social Forces*, 56, 148–65.

Schwendinger, H., & Schwendinger, J. S. (1985). *Adolescent subcultures and delinquency: Research edition*. New York: Praeger.

Scully, D., & Marolla, J. (1984). "Convicted rapists' vocabulary of motive: Excuses and justifications." *Social Problems*, 31, 530–44.

———. (1985). " 'Riding the bull at Gilley's': Convicted rapists describe the rewards of rape." *Social Problems*, 32, 251–63.

Sherman, L. W., & Berk, R. A. (1984). "The specific deterrent effects of arrest for domestic assault." *American Sociological Review*, 49, 261–71.

Shotland, R. L., & Goodstein, L. (1983). "Just because she doesn't want to doesn't mean it's rape: An experimentally based causal model of the perception of rape in a dating situation." *Social Psychology Quarterly*, 46, 220–32.

Sigelman, Carol K., Berry, Carol J., & Wiles, Katherine A. (1984). "Violence in college students' dating relationships." *Journal of Applied Social Psychology*, 5(6), 530–48.

Simmel, Georg. (1955). *Conflict and the web of group affiliation*. New York: Free Press.

Skipper, J. K., & Nass, G. (1966). "Dating behavior: A framework for analysis." *Journal of Marriage and the Family*, 28, 412–20.

Smith, E. A. (1962). *American youth culture: Group life in teen-age society*. New York: Free Press.

Sorensen, R. C. (1973). *Adolescent sexuality in contemporary America.* New York: World.

Spanier, G. B. (1983). "Married and unmarried cohabitation in the United States: 1980." *Journal of Marriage and the Family,* 45, 277–88.

Sprey, J. (1979). "Conflict theory and the study of marriage and the family." In W. R. Burr, R. Hill, F. I. Nye, & I. L. Reiss (eds.), *Contemporary theories about the family,* volume 1, pp. 130–59. New York: Free Press.

Starr, B., Clarke, C. B., Goetz, K. M., & O'Malia, L. (1979). "Psychosocial aspects of wife-battering." *Social Casework,* 60, 479–87.

Steinmetz, Suzanne K. (1978). "The battered husband syndrome." *Victimology,* 2, 499–509.

Stets, Jan E. (1988). *Domestic violence and control.* New York: Springer-Verlag.

Stets, Jan E., & Pirog-Good, Maureen A. (1987). "Violence in dating relationships." *Social Psychology Quarterly,* 49, 63–71.

———. (1989). "Patterns of physical and sexual abuse in dating relationships." *Journal of Family Violence.*

Stets, Jan E., & Straus, Murray A. (1989). "Gender differences in reporting marital violence and its medical and psychological consequences." In Murray A. Straus and R. J. Gelles (eds.), *Physical violence in American families: Risk factors and adaptations to violence in 8,145 families,* Chapter 9. New Brunswick, NJ: Transaction Press.

Straus, Murray A. (1976). "Sexual inequality, cultural norms, and wife beating." *Victimology,* 1, 54–76.

———. (1979). "Measuring intrafamily conflict and violence: The conflict tactics (CT) scales." *Journal of Marriage and the Family,* 41, 75–86.

———. (1980). "Social stress and marital violence in a national sample of American families." *Annals of the New York Academy of Science,* 347, 229–50.

———. (1980). "The marriage license as a hitting license: Evidence from popular culture, law, and social science." In M. A. Straus & G. T. Hotaling (eds.), *The social causes of husband-wife violence,* pp. 39–50. Minneapolis, MN: University of Minnesota Press.

———. (1980). "Victims and aggressors in marital violence." *American Behavioral Scientist,* 23, 681–704.

Straus, Murray A., & Gelles, Richard J. (1986). "Societal change and change in family violence from 1975 to 1985 as revealed by two national surveys." *Journal of Marriage and the Family,* 48, 465–79.

———. (1988). "How violent are American families? Estimates from the national family violence resurvey and other studies." In G. T. Hotaling et al. (eds.), *New directions in family violence research.* Beverly Hills, CA: Sage.

Straus, Murray, A., Gelles, Richard J., & Steinmetz, Suzanne K. (1980). *Behind closed doors: Violence in the American family.* Garden City, NY: Anchor.

Straus, Murray A., & Hotaling, Gerald T. (1980). "Culture, social organization, and irony in the study of family violence." In M. A. Straus & G. T. Hotaling (eds.), *The social causes of husband-wife violence,* pp. 3–22. Minneapolis, MN: University of Minnesota Press.

Straus, M. A., & Lincoln, A. J. (1985). "A conceptual framework for understanding crime and the family." In A. J. Lincoln & M. A. Straus (eds.), *Crime and the family.* New York: C. C. Thomas.

Strube, M. J., & Barbour, L. S. (1984). "Factors related to the decision to leave an abusive relationship." *Journal of Marriage and the Family*, 46, 837–44.

Sugarman, David B., & Hotaling, Gerald, T. (In press). "Violent men in intimate relationships: An analysis of risk markers." *Journal of Applied Social Psychology*.

Surra, C. A. (1987). "Reasons for change in commitment: Variations by courtship type." *Journal of Social and Personal Relationships*, 4, 17–34.

Szinovacz, M. E. (1983). "Using couple data as a methodological tool: The case of marital violence." *Journal of Marriage and the Family*, 45, 633–44.

Tedeschi, J. T., Smith, R., & Brown, R. (1974). "A reinterpretation of research on aggression." *Psychological Bulletin*, 81, 540–62.

Thompson, W. E. (1986). "Courtship violence: Toward a conceptual understanding." *Youth and Society*, 18, 162–76.

Thornton, B. L., Robbins, M. A., & Johnson, J. A. (1981). "Social perceptions of the rape victim's culpability: The influence of respondents' personal-environmental causal attribution tendencies." *Human Relations*, 34(3), 225–37.

Toby, Jackson. (1966). "Violence and the masculine ideal: Some qualitative data." *Annual American Academic Political Social Science*, 364, 19–28.

Trepper, T. S., & Barrett, M. J. (1986). "Conceptual framework for the assessment of intrafamily sexual abuse." In T. S. Trepper & M. J. Barrett (eds.), *Targeting incest: A multimodal systems perspective*, pp. 13–25. New York: Haworth.

Ulbrich, Patricia, & Huber, Joan. (1981). "Observing parental violence: Distribution and effects." *Journal of Marriage and the Family*, 44, 623–31.

Walker, Lenore E. (1979). *The battered woman*. New York: Harper & Row.

Waller, W. (1937). "The rating and dating complex." *American Sociological Review*, 2, 727–34.

Wiener, R. L. & Rinehart, N. (1986). "Psychological causality in the attribution of responsibility for rape." *Sex Roles*, 14(7/8), 369–82.

Williams, Linda. (1984). "The classic rape: When do victims report? *Social Problems*, 31, 459–67.

Wilson, Kenneth, Faison, Rebecca, & Britton, G. M. (1983). "Cultural aspects of male sex aggression." *Deviant Behavior: An Interdisciplinary Journal*, 4, 241–55.

Wilson, W., & Durrenberger, R. (1982). "Comparison of rape and attempted rape victims." *Psychological Reports*, 50, 198.

Wolfgang, M. E., & Ferracuti, F. (1967). *The subculture of violence*. New York: Tavistock.

Wolfe, J., & Baker, V. (1980). "Characteristics of imprisoned rapists and circumstances of the rape." In C. G. Warner (ed.), *Rape and sexual assault*, pp. 265–78. Germantown, MD: Aspen.

Wydra, A., Marshall, W. L., Earls, C. M., & Barbaree, H. E. (1983). "Identification of cues and control of sexual arousal by rapists." *Behavior Research and Therapy*, 21, 469–76.

Yllo, Kersti, & Straus, Murray A. (1981). "Interpersonal violence among married and cohabiting couples." *Family Relations*, 30, 339–47.

Zillmann, D. (1979). *Aggression and hostility*. Hillsdale, NJ: Erlbaum.

Index

About the Editors and Contributors

ABOUT THE EDITORS

MAUREEN A. PIROG-GOOD is professor of public and environmental affairs at Indiana University. She has published in a wide variety of important public policy areas including teenage parenting, child support enforcement, employment and crime, the effectiveness of programs for male batterers, and premarital dating violence. Articles have appeared in *Social Science Quarterly, Social Psychology Quarterly, Contemporary Policy Issues, American Journal of Economics and Sociology, Journal of Quantitative Criminology,* and *Journal of Family Violence.*

Dr. Pirog-Good earned a B.A. and an M.A. in economics from Boston College. She holds a Ph.D. in public policy analysis from the University of Pennsylvania.

JAN E. STETS is professor of sociology at Washington State University. For the year 1987–88, she held a post-doctoral fellowship at the Family Research Laboratory at the University of New Hampshire where she conducted research on marital and dating violence.

She has published widely in the area of interpersonal violence. Her work has included an analysis of domestic violence, male battering programs, and premarital physical, sexual, and psychological abuse. She is author of *Domestic Violence and Control* (1988). Her articles have appeared in *Social Psychology Quarterly, Victimology: An International Journal, Journal of Family Violence,* and several books.

Dr. Stets earned a B.A. in sociology from the University of Dayton. She holds an M.A. and a Ph.D. in sociology from Indiana University.

ABOUT THE CONTRIBUTORS

JOANNE BELKNAP is a professor in the School of Criminal Justice at the University of Cincinnati.

RODNEY M. CATE is a professor and chair of the Department of Child and Family Studies at Washington State University. He conducts research on premarital relationships and examines violence in dating relationships.

SARAH FENSTERMAKER is a professor of sociology at the University of California-Santa Barbara. Her research focuses on women, work, and family.

ROBERT GEFFNER is a professor of psychology and director of the Family Violence Research Program at the University of Texas-Tyler. He directs research and treatment programs on physical and sexual abuse.

PATRICIA GWARTNEY-GIBBS is a professor of sociology at the University of Oregon. She conducts research on women and work and has published other work on dating violence.

GERALD T. HOTALING is a professor of sociology at the University of Lowell and is a research scientist at the Family Research Laboratory at the University of New Hampshire. He has published widely in the area of family violence.

MARY P. KOSS is a professor at the University of Arizona Medical School. She has published widely in the area of date rape and sexual victimization.

JAMES E. KOVAL is a professor in the Department of Home Economics, Child Development, and Family Studies at California State University-Long Beach. His research examines premarital violence and interpersonal relationship development, as well as counseling and intervention, with premarital couples.

SALLY A. LLOYD is a professor in the Department of Family and Consumer Studies at the University of Utah. Her research focuses on premarital violence and the development of conflict in premarital relationships.

PAULA LUNDBERG-LOVE is a professor of psychology and associate director of the Family Violence Research Program at the University of Texas-Tyler. Her current research focuses on sexual abuse.

NEIL M. MALAMUTH is a professor of psychology and communications at the University of California-Los Angeles. He has written extensively on sexual aggression and pornography.

JAMES MAKEPEACE is a professor of sociology at the College of Saint Benedict. He has published extensively on dating violence.

CHARLENE L. MUEHLENHARD is a professor of psychology and women's studies at the University of Kansas. Her research examines dating behavior and date rape.

K. DANIEL O'LEARY is a professor of psychology and past chairman of the Psychology Department of the State University of New York at Stoney Brook. His research focuses on marital therapy, the relationship between marital and child problems, and spouse abuse.

DAVID S. RIGGS is affiliated with the Medical University of South Carolina. His research addresses physical and sexual aggression in dating relationships.

JEAN STOCKARD is a professor of sociology at the University of Oregon.

MURRAY A. STRAUS is a professor of sociology and director of the Family Research Laboratory at the University of New Hampshire. He has authored numerous books and articles on family violence.

DAVID B. SUGARMAN is a professor of psychology, Rhode Island College. He conducts research in the areas of domestic violence and interpersonal attraction.